THE USE OF THE OLD TESTAMENT
IN THE NEW AND OTHER ESSAYS

THE USE OF
THE OLD TESTAMENT
IN THE NEW AND
OTHER ESSAYS

STUDIES IN HONOR OF
WILLIAM FRANKLIN STINESPRING

Edited by
JAMES M. EFIRD

DUKE UNIVERSITY PRESS
Durham, N. C. 1972

© 1972, Duke University Press

L.C.C. card no. 70–185463

I.S.B.N. 0–8223–0288–8

PRINTED IN THE UNITED STATES OF AMERICA

Composition by Maurice Jacobs, Inc.

DEDICATION

For many years Professor W. F. Stinespring has encouraged, stimulated, and inspired students in the Divinity School at Duke University. His knowledge, his devotion to scholarship, and his ability to communicate have won him great respect and admiration from many student generations, and his genuine interest in and concern for individual students have left many of us with a debt which can never be repaid but will always be acknowledged and appreciated.

Throughout his teaching career Dr. Stinespring has had two main interests: a love for Semitic languages, especially the teaching of introductory Hebrew, and a concern that Christians remember that the Old Testament and the New Testament are not separate entities but integrally related documents witnessing to *one* religious faith and the same God! This collection of essays focuses upon the latter interest and reflects the admiration, esteem, and genuine affection for him of all those who have in any way contributed to this volume. We hope that these essays will in some way do honor to him who has meant so much to so many.

TABLE OF CONTENTS

LIST OF ABBREVIATIONS

AJ   "The Apocryphon of John"

ANET   J. B. Pritchard, ed., *Ancient Near Eastern Texts Relating to the Old Testament*, 2nd ed. (Princeton: Princeton University Press, 1955)

ATD   *Das Alte Testament Deutsch*

BASOR   *Bulletin of the American Schools of Oriental Research*

BT   Babylonian Talmud

BZAW   Beihefte zur Zeitschrift für die alttestamentliche Wissenschaft

CBQ   *Catholic Biblical Quarterly*

CDC   Cairo Fragments of a Damascus Covenant

HA   "The Hypostasis of the Archons"

IB   *The Interpreter's Bible*, ed. G. A. Buttrick, 12 vols. (New York: Abingdon, 1951–1957)

IDB   *The Interpreter's Dictionary of the Bible*, ed. G. A. Buttrick, 4 vols. (New York: Abingdon, 1962)

JBL   *Journal of Biblical Literature*

NTS   *New Testament Studies*

OW   "On the Origin of the World"

RB   *Revue Biblique*

RGG   *Die Religion in Geschichte und Gegenwart*

SBT   *Studies in Biblical Theology*

StTh   *Studia Theologica*

SVT   *Supplement of Vetus Testamentum*

TLZ   *Theologische Literaturzeitung*

TZ   *Theologische Zeitschrift*

ZAW   *Zeitschrift für die alttestamentliche Wissenschaft*

ZDMG   *Zeitschrift der deutschen morgenländischen Gesellschaft*

ZNTW   *Zeitschrift für die neutestamentliche Wissenschaft*

EDITOR'S NOTE

It is a rare privilege to be associated with a group of persons of such stature and competence as those who have contributed to this volume. The editor would like to take this opportunity to thank the many persons who have so graciously worked for the success of this project. First of all there are the authors of the various essays. For them this has been a labor of love in honor of a former teacher and/or colleague. The quality of their offerings has been such that the usually tedious task of editing has been made quite minimal. The articles were submitted by May, 1970; the authors have been exceedingly patient with the usual delays. Second, the editor wishes to thank the former Dean of the Duke University Divinity School, Dr. Robert E. Cushman, and those connected with the Duke University Press for their support, encouragement, and general helpfulness from the initiation of this project to its completion.

There are, in addition, a number of individuals who deserve special mention. To my friend and colleague, Dr. D. Moody Smith, Jr., a word of appreciation is extended for his support and helpful suggestions along the way. Mr. Jerry Campbell, my student assistant, contributed much with his attention to detail in the final editing and proofing work. Mr. Donn Michael Farris and his fine staff of the Divinity Library of Duke University have been of great assistance especially in compiling the bibliography of Dr. Stinespring's publications. To my dear friend and competent secretary, Mrs. Vivian Crumpler, go heartfelt thanks for her many abilities and talents without which this volume would not have been possible, and for her patience and tolerance with me in this task.

But the deepest appreciation must go to the man to whom this volume is dedicated. The editor has been related to Dr. Stinespring as student, colleague, and friend, and is indebted to him for his wealth of knowledge, his patience and understanding, and his wise counsel. It is the hope of all connected with this volume (and many who are not) that his retirement may be as satisfying and fruitful as his active teaching career.

Εὖ δοῦλε ἀγαθὲ καὶ πιστέ, καὶ φίλε ἀγαπητέ.

WILLIAM FRANKLIN STINESPRING

Born: Harrisonburg, Virginia, September 24, 1901.

Academic Training: University of Virginia, 1924, B.A.; 1929, M.A.
Peabody Conservatory of Music, Baltimore, Maryland.
Yale University, 1932, Ph.D. (Semitics and Biblical Languages).
American School of Oriental Research, (Jerusalem) 1932–35, Fellow and Assistant Director.

Career: *Smith College:* Assistant Professor, 1935–36.
Duke University Divinity School: Assistant Professor, 1936–39; Associate Professor, 1939–44; Professor, 1944–71.
Visiting Professorships: University of North Carolina, 1939, 1966. University of Chicago, 1943.
Pacific School of Religion, 1944.
Iliff School of Theology, 1948.
American School of Oriental Research, Jerusalem, 1963.
Research Assistant: State Department, Anglo-American Committee on Palestine, 1946.

Family: Married: Mary Foxwell Albright, April 2, 1928.
Children: W. Forrest Stinespring, born March 16, 1929.
John A. Stinespring, born December 8, 1935.

Church Affiliation: Licensed and ordained September 30, 1940, by Granville Presbytery, Presbyterian Church in the United States.

Societies: Phi Beta Kappa (Senator, South Atlantic District, 1971–)
Society of Biblical Literature and Exegesis (Honorary President, 1971)
American Friends of the Middle East
American Oriental Society
National Association of Biblical Instructors (Now American Academy of Religion)

BIBLIOGRAPHY

BOOKS

Joseph Klausner. *From Jesus to Paul.* Trans. from the Hebrew by W. F. Stinespring. New York: Macmillan, 1943. 624 pp.

Anglo-American Committee of Inquiry on Jewish Problems in Palestine and Europe. *Report to the United States Government and His Majesty's Government in the United Kingdom.* Washington, D. C.: United States Government Printing Office, 1946. (On research staff and assisted in preparing report.)

Joseph Klausner. *The Messianic Idea in Israel.* 3rd ed. Trans. from the Hebrew by W. F. Stinespring. New York: Macmillan, 1955.

ARTICLES

"Light on an Old Inscription from Jerash," *Bulletin of the American Schools of Oriental Research,* no. 54 (April, 1934), 21–24.

"The Inscription of the Triumphal Arch at Jerash," *Bulletin of the American Schools of Oriental Research,* no. 56 (December, 1934), 15–16.

"Jerash in the Spring of 1934," *Bulletin of the American Schools of Oriental Research,* no. 57 (February, 1935), pp. 3–9.

"The History of Excavation at Jerash." In *Gerasa: City of the Decapolis.* Ed. Carl H. Kraeling, pp. 1–10. New Haven, Conn.: American Schools of Oriental Research, 1938.

"Hadrian in Palestine 129/130 A.D.," *Journal of the American Oriental Society,* 59 (September, 1939), 360–65.

"The Critical Faculty of Edward Robinson," *Journal of Biblical Literature,* 58 (December, 1939), 379–387.

"Some Archaeological Problems of Jerusalem," *Journal of Bible and Religion,* 9 (May, 1941), 89–93.

"Note on Ruth 2:19," *Journal of Near Eastern Studies,* 3 (April, 1944), 101.

"Palestine: Land of Hope and Trouble," *Social Action,* vol. 13, no. 10 (December 15, 1947), 4–34.

"Hosea, Prophet of Doom," *Crozer Quarterly,* 27 (July, 1950), 200–7.

"History and Present Status of Aramaic Studies," *Journal of Bible and Religion*, 26 (October, 1958), 298–303.

"Eschatology in Chronicles," *Journal of Biblical Literature*, 80 (September, 1961), 209–19.

"The Active Infinitive with Passive Meaning in Biblical Aramaic," *Journal of Biblical Literature*, 81 (December, 1962), 391–94.

G. A. Buttrick, ed. *Interpreter's Dictionary of the Bible*. New York and Nashville: Abingdon Press, 1962. 4 vols. Articles: "Ashdod," 1:248–49; "Ashkelon," 1:252–54; "Beth-eglaim," 1:389–90; "Ekron," 2:69; "Gath," 2:355–56; "Gaza," 2:357–58; "Humor," 2:660–62; "Irony and Satire," 2:726–28; "Soco," 4:395; "Solomon's Portico," 4:408; "Temple, Jerusalem," 4:534–60.

H. G. May and B. M. Metzger, eds. *The Oxford Annotated Bible*. New York: Oxford University Press, 1962. Articles: "First Samuel," "Second Samuel," "First Kings," "Second Kings," "First Chronicles," "Second Chronicles."

"Temple Research in Jerusalem," *The Duke Divinity School Review*, 29 (Spring, 1964), 85–101.

F. C. Grant and H. H. Rowley, eds. *Hasting's Dictionary of the Bible*. Revised ed. New York: Charles Scribner's Sons, 1963. Articles: "Adam in the New Testament," p. 9; "Congregation, Assembly," p. 173; "Dagon," pp. 197–98; "Education," pp. 230–31; "Elijah," pp. 242–43; "Elisha," pp. 244–45; "Fringes," p. 308; "Law in the Old Testament," pp. 567–69; "Oaths," pp. 707–8; "Salt," pp. 878–79; "Talmud," pp. 954–56.

"No Daughter of Zion: A Study of the Appositional Genitive in Hebrew Grammar," *Encounter*, 26 (Spring, 1965), 133–41.

"Wilson's Arch Revisited," *Biblical Archaeologist*, 29 (February, 1966), 27–36.

"Wilson's Arch and the Masonic Hall, Summer 1966," *Biblical Archaeologist*, 30 (February, 1967), 27–31.

Encyclopedia International, 20 vols. New York: Grolier Inc., 1963–68. Fifty articles on biblical subjects.

"The Participle of the Immediate Future and Other Matters Pertaining to Correct Translation of the Old Testament." In *Translating and Understanding the Old Testament*. Ed. H. T. Frank and W. L. Reed, pp. 64–70. New York and Nashville: Abingdon Press, 1970.

"Prolegomenon." In C. C. Torrey, *Ezra Studies*, pp. xi–xxviii. 1910. Reprint ed. New York: KTAV Publishing House, 1970.

THE USE OF THE OLD TESTAMENT
IN THE NEW AND OTHER ESSAYS

THE USE OF THE OLD TESTAMENT
IN THE NEW

D. MOODY SMITH, JR.

Professor William F. Stinespring's career has been an expression of his commitment both to biblical scholarship and to the Christian faith. It has been his steady conviction that the study of the Old Testament and of Semitic languages is directly important for, and ultimately indispensable to, the right understanding of the New Testament and hence of Christianity. Therefore, the question of the Old Testament in the New goes to the heart of Professor Stinespring's own interests and concerns. This article, in tribute to him, is an attempt to reopen and review that important question in the light of recent research. Our purpose cannot be to bring forth in detail or on a large scale the results of recent scholarly effort. Concentrating primarily upon explicit usage or citation, we shall attempt to sketch the main lines of development since the publication of Tasker's general book on this subject in 1946, and especially since its revision in 1954.[1]

The phrase "the Old Testament in the New" is, of course, an anachronism on two counts. First, and most importantly, the concept of an "Old Testament" depends upon the existence of a "New

1. R. V. G. Tasker, *The Old Testament in the New*, 2nd ed. (Grand Rapids, Mich.: Eerdmans, 1954). Hopefully this book will also serve as a guide to recent literature in this field. Other bibliographical data may be found in the preface to Krister Stendahl's *The School of St. Matthew and its Use of the Old Testament* (1954; reprinted, Philadelphia: Fortress, 1968) pp. i–xiv. Note also the article by Gottlieb Schrenk, "γράφω . . . ," *Theological Dictionary of the New Testament*, trans. G. W. Bromiley and ed. Gerhard Kittel (Grand Rapids, 1964–69), 1, 742 ff. Principal items of the earlier literature are cited by L. Venard, "Citations de l'Ancien Testament dans le Nouveau Testament," *Dictionnaire de la Bible: Supplément*, ed. L. Pirot (Paris: Librarie Letouzey, 1934), 2, 23–51, esp. 50–51.

Only after the completion of my article was I able to see C. K. Barrett's essay, "The Interpretation of the Old Testament in the New," in *The Cambridge History of the Bible*, vol. I, *From the Beginnings to Jerome* (Cambridge: Cambridge University Press, 1970), pp. 377–411. Important also is the even more recent article by Merrill P. Miller, "Targum, Midrash and the Use of the Old Testament in the New Testament," *Journal for the Study of Judaism*, 2 (1971), 29–82, containing extensive bibliographical information. Note also P. Nickels, *Targum and the New Testament: A Bibliography together with a New Testament Index* (Rome: Pontifical Biblical Institute, 1967).

Testament." Therefore, we should not expect any reference to the
Hebrew Scriptures as Old Testament until the formation of the
New Testament canon was well under way.[2] Nevertheless, Paul
already speaks of the reading of the Old Covenant (II Cor. 3:14),
by which he certainly means part, if not all, of the Scriptures,
and thus prepares the way for the adoption of the term *Old Testament*. In the second place, the canon of the Old Testament was not
officially closed on the Jewish side at the time many New Testament books were being written; thus it is incorrect to imply that
it was completely fixed at the time of Christian origins. Moreover,
some fluidity in Christian usage continued well past the official
establishment of the Jewish canon in A.D. 90 or 100. Nevertheless,
the authority of the Law and the Prophets (Matt. 5:17; 7:12;
Luke 16:16; John 1:45; Rom. 3:21) or the Scriptures (plural,
Matt. 21:42; Mark 12:24; Acts 17:2; or sing., Acts 8:32; John 20:9;
Rom. 4:3) had long been acknowledged within Judaism when
Christianity appeared upon the scene. Such fluidity as there was
pertained only to the Hagiographa, but even there usage had
established the authority of a number of books. Luke refers to the
Law, the Prophets and the Psalms (Luke 24:44), and New Testament usage generally confirms the existence of a threefold canon.
The prologue to the wisdom of Jesus ben Sirach, almost two centuries older than any New Testament book, confirms the general
use of a threefold canon in early Christian times as does the usage
of Philo, who quotes from the Law, Prophets and Writings, and
Josephus (cf. *Against Apion* I:8), whose use of apocryphal material
may be significant.[3]

The Old Testament at the Beginning
of the Christian Era

The problem of the Old Testament canon

The preceding observations are sufficient to justify speaking of
the Old Testament in relation to the New. The term refers to a

2. Perhaps the earliest reference to the Hebrew scriptures as "Old Testament" is
to be found in Melito of Sardis (ca. A.D. 180), who sets forth a list of books τῆς παλαιᾶς
διαθήκης. Cf. W. G. Kümmel *Introduction to the New Testament*, founded by Paul Feine
and Johannes Behm and trans. A. J. Mattill, Jr., 14th ed. rev. (Nashville: Abingdon,
1966), p. 344.

3. Cf. R. H. Pfeiffer, *Introduction to the Old Testament* (New York: Harper and
Brothers, 1941), pp. 67 f.

body of canonical Scriptures whose existence, if not its exact delimitation, was scarcely in doubt. Yet the question of the exact delimitation of the Old Testament in the New Testament period is real and should not simply be bypassed. Because of the predominance of septuagintal quotations, as opposed to quotations which reflect the Hebrew in distinction from the Septuagint, it has been widely assumed that the Septuagint was the Bible of the primitive church. This is by no means an erroneous assumption. On the other hand, the corollary that the Christian church adopted an Alexandrian canon consisting of the books of the Hebrew Old Testament finally accepted at Jamnia (c. A.D. 90) plus the Apocrypha (included in one form or another in extant Septuagint manuscripts) has recently been opposed by A. C. Sundberg.[4] Sundberg argues that such a Hellenistic-Jewish canon never existed at all. The Christian canon, based upon pre-Jamnian Jewish usage, consists of the Law, the Prophets and a more broadly based collection of Hagiographa than was finally admitted by the rabbis at Jamnia. But this canon does not represent an earlier, official Alexandrian canon, as opposed to a narrower Palestinian one. Rather, the septuagintal canon reflects a pre-Jamnian Jewish situation fully as common to Palestine as to the Hellenistic environment of Alexandria. This earlier period in Palestine is reflected also in the Qumran scrolls, where canonical and extracanonical materials existed together with little indication that the Qumraners respected the bounds of canonicity as they were to be later defined. Moreover, the usage of the New Testament, as reflected in Nestle's marginal notes, shows that these earliest Christian writers did not

---

4. *The Old Testament of the Early Church*, Harvard Theological Studies, no. 20 (Cambridge: Harvard University Press, 1964). Sundberg discusses the development of the Alexandrian canon hypothesis on pp. 7–24 and its general acceptance on pp. 25–40. A reserved proponent of the Alexandrian canon hypothesis is R. H. Pfeiffer; see his *Introduction to the Old Testament*, pp. 65–70, and his article "Canon of the Old Testament," *IDB*, 1:510 f. On the other hand, no less an authority than H. E. Ryle, *The Canon of the Old Testament*, 2nd ed. (London: Macmillan, 1914), rejected the Alexandrian canon hypothesis quite emphatically (pp. 156, 180).

Sundberg, "Towards a Revised History of the New Testament Canon," *Studia Evangelica* (Oxford Congress, 1965), vol. 4, which is *Texte und Untersuchungen*, ed. F. L. Cross (Berlin, 1968), 102:452–61, has recently argued that the frequent identification of "canon" and "scripture" is misleading, since in the New Testament γραφή is not the equivalent of "canon." Rather, all the instances of γραφή which are usually cited as carrying the meaning of "canon" can be shown to carry instead the meanings of "specific writing" or "book." The plural γραφαί, moreover, refers to the sacred writings taken together, but not necessarily to the canon.

confine themselves to the Jamnian canon.[5] Earliest Old Testament canonical lists of the church fathers show considerable variation, an unlikely phenomenon if there had been a Hellenistic–Jewish Alexandrian canon of recognized status. The probability that there never was such a canon is further strengthened by the unlikelihood of such a canon's being established independently of Palestinian Judaism.

While Sundberg's case for a certain fluidity in the Hagiographa of Palestine as well as Alexandria seems to be well made, the impression he leaves concerning the early Christian use of extra-canonical (by Jamnian standards) books is not entirely felicitous.[6] Robert A. Kraft has raised some pertinent issues about Sundberg's procedures. He questions "his appeal to the passages from 'non-canonical' Jewish literature listed in the margins of Nestle's 22nd edition of the New Testament (!) as evidence for 'the canon' received by 'the church' from Judaism." Moreover, he asks: "Do alleged parallels in wording and thought indicate actual use? Does actual use indicate canonical status. . . ? Does canonical status for Jude necessarily indicate the same for Paul, or for the whole of early Christianity?"[7] It seems to be a fact that although a few passages from outside the Hebrew or Jamnian canon are cited as scripture in the New Testament, none of these is from the Apocrypha. The New Testament gives the impression that the Old Testament acknowledged by its writers was virtually the same as that adopted by Judaism in the early years of our era.[8] Neverthe-

5. The precise role and importance of Jamnia is a matter of dispute. Sundberg, *The Old Testament of the Early Church*, pp. 113 ff., takes the more-or-less orthodox critical view that the council meeting there ca. A.D. 90 set the bounds of the Hagiographa, confirming some books (e. g., Ecclesiastes, Esther, Song of Songs) and eliminating Sirach and those books known to have been of recent origin. On the other hand, Jack P. Lewis, "What Do We Mean by Jabneh?" *The Journal of Bible and Religion*, 32 (1964), 125–32, points out that the traditional view of Jamnia is largely inference and conjecture. While this may be so, "Jamnia" apparently does point to an actual stabilization of the canon which took place at the end of the first century or shortly thereafter. The second-century proscription of the Septuagint and the Jewish adoption of the Greek version of Aquila (whose limitations correspond to the Jamnian canon) would seem to indicate that such a stabilization had taken place.

6. *The Old Testament of the Early Church*, pp. 53 ff., 81–103.

7. Review of Sundberg, *The Old Testament of the Early Church*, in *JBL*, 85 (1966), 259.

8. In a 1965 Ph.D. dissertation written under the direction of Professor Stinespring, I. H. Eybers has argued forcefully that the books regarded as canonical in Palestine in 100 or even 150 B.C. were virtually the same as those approved at Jamnia at the the end of the first Christian century ("Historical Evidence on the Canon of the Old

less, the apparent absence of apocryphal citations as such in the New Testament does not necessarily mean that the New Testament writers did not acknowledge the apocryphal books as canonical. In point of fact, a number of Old Testament books are not cited as scripture in the New Testament, especially those from the Hagiographa, which was precisely the part of the canon still in a fluid state during the early Christian period.[9] The situation with respect to those books is no different from that of the Apocrypha. There are similarities of language and allusions in the New Testament, but no explicit quotations as scripture. If citation as scripture in the New Testament were made the touchstone of canonicity of the Old, the latter would be significantly smaller.[10] Still, the only certain indication that a book was regarded as canonical is its citation as scripture. (Although one will scarcely doubt that I Samuel and II Kings, neither of which is cited explicitly as scripture, were regarded by the early Christians as a part of their Bible.)

The only safe generalization, then, would go something like this: the Law, the Prophets and a number of the Writings—the exact number being a matter of dispute—were regarded as canonical by the Christians (and Jews) of the New Testament period, but from

---

Testament with Special Reference to the Qumran Sect"). Josephus, Philo, the New Testament, IV Ezra, and especially Qumran are cited in support of this contention. Eybers maintains that the Septuagint can scarcely be adduced as evidence of a broader canon in Hellenistic Judaism, since the manuscripts and lists show its contents to have been very uncertain (pp. 53, 59). Moreover, almost all the important evidence for the Septuagint comes from Christian sources (pp. 61 f.). Nevertheless, Eybers must admit that several documents such as Jubilees, the Testament of the Twelve Patriarchs, Enoch, and Sirach may have been regarded as canonical, or at least authoritative, at Qumran.

While his argument for the prevalence of the Palestinian canon in Greek-speaking Judaism is impressive, Eybers never fully explains why the Christian church, which did not widely use the Apocrypha in the New Testament, would have introduced it into its Old Testament unless it were in use by Hellenistic Jews already.

9. According to the Nestle *index locorum*, Proverbs is cited only four times as Scripture, Job once, and Ecclesiastes and Song of Songs not at all. Psalms on the other hand is cited fifty-five times, or more than any other book in the Old Testament. Thus the casual reference in Luke 24:44 to "the Law of Moses, the Prophets, and the Psalms" seems to be very close to an accurate description of the canon of the New Testament writers. Of course, Kraft's point (above) that the limits of the canon may have differed for individual New Testament writers is well taken.

10. By my count about seventeen Old Testament books are not explicitly cited as Scripture in the New Testament, although only four are not represented at least once in bold-face type in the Nestle text (Ruth, Ezra, Ecclesiastes, Song of Songs).

among those writings the New Testament authors tended to quote
mostly from the Pentateuch, certain of the Prophets, especially
Isaiah, and the Psalms. Moreover, they afford no sure evidence
for the canonicity of the books of the Apocrypha.

Principal texts and versions

That the Hebrew text existed in a form not too different from
the Masoretic text during the New Testament era has now been
shown by the discovery of the Qumran Scrolls. Yet the scrolls also
attest the existence of near prototypes of the Samaritan Pentateuch
and the Septuagint. B. J. Roberts observes that the Qumraners
were little disturbed by the existence of competing textual traditions; in fact, they made the most of them.[11] More conservative
treatment of the textual tradition is attested by the manuscript
finds at Wadi Murabba'at. These manuscripts belong to the period
of the Bar Cocheba Revolt (A.D. 132–135), and the association of
the eminent Rabbi Akiba with that uprising would lead us to expect a closer conformity with the emerging textual "orthodoxy."
Roberts believes that the text-form of the Torah was fairly well
established, with some variation, in pre-Christian times, but that
there were major divergences in other parts of the Old Testament.[12]
But no unified textual tradition at the beginning of the Christian
era can be posited as the beginning point for work upon the problem of the Old Testament in the New. The divergences of the
Septuagint from the Masoretic text already invite such a conclusion.

The Septuagint. The Septuagint is, of course, the immediate
source for most of the Old Testament quotations in the New.
According to R. H. Pfeiffer, eighty percent of the Old Testament
quotations in the New are drawn from the Septuagint.[13] This
figure, presumably based upon agreement or near agreement with
some known septuagintal text-form, may be a bit high, but it is
probably not misleading. In many or even most of these instances
there is little or no disagreement between the Septuagint and the

11. "Text: Old Testament," *IDB*, 4, 583; cf. Stendahl, *The School of St. Matthew*,
esp. pp. 183 ff.
12. Roberts, 4: 583. On the text of the Old Testament compare his earlier work,
The Old Testament Text and Versions (Cardiff: University of Wales Press, 1951).
13. Pfeiffer, 1: 511.

Masoretic text. This does not, of course, mean that the quotation could have just as well been made from the Hebrew, for no two translators are likely to render the same sentence in exactly the same way. Moreover, there are numerous instances in which a New Testament writer obviously follows the Septuagint in distinction from the Hebrew.[14] The dictum that the Septuagint was the Bible of the early Christian community and of the New Testament writers is not false. To repeat this, however, does not solve every problem, for the state of the septuagintal text in early Christian times is itself a far-reaching, highly complex, and important question. Moreover, it is quite clear that not only the Septuagint, but also the Hebrew text and the Targums have had some influence upon the writings of the New Testament.

The question of the nature of the Greek translation we know as the Septuagint has been much debated in the last few decades. Perhaps the chief impetus for this debate has been the theory of Paul Kahle, according to which the Septuagint arose out of a welter of Greek Targums to the various parts of the Old Testament.[15] In Kahle's view, the Letter of Aristeas was intended to propagandize for a standard Jewish translation of the Torah (Pentateuch) into Greek at about the end of the first century B.C. The claims which it makes for the Pentateuch were later extended to the entire Greek translation and the name derived from it applied to the entire body of scriptures by Christians. In point of fact, the Septuagint Old Testament is a creation of second-century Christians out of various Jewish translations of portions of the Old Testament, none of which had previously attained undisputed authoritative status, except perhaps the pentateuchal translation promoted by Aristeas. Evidence for this view is adduced from a number of sources and considerations: the existence of various textual traditions of the Septuagint designated by Jerome (Hesy-

14. For a very convenient and useful assembly of the New Testament, septuagintal, and Masoretic materials see W. Dittmar, *Vetus Testamentum in Novo: Die alttestamentlichen Parallelen des Neuen Testaments im Wortlaut der Urtexte und der Septuaginta* (Göttingen: Vandenhoeck & Ruprecht, 1903). C. H. Toy's older work, *Quotations in the New Testament* (New York: Scribner's, 1884) gives English translations as well as the original New Testament, Hebrew, and septuagintal texts.

15. See *The Cairo Geniza*, The Schweich Lectures of the British Academy, 1941 (London: Oxford University Press, 1947), pp. 132–79, esp. 157 f., 165, 174 ff. Kahle published a second edition of this book a decade later (Oxford: Blackwell, 1959), in which see esp. pp. 235 ff.

chius, Lucian, and Origen); the likelihood that earlier translation work underlies the three second-century Greek versions of Aquila, Theodotion, and Symmachus (not to mention the anonymous translations cited in Origen's Hexapla); and the numerous New Testament quotations which do not correspond to the text of the Septuagint.[16] Kahle also maintains that in dealing with a translation it is fallacious to assume a single *Urtext* as one does when dealing with an original text. It is rather *prima facie* possible that translations of such a work as the Old Testament would spring up quite independently. Kahle cites the growth of the Targums and of the Latin and Syriac versions of the Bible as evidence of his contention that in the case of translations, standardization of the text follows upon a period of freedom and even confusion in its transmission.[17]

Although Kahle's position seems plausible, the prevailing tide of contemporary scholarship is against it.[18] Major objections are raised on several counts. First, the recently discovered Greek Old Testament fragments from Qumran and elsewhere seem to confirm the existence of a standardized Greek text in the pre-Christian period, although Kahle has not conceded this.[19] Secondly, evidence is lacking for the process of standardization in the second-century Christian church. Moreover, the second-century B.C. prologue to the Wisdom of Sirach speaks of the translation of the threefold canon in such a way as to imply something more than a collection of more or less unofficial Targums, and there is some doubt that the evidence of Philo and Josephus can be disposed of in such a way as to accommodate Kahle's theory.[20] As for the New Testa-

16. Note especially Alexander Sperber, "New Testament and Septuagint," *JBL*, 59 (1940), 193–293; cf. his earlier article "The New Testament and the Septuagint," in the Hebrew quarterly *Tarbiz*, 6 (1934), 1–29 (*non vid.*).

17. *Cairo Geniza*, 1st ed., p. 175.

18. Roberts, *The Old Testament Text and Versions*, pp. 111–15; Sidney Jellicoe, *The Septuagint and Modern Study* (Oxford: Clarendon Press, 1968), pp. 59–63, catalogues older and more recent opposition to Kahle (H. M. Orlinsky, Peter Walters (Katz), D. Barthélemy, F. L. Cross, and H. H. Rowley).

19. F. L. Cross, "The History of the Biblical Text in the Light of Discoveries in the Judean Desert," *Harvard Theological Review*, 57 (1964), 281–99, esp. 281–84. Cf. Kahle, *The Cairo Geniza*, 2nd ed., pp. 246 f.

20. *Cairo Geniza*, 1st ed., pp. 141 ff., 150 ff.; 2nd ed., 229 ff., 247 ff. Cf. Peter Katz, *Philo's Bible: The Aberrant Text of Bible Quotations in Some Philonic Writings and its Place in the Textual History of the Greek Bible* (Cambridge: Cambridge University Press, 1950), who believes the variations in Philo's Old Testament texts have been introduced from later translations.

ment quotations, most do not differ materially from the Septuagint,[21] and there are a number of possible explanations for those that do: quotation from memory, influence of Masoretic or other Hebrew traditions or of the Aramaic Targums. But such reservations regarding Kahle's denial of the existence of a non-Christian Septuagint do not necessarily rule out other aspects of his hypothesis. In his criticism of the predominant theory identified with Paul de Lagarde, Kahle rightly objects to the assumption that a translated text must, like an original text, have a single *Urtext* or *autographon.* Independent translations could arise, and apparently did.[22] Certainly it is reasonable to suppose that traces of variant readings arising from such processes may be found in the New Testament.

The implications of the present state of Septuagint studies for New Testament exegesis generally are thus difficult to assess. Even if Kahle's thesis is rejected, a certain fluidity in the Greek text of the Old Testament, if not distinct traditions of translation, remains a certainty. Accordingly, variations in New Testament quotations from the principal Septuagint manuscripts may in any instance simply indicate reliance upon a variant Greek translation. Needless to say, each such instance is to be judged on its own merits.

The Targums. While the importance of the Septuagint for the investigation of the use of the Old Testament in the New has long been recognized, the question of the bearing of the Aramaic Targums upon this problem is still in relatively early stages of exploration. There is, first of all, the matter of which Targums are most useful in New Testament study. (Of course, the Targums of the Hagiographa are generally rather late.) Gustaf Hermann Dalman threw his prestige behind the value of the official Pentateuchal Targum of Onkelos and the Prophetic Targum of Jonathan, which

21. Sperber, "New Testament and Septuagint," p. 204, cites Turpie, *The Old Testament in the New* (London, 1868) to the effect that the New Testament departs from the Septuagint in 185 instances, but he also cites Grinfield, *Apology for the Septuagint* (1841), who finds only about fifty quotations that differ materially from the Septuagint.

22. Saul Lieberman, *Greek in Jewish Palestine: Studies in the Life and Manners of Jewish Palestine in the II–IV Centuries C.E.* (New York: Jewish Theological Seminary, 1942), pp. 47 ff., adduces evidence of the use of Greek translation(s) of the Scriptures by Palestinian rabbis. W. D. Davies, "Law in First-Century Judaism," *IDB*, 3: 90, refers to a statement on translating the law by Rabban Simeon Gamaliel, who is reported to have said that such a translation could be written only in Greek.

he regarded as representative of the early Targumic tradition of Palestine, despite the fact that he was well aware of their immediate Babylonian provenance. More recent research, especially that of Paul Kahle, has emphasized the scholastic and standardizing tendencies at work in Onkelos especially, and has turned to the Palestinian Targum as a better representative of the speech and thought of first-century Palestine.[23] With the further support afforded by the discovery of the Neofiti Codex of the Palestinian Targum, Kahle's views have in this case won wide acceptance. The recent monograph of Martin S. McNamara seeks to vindicate the early date of the Palestinian Targum and its importance for early Christianity by examining certain texts and motifs of the New Testament against that background.[24]

I am unable to offer the critical evaluation which McNamara's significant work deserves. Obviously, however, he has shown that there are affinities of various sorts between the New Testament and the Palestinian Targum, and thus he has reason to think that he has vindicated the statement of Kahle which he quotes toward the beginning and end of his work:

> "We can learn many more details from them [the PT texts] than from the material collected by Billerbeck and Bonsirven. ... In the Palestinian Targum of the Pentateuch we have in the main material coming down from pre-Christian times which must be studied by everyone who wishes to understand the state of Judaism at the time of the birth of Christianity. And we possess this material in a language of which we can say that it was similar to that spoken by the earliest Christians. It is material, the importance of which can scarcely be exaggerated."[25]

Needless to say, the value of the Targums for New Testament investigation is not limited to what light they may shed upon the

23. *Cairo Geniza*, 1st ed., pp. 117 ff.; 2nd ed., 191 ff. Nevertheless, discussion continues among the experts as to the antiquity of this Targum. See the articles by Malcolm C. Doubles, "Toward the Publication of the Extant Texts of the Palestinian Targum(s)," *Vetus Testamentum*, 15 (1965), 16–26, and "Indications of Antiquity in the Orthography and Morphology of the Fragment Targum," *In Memoriam Paul Kahle*, ed. Matthew Black and Georg Fohrer (Berlin: Töpelmann, 1968), pp. 79–89.

24. *The New Testament and the Palestinian Targum to the Pentateuch*, Analecta Biblica, no. 27 (Rome: Pontifical Biblical Institute, 1966), pp. 33 ff.

25. *Ibid.*, pp. 34, 253; *The Cairo Geniza*, 2nd ed., p. 208.

use of the Old Testament in the New. They afford a rich resource of material relating to the language, conceptuality, and religion of the Judaism of New Testament times. With the publication of critical texts of Onkelos and Jonathan,[26] as well as the forthcoming Madrid edition of the Palestinian Targum, elicited by the discovery of its complete text in the Neofiti Codex,[27] the Targums are now more than ever before becoming accessible for New Testament and cognate research.

The use of the Old Testament in late Judaism

The consideration of the questions of the canon, text, and versions of the Old Testament in the first Christian century provides the necessary framework for any discussion of the use of the Scriptures of Judaism in the books of the New Testament. Yet it does not supply the key to understanding the motives, methods, and purposes that govern their use. Such a key is perhaps to be found in the investigation of the use of the Old Testament in contemporary Judaism. Yet to gain access to such a key is no simple task. For one thing, it is perhaps easier to ascertain the typical uses of the Old Testament in first-century Christianity than in first-century Judaism. For example, the New Testament affords a fairly comprehensive picture of the use of the Old Testament in the theology and practice of the early church. On the other hand, the rabbinic literature is organized around interests and perspectives of post-Jamnian Judaism, which was predominantly Pharisaic. While Philo utilizes exegetical methods and perhaps traditions common also to the rabbis, he is apparently an original if not an entirely isolated figure. Josephus' interests in Old Testament texts are primarily those of a historian, albeit a first-century historian with apologetic motivation. The Qumran literature probably furnishes the most fruitful parallels to the New Testament and

26. Alexander Sperber, *The Bible in Aramaic*, 3 vols. (Leiden: Brill, 1959–62). See also J. W. Etheridge, trans., *The Targums of Onkelos and Jonathan Ben Uzziel on the Pentateuch with the Fragments of the Jerusalem Targum from the Chaldee*, 2 vols. in 1 (1862, 1865; reprint ed., New York: KTAV Publishing House, 1971).

27. A. D. Macho, ed. *Neophyti 1: Targum Palestinense, Ms de la Biblioteca Vaticana*, Textos y Estudios, nos. 7 ff. (Madrid: Consejo Superior de Investigaciones Científicas, 1968–). The first two volumes have appeared, but I was able to see them only after the completion of this article.

early Christian usage.[28] True, the Essenes or Qumraners do not represent a main line of Jewish piety, but a sect. Yet precisely their sectarian character affords an analogy with earliest Christianity, which was also, if in a somewhat different way, a sect of Judaism.

In addition to these frequently cited representatives of first-century Judaism, a consideration of the use of the Old Testament in the so-called Apocrypha, or even the use or reappropriation of the earlier books or traditions of the Old Testament in later books or recensions, might be relevant and worthwhile. It is arguable, however, that such instances are qualitatively different from those previously mentioned, since many of the apocryphal books, as well as the later Old Testament books, were very likely written before the Old Testament canon was closed. Of course, a number of the writings of the New Testament, Qumran, and Philo were composed before the Old Testament canon (particularly the contents of the Hagiographa) was firmly fixed, so any such distinction is less than absolute. Nonetheless, the Apocrypha differs from the New Testament, Philo, the rabbinic sources, and Qumran, not only in being for the most part somewhat earlier, but also in lacking any clear differentia from the later Old Testament books themselves —witness their inclusion in the Septuagint.[29] The apocryphal writers are not so clearly concerned with coming to terms with or expounding a body of accepted scripture. Neither do they feel the need to reinterpret the scriptures in the light of a new historical situation (Qumran, the New Testament) or a new perspective or insight (Philo). Therefore, the relative scarcity of explicit Old Testament citations, in comparison to numerous references and allusions, is not surprising.

The most important witnesses to the use of the Old Testament in Jewish religious literature contemporary with the New Testament (i. e. the rabbis, Philo, and Qumran) all manifest some similarities to the New Testament. Needless to say, they also display

---

28. Cf. J. A. Fitzmyer, "The Use of Explicit Old Testament Quotations in Qumran Literature and in the New Testament," *NTS*, 7 (1961), 297 f.

29. Cf. J. L. Zink, "The Use of the Old Testament in the Apocrypha" (Ph.D. diss., Duke University, 1963). In an otherwise careful study Zink pays too little attention to the implications of the obvious but important fact that the apocryphal writers could not know that they were writing "apocryphal" rather than "Old Testament" books.

some important differences, inasmuch as the appropriation of the Old Testament in the New presupposes Jesus Christ as its central organizing point. These similarities and differences have been studied with respect to various documents of early Christianity and late Judaism.[30] Sweeping generalizations regarding the use of the Old Testament in, let us say, the rabbis and the New Testament are probably not very helpful, and, while unnecessary for the scholar, may prove misleading to the novice. More profitable are comparisons of specific authors or documents and the use of contemporary and cognate materials, for instance, from Philo or Qumran, to illuminate specific instances of the use of the Old Testament in the New. With this caveat in mind and with appropriate disclaimers to completeness, it may nevertheless be useful to record a few observations about the use of the Old Testament in Judaism.

The use of the Old Testament in rabbinic materials in comparison to its use by Paul has been extensively treated by Joseph Bonsirven, whose work is useful for obtaining a grasp of rabbinic exegesis generally.[31] Bonsirven is able to show many affinities between Paul and the rabbis, especially in exegetical method and technique, introductory formulas, and the like. What is true for Paul, moreover, holds good for much of the remainder of the New Testament. With good reason Géza Vermès sees in the New Testament material for the reconstruction of methods and traditions of Jewish exegesis in the first century of our era.[32] Moreover, the relationships in exegetical method among the documents of this period are complex. For example, there are remarkable affinities not only between the rabbis and the New Testament, but also between the

30. See, for example, the recent monographs of S. G. Sowers, *The Hermeneutics of Philo and Hebrews: A Comparison of the Interpretation of the Old Testament in Philo Judaeus and the Epistle to the Hebrews*, Basel Studies of Theology, no. 1 (Zurich: EVZ Verlag, 1965) and Peder Borgen, *Bread From Heaven: An Exegetical Study of the Concept of Manna in the Gospel of John and the Writings of Philo*, Supplements to Novum Testamentum, no. 10 (Leiden: Brill, 1965). J. W. Doeve, *Jewish Hermeneutics in the Synoptic Gospels and Acts* (Assen: van Gorcum, 1954), has provided an introduction to the use of Jewish materials for understanding Old Testament exegesis in the narrative books of the New Testament. See also B. M. Metzger, "The Formulas Introducing Quotations of Scripture in the New Testament and the Mishnah," *JBL*, 70 (1951), 297–307.

31. *Exégèse Rabbinique et Exégèse Paulinienne*, Bibliothèque de Théologie historique (Paris, Beauchesne, 1938).

32. *Scripture and Tradition in Judaism: Haggadic Studies*, Studia Post-Biblica, vol. 4 (Leiden: Brill, 1961), p. 8.

rabbinic literature and the Dead Sea Scrolls.[33] Since the hallmarks
of rabbinic exegesis have been set forth in great detail by Bonsirven[34] and summarized by others,[35] there is no need to rehearse
them here. Suffice it to say that despite many points of contact,
one receives rather divergent impressions of the Old Testament
from Paul and the rabbis.[36] The disparity between them doubtless
has something to do with Paul's Christocentrism and the centrality of the Torah in the rabbis. For Paul the Old Testament is
no longer primarily law, in the sense of commandment, although
it certainly was and remains, that. It is primarily promise and the
prefiguration of the salvation event of the coming of Christ. Its
prophetic and eschatological potentialities are utilized to the fullest.
While Paul can and does use the Old Testament commandments
in a prescriptive sense (e. g. Rom. 12:20; cf. also I Cor. 9:9 where
the Old Testament is used in precisely this way, even though Paul
insists it now applies to Christians), this is not the style most characteristic of him (cf. Rom. 10:6 ff., where Paul takes a word about
the law from Deut. 30:12 ff. and applies it to Christ). For the rabbis, on the other hand, the Old Testament is above all God's commandments; their energies are tirelessly devoted to the exegesis of
the commandments for prescriptive application to specific situations. Perhaps it is not misleading to say that while the rabbis tend
to read the Old Testament as law,[37] Paul (and with him the other
New Testament writers) reads the Old Testament as prophecy
and even transforms specific commandments and narrations into
prophetic words (e. g. I Cor. 9:9 and 10:1 ff., which although
taken in something like their original sense are thought to point
forward to the Christian community).

Possibly Philo's use of the Old Testament ought to be studied as
an instance of highly creative Hellenistic rabbinic exegesis. Yet
because Philo seems so distinctive in comparison to the rabbis
whom we know through the Mishnah and Talmud there is good

33. Fitzmyer, "The Use of Explicit Old Testament Quotations," pp. 304 f.
34. Pt. 1, esp. 252 ff.
35. E. g., E. Earle Ellis, *Paul's Use of the Old Testament* (Grand Rapids, Mich.:
Eerdmans, 1957), pp. 45 ff., 54 ff.
36. Noted also by Bonsirven, pp. 324, 348 ff.
37. Cf. Bonsirven, p. 252: "Le Judaïsme est la Religion de la Tora, comportant
pour la Loi divine un culte savant et pieux: de cette propriété fondamentale dérivent
tous les caractères de l'exégèse juive."

reason for considering him as a special instance. Since the precise delineation of Philo's whole orientation and purpose has been a matter of dispute, unanimity over his exegetical method ought not to be expected. Be that as it may, there is little inclination to deny to Philo the title of the leading exponent of allegorical exegesis in first-century Judaism. His methods or those of his school were later taken up by Christian exegetes and became common currency in the church for centuries. The kind of allegorical exegesis we find in Philo is not utterly without representation in the New Testament (see Gal. 4:21–31), and there are weighty reasons for seeing a certain positive relation between his biblical exegesis and what we find in the Epistle to the Hebrews. Yet the total impression conveyed by Philo's exegetical procedure is very different from that obtained from the New Testament, and indeed from the main line of rabbinic exegesis. While the New Testament and the rabbis may differ in emphasizing the prophetic and legal aspects of the scriptures respectively, they lack the Philonic penchant for using the facts, figures, words, and whole passages of scripture as ciphers or symbols designating some less obvious reality to be grasped by either mystical or philosophical insight. Both Paul and the rabbis appear confident that the scriptures have some rather clear and direct message, while for Philo their meaning is of a more recondite character and requires a unique insight or inspiration as the prerequisite of interpretation. Still, in just this fact there is a point of contact between Philo and the New Testament. For both, a proper perspective is required before the scriptures can be understood. In the New Testament, of course, this perspective is given in the central, saving event. In Philo it is less concrete, but nonetheless real. Whoever does not read the Old Testament by the light of that mystical and divine revelation which Philo associates with λόγος, νοῦς, or φῶς will not find its more important meaning. Like the rabbinic literature, however, Philo's writings lack the New Testament's emphasis upon the prophetic and eschatological dimensions of the Hebrew Scriptures.[38] For Philo the necessary perspective on the Old Testament is not so integrally related to eschatology and historical revelation.

38. Thus C. F. D. Moule in his important article, "Fulfillment-Words in the New Testament: Use and Abuse," *NTS*, 14 (1967/68), 311, points out that there is in Philo virtually no use of the πληροῦν-words so common in the New Testament.

The most striking similarities to the New Testament's use of the Old are probably to be found in the Qumran Scrolls. The affinity between the use of the Old Testament in the scrolls and in the New Testament doubtless hinges upon the fact that both the Qumran community and the primitive church saw in their own times and among themselves the fulfillment of biblical prophecy.[39] One might characterize both the New Testament and the Qumran use of the scriptures as historical, prophetic, or eschatological. 't is historical in the sense that the historical and revelatory situation in which the community finds itself is the indispensable ingredient of the hermeneutical process; prophetic in that the scriptures are seen as written about or directed toward the events transpiring in and around the community;[40] eschatological in that these events are understood as the culmination, or the anticipation of the culmination, of God's sovereign activity as Lord of history. It is no

39. Cf. Herbert Braun, *Qumran und das Neue Testament* (Tübingen: Mohr, 1966), 2: 306. For a summary of the literature on the use and exposition of the Scriptures at Qumran, see pp. 301–25. A brief, but illuminating discussion of Qumran biblical interpretation is to be found in Géza Vermès, "The Qumran Interpretation of Scripture in its Historical Setting," *The Annual of Leeds University Oriental Society*, 6 (1966–68; *Dead Sea Scroll Studies 1969*), 84–97. Cf. also the substantial work of O. Betz, *Offenbarung und Schriftforschung in der Qumransekte*, Wissenschaftliche Untersuchungen zum Neuen Testament, no. 6 (Tübingen: Mohr, 1960), and L. H. Silberman, "Unriddling the Riddle: A Study in the Structure and Language of the Habakkuk Pesher," *Revue de Qumran*, 3 (1961), 323–64.

With good reason Moule, "Fulfillment-Words in the New Testament," p. 311, speaks of a greater sense of completeness in the New Testament than in the Qumran sources, a situation doubtless indicative of the difference between Qumran and New Testament eschatology.

40. In this connection F. F. Bruce, *Biblical Exegesis in the Qumran Texts* (Grand Rapids, Mich.: Eerdmans, 1959), pp. 67 f., compares I Pet. 1:10–12 and 1 Qp Hab. vii. 1–5.

According to I Pet. 1:10–12a, "The prophets who prophesied of the grace that was to be yours searched and inquired about this salvation; they inquired what person or time was indicated by the Spirit of Christ within them when predicting the sufferings of Christ and the subsequent glory. It was revealed to them that they were not serving themselves, but you. . . ."

The Qumran community (1 Qp Hab. vii. 1–5) had a similar view: "God commanded Habakkuk to write the things that were coming upon the last generation, but the fulfillment of the epoch he did not make known to him. And as for the words, 'so he may run may read,' their interpretation concerns the teacher of Righteousness, to whom God made known all the mysteries of the words of his servants the prophets."

In the latter text Vermès, "The Qumran Interpretation of Scripture," p. 91, sees the following assumptions or principles of Qumran prophetic exegesis at work: the mysterious character of the prophetic word; its reference to end-events; the imminence of those events for the contemporary generation; the revelation of the mysteries in question to the Teacher of Righteousness.

coincidence that both the Qumran community and the primitive church saw in Isa. 40:3 a direct command or prophecy relating to their own times (1QS viii, 13–16; cf. Mark 1:3; Luke 3:4–6; John 1:23). Nor is it a matter of chance that both the Qumran commentator and the apostle Paul saw in Hab. 2:4 a reference to faith in their own founder or Lord (1Qp Hab. viii, 1–3; cf. Rom. 1:17; Gal. 3:11). Moreover, similar patterns in the use of the Old Testament emerge in both the scrolls and the New Testament, despite the differences in literary genre. (There are, for example, no biblical commentaries, strictly speaking, in the New Testament.) Joseph Fitzmyer has classified the non-*pesher* scroll quotations into four basic types: the literal or historical class, in which the original sense of the text is preserved; the modernized texts, which are applied to new situations in the life of the community (Hab. 2:4 in 1Qp Hab. viii, 1–3 would presumably fit this category also); the accommodated texts, which are taken out of context or essentially modified; and the eschatological texts, in which an original promise or threat is applied to the yet outstanding culmination of history toward which the community is pointing. Fitzmyer[41] sees these same basic types occurring frequently in the New Testament, although he wisely hesitates to claim that these categories exhaust the full range of the use of the Old Testament by New Testament writers.[42] Nevertheless, in view of the similarities in eschatology and historical situation, it is not surprising that a related similarity in the ways of adopting and adapting the Scriptures can also be perceived.

In a more technical vein, recent research has also uncovered some striking similarities between the text-form of the New Testament quotations and those of Qumran.[43] The investigation and comparison of these text-forms may prove to be an interesting and significant aspect of the study of the Old Testament text in Qumran. The intriguing question stimulating—or plaguing—such investigation will be whether affinities in such text-forms between

41. "The Use of Explicit Old Testament Quotations," pp. 297–333.
42. *Ibid.*, p. 330, esp. n. 2.
43. J. de Waard, *A Comparative Study of the Old Testament Text in the Dead Sea Scrolls and in the New Testament*, Studies on the Texts of the Desert of Judah, no. 4 (Leiden: Brill, 1965), discerns evidence of a relationship between the Qumran text and Old Testament quotations in the New, particularly in the speeches of Acts; see pp. 17–26, 41 ff., 78 ff.

the New Testament and Qumran mean that the New Testament
writers or speakers knew the Hebrew text in forms similar to those
known at Qumran or that the Qumran text-form or something
similar underlies the Greek translations employed by the New
Testament writers. Already de Waard has attacked the well-known
view that the speeches of Acts are Luke's composition with the
argument that affinities with Qumran text-forms indicate that an
Aramaic tradition at least stands as the basis of the speeches.[44]

Although the early Christian appropriation of the Old Testament cannot be explained solely on the basis of documents of
contemporary Judaism, indispensable light is shed upon the New
Testament by them. Clearly they show that the ways in which the
New Testament writers put the Old Testament to use are not at
all unprecedented. While this usage may seem at places arbitrary
enough, it is by and large neither more nor less arbitrary than the
contemporary use of the Old Testament among Jews. Against this
background it is to be understood and appreciated.[45]

THE USE OF THE OLD TESTAMENT IN PRIMITIVE CHRISTIANITY

The use of the Old Testament by Jesus

Is the use of the Old Testament in the New Testament grounded
upon its prior use in the primitive church? Most critics would
surely answer affirmatively, regardless of how many reservations
they might hold regarding some recent theories of its use. Is the
primitive church's use of the Old Testament grounded upon
Jesus' own understanding and interpretation of the Old Testament?
On this question there is not even the most general kind of consensus. Only sheer temerity would deny that Jesus was familiar

---

44. Pp. 78 ff.

45 A rapidly developing interest in Jewish exegetical techniques in the period of
Christian origins is strongly reflected in recent research and publication. Along with
the earlier work of Doeve, Vermès and Borgen mentioned elsewhere, the following
recent articles exemplify this interest: R. Le Déaut's review of A. G. Wright's *The
Literary Genre of Midrash* (Staten Island: Alba House, 1967), translated and published
as "Apropos a Definition of Midrash" in *Interpretation*, 25 (1971), 259–82; J. W.
Bowker, "Speeches in Acts: A Study in Proem and Yellammedenu Form," *NTS*, 14
(1967/68), 96–111; E. Earle Ellis, "Midrash, Targum and New Testament Quotations," *Neotestamentica et Semitica: Studies in Honour of Matthew Black*, ed. Ellis and M.
Wilcox (Edinburgh: Clark, 1969), pp. 61–69; *idem*, "Midraschartige Züge in den
Reden der Apostelgeschichte," *ZNTW*, 62 (1971), 94–104.

with the Old Testament, regarded it as God's word, and reflected upon his own mission in the light of a religious perspective fundamentally informed by it. On the other hand, there is a real problem as to the extent to which the use of the Old Testament in the New— even in the Gospels—reflects directly or indirectly Jesus' own meditation over, and interpretation of, the Scriptures.

To attempt to adjudicate this question is too great a task for a general essay such as this. But since the question cannot ultimately be skirted, it is therefore incumbent upon us at least to describe the present state of affairs and to venture an opinion concerning it. While there may be a great variety of viewpoints on this question, there seem to have developed two basic positions around which, or between which, others take their place. For convenience we may call these the conservative and the radical views, recognizing the lack of precision inherent in such a characterization. According to the conservative view, represented particularly by such luminaries as Dodd, the two Mansons, and Hoskyns, Jesus very carefully thought out his mission and message in reflection upon the Old Testament, and his line of thought can be recovered from the New Testament (and the Old). This view has had considerable popularity also in America. According to the more radical position current in the Bultmann school and espoused by a number of other scholars, including some in the English-speaking world, the Old Testament quotations in the Gospels are largely the result of the interpretative work of the early Christian church, which used the Old Testament to prove the messiahship of Jesus and to make other points in controversy with Judaism. Bultmann's view that Jesus was a first-century Palestinian rabbi as well as an apocalyptic prophet would seem to imply that Jesus was an interpreter of the will of God found in the Scriptures. Bultmann does not deny this, but maintains a profound skepticism as to the possibility of recovering Jesus' own interpretations of the Scriptures from the New Testament, which is "Christian" in a sense in which Jesus was not.[46]

46. Bultmann's own position on Jesus' use of the Old Testament is implicit in his *Die Geschichte der synoptischen Tradition*, Forschungen zur Religion und Literatur des alten Testaments, n.s. 12; 4th ed. (Göttingen: Vandenhoeck & Ruprecht, 1958), although he does not set it forth in a comprehensive statement. On pp. 51 f., however, he indicates how in the context of *Streitgespräche* Old Testament words are attributed to Jesus, without denying that some may actually go back to him (see also pp. 272 ff.,

These two positions are closely but not inextricably bound to the question of whether Jesus understood his earthly ministry as messianic. The synoptic Gospels, beginning with Mark, certainly interpret this ministry in that way in accord with their Christian faith. Yet the problems of taking the Gospels', particularly Mark's portrayal, as historical fact have often been pointed out.[47] Certainly they bear the imprint of faith's later interpretation, whatever the facts may have been. If one accepts the Gospels' portrayal as basically historical, one is likely also to take seriously the several hints and indications that Jesus performed his messianic role in fulfillment of the Scriptures, especially insofar as he took it upon himself to suffer and die. Thus those who accept the Gospel picture of a deliberately messianic ministry are inclined also to believe that Jesus thought of his suffering as a fulfillment of Scripture, and particularly a fulfillment or representation of the Suffering Servant motif of Isaiah. Those who are skeptical of Jesus' explicitly messianic consciousness—or at least skeptical of recovering it—tend to regard the Scripture fulfillment motif as a theologoumenon of the earliest church and to question the view that Jesus thought of himself as Suffering Servant.

In this connection, it is remarkable that there has lately been some breaking of ranks, especially on the conservative side. Two British scholars who have come to maturation in America have in recent years gone over to the more radical (or Bultmannian) posi-

---

302 ff., and 329). On Bultmann's view of Jesus as rabbi see *Jesus and the Word*, trans. L. P. Smith and E. H. Lantero (New York: Scribner's, 1934), pp. 57 ff.; for his understanding of the relation between the historical Jesus and the Christian kerygma consult his *Theology of the New Testament*, trans. Kendrick Grobel (New York: Scribner's, 1951), 1: 3–52.

47. Perhaps most memorable is Albert Schweitzer's *The Quest of the Historical Jesus*, trans. William Montgomery (New York: Macmillan, 1954), pp. 330 ff., essentially agreeing with W. Wrede's *Das Messiasgeheimnis in den Evangelien*, 2nd ed. (Göttingen: Vandenhoeck & Ruprecht, 1913), esp. pp. 9–22. The most thoroughgoing critique of the Marcan framework is K. L. Schmidt, *Der Rahmen der Geschichte Jesu: Literarische Untersuchungen zur ältesten Jesusüberlieferung* (Berlin: Trowitzsch, 1919). The difficulties of taking the Marcan framework as historical have been reiterated by D. E. Nineham, "The Order of Events in St. Mark's Gospel—An Examination of Dr. Dodd's Hypothesis," in his *Studies in the Gospels* (Oxford: Oxford University Press, 1955), and J. M. Robinson, *A New Quest of the Historical Jesus*, Studies in Biblical Theology, no. 25 (London: SCM, 1959), pp. 35 ff. For a brief summary of a wide consensus of opinion concerning the nature of the Marcan framework by a "conservative" scholar, see Joachim Jeremias, *The Eucharistic Words of Jesus*, trans. Norman Perrin (New York: Scribner's, 1966), pp. 91 f., esp. p. 92, n. 1.

tion, namely, R. H. Fuller and Norman Perrin.[48] Moreover, the view once common among English scholars that Jesus thought of himself in terms of the Isaianic Suffering Servant has been subjected to searching scrutiny by the Englishwoman M. D. Hooker, who has pronounced a negative judgment upon it.[49] Moreover, Miss Hooker's negative conclusions are now reflected in the work of the distinguished British scholar, C. K. Barrett.[50] Also, the Anglican Barnabas Lindars, whose stimulating monograph on the use of the Old Testament in the New generally takes up and affirms the earlier work of Dodd, discreetly demurs at accepting the latter's suggestion that Jesus is the originator of the exegetical methodology of the New Testament writers.[51]

The present state of affairs admits of few unexceptionable generalizations on the question of Jesus' use of the Old Testament beyond the acknowledgment that he in fact interpreted it. Thus scholars of diverse perspectives such as W. D. Davies and Rudolf Bultmann can agree in describing Jesus as a rabbi.[52] While recent

48. Fuller, *The Foundations of New Testament Christology* (New York: Scribner's, 1965), *passim*, but especially pp. 108 f. and pp. 18 f., where Fuller adumbrates his tendency to ascribe scripture fulfillment to the early church. Perrin's most recent statement of his position is to be found in *Rediscovering the Teaching of Jesus* (New York: Harper & Row, 1967). He does not deny that Jesus used the Old Testament (p. 66) but, like Fuller, tends to ascribe Old Testament exegetical work to the traditions of the early church (pp. 27 f., 176 f., 185). Both Fuller and Perrin have departed from the predominant Anglo-Saxon affirmation of the explicitly messianic consciousness of Jesus.

49. *Jesus and the Servant: The Influence of the Servant Concept of Deutero-Isaiah in the New Testament* (London: S.P.C.K., 1959). Miss Hooker therefore brings into question the view of the distinguished Göttingen New Testament scholar Joachim Jeremias that Jesus identified with the Servant; cf. Jeremias and Walther Zimmerli, *The Servant of God*, Studies in Biblical Theology, no. 20 (London: SCM, 1957). Jeremias has replied in a review of Hooker, *Journal of Theological Studies*, n.s. 11 (1960), 140–44, and the continuation of the discussion scarcely permits us to treat the matter as settled.

50. *Jesus and the Gospel Tradition* (London: S.P.C.K., 1967), pp. 39 f.

51. *New Testament Apologetic: The Doctrinal Significance of the Old Testament Quotations* (Philadelphia: Westminster, 1961), p. 30.

52. Bultmann, *Jesus and the Word*, esp. pp. 57 ff., and W. D. Davies, *The Sermon on the Mount* (New York: Oxford, 1966), pp. 129 ff. and 154 ff. A helpful inventory and initial discussion of the Old Testament in the sayings of Jesus has been made by T. W. Manson, "The Old Testament in the Teaching of Jesus," *Bulletin of the John Rylands Library*, 34 (1951/52), 312–32. Two more recent works, Perrin, *Rediscovering the Teaching of Jesus*, (see above, n. 48) and L. Hartman, *Prophecy Interpreted: The Formation of Some Jewish Apocalyptic Texts and of the Eschatological Discourse Mark 13 par*, Coniectanea Biblica: New Testament Series, no. 1 (Lund: CWK Gleerup, 1966), in rather different ways undertake investigations of Old Testament material attributed to Jesus. While Perrin's work follows well-established form- and redaction-critical lines, Hartman concentrates on the relation of the material in question to Jewish

criticism manifests a discernible trend toward greater recognition
of the role of the early church in the development of Christology
generally, as well as in the christological use of the Old Testament,
it scarcely justifies the assumption that Jesus did not reflect upon
his own mission in light of the Scriptures. At least his authoritative
interpretation of Scripture implies a uniquely authoritative, if not
an explicitly messianic, self-consciousness. The problem of Jesus'
use of the Old Testament, particularly in connection with his own
self-understanding, is difficult for almost the same reason that the
problem of his messianic self-consciousness is difficult. For at points
in the Gospel where Jesus speaks in terms later employed by the
Christian community it is often hard to decide what, if anything,
goes back to the historical Jesus. This is especially true if the critic
eschews both the orthodox and the critically orthodox ways of cutting the Gordian knot, that is, either, to maintain that the Gospels
accurately portray Jesus' own mind or, alternatively, to regard all
explicit—and some implicit—expressions of Christology (or mes-
sianology) as the work of the later church. In this connection Jesus'
use of the Old Testament might profitably be made the subject of
further investigation, since it represents an important instance in
which an external criterion, i. e. the textual traditions of the Old
Testament, can serve as a check and a guide for the judgments of
the critic. (For example, an Old Testament reference reflecting
the Hebrew text or the Targums will presumably have a higher
claim to authenticity than one reproducing the Septuagint.)
Naturally, the investigator would do well to begin with those
citations which do not relate directly to the questions of Jesus'
messianic consciousness and his death and thereby attempt to
establish a basis for further, more difficult, judgments.

For our present purposes the obvious impossibility of adjudi-
cating the questions and issues surrounding Jesus' use of the Old
Testament is not an insurmountable obstacle. Although this is an
important area for research and theological reflection, it is nevertheless possible and legitimate to circumvent it in order to deal

---

exegetical or midrashic techniques. In a similar fashion Birger Gerhardsson has
investigated the temptation narratives in *The Testing of God's Son (Matt 4:1–11 &
Par): An Analysis of an Early Christian Midrash* (Coniectanea Biblica: New Testament
Series, no. 2; Lund: CWK Gleerup, 1966).

with the use of the Old Testament in the New Testament books. For most of what can be said on that subject will stand whatever may be decided about historical origins, whether with Jesus or the early church.

The use of the Old Testament in the primitive church

The use of the Old Testament in the earliest preaching is amply attested in the Books of Acts. While the role of Luke in the composition of the speeches was certainly considerable, recent research tends to confirm the judgment of Martin Dibelius, as well as Dodd, that they are based on earlier tradition.[53] That this should be the case may also be inferred from I Cor. 15:3 f., where Paul recites the basic elements of the kerygmatic tradition, which are affirmed to be—doubtless in the tradition as well as in Paul's own view—"according to the scriptures." The way in which not only direct scripture quotations but also implicit ones and allusions are imbedded in the narratives of the Gospels, especially the Passion narratives, also attests the widespread and primitive use of the Old Testament in the early church. The fact of this extensive use of the Old Testament is relatively easy to confirm. All one really has to do is read the New Testament. The purpose, manner, and origin of this usage are another matter.

Whoever addresses himself to this series of problems has eventually to deal with the matter of the exact source of the Old Testament material in the New. Since the invention of printing in relatively modern times the availability, transport, and storage of the Bible has not been a significant difficulty for Christians, Jews, and biblical scholars. But prior to the printing press books were relatively scarce and literally weighty, so that carrying around the Old Testament would have been a considerable job. This consideration alone might have prompted itinerant Christian mis-

---

53. Martin Dibelius, *From Tradition to Gospel*, trans. B. L. Woolf (New York: Scribner's, 1935), pp. 15 ff., and C. H. Dodd, *The Apostolic Preaching and its Developments* (New York: Harper & Row, 1936), pp. 17 ff. More recently de Waard has argued for primitive tradition in the speeches on the basis of affinities with the Qumran Old Testament textual tradition (see above, n. 42). Lindars, pp. 38–45, shows the traditional character of the Old Testament quotations, particularly in the Pentecost speech of Peter. Cf. also Max Wilcox, *The Semitisms of Acts* (Oxford: Clarendon, 1965), especially pp. 49, 180–86.

sionaries to make notes on the Old Testament texts most useful in proclaiming and proving the truth of the Gospel. On grounds of other and more scholarly evidence Rendel Harris several decades ago suggested that they did just that. On the basis of evidence adduced from the New Testament, patristic, and later documents, he propounded his theory of a "testimony book" of Old Testament quotations widely used in the early church.[54] Harris began from the fact that there exists a third-century collection of testimonies attributed to Cyprian. On the basis of such criteria as recurring peculiar texts, sequences of texts, erroneous ascriptions of authorship, editorial prefaces, comments or conclusions, especially polemical ones—the testimony book was originally directed against the Jews—Harris discerned traces of the testimony book in Tertullian, Irenaeus, and Justin, not to mention Bar Salibi and Matthew the Monk! Turning to the New Testament he found there similar evidences of a testimony book: the same passage is frequently quoted by New Testament writers; sometimes it appears in an identical or similar form differing from the Septuagint; certain passages appear in combination in more than one New Testament text (notably Isa. 28:16 and 8:14, in I Pet. 2:8 ff. and Rom. 9:32 f.); sometimes passages are ascribed to the wrong Old Testament book (the famous instance of the Malachi passage ascribed to Isaiah in Mark 1:2, 3; there is also the problem of the Zechariah quotation attributed to Jeremiah in Matt. 27:9); occasionally passages seem to have been brought together on the basis of some key word (e. g. the passages governed by the term *stone* in I Pet. 2:6–8; Rom. 9:32 f.; Mark 12:10–11 ff.; Acts 4:11).

Harris argued his case with great deftness and erudition. His proposal was taken very seriously in almost all quarters and accepted in some.[55] For most, however, it remained in the kind of

54. J. Rendel Harris, with the assistance of Vacher Burch, *Testimonies*, 2 vols. (Cambridge: Cambridge University Press, 1916). Harris's book is not easily available, but a brief summary is to be found in C. H. Dodd, *According to the Scriptures: The Substructure of New Testament Theology* (London: Nisbet, 1952), pp. 23 ff.

55. It should be noted, however, that Harris's proposal was not without its forerunners; for example, A. Freiherr von Ungern-Sternberg, *Der traditionelle alttestamentliche Schriftbeweis "de Christo" und "de evangelio" in der alten Kirche bis zur Zeit Eusebs von Caesarea* (Halle: Niemeyer, 1913), argues for the existence of a testimony tradition with roots in the New Testament community, but not for a pre-New Testament testimony book. Earlier Edwin Hatch, *Essays in Biblical Greek* (Oxford: Clarendon Press,

limbo to which the proposals of very learned men are often relegated for lack of a competent critic, until the publication in 1957
of C. H. Dodd's slim but important volume *According to the Scriptures: The Substructure of New Testament Theology*. Dodd acknowledged
the significance of the hypothesis set forth by Harris insofar as it
underlined the evidence for the primitive and traditional character
of the use of the Old Testament in the New, as well as the widespread agreement among early Christians as to the importance
and application of certain scriptures. For Dodd the most primitive
Christian tradition was the kerygma,[56] the generally uniform an-
nouncement of the grace of God in Christ. But this aboriginal
proclamation was, according to Dodd, given its original significance and exposition through the Old Testament scriptures. By
the time of the earliest New Testament authors much of the fundamental exegesis and interpretation of the Scriptures had already
been done and could be presupposed as agreed upon. Dodd points
to the fact that the Lo-Ammi passage from Hosea (2:23) and the
Isaiah passages concerning the remnant (10:22 f.; cf. 1:9), the
foundation stone of Zion (28:16), and the stone of stumbling (8:14)
are in Romans (9–11) all assumed to apply to the situation brought
about by the coming of Christ. Moreover, all these passages save
one are used, under the same assumption, in I Peter.[57]

Despite his recognition of the significance of Harris's proposal,
Dodd nevertheless rejected the testimony book hypothesis. While
in his view the same Old Testament passages occur in different,
and apparently unrelated, New Testament books with significant
frequency, the recurrence of common textual variations, the same
combinations of passages and the like are not so frequent as to

---

1889), p. 203, suggested that Greek-speaking Jews probably produced propaganda
manuals consisting of extracts from the Old Testament.

Harris's proposal of a Testimony Book has been accepted more or less completely
by D. Plooij, *Studies in the Testimony Book* (Amsterdam: Noord-Hollandsche Uitgevers-
Maatschappij, 1932), and by B. P. W. Stather Hunt, *Primitive Gospel Sources* (New
York: Philosophical Library, 1951), who makes it the basis of his research into the
Gospels. Robert A. Kraft, "Barnabas' Isaiah Text and the 'Testimony Book' Hypothesis," *JBL*, 79 (1960), 336–50, does not find support for Harris's theory in the Epistle
of Barnabas, but rather discovers evidence for the existence of a variety of briefer
"testimony note sheets" (cf. 4Q Test).

56. *The Apostolic Preaching*, pp. 7 ff.; cf. *According to the Scriptures*, p. 12, n. 1.

57. *According to the Scriptures*, p. 23.

justify the testimony book hypothesis. In other words, the kind of evidence that scarcely admits of any other explanation than a common, written source is too sparse to support the hypothesis of an extensive testimony book. Aside from this important fact, the lack of concrete evidence for the existence of such a book in the first two centuries makes the hypothesis questionable. So widely-known a book would surely have been widely and explicitly cited.[58] One could even imagine that it would have been incorporated into the New Testament.

Dodd seeks, however, to incorporate the valid aspects of Harris's testimony book theory into his own counter-proposal. Not a fixed book of Old Testament quotations, but a nonetheless real, if largely oral, consensus concerning the important Old Testament texts lies behind the New Testament, and is reflected in the repeated use of the same and neighboring texts in the various books.[59] Dodd adduces about fifteen important texts which are used more than once in the New Testament. He then shows how these and related or contiguous texts fall into three groupings (apocalyptic-eschatological scriptures, scriptures of the New Israel, scriptures of the Servant of the Lord and Righteous Sufferer) which taken together form the Bible of the early church. He also relates the use of the Old Testament to the principle doctrines of early Christian theology (the church, the messianic titles, the death of Christ).[60] Further, Dodd maintains that there was agreement not only on the choice and extent of scriptural texts, but also on the methods of exegesis and other uses of those texts. Isolated quotations are generally not intended as proof-texts, but as pointers to whole Old Testament contexts, knowledge of which is assumed. This consistent usage of the Old Testament, which at bottom was intended to manifest the ground of the Christian message in "the determinate counsel of God," is common to all the major portions of the New Testament. As the basic interpretative mode of the early Christian kerygma, it is the substructure of New Testament theology.[61]

In opposition to much modern critical opinion concerning the

58. *Ibid.*, pp. 26 f.
59. *Ibid.*, pp. 28 ff.
60. *Ibid.*, chap. 4, "Fundamentals of Christian Theology."
61. *Ibid.*, pp. 126 f.

use of the Old Testament by the New Testament writers, Dodd contends that it was not fundamentally arbitrary: "In general . . . the writers of the New Testament, in making use of passages from the Old Testament, remain true to the main intention of their writers."[62]

Dodd's work received a favorable reception, especially in the English-speaking world,[63] and stimulated renewed interest in this aspect of biblical study. Nevertheless, some doubt remains as to whether all his major contentions have been equally well established. Since the discovery of relatively brief collections of Testimonia at Qumran (4Q Test; cf. 4Q Flor), Dodd's arguments against Harris's testimony book hypothesis may stand in need of some qualification.[64] Whether Dodd's own proposal of a consensus or established tradition is less vulnerable to criticism is a matter of debate. Over a decade ago A. C. Sundberg registered a strong demurral, pointing out that 42 percent of the Old Testament chapters cited in the New are cited by more than one author, including 71 percent of the 56 chapters of Isaiah that are cited and one-third of the Psalms.[65] Against such a statistical background, instances of the use of the same or proximate Old Testament texts in different New Testament books seem less impressive as evidence of a common tradition. Moreover, Sundberg maintained on the basis of another statistical reckoning that those books which on Dodd's accounting comprise the Bible of the early church do not actually predominate in the entire New Testament.[66] While Sundberg's statistics seem at first to be devastating to Dodd's theory, one must bear in mind that the latter's proposal was not based primarily on a statistical survey of individual instances, but involved judgments about the ways in which portions of the Old Testament were used repeatedly to confirm certain central doctrines of primitive Christianity. Additionally, however, Sundberg has questioned Dodd's contention that most Old Testament quotations in the New are dependent on

62. *Ibid.*, p. 130.
63. Cf. Lindars, p. 14; Bruce, *Biblical Exegesis in the Qumran Texts*, p. 68.
64. Cf. J. A. Fitzmyer, "4Q Testamonia and the New Testament," *Theological Studies*, 15 (1957), 513–37.
65. "On Testimonies," *Novum Testamentum*, 3 (1959), 268–81. Cf. the negative comments of Alfred Suhl, *Die Funktion der alttestamentlichen Zitate und Anspielungen in Markusevangelium* (Gütersloh: Gütersloher Verlaghaus, 1965), pp. 32 f.
66. These statistical phenomena are displayed in two tables; Suhl, pp. 272 f.

their Old Testament context for proper understanding[67] and denied that it is possible to discern an agreed-upon or uniform method of exegesis. Divergent uses of the same text argue against the theory of a widespread and primitive common exegetical method. Concerning these matters it is difficult to make an overall judgment, but Sundberg at least points to aspects of Dodd's position which have not as yet been clearly established.

The function of the Old Testament in early Christian preaching and teaching

The question of the exact source of most, or even a great many, of the Old Testament quotations in the New may not be amenable to solution by any comprehensive theory. Dodd's approach is not so neat as Harris's, for example, in view of its exclusion of the testimony book hypothesis, and really leaves undecided the exact nature of the sources upon which the New Testament writers drew. Interest has actually been moving in the direction of Dodd's own principal focus upon the manner and purpose of the appropriation of the Old Testament. Not surprisingly, Dodd contended that the primal function of the Old Testament in primitive Christianity was to support the assertions of the kerygma—originally, of course, in a Jewish context—to show that they were in accord with the determinate council of God. Allowing for legitimate debate over the content and possible variety of the kerygma, one must at the same time acknowledge the fundamental rightness of Dodd's proposal. Beyond this, however, much remains to be clarified concerning the manner and motivations of the use of the Old Testament in the developing church, which had many needs and functions other than the promulgation and demonstration of its missionary preaching, important as that remained.

Two subsequent and rather more technical works have elaborated or modified Dodd's position. Krister Stendahl analyzed a special class of Old Testament quotations in Matthew with a view to recovering their function and *Sitz im Leben* there and in the pre-

---

67. On the question of "respect for context" in the use of the Old Testament in the synoptics, see R. T. Mead, "A Dissenting Opinion about Respect for Context in Old Testament Quotations," *NTS* 10 (1963/64), 279–89, who takes issue with S. L. Edgar, "Respect for Context in Quotations from the Old Testament," *NTS*, 9 (1962/63), 55–62, and denies that such respect characterizes instances of Old Testament citation attributed to Jesus.

Matthean tradition, and Barnabas Lindars refined Dodd's position in attempting to account for the fact (pointed out by Sundberg) that the same Old Testament quotations are often put to different uses in the New Testament. Since Stendahl's work is much more circumscribed in focus, we shall consider it in connection with the use of the Old Testament in the Gospel according to Matthew. Lindars's work, however, takes up and develops the proposals of Dodd directly and comprehensively.

Accepting Dodd's repudiation of Harris's hypothesis, Lindars undertook to refine Dodd's rather general proposals concerning the use of the Old Testament in primitive Christianity. It is hardly possible to do justice to Lindars's work apart from a consideration of the detail and nuances of his arguments. Nevertheless, the main thrust of his investigation is clear enough. Beginning from Dodd's insights that early Christians used the Old Testament to support and defend the kerygma and that the blocks of material from which the specific quotations are drawn are of very great importance for the understanding of their appropriation and function, Lindars moved forward along lines suggested by the Qumran scrolls and particularly Stendahl's work *The School of St. Matthew* to formulate an initial conception of early Christian exegesis.[68] Qumran *pesher* exegesis, in which texts and textual traditions were chosen and even modified to fit the theological needs and historical situation of the community, provides a fruitful model for understanding the development of Old Testament exegesis within the primitive church. (The relevance of Qumran to Matthew has been suggested by Stendahl, who proposed that similar exegesis is to be found also in John,[69] and Ellis adduced evidence for the same phenomenon in or behind Paul's use of the Old Testament.[70]) The analogy of Qumran provides historical precedent for the kind of development which Lindars projected for primitive Christianity, a development which involves modification of the Old Testament text, but more importantly, a shift in application of those texts in accord with the changing situation of the church.[71] This shift in

68. Cf. Lindars, pp. 13 ff.
69. Pp. 162 f.
70. Pp. 139 ff.
71. On modification of the text, see Lindars, pp. 17, 24 ff.; on shift of application see pp. 17 ff. Lindars recognizes the difficulty of moving too quickly from the Qumran *pesher* model to New Testament exegesis of the Old.

application is generally a departure from an earlier evidenced or putative use of the Old Testament to support or defend the kerygma. The presumptive occasion for such a shift is the need for a relevant apologetic to meet new situations.[72] For example, Isaiah 53 was almost surely used at a very early time in connection with Jesus' Passion. But explicit citations of it in the New Testament and other early literature have to do with his miracles (Matt. 8:17) or with the lesson of humility that may be drawn from his silent suffering (I Clement 16).[73]

As will be apparent, Lindars's view of the early Christian use of the Old Testament is more complex than C. H. Dodd's, for developments in the use of texts are described in great detail. Indeed, he sees a development within the primitive kerygma concomitant with, and related to, the use of the Old Testament. Fundamental in his view is the proclamation that Jesus has been raised from the dead and its corollary, deduced with the help of Old Testament texts, that he is the Messiah. How this inference was drawn is explained by Lindars with particular reference to the use of Ps. 16:8–11 in the Pentecostal speech of Peter (Acts 2:22–36).[74] Although the Resurrection itself was proclaimed as the literal fulfillment of Old Testament prophecy, this most primitive use of the Old Testament is often submerged in the New. For example, Hos. 6:2, which was likely used as the scripture proof of the tradition of Jesus' Resurrection on the third day, is not explicitly cited in the New Testament.[75] No sooner was Jesus proclaimed as raised from the dead and as the Messiah than it became necessary to explain his ignominious death. Within a Jewish context the idea of a crucified Messiah rejected by his own people was, as Paul recognized (I Cor. 1:23), an offense. The early Christians' response to the objection elicited by this state of affairs was the development of a Passion apologetic, by which they sought to show that the

---

72. *Ibid.*, p. 30.

73. *Ibid.*, pp. 20–22.

74. *Ibid.*, pp. 36 ff. Recently, H. W. Boers has sought to discern in Psalm 16 the scriptural basis for the disciples' reflection upon Jesus' death, which in turn created the psychological state of expectation leading to the resurrection experiences: see "Psalm 16 and the Historical Origin of the Christian Faith," *Zeitschrift für die neutestamentliche Wissenschaft*, 60 (1969), 105–10.

75. Lindars, pp. 59 ff.

suffering of the Messiah was anticipated, and therefore vindicated, by Scripture. In this Passion apologetic such passages as Isaiah 53; Psalms 22, 31, 34, 41, 69, and 109; and the book of Zechariah played a prominent role. Lindars endeavors to show through close examination of quotations in the New Testament how these passages were used in the Passion apologetic. In some cases this usage must be inferred from such subtle matters as interpretative variations in the text, especially when the New Testament contains no instances of the use of a given quotation in direct connection with the Passion. This Passion apologetic was in no sense an afterthought, presupposing the developed *theologia crucis*. Rather, it was the seedbed in which the doctrine of the atonement, already stated in the tradition behind I Cor. 15:3, grew.[76]

Only after the application of the Old Testament to the Resurrection and death of Jesus did attention turn to his earthly ministry. Then the Old Testament (Ps. 2:7; Isa. 42:1) was first used in connection with Jesus' baptism (cf. Mark 1:11) to help demonstrate the messianic character of his entire ministry.[77] A similar motivation helps explain the conflation of these same texts in the transfiguration scene (Mark 9:7). What Lindars calls the "apologetic of response" grew up in direct relation to the portrayal of the earthly ministry as the arena of messianic revelation, for the latter naturally raises the question of the culpability of those who fail to recognize the messianic character of Jesus' work.[78] This question tends ultimately to be resolved in the direction of the theory of a deliberate policy of self-reservation or concealment on the part of Jesus, the messianic secret.[79] In the process, however, the Scriptures (e. g. Isa. 6:9; 28:16) are adduced to show that the rejection of Jesus by the greater part of his people in no wise affects adversely his messianic claim, but is rather the fulfillment of Scripture.

The final chapters of Lindars's book are devoted to a consideration of the Old Testament in the development of the tradition concerning Jesus' birthplace (chap. 5), quotations in Paul (chap. 6),

76. *Ibid.*, p. 134: "Atonement theology and Passion apologetic are worked out together, and naturally the same scriptures are useful for both."
77. *Ibid.*, pp. 138 ff.
78. Cf. *ibid.*, pp. 155, 187 f.
79. *Ibid.*, pp. 158 f.

and in the early church generally, especially in Matthew and
John (chap. 7). He finds that the tradition of Jesus' birth in Bethlehem has actually replaced an older tradition of his origin in
Nazareth. Although Paul's use of the Old Testament has its place
in the line of the church's exegetical work, Lindars finds that "he
does not reproduce the christological texts nor argue that Jesus is
the Messiah. This is simply taken for granted as an assured fact."[80]
Strikingly, he maintains that the use of the Old Testament quotations in John represents more nearly the older apologetic tradition
than in Matthew, and that the latter really does not understand
the *pesher* quotations which Stendahl ascribed to the Matthean
school.[81]

The most notable aspect of this important book is Lindars's
effort comprehensively to grasp the Old Testament quotations in
the New in the light of their *Sitz im Leben* in the development of
early Christian preaching and theology. Whether the picture which
Lindars has drawn, admittedly in a hypothetical way,[82] will stand
the test of further investigation remains to be seen. Many of his
individual exegetical insights are extremely perceptive and suggestive, while others are somewhat conjectural. But the attempt to
probe into and behind the New Testament in order to trace the
development of primitive Christian reflection in and through the
Old Testament quotations is an exceedingly stimulating exercise
and one that should prove quite fruitful. The reader familiar with
form criticism will doubtless notice how Lindars's work seems to
confirm the perspectives and insights of that discipline. To what
extent this is an independent corroboration of the basic insights of
form criticism is, however, difficult to say, since Lindars to some
extent shares its basic presuppositions and methods. The idea that
the use of the Old Testament in the New is fundamentally apologetic will doubtless bear further scrutiny, although there is little
doubt of the importance of the apologetic factor, especially in the
original Jewish milieu. That further work remains to be done in
this obscure but important area scarcely needs to be said, but the

80. *Ibid.*, p. 247.
81. *Ibid.*, pp. 259 ff.
82. *Ibid.*, p. 9.

contributions of Harris, Dodd, and Lindars certainly provide a basis and stimulus for future investigations.

THE USE OF THE OLD TESTAMENT BY THE
NEW TESTAMENT WRITERS

In the preceding section we have surveyed the problem of the use of the Old Testament in primitive Christianity, focusing attention particularly on the works of Dodd and Lindars. The use of the Old Testament by the New Testament writers is a distinguishable, if finally an inseparable, question, for the history of the use and exegesis of the Old Testament by the early church antedates its appropriation in the earliest New Testament documents by at least two decades.[83] Therefore the texts of the Old Testament as appropriated by the New Testament writers may well have been understood, interpreted, and even altered, along lines already laid down by traditional exegesis. As we have already noted, Dodd pointed to this phenomenon, Lindars made it the basis for his study, and Stendahl showed its peculiar relevance to Matthew. Recently Edwin Freed has investigated the use of the Old Testament in John to ascertain its relation to an earlier textual and exegetical tradition,[84] while E. Earle Ellis has made proposals along these lines with respect to Paul.[85] Although the use of the Old Testament in the New must always be seen against this background, it is also clear that various New Testament writers understand and make use of the Old Testament in distinctive ways. Our purpose here is not to engage in the kind of thoroughgoing consideration or exegetical study that might be expected to advance our knowledge, but rather to point to the more salient, and perhaps in some instances obvious, features of the use of the Old Testament by the major New Testament authors or traditions in the light of recent research.

83. I and II Thessalonians which may be earlier scarcely come into consideration, since, with the exception of II Thessalonians 2, Paul makes little use of the Old Testament in them.

84. *Old Testament Quotations in the Gospel of John*, Supplements to Novum Testamentum, no. 2 (Leiden: Brill, 1965).

85. Pp. 139 ff.

Paul

The ground-breaking work on Paul's use of the Old Testament is Otto Michel's *Paulus und seine Bibel* (1929).[86] It was followed a decade later by Bonsirven's exhaustive comparison of Pauline usage with rabbinic exegesis. More recently Ellis has brought matters up to date with his very useful book, *Paul's Use of the Old Testament* (1957).

There is little question of the importance of the Old Testament in the development of Paul's thought. Despite the absence of Old Testament quotations from I Thessalonians, Philippians, and much of I and II Corinthians, Harnack's view that Paul valued the Old Testament only for polemical use against Jews or Jewish-Christian opponents is no longer widely held.[87] Moreover, one may be quite certain that Paul's exegesis finds its place in his own world, with real and obvious connections with his contemporaries, within the church and outside. While he differs from the rabbis in his total perspective on the Old Testament,[88] this is rather because of his different eschatological and christological perspective than on account of a deliberately different method of dealing with scripture. Victor P. Furnish, who is disinclined to view Paul as a rabbi,[89] concedes Paul's kinship with the rabbinic style of biblical exegesis.[90] In all probability, however, Paul's peculiar slant on scripture is more closely paralleled in the Qumran community. Not only the *pesher* exegesis,[91] but the conviction that the Old Testament finds its fulfillment in a new event or series of events which have occurred

---

86. Beiträge zur Förderung christlicher Theologie, no. 18 (Gütersloh: Bertelsmann, 1929). Although Bultmann's review in *Theologische Literaturzeitung*, 58 (1933), 157–59, was scarcely friendly, he at least granted the value of the volume as a summation of scholarship.

87. "Das Alte Testament in den Paulinischen Briefen und in den Paulinischen Gemeinden," *Sitzungsberichte der Preussischen Akademie der Wissenschaften zu Berlin*, Sitzung der philosophisch-historischen Klasse, 1928, pp. 124–41. Yet Harnack himself did not doubt the importance of the scriptures in Paul's own thought. His theory applied only to Paul's missionary churches.

88. Cf., in addition to Bonsirven, Victor P. Furnish, *Theology and Ethics in Paul* (Nashville: Abingdon, 1968), pp. 33 f.

89. Contrast W. D. Davies, *Paul and Rabbinic Judaism: Some Rabbinic Elements in Pauline Theology*, 2nd ed. (London: S.P.C.K., 1955).

90. Pp. 33, 40; cf. Furnish's brief but useful treatment of the Old Testament as a source of Paul's ethical teaching (pp. 28–34, 42 f.).

91. Ellis, pp. 139 ff. Such exegesis probably indicates Paul's connection with earlier exegetical tradition.

or are about to occur, is a common factor binding Qumran exegesis to that of Paul and much of the New Testament. But despite the similarities, which are related to their prophetic-eschatological viewpoint, Paul's Christology gives to his exegesis an emphasis on present eschatological fulfillment absent from Qumran.

> At the acceptable time I have listened to you,
> and helped you on the day of salvation.

So writes Second Isaiah (49:8), and Paul (II Cor. 6:2) comments, "Behold, now is the acceptable time; behold, now is the day of salvation."[92]

Paul's use of the Old Testament may be summarized under four heads. First, and most important, there is his general prophetic and kerygmatic understanding of the Old Testament as the precursor, prefiguration, and promise of the Gospel. Thus the Gospel was "promised beforehand through his prophets in the holy scriptures" (Rom. 1:2) and "the law and the prophets bear witness to it" (Rom. 3:21). As we have already noted in the case of the quotation from II Cor. 6:1 f., the Gospel can be announced in the language of the Old Testament. Moreover, Adam is said to be a τύπος of the one who was to come (Rom. 5:14), and Abraham, as the type or model of the man of faith, prefigures the Gospel (Romans 4; Galatians 3).[93] The Scripture is said to preach the Gospel to him, saying (in the words of Gen. 12:3), "In you shall

92. Despite points of contact (Michel, pp. 107 f.), Paul's approach to the Old Testament is rather different from Philo's, for the latter largely lacks appreciation for the historical and eschatological dimensions of the Old Testament. Probably Philo is not altogether typical of Hellenistic Judaism. Yet the Wisdom of Solomon also shows relatively little of Paul's prophetic eschatological viewpoint, despite its well-known similarities to Paul's diagnosis of man's sinfulness.

93. This use of the Old Testament may be distinguished from the purely prophetic as "typological." Yet typology seems to be based on the premise of prophecy and fulfillment, particularly in Paul. Probably L. Goppelt, *Typos: Die typologische Deutung des Alten Testaments in Neuen*, Beiträge zur Förderung christlicher Theologie, no. 43 (Gütersloh: Bertelsmann, 1939), goes too far in seeing typology as the dominant form of the use of the Old Testament in the New (p. 239). Nevertheless, typology may well be the distinctly Christian form of the appropriation of the Old Testament. Cf. G. W. H. Lampe and K. J. Woollcombe, *Essays on Typology*, Studies in Biblical Theology, no. 22 (London: SCM, 1957): "While it is indisputably convenient to use one word to embrace the study of all such linkages [between the Old Testament and the New], it is open to question whether typology is the right word" (p. 39). "The methods of handling the Old Testament which were already practised in Judaism were allegorism and the study of the fulfillment of prophecy. Historical typology, as defined above, came into existence with Christendom" (p. 42).

all the nations be blessed" (Gal. 3:8). In somewhat less explicit or emphatic ways, Paul also uses the language of the Old Testament to characterize the eschatological consummation (Phil. 2:10 f.; cf. Isa. 45:23; I Cor. 15:27; and Ps. 8:7) and to interpret Jesus' ministry (Rom. 15:3; cf. Ps. 69:9).

A second typical Pauline usage might be called ecclesiastical-parenetic. Paul uses the Old Testament as a source for the ethical instruction and edification of the church.[94] He may do this in a variety of ways. Most simply Paul continues to apply individual commandments of the law to specific problems (cf. II Cor. 13:1), although he may shift the application of the law in the light of his new situation (I Cor. 9:8–10). Of course, it is not the case that the law simply remains in force. In light of the demonstration of God's love in Christ's cross (cf. Rom. 5:8), the man of faith has a new perspective from which to view even the law (Rom. 13:8–10; Gal. 5:13–15). Its entire meaning is love of neighbor; love is the fulfillment of the law. Paul can also use the Exodus traditions in haggadic fashion to admonish the church (I Cor. 10:1–13), as he can use the Old Testament to express exhortations or warnings (Rom. 12:19 f.; I Cor. 5:15; II Cor. 6.16–18) or to support them (II Cor. 8:15; 9:9; Rom. 14:11).

A third distinguishable use of the Old Testament is found in Paul's interpretation of the historical or historical-eschatological situation in which he finds himself. Although it is not always possible clearly to distinguish this usage from the christological or kerygmatic one, since the historical-eschatological situation is fundamentally conditioned by the coming of Christ, the appropriation of the Old Testament as the key to the unfolding course of events is a clear feature of several Pauline passages, particularly Romans 9–11 (cf. also Rom. 15:8 ff.; Gal. 4:21 ff.; Phil. 2:10 ff.). Here Paul's conception of the interplay between Israel and the Gentiles in the history of salvation is based upon his exegetically grounded discussion of the present state of affairs between Israel and the church. Moreover, his last word concerning the mystery of God's working in history is taken from the Old Testament (Rom. 11:34 f., quoting Isa. 40:13 and Job 35:7).

A fourth and final category of Paul's use of the Scriptures is

94. Cf. Furnish, pp. 25 ff.

probably best left unlabelled. It comprises a variety of instances in which Paul uses the Old Testament to prove a point, on the assumption that Scripture is God's word. Particularly interesting subcategories are Paul's use of the Old Testament in connection with wisdom (I Cor. 1:19, 31; 2:9, 16; 3:19 f.) and in his description of the human situation (see esp. Rom. 3:9–20). Otherwise, Paul can make use of the Old Testament to uphold Christian freedom (I Cor. 10:26); to give guidance concerning tongues (I Cor. 14:21); to expound his eschatology (I Cor. 10:27, 54 f.); or to illuminate the relation of Christ and Adam (15:45). This category naturally shades over into Paul's ethical and parenetic use of the Old Testament, where he often quotes the Old Testament in order to add force to his argument.

There are, moreover, several passages in which Paul becomes rather explicit in stating the role and status of the Old Testament in the light of the Gospel. To say that he regards the Old Testament as a Christian book would be anachronistic. Yet Paul evidently felt peculiarly empowered to apply the Old Testament to Christ and to the church (see I Cor. 9:8–10; 10:11), and he makes this fact quite explicit. As far as Paul was concerned, the Old Testament could not be rightly read apart from Christ and his spirit (II Cor. 3:12–18). For the earlier preaching and exegetical tradition the Old Testament was the key to Christ in that it provided both a framework for understanding him and the promises and other adumbrations of his coming. Already for Paul, however, a subtle shift is taking place.[95] For he can claim that the ancient scriptures themselves are not rightly understood apart from Christ, a claim that was to be reiterated in the early church (cf. John 5:38 ff.). For Paul, as a Jew, Christ still gained intelligibility from the Old Testament; but a generation later, when most Christians were not Jews, the shoe would be on the other foot.[96]

The form of Paul's Old Testament quotations is predominantly septuagintal, although there are a significant number which depart

95. Lindars, pp. 17 f., sees the recognition of a shift in the application of Old Testament quotations as basic to a right understanding of their history in early Christianity.

96. Rom. 16:25–27 is intentionally omitted from this discussion because it is usually regarded as secondary and non-Pauline. Cf., for example, C. K. Barrett, *The Epistle to the Romans*, Harper's New Testament Commentaries (New York: Harper & Row, 1958), pp. 10–13, 286 f.

from any known Septuagint textual tradition.[97] Agreement with the Masoretic text against the Septuagint is not frequent, although a number of Paul's *pesher* quotations may have been influenced by a form of the Hebrew text. Ellis finds that Paul's conflated or combined quotations show a much higher than normal degree of deviation from the Septuagint,[98] a fact which suggests their origin and transmission in the exegetical tradition of primitive Christianity.

Mark

Mark's use of the Old Testament is hard to isolate and characterize.[99] Apparently he and the church standing behind him regard the Old Testament as holy Scripture, divine revelation; yet even this is not undisputed,[100] for he at least represents Jesus as taking a position in seeming opposition to some parts of scripture (7:14 ff.), albeit sometimes on the basis of scripture (10:5 ff.).

Similarly, Mark apparently relies on a Christian tradition of Old Testament interpretation. The combination of Malachi and Isaiah in a probable *pesher* quotation and Mark's ignorance of its exact origin both point in that direction. Moreover, the use of the Old Testament in Mark's passion narrative is in all probability of

97. Ellis, *Paul's Use of the Old Testament*, p. 12, gives the number of these as thirty-eight.

98. *Ibid.*, p. 12 (see esp. n. 5).

99. Since we are concerned primarily with the explicit use of the Old Testament in the New, we shall not go into the question of the more subtle influence of the Old Testament upon Mark, as important as that may be for the understanding of the whole Gospel and for the question of the historical Jesus. Quite thoroughgoing in interpreting Mark in terms of Old Testament typology is Austin Farrer, *A Study in St. Mark* (London: Dacre, 1951). His approach has not, however, gained wide acceptance. Ulrich Mauser, *Christ in the Wilderness: The Wilderness Theme in the Second Gospel and its Basis in the Biblical Tradition*, Studies in Biblical Theology, no. 39 (London: SCM, 1963), develops the theme of the wilderness in Mark's theology. His theses, however, have also met some opposition; cf. Ernest Edwin Best, *The Temptation and the Passion: The Marcan Soteriology*, Society for New Testament Studies, Monograph Series, no. 2 (Cambridge: Cambridge University Press, 1965), pp. 25 ff. On Mark's use of the Old Testament see further Best, pp. 134–59 and the literature cited there.

Regrettably, Manfred Karnetzki's Tübingen dissertation, "Die alttestamentlichen Zitate in der synoptischen Tradition" (1955) has not been published. Apparently he has undertaken to trace the history of the Old Testament material in the synoptic Gospels on form-critical grounds. See Joachim Rohde, *Rediscovering the Teaching of the Evangelists*, trans. D. M. Barton (Philadelphia: Westminster, 1968), p. 27, n. 96.

100. Cf. the position of Samuel Schultz, "Markus und das Alte Testament," *Zeitschrift für Theologie und Kirche*, 58 (1961), 184–97, who thinks that Mark has a canon within the canon of the Old Testament and does not regard the corpus of scriptures *per se* as authoritative.

pre-Marcan origin.[101] Here the frequency of Old Testament allusions and quotations in comparison to the rest of the Gospel increases markedly. Strangely enough, however, most of these references are not in any way noticed or marked as such. Likely they belong in large measure to the very early tradition of the passion, which was deeply influenced by the Old Testament. The earliest disciples and their contemporaries doubtless searched the Scriptures in order to unlock the secrets of Jesus' suffering and death. Also rather striking is the absence in Mark of any reference to the Scriptures in the Resurrection narrative (16:1–8; cf. Luke 24:25–27; John 20:9; I Cor. 15:4; Acts 2:25–28), an absence, however, which is paralleled in Matthew.

Mark's Old Testament quotations are taken primarily from the Septuagint, although there are variations.[102] In several instances Jesus seems to quote the Old Testament in its septuagintal form.[103] At first glance this would seem to indicate that these quotations had been placed on Jesus' lips by the evangelist or by the Hellenistic church. Yet this conclusion is inevitable only in instances in which the argument of a pericope is based upon the Septuagint.[104] Otherwise, it is quite possible that such quotations have been assimilated to the Septuagint, a procedure with ample precedent. Josephus, whose native language was Aramaic, generally chose to quote the Bible according to the Septuagint in his works, which were published in Greek.

The question of Mark's purpose in quoting the Old Testament has recently become the subject of discussion.[105] It has ordinarily been assumed that the New Testament writers see the Old Testament standing in a relation of prophecy and fulfillment to the coming of Christ, the growth of the church, and so on. Alfred Suhl,

101. For a discussion of this question with citation of relevant literature, see Suhl, pp. 45–56. Admittedly, there is a difference of opinion as to when the Old Testament quotations and allusions entered into the formation of the tradition.

102. Cf. R. H. Gundry, *The Use of the Old Testament in St. Matthew's Gospel*, Supplements to Novum Testamentum, no. 18 (Leiden: Brill, 1967), pp. 5, 9, 28, 147 ff.; also Henry Barclay Swete, *The Gospel According to St Mark: The Greek Text with Introduction, Notes and Indices* (London: Macmillan, 1898), pp. lxx–lxxiv. On variations in the direction of the Hebrew and the targums in the words of Jesus, see T. W. Manson, "The Old Testament in the Teaching of Jesus," esp. pp. 314 ff.

103. E. g. Mark 7:6 f.; 7:10; 10:6 f.

104. As seems to be the case in Mark 7:6 f.

105. Suhl's work is fundamentally concerned with this question. Cf. Hugh Anderson's essay on Mark's use of the Old Testament in this volume.

however, has sought to show that Mark's intention in appropriating the Scriptures is only to show the *Schriftgemässheit* of events in Jesus' ministry and that it is therefore wrong to impute to him a view of salvation history and a scheme of prophecy and fulfillment that is really derived from Matthew and Luke. Suhl's position is well taken in so far as he seeks to differentiate Mark from the much more pointed use of the Old Testament and Old Testament themes in the other Gospels. Nevertheless, his case is somewhat distorted by dependence on Willi Marxsen's view of Mark's Gospel as evangelical proclamation decisively conditioned by the expectation of the imminent Parousia of Jesus in Galilee.[106] The denial that Mark is interested in prophecy and fulfillment is tied to a denial that Mark is interested in salvation history. Perhaps Mark does not have the historical sensibilities of Luke. Yet it is scarcely possible that his work does not embody the more primitive Christian idea that the kerygma as presently announced fulfills the past prophetic Scriptures (I Cor. 15:3 ff.), and scarcely credible that the primitive references to the Scriptures (e. g. in I Cor. 15:3 ff.) have no specific Scripture prophecies in view, but express only the community's faith in the *Schriftgemässheit* of the salvation events. Mark's Gospel begins with an Old Testament quotation whose most obvious significance is to indicate the fulfillment of prophecy, a motif which occurs relatively seldom, but nevertheless explicitly (9:11–13; cf. 12:10 ff.). Suhl's position must be regarded as an overstatement of a valid insight, namely, that Mark's view of the Old Testament is much less refined and programmatically formulated than that of his successors.

Although Mark (through his introductory quotation and his appropriation of a traditional passion narrative replete with Old Testament references or allusions) reflects the primitive Christian idea that the event of Jesus' coming is the fulfillment of Scripture and portrays Jesus as debating about the bearing of Scripture (especially the Law), he does not generally use the Old Testament to embellish and interpret the events of Jesus' Galilean ministry as extensively as does Matthew. This relative omission is perhaps of a piece with his omission of the teaching tradition we know from

---

106. *Mark the Evangelist: Studies on the Redaction History of the Gospel*, trans. James Boyce *et al.* (Nashville: Abingdon, 1969). (The English translation is based upon the 1959 German edition.)

the other Gospels. Furthermore, it is consonant with the kerygmatic character of Mark's Gospel, which concentrates on the saving event and person, eschewing any broader historical interest, in essential correspondence with the primitive kerygma. In emphasizing the kerygmatic character of Mark as compared with Matthew and Luke, Suhl is surely right, whether one refers "kerygma" here to the primitive kerygma of the apostolic preaching (Dodd) or to the Hellenistic kerygma of the Gentile-oriented church. Mark's total theological interest appears to be in accord with his use of the Old Testament.

To what extent Mark preserves an accurate picture of Jesus' attitude toward, and use of, the Old Testament is a good question. Long-standing conceptions of Jesus' most fundamental insights into the will of God rest largely upon the assumption that Jesus actually spoke as Mark reports him to have spoken, for example, in chapters 7 and 10. Some recent research has made this assumption appear invalid, however, precisely insofar as it has emphasized Mark's kerygmatic interest in contradistinction to any historical interest.[107] Such a state of affairs is at least superficially supported by the septuagintal flavor of Mark's Old Testament. Yet on the other hand one may cite the affinity of Jesus' free use and interpretation of the Old Testament in Mark with what appears to be a similar stance in the Sermon on the Mount. Indeed, the authoritative posture of the Jesus of the Sermon on the Mount is even more pronounced than in Mark's Gospel. So even if the kerygmatic, and Hellenistic or Gentile character of Mark's Gospel is emphasized and his historical interests minimized, it is still not too much to think that he conveys the spirit of the historical Jesus, particularly his attitude toward the Old Testament law.[108]

Matthew

Matthew[109] generally reproduces Mark's explicit Old Testament quotations. There are four formal Old Testament quotations pe-

107. This position is characteristic of the work of Suhl and, to a lesser degree, of Schulz.

108. This much, at least, is granted by Schulz, p. 197.

109. There has recently been published extensive work on Matthew's use of the Old Testament, much of it stimulated by Stendahl's monograph. Aside from Gundry (n. 102 above), see R. S. McConnell, *Law and Prophecy in Matthew's Gospel: The Au-*

culiar to Matthew and Luke and twenty peculiar to Matthew. These last represent a variety and mixture of text types.[110] Among these eleven (or twelve) are of particular interest. They are introduced by special fulfillment formulas, indicating that the events relating to Jesus' life or ministry fulfill Old Testament prophecy, and represent unique textual traditions.[111] In *The School of St. Matthew* Stendahl paid particular attention to these formula quotations, which he likened to the *pesher* quotations of the Habakkuk Commentary of Qumran, in developing his thesis regarding the origin of the First Gospel. Stendahl believes that Matthew originated in a school or circle of early Christian Old Testament interpretation analogous to that of Qumran. The interpretation of the special formula quotations in Matthew's school accounts for their special form, just as the Qumran *pesher* activity accounts for aberrant Old Testament text-forms. Moreover, the formula quotations in Matthew show Semitic influence, whereas the other Old Testament quotations in Matthew are predominantly septuagintal.[112]

Stendahl's thesis has proved stimulating, not only for Matthean studies, but also for attempts to understand the use of the Old Testament in primitive Christianity. For example, Lindars's work on the apologetic use of the Old Testament in the early church was inspired largely by Stendahl's research. Nevertheless, his position has met with criticism as well as assent.[113] Lindars, although finding his research stimulating, does not believe that the evan-

---

thority and Use of the Old Testament in the Gospel of St. Matthew, Theologishe Dissertationen, no. 2 (Basel: Reinhardt, 1969), and W. Rothfuchs, *Die Erfüllungszitate des Matthäus-Evangeliums: Eine biblisch-theologische Untersuchung*, Beiträge zum Wissenschaft vom Alten und Neuen Testament, ser. 5, no. 8 (Stuttgart, Kohlhammer, 1969); also earlier G. D. Kilpatrick, *The Origins of the Gospel According to St. Matthew* (Oxford: Clarendon, 1946), *passim*.

110. *Ibid.*, pp. 148 f.

111. The formula quotations are 1:23; 2:6, 15, 18, 23; 4:14 f.; 8:17; 12:18–21; 13:35; 21:5; 27:9 f. by Stendahl's accounting, pp. 97–127. Matt. 3:3 is also introduced by the peculiar formula, but has synoptic parallels.

112. Gundry, however, criticizes Stendahl for ignoring the nonseptuagintal elements in other Matthew quotations (pp. 157 f.). In his view only the parallels to Mark's formal quotations should be characterized as septuagintal.

113. Lindars, pp. 259 ff. Note also Bertil Gärtner's far-reaching criticisms, particularly of Stendahl's attempt to explain the Matthean quotations on the basis of Qumran, in "The Habakkuk Commentary (DSH) and the Gospel of Matthew," *S. T.*, 8 (1954), 1–24. Stendahl opens the preface of the Fortress edition of his work with a candid acknowledgment of the weight of such criticisms, indicates some reservation of his own about the Matthean school hypothesis, and avers that the principal justification of the study was and is the analysis of the Old Testament text in the Gospel.

gelist himself appreciated the exegetical work lying behind the formula quotations, but rather understood them pictorially, that is, as depicting in advance events to be fulfilled in Jesus' life and ministry. Thus, in his view Matthew the evangelist does not really belong to the school of that name! At least he ignores it in the use of these Old Testament quotations. In a more negative vein, Gundry rejects Stendahl's whole thesis (along with Lindars's) on the principal ground that he fails to note the pervasiveness of non-septuagintal influence on all Matthew's quotations except those in which he is simply following Mark. Gundry takes the position that the apostle Matthew is responsible for the present text-forms.[114] In the new preface (Fortress edition, pp. vi–ix) of his work, however, Stendahl guardedly reiterates his view that the formula quotations are the ambiance of the evangelist and in their present text-form provide a key to understanding Matthew's Gospel. Stendahl is, in fact, responding specifically to Strecker,[115] yet in effect he responds also to the criticism of Lindars. Although Stendahl has not yet replied to Gundry's attack, he promises a detailed analysis of the latter's book in a forthcoming issue of *Biblica*. So the debate over Matthew's special quotations continues. That it is not a merely technical matter is clear enough, for at stake is the problem of Matthean origins and therefore Matthean interpretation.

In view of the unsettled state of research, is it possible to characterize Matthew's use of the Old Testament with any felicity? Probably so, for despite debated issues, major aspects of his use of the Old Testament stand out clearly. Moreover, even scholars who, for example, deny that Matthew is a "Jewish gospel" agree that it at least embodies elements of a Jewish-Christian tradition, while those who regard it as Jewish-Christian often grant that it was composed in a Hellenistic environment.[116]

114. See pp. 181 ff. While Gundry's labors in collecting and sorting out the Old Testament textual materials relating to Matthew have won critical approval, the same cannot be said for his own position. See, for example, the review by Lindars, *Journal of Theological Studies*, n.s. 20 (1969), 282–84. It has been observed that Gundry's consideration of Old Testament allusions as well as quotations has given rise to the theory of pervasive mixed text-forms, but that the nature of the possible allusions scarcely admits of inference about text-forms.

115. Strecker, *Der Weg der Gerechtigkeit: Untersuchungen zur Theologie des Matthäus*, Forschungen zur Religion und Literatur des Alten und Neuen Testaments, no. 82; 2nd ed. (Göttingen: Vandenhoeck & Ruprecht, 1966).

116. Note Stendahl's preface to the new Fortress edition of his work, pp. viii, n. 3; xii, n. 1; xiii. Stendahl has sympathy with Davies's position that Matthew is a response

Matthew's use of the Old Testament is a problem with at least two foci. First, and more generally, how does Matthew relate the Old Testament to his account of Jesus' ministry? Second, what is the Matthean position toward the Law? The second question is not really separable from the first, but since we are primarily interested in the use and functioning of the Old Testament we shall concentrate upon the first and deal with the second only insofar as it impinges upon it. As was the case with Paul, a thorough pursuit of the question of the Law would entail a treatment of the total theological perspective of the author.[117]

Matthew takes up most of the Marcan Old Testament quotations and thus apparently endorses them. Over and beyond this he has about two dozen formal quotations, four of which he shares with Luke and ten or eleven of which fall into the category of the Matthean formula quotations. Whatever their origins, these last seem most typical of Matthew. The occurrence of five of these special quotations in Matthew's distinctive birth narrative, where they follow hard on the heels of the Matthean genealogy, tends to confirm this judgment. Where Matthew constructs his own narrative episodes in relative independence (although he probably knew an earlier tradition) his historical narration stands in closest relation to Old Testament testimonies.[118]

The events are portrayed as the fulfillment of the prophetic words of Scripture. Naturally, not every detail of the narrative is

---

to Jamnian Judaism. Yet he doubts that "the influence of Palestinian Judaism on the Gospel of Matthew can ... be as direct as Davies's study [*The Setting of the Sermon on the Mount*] presupposes" (p. xii, n. 1). On the other hand, scholars such as Strecker and Wolfgang Trilling, *Das Wahre Israel: Studien zur Theologie des Matthäus-Evangeliums*, Studien zum Alten und Neuen Testaments, no. 10; 3rd ed. (Munich: Kösel, 1964), who regard Matthew as the product of a church fully separated from Judaism, grant the Jewishness of much of Matthew's tradition. In fact, the distinction between the viewpoint of this tradition and that of the final redaction is the basis of their positions.

117. H. Freiherr von Campenhausen discusses the use of the Old Testament in Paul and Matthew in relation to the question of Law and Gospel: *Die Entstehung der christlichen Bibel*, Beiträge zur historischen Theologie, no. 39 (Tübingen: Mohr, 1968), pp. 16 ff., 32 ff.

118. On the Matthean infancy narratives and particularly their use of the Old Testament, see Stendahl, "Quis et unde? An Analysis of Mt 1–2," *Judentum, Urchristentum, Kirche: Festschrift für Joachim Jeremias*, Beihefte zur Zeitschrift für die neutestamentliche Wissenschaft, no. 26; 2nd ed. (Berlin: Töpelmann, 1964), pp. 94–105; Strecker, pp. 51–63; and especially W. Barnes Tatum, "The Matthean Infancy Stories: Their Form, Structure, and Relation to the Theology of the Evangelist" (Ph.D. diss., Duke University, 1966), esp. pp. 83–85 ff., 99.

supported by Scripture, but the Scripture quotation seems to lift out and underline principal points of each pericope: "A virgin shall conceive . . ."; Christ is to be born in Bethlehem; the Son of God is called out of Egypt; and so on. That all of these events happen according to prophecy and not fortuitously means, of course, that they are ordained of God and, moreover, that they constitute an extension of the holy history into the period of Jesus' life and ministry. That this last is not a purely Lucan idea (Conzelmann) would seem to be indicated by the opening genealogy, through which the continuity of the New with the Old is assured.

When Matthew passes from the birth narrative to the account of Jesus' ministry, he picks up and rearranges the Marcan quotation of Malachi and Isaiah which introduces the Baptist narrative, correcting Mark's erroneous ascription of the whole passage to Isaiah. There follows the Q narrative of the temptation of Jesus, already replete with Old Testament themes and allusions (4:1–11). Then begins Jesus' public ministry in Galilee, introduced by Mark (1:21) with a simple transitional statement of place, but by Matthew with an extensive formula quotation (4:15–17), which establishes the Galilean locus of Jesus' ministry as the fulfillment of Isaiah's prophecy. One hesitates to attribute to Matthew's deliberate intention what may be merely the result of chance, but the remainder of the formula quotations are distributed among various important phases or aspects of Jesus' ministry: his healings (8:17); his self-concealment (12:18–21); his parables (13:35); the preparation for his entry into Jerusalem (21:5); Judas' fate (27:9 f.). The formula also occurs to introduce the famous Isaiah passage (40:3) used in connection with the appearance of the Baptist (3:3), although in this instance there is a Marcan parallel. Rather striking, however, is the relative scarcity of distinctly Matthean quotations with the fulfillment formula in the passion narrative (cf. 27:9 f.), where it might have been expected to appear more often in connection with Jesus' death.

Matthew very deliberately introduces his Gospel narrative with extensive references to the Old Testament. In general these Old Testament references extend and refine the common early Christian idea that the Gospel is the fulfillment of the Scriptures, but in the precise sense that the events of Jesus' life and ministry—particularly its beginnings—are prophesied therein. Thus he extends the familiar motif of Jesus as the one announced by Scripture, a motif already present in Mark, but, interestingly enough, absent from Q.[119]

The high regard for the Old Testament which Matthew manifests in his portrayal of Jesus is reflected also in his attitude toward the law.[120] Probably Matthew's handling of this issue places him in a Jewish-Christian milieu.[121] But Matthew's exact attitude toward the Old Testament, and particularly the Law, is not always easy to deduce, since he appropriates traditions embodying varying viewpoints. Yet it may be inferred from the content and structure of the Sermon on the Mount that Jesus stands over and above the Law, the Old Testament Torah per se, not just its traditional interpretation. This is particularly clear from the antitheses.[122] Moreover, Matthew keeps the Marcan instances in which Jesus breaks the sabbath or purification commandments, although he tends to soften them.[123] While he also transmits the strict or conservative line, attributed to Jesus, on the keeping of the Law (5:17–20; see also 23:3), he tempers this position with the repeated quotation of Hos. 6:6, "I desire mercy, and not sacrifice" (Matt. 9:13; 12:7), and sharply distinguishes between the trivial and the weightier matters of the Law (23:23). Yet in the same breath in which he makes that distinction he also insists upon observance. The whole Law, however, "hangs" upon the double commandment of love of God and love of neighbor (22:40), which provides the hermeneutical fulcrum for the interpretation of the individual commandments. Yet the allegiance which Matthew commends is

119. Trilling sees as the peculiarly Matthean contribution in the appropriation of the Old Testament the evangelist's interpretation of the Christian church, rather than the synagogue, as the true continuation of the Old Testament people of God, "The True Israel." On the absence of christological proof from prophecy from Q, see von Campenhausen, p. 13, n. 32; but Matt. 11:4–6 / Luke 7:22 f., with obvious references to Isaiah (29:18 f.; 35:5 f.; 61:1), seems to constitute an exception.

120. Note especially Gerhard Barth, "Matthew's Understanding of the Law," in Günther Bornkamm, Barth, and H. J. Held, *Tradition and Interpretation in Matthew*, trans. P. Scott (London: SCM, 1963), pp. 58, 164: "The Law of Moses is for him unquestionably the law of God, and also for the church" (p. 158). Cf. also Trilling, pp. 165–224, and Reinhart Hummel, *Die Auseinandersetzung zwischen Kirche und Judentum in Matthäusevangelium*, Beiträge zur evangelischen Theologie, no. 33; 2nd ed. (Munich: Kaiser, 1966), pp. 34–75.

121. So von Campenhausen, p. 22.

122. *Ibid.*, pp. 18 f.

123. *Ibid.*, pp. 20 f. Cf. Bornkamm, Barth, and Held, pp. 24 f., on Matthew's strict interpretation of the law.

not to the Law, but to Christ. One can certainly not hide behind any legalism in order to protect himself from the hard demands of God's will (cf. 3:7–10) promulgated definitively by Jesus. Matthew teaches a Christianity that is discipleship, following Christ, the way of righteousness (Strecker), to a community with deep roots in its Jewish past (Stendahl, Davies, von Campenhausen, *et al.*), probably one in which these roots have not been completely broken. Yet in principle Matthew's position makes such a break inevitable, for in his view adherence to the commandment as commandment is no longer the fundamental organizing principle and ground of inspiration or exhortation, but loyalty and obedience to Christ (7:24–27; 11:25–30; 28:18–20). On the other hand, this loyalty is itself defined by an understanding of obedience or righteousness which is intelligible only against an Old Testament and Jewish background.

Luke

The Old Testament quotations, references, and allusions in Luke's Gospel are concentrated largely in the introduction (the nativity and Jesus' preaching in Nazareth), and in the Passion and Resurrection accounts. In Acts they are most frequent in the initial section dealing with the Jerusalem church (chaps. 1–7) and at the end (28:23 ff.). Moreover, they tend to fall in the speeches. The similar tendency in the Gospel for Old Testament quotations to appear on Jesus' lips is due mainly to the precedents established by Mark and Q. Nevertheless, it is significant that in his initial sermon at Nazareth (cf. 4:18 f.) and in his final utterance on the cross (23:46) Jesus quotes the Old Testament, since both instances are unique with Luke. Surely it is also not a happenstance that the Risen Jesus interprets the Scriptures to his disciples in Luke alone (24:27, 32, 44 ff.).

It is usually said that Luke's Bible is the Septuagint, and the predominance of quotations from the Septuagint is real. Luke's imitation of the style of the Septuagint has also been noted.[124] Recently, however, Traugott Holtz has advanced the thesis that only Luke's quotations from Isaiah, the Minor Prophets, and the Psalms are taken directly from the Septuagint; and that his other Old Testa-

---

124. Kümmel, pp. 95, 98, 123.

ment quotations, if not simply drawn from Mark, follow the text-forms of primitive Christian testimonia.[125] While Holtz's theory will bear further critical scrutiny, its correspondence with the textual evidence of Luke-Acts is striking. Already Lindars and de Waard have drawn attention to the primitive, traditional char-acter of the Old Testament testimonia in some of the Acts speeches. Moreover, it is a real question whether at this stage in the develop-ment of early Christianity (the latter part of the first century) authors would have had easy access to the entire Old Testament— a considerable library—particularly if they belonged to churches which had already separated from the synagogue.

As a Gentile Christian in the Pauline sphere of influence, Luke doubtless belonged to such a separated Christian church. Luke looks back on the period of most intense struggle with (and within) Judaism over the new Christian Gospel and its interpretation. For him the controversy over the law within Christianity—Luke adumbrates the term in referring to χριστιανοί—was a matter of historical interest except insofar as it had left wounds which still needed to be healed. Yet his feeling for the continuity between Israel and the church was real and deep. Although he was scarcely the originator of the concept of salvation-history,[126] he brought it to clear articulation in his two-part narrative which is so explic-itly and consciously rooted in the Scriptures of Israel. The discus-sion of the finer points of Conzelmann's comprehensive portrayal of Lucan theology does not need to be taken up here. While we may reserve judgment on the precise periodization of salvation-history in Luke's own intention, the main lines of Conzelmann's Lucan interpretation surely point us in the right direction. This is particularly so in regard to the place and importance of Israel, and concomitantly of Israel's Scriptures, in Luke's overall con-ception.

The prominence of the Old Testament at two crucial points in Luke's work is obvious. First of all, the Acts speeches emphasize

125. *Untersuchungen über die alttestamentlichen Zitate bei Lukas*, Texte und Unter-suchungen, no. 104 (Berlin: Akademie-Verlag, 1968). I have not been able to see the Bonn dissertation of M. Rese, *Alttestamentliche Motive in der Christologie Lukas* (Bonn, 1965); cf. the brief summary in Rohde, pp. 217–19.

126. Cf. Ulrich Wilckens, "Interpreting Luke-Acts in a Period of Existentialist Theology," *Studies in Luke-Acts*, eds. L. E. Keck and J. L. Martyn (Nashville: Abingdon, 1966), pp. 60–83, esp. 72 ff.

that Christ's coming and the coming of the Spirit in the church are the fulfillment of prophetic Scripture (see, for example, Acts 2). Probably these speeches embody primitive tradition, but to the degree that they are Luke's own composition they attest his conviction that God's ancient word has found its fulfillment in Christ and his church. In the second place, there are the initial chapters of the Gospel, including the birth narratives and Jesus' preaching in Nazareth, which are full of Old Testament allusions and quotations. It will be instructive to look briefly at these opening chapters, since they afford an interesting comparison with Matthew's.[127]

Anyone who reads the Lucan birth narrative is immediately struck by its style and tone, which is deliberately contrived to evoke the narratives of the Old Testament. Also the great hymns or canticles uttered by the angel Gabriel, Mary, Zechariah, and Simeon are reminiscent of hymns and Psalms of the Old Testament. These similarities have, of course, often been noted by commentators. The whole narration is clearly designed to anchor the birth of Jesus the Christ in the faith and piety of Israel, in the Hebrew Scriptures, and thus in the plan and purpose of God. Generally its function is not unlike that of the Matthean birth narrative. On the other hand, the formal contrast is considerable. Whereas Matthew accomplishes his purpose by punctuating his narrative with Old Testament testimonies—indeed, they may provide the framework of his account—Luke has not a single formal Old Testament quotation. The difference is rather typical of the Gospels, for Matthew continues to introduce such Old Testament testimony on a much larger scale than Luke.

But surely Luke is just as much interested in portraying Jesus as fulfilling the Scriptures.[128] This intention becomes quite explicit in the famous scene in the Nazareth synagogue (4:16–30) where Jesus begins his public ministry. Luke has apparently taken the

127. On Luke's birth narratives, see W. Barnes Tatum, "The Epoch of Israel: Luke i–ii and the Theological Plan of Luke-Acts," *NTS*, 13 (1966–1967), 184–95, who cites the recent literature fully. Tatum argues persuasively that "St. Luke uses the birth stories to characterize that period in salvation-history before the ministry of Jesus as the Epoch of Israel" (pp. 190–93 f.).

128. Paul Schubert, "The Structure and Significance of Luke 24," *Neutestamentliche Studien für Rudolf Bultmann*, Beihefte zur Zeitschrift für die neutestamentliche Wissenschaft, no. 21; 2nd ed. (Berlin: Töpelmann, 1957), pp. 165–86, has underlined the central place of Old Testament (but not only Old Testament) proof from prophecy in Luke's theology.

Marcan account of Jesus' preaching in the synagogue at Nazareth (Mark 6:1–6), modified it and enlarged it greatly to suit his own ends, and introduced it at the opening of the ministry. Since Luke has acted so deliberately, we are justified in assuming that he thereby reveals his own outlook and viewpoint. Thus it would seem he takes this occasion to have Jesus announce the fulfillment of Isaiah's prophecy (61:1–2) in his own public activity (Luke 4:18–21). The words of Isaiah in the mouth of Jesus answer to the fulfilled expectation which is expressed in the joyous hymns of the infancy narrative. These hymns reveal the fervid expectancy which for Luke characterizes the time of Israel, the first epoch in the history of salvation.

Yet the account does not simply end with Jesus' own proclamation of himself as the fulfillment of prophecy. Another characteristic Lucan motif finds expression as in response to Jesus' sharp retort (vv. 23 ff.), anticipating his rejection by Israel and acceptance by Gentiles—a retort which is really unjustified in the context[129]—his fellow townsmen turn violently against him (vv. 28–30). At this point Jesus simply departs to Capernaum (and Luke takes up the Marcan account). This account may make little sense historically, but it is a perfect expression of Luke's own view that the Gospel is offered first to Jews, preserving the continuity of salvation history, and, when rejected by them, to Gentiles. This pattern emerges again and again in Acts and provides the note on which the entire narrative concludes (28:23–28).

Thus Luke 4:16–30 affords an excellent illustration of Luke's attitude both toward the Scriptures and toward Judaism. Jesus' coming is the fulfillment of Scripture. At the same time, his rejection by Israel—a historical fact in Luke's own time—is anticipated at the very beginning of Jesus' ministry. Thus the continuity of redemptive history is maintained both in the appropriation of the Scriptures and in the conviction that the rupture between synagogue and church is the result of the peculiar hostility of a particular generation of Jews.[130]

129. By mentioning Capernaum (v. 23) Luke implies that Jesus' public ministry had already previously commenced. Probably this incongruity is Luke's own, revealing his awareness of having transposed the whole incident (cf. vv. 31 ff.), and not an indication of reliance upon an earlier source (whose mention of Jesus' activity at Capernaum Luke would have then suppressed).

130. Yet this obduracy is not without precedent, but in Luke's view has a signifi-

John

For John the question of the Old Testament as Law is a dead issue, reflected only occasionally in passages such as 1:17, where the author seems to be pointing to successive epochs if not setting up a deliberate antithesis. References to "your law" in Jesus' debate with the Jews (8:17; 10:34) indicate that for John's church, and in John's theological perspective, the Law belongs to the Jews. And while salvation may be "of the Jews" (4:22), it is actually "of them" and no longer "in them." For the Jews in John's Gospel represent the world's rejection of Jesus.[131]

The disciples' obedience is no longer defined, even in concrete or practical instances, in terms of the Old Testament law. Rather they are given a new commandment, the love commandment, by Jesus (13:34 f.). Yet in some sense the validity of the law is acknowledged in just those instances in which it is referred to as "your law," and Nicodemus' appeal to the law in 7:51 is clearly set in a positive light by the evangelist. Moreover, John holds that Moses himself wrote about Jesus in the law (1:45; 5:46). Very likely this ambiguity toward the law reflects the history of the Johannine Christianity's conflict with the synagogue, in which it has been alienated from Judaism, all the while appealing to the Jewish Law in its own defense.[132]

Paradoxically, John evinces a more positive attitude to the Scriptures than to the Law per se (or to the Scriptures considered as Law). This comes about in two ways, which we shall examine briefly. First, John appropriates the Old Testament testimony tradition of primitive Christianity reflected elsewhere in the New

cant history which he rehearses in Acts 7 (see esp. 7:51–53). While Luke obviously employs traditional material, D. C. Arichea, "A Critical Analysis of the Stephen Speech in the Acts of the Apostles" (Ph.D. diss., Duke University, 1965), is doubtless correct in maintaining that the most fruitful approach to the speech relates it to Luke's purpose (pp. 237 ff.).

131. Cf. von Campenhausen, p. 62, and especially the discussion of Bultmann, *Theology of the New Testament*, trans. Kendrick Grobel (New York: Scribner's, 1953), 2: 26–32.

132. For an analysis of crucial aspects of the Fourth Gospel as the direct or indirect expression of this conflict, see J. Louis Martyn, *History and Theology in the Fourth Gospel* (New York: Harper & Row, 1968). On the ambivalence of the relationship of the law to Jesus in John, see Wayne A. Meeks, *The Prophet-King: Moses Traditions and the Johannine Christology*, Supplements to Novum Testamentum, no. 14 (Leiden: Brill, 1967), pp. 288 ff.

Testament.[133] Second, John sets his Gospel against the background of Old Testament Judaism. Old Testament figures, Old Testament places, Old Testament symbols and institutions are woven into its very fabric, sometimes as the antitypes of John's Jesus, but not always so.[134]

The variety of text-forms in John's Old Testament[135] testimonia probably means that they have been derived from traditional sources. Particularly noteworthy are the Passion testimonies of John. In several instances John has an explicit testimony that is only suggested in Mark (cf. Mark 15:24; 15:36; and John 19:24;

133. M. Dibelius, "Die alttestamentlichen Motive in der Leidensgeschichte des Petrus- und des Johannes-Evangelium," in *Botschaft und Geschichte: Gesammelte Aufsätze* (Tübingen: Mohr, 1953), 1: 221–47, drew attention to the traditional character of the Johannine Old Testament quotations in the Passion narrative. Cf. Lindars, *New Testament Apologetic*, pp. 265–72, on the traditional character of the formula quotations related to the Passion, as well as their apologetic tendency. Very recently Rothfuchs has observed that these quotations deal with and interpret the enemies of Jesus and their actions (pp. 170 ff.).

John's explicit quotations are predominantly from the Prophets (cf. 12:15, 38, 40; 19:37 f.) and the Psalms (2:17; 13:18; 15:25; 19:24, 28 f., 36).

134. The Old Testament matrix of Johannine thought is frequently pointed out by E. C. Hoskyns, *The Fourth Gospel*, ed. F. N. Davey (London: Faber and Faber, 1947). A good summary treatment of this phenomenon has been set forth by C. K. Barrett, "The Old Testament in the Fourth Gospel," *Journal of Theological Studies*, 48 (1947), 155–69. Much more extensive is François Marie Braun, *Jean le Théologien: Les grandes traditions d'Israël et l'accord des Écritures selon le Quatrième Évangile*, Etudes Bibliques (Paris: Gabalda, 1964), the second volume of Braun's trilogy on the Fourth Gospel. Borgen, p. 27, n. 1, cites major contributions to the question of John's use of the Old Testament, of which he is generally critical for their failure to take account of contemporary Jewish midrashic exposition.

Aileen Guilding in an elaborate and erudite study, *The Fourth Gospel and Jewish Worship: A Study of the Relation of St. John's Gospel to the Ancient Jewish Lectionary System* (Oxford: Clarendon Press, 1960), attempts to account for John's Old Testament substructure by understanding the Gospel as a series of meditations upon a triennial cycle of Old Testament lections. Her conclusions have not, however, been widely accepted; cf. Ernst Haenchen, *Theologische Literaturzeitung*, 86 (1961), 670–72; Leon Morris, *The New Testament and the Jewish Lectionaries* (London: Tyndale, 1964); and D. Moody Smith, Jr., *The Composition and Order of the Fourth Gospel: Bultmann's Literary Theory*, Yale Publications in Religion, no. 10 (New Haven: Yale University Press, 1965), pp. 102–5.

135. Pointed out by Charles Goodwin, "How Did John Treat His Sources?", *JBL*, 73 (1954), 61–75, who suggests that John may cite from memory (p. 73). More recent research such as Lindars's and Edwin D. Freed's has, however, made this originally plausible suggestion appear less likely. Freed proposes a background of the Old Testament quotations analogous to Stendahl's school of St. Matthew (p. 130). Thus his conclusion that John probably did not use written testimonia (p. 128) does not deny John's dependence on tradition in the broader sense. Freed's research suggests that at points John's use of the Old Testament is in contact with the Hebrew original or the Targums, although his literal agreements are mostly with the Septuagint. A Semitic background for some of John's Old Testament quotations is also proposed by Borgen, esp. pp. 64 f.

19:28 f.), and John makes very clear the Christian conviction that the Scriptures point to Christ (1:45; 5:39; 5:46 f.). Major events of Jesus' career are said to have occurred in fulfillment of Scripture. Usually the specific Scripture is cited (e.g. 2:17; cf. vs. 22; 12:14–16), but in the case of the Resurrection it is not (20:9). The apologetic of response, a major motif of the early Christian testimony tradition, occurs also in John (12:39 f.).[136] Moreover, the Johannine use of these and other testimonies may reflect an intimate acquaintance with their traditional use.[137] Major Old Testament figures are said to have written about Jesus (Moses in 5:46 f.) and to have seen his day (Abraham in 8:56) or his glory (Isaiah in 12:38). Although the Scripture passages cited may be drawn largely from the testimony tradition of early Christianity, probably the explicit statements regarding the remembering of the Scriptures (e.g. 2:17, 22) and the references to Moses, Abraham and Isaiah are to be ascribed to the fertile and creative mind of the author.

Significant as such instances of the use of the Old Testament as cited above may be, both in showing John's debt to tradition and his originality, they are of secondary importance in comparison with the way in which the movement and framework of the Gospel are set against a Jewish and Old Testament background. The prologue's (1:1–18) depiction of the role of the Logos (Word) in creation—note the light-darkness motif—is reminiscent of the Genesis creation story, where also "in the beginning" God speaks and separates light from darkness. The subsequent account of John the Baptist and the calling of the disciples (1:19–51) is replete with Old Testament references and allusions. The very purpose of John's baptism is the revelation of Jesus (as the Christ) to Israel (v. 32). In this episode a whole series of Old Testament or traditional Jewish titles are ascribed to Jesus: Lamb of God (vv. 29–36), Son of God (v. 34), Rabbi (v. 38), Messiah (v. 41), the one "of whom Moses in the law and also the prophets wrote," the King of Israel (v. 49), and the Son of man (v. 51). The positive relation of Jesus to the Old Testament tradition is affirmed, despite—or perhaps because of—the polarity between Jesus and Moses described in 1:17.

Following this lengthy introduction Jesus proceeds to turn the

---

136. Lindars, *New Testament Apologetic*, pp. 18, 159–61.
137. *Ibid.*, pp. 265 ff.

water intended for use in Jewish rites of purification into the wine symbolic of his own divine revelation (2:1–11). After this he cleanses the temple (2:13–22), but indicates that he will ultimately replace it (2:19 ff.; cf. 4:21 ff.)! There follows an encounter with Nicodemus, the representative of main-line Judaism (3:1–21), after which Jesus confronts the Samaritan woman (4:1–42), who epitomizes Jewish apostasy. The miracle at Bethzatha Pool (5:1–9) becomes the occasion for Jews to persecute Jesus for working on the Sabbath and thus violating Old Testament law. This in turn leads to a christological discussion in which Jesus' work is compared with the Father's. Chapter 6, which finds Jesus suddenly in Galilee, continues much the same level of christological discussion, although in a different theological as well as geographical setting. Here the Exodus tradition is invoked as Jesus and his interlocutors discuss the real meaning of Exod. 16:4 (cf. Ps. 78:24, etc.): Who or what is the true bread from heaven?[138] After the withdrawal of many of his disciples at the end of this episode, Jesus goes again to Jerusalem, where a crucial conflict with the Jewish officialdom takes place (chaps. 7, 8). And one could trace this thread through the remainder of Jesus' public ministry, for it is a major motif of the Johannine framework.

This framework itself is marked by repeated appearances of Jesus in Jerusalem for the Jewish feasts (2:13, 23; 5:1; 6:4; 7:2, 37, etc.). There are also other instances in which events or symbols from the Old Testament are used by Jesus in a way that might be described as typological, for example, the comparison of Jesus' crucifixion to Moses' lifting up the serpent in the wilderness (3:14 f.).[139] Further, it may be possible to trace the influence of

138. *Bread From Heaven* by Borgen is the most thorough recent discussion of John 6. It is, of course, especially valuable for the way in which John's method of dealing with the Old Testament is placed over against contemporary Jewish homiletical practice.

139. The possibility that the signs of John's Gospel stand in an intentional typological relation to the "signs" or "signs and wonders" of Moses in the exodus tradition of the Old Testament has been put forward by Robert H. Smith, "Exodus Typology in the Fourth Gospel," *JBL*, 81 (1962), 329–42. He reviews and criticizes the earlier proposals of J. J. Enz, B. P. W. Stather Hunt, and Harold Sahlin. Whether his own theory is a plausible one is a question that deserves more extended treatment than can be given here. While I do not find it convincing in detail, a typological relation between Jesus and Moses certainly cannot be dismissed. (See John 1:17; 6:32 f. and 9:25 f. as well as 3:14). On the figure of Moses in the Fourth Gospel see also Martyn, pp. 88, 91 ff.; T. F. Glasson, *Moses in the Fourth Gospel*, Studies in Biblical Theology, no. 40 (London: SCM, 1963) and especially now the important work of Meeks, *The Prophet-King*.

the language and thought of certain Old Testament traditions or books, particularly Isaiah, through John's Gospel.[140]

In a variety of ways John seems the most *alttestamentlich* of New Testament books. This is not, however, the result of a simple idea of continuity between the Old Testament, the Judaism of Jesus' or John's day, and the Gospel. In fact, John sets up the sharpest antithesis between the Old and the New that is to be found in the New Testament. One has the impression that the New—Jesus Christ as God's word, as Light, Truth and Life—is not in fact rightly known on the basis of a prior understanding of the Old Testament or the institutions of Judaism. Rather, faith in Jesus, which is the one indispensable thing in John's view, opens up the possibility for a proper understanding of the Scriptures as pointing to him, and of the institutions of Judaism as finding fulfillment in him. Such an understanding ought perhaps to have been present in Jesus' own contemporaries, but in fact it was not (5:39 f.; 5:46 f.). On the contrary, a whole series of "testimonies" is brought forth by the Jews in order to disprove Jesus' claims (e. g. 7:42, 52; 12:34). These, however, represent the unenlightened reading of the Scriptures that is bound to err because it does not recognize and acknowledge in Jesus the source of true light and life. Thus even Nicodemus seems farther from the truth initially than the Samaritan woman, despite his rabbinic learning, and those who reject Jesus most vehemently are the learned representatives of Jewish officialdom (7:45–52; 11:45–53).

In light of this state of affairs, Jesus' turning away from "the Jews" to "his own," already adumbrated in 1:11 f., becomes intelligible. Yet after Jesus turns from the Jews, who have become the representatives of a hostile world, to his own disciples (esp. chaps. 13–17, 21), he turns again with them toward the world, sending them into the world as he was sent (3:13; 17:20 ff.; 20:21). The destiny of Jesus' disciples is a mission to and for the world. It is, however, a real question whether for Johannine Christianity the explicit use of the Old Testament is any longer a necessity for missionary preaching and the ordering of church life. The answer depends in part on whether one sees the Fourth Gospel as representative of a church still in some positive contact with Judaism or

140. F. W. Young, "A Study of the Relation of Isaiah to the Fourth Gospel," *Zeitschrift für die neutestamentliche Wissenschaft*, 46 (1955), 215–33.

as the product of a dialogue that has resulted in alienation, without, however, producing the thoroughgoing rejection of the Old Testament and of creation as divinely ordered that is found in Gnosticism. In my view the latter alternative is more probable. If so, it may be that Johannine Christianity could come to expression apart from its Old Testament basis, as in fact seems to have happened in the Johannine Epistles, as well as the farewell discourses of the Gospel. While the Gospel is built upon a foundation of Old Testament allusion and imagery, especially in chapters 1–12, the Epistles, likely the work of another author or authors, may represent a stage of development in which this Jewish, Old Testament matrix has been attenuated. It is noteworthy that in the Pastorals, documents of comparable date and *Sitz im Leben*, there is a similar dearth of Old Testament references. Conversely, however, other later New Testament documents such as Hebrews, Revelation, and James, not to mention the Apostolic Fathers (see esp. I Clement and Barnabas), attest that the separation of the church from Judaism did not result in the downgrading of the Old Testament. Instead, in many ways it paved the way for the adoption of the Old Testament as a Christian book. In a certain sense it is already that for the Fourth Evangelist, and as such indispensable to the presentation of Jesus which he gives us.

Hebrews and Revelation

This survey of the use of the Old Testament in the New may at best be suggestive of the main lines and results of relevant research, and hopefully also of areas needing further study. As such it is necessarily incomplete. We cannot, however, conclude without mentioning two other New Testament books. Much significant research has recently been done on the one; the other has lately been overlooked. These are, respectively, the Epistle to the Hebrews and the Revelation to John.[141] Each makes as much or more use of the Old Testament as any New Testament document, yet in very different ways. Hebrews contains a great number of rather explicit verbatim scriptural quotations, most of which are attributed directly to God, Christ, or the Holy Spirit. Thus Hebrews'

141. One might also find it fruitful to investigate I Peter in this connection, since the use of the Old Testament in that document appears to bear traces of an earlier tradition (e. g., compare the use of Isaiah in I Pet. 2:6 and Rom. 9:33).

introductory formulas indicate that the author regards the text as God's own speaking. Revelation contains not a single formal citation, but it is just as full of Old Testament language, phraseology, and allusions as Hebrews.[142]

Since so much of Hebrews is biblical exegesis, or at least application, and since we have rather copious Jewish exegetical materials dating from the contemporary period, much recent interest has focused upon locating its precise background. While rabbinic methods of exegesis find extensive parallels in Hebrews,[143] much recent investigation has focused upon Philo[144] or Qumran.[145] Yet neither Qumran nor Philo provides the key to understanding the complex patterns of exegetical discussion in Hebrews, for the author was an original thinker and writer, and a Christian as well. Although he obviously owes something to the exegetical traditions of early Christianity, the attempt to make Hebrews dependent upon the hypothetical primitive testimony book (Harris) scarcely succeeds.[146] Actually, it seems that the author of Hebrews was not greatly dependent upon his Christian predecessors. He appears to have used a form of the Septuagint for most, if not all, of his thirty-odd Old Testament quotations.[147] Probably the key to Hebrews does not lie outside the book itself, but is to be found in an analysis of the author's use of the Scriptures in the context of his total work.

Despite certain affinities with Philonic exegesis, the basic form of the appropriation of the Old Testament in Hebrews is not alle-

142. For the following discussion I am largely indebted to excellent seminar papers (spring semester, 1969) of two graduate students in New Testament at Duke: C. Denny White, "The Use of the Old Testament in the Epistle to the Hebrews," and James S. Aull, "The Use of the Book of Jeremiah in the Apocalypse of John."

143. Richard Reid, "The Use of the Old Testament in the Epistle to the Hebrews" (Th.D. diss., Union Theological Seminary, N. Y., 1964), pp. 72–97, esp. 73, 80–97.

144. See Sowers (above, n. 30).

145. For example, Hans Kosmala, *Hebräer-Essener-Christen: Studien zur Vorgeschichte der frühchristlichen Verkündigung*, Studia Post-Biblica, no. 1 (Leiden: Brill, 1959), esp., pp. 1–43; cf. S. Kistemaker, *The Psalm Citations in the Epistle to the Hebrews* (Amsterdam: Wed. G. van Soest, 1961), pp. 64–70 *et passim*; also George Howard, "Hebrews and the Old Testament Quotations," *Novum Testamentum*, 10 (1968), 208–16, who attempts to make the textual evidence of Qumran profitable for the determination of the Old Testament text-form of Hebrews (but cf. n. 147 below).

146. F. C. Synge, *Hebrews and the Scriptures* (London: S.P.C.K., 1959); Reid, pp. 66–71, also Kistemaker, pp. 91 f.

147. A recent and very full treatment of the use of the Old Testament in Hebrews, Friedrich Schröger, *Der Verfasser des Hebräerbriefes als Schriftausleger*, Biblische Untersuchungen, no. 4 (Regensburg: Friedrich Pustet, 1968), confirms the generally held view that the author relies upon the Septuagint (see pp. 248 ff., 262–65).

gory, but typology. Although Hebrews has a forerunner in Paul (cf. Romans 4; Galatians 3), the author is certainly the master of typology among New Testament writers. There are several important typologies in Hebrews: the Moses-Christ typology (3:2 ff.); the Israel-Church typology (3:7–4:11); the Melchizedek-Christ typology (chap. 7). They all, however, seem to revolve about the basic typology of the Old and New Covenants.[148] This typology is not only implicit in the entire argument of Hebrews, but becomes quite explicit in 8:8–13, for there the author quotes the famous new covenant passage of Jer. 31:31–34 in its entirety. Within this overall typology, the exegesis of several Psalms plays an important role. In 2:6–8 Ps. 8:4–6 is adduced to make the point that Christ identifies with humanity. In 3:7–11 Ps. 95:7–11 is adduced to warn the church by means of the example of Israel's apostasy. In 1:13 and 5:6 Ps. 110:1,4 is used to underline Jesus' exaltation. Finally, in 10:5–7 (Ps. 40:6–8) the exact means of transition from the Old Covenant into the realm of holiness of the New is specified: "through the offering of the body of Jesus Christ once for all."[149] The themes of these Psalm quotations are summarized in 2:17.

If one speaks of the purpose of the author of Hebrews in using the Old Testament, he must distinguish two levels. There was the practical and overall purpose of the letter to encourage and warn Christians wavering in their faith, perhaps in danger of persecution, perhaps in greater danger of falling, or falling back, into Judaism because of their general lassitude and disappointment over the delay in the Parousia. To this end the Old Testament is sometimes applied directly (e. g. 3:7–11; chap. 11). More often, however, the Old Testament is used to develop the theological argument concerning the superiority of Jesus, the high priestly mediator of the New Covenant, over the sacrificial system of the Old. (The messiahship of Jesus is simply assumed. What is demonstrated is his high priestly function.) The faith conviction that underlies this argument is the grounds upon which the author of Hebrews can comfort, exhort, and warn the wavering community which he addresses. The Old Testament provides not only the framework

148. Cf. Sowers, pp. 91 ff.
149. This is the discovery of Kistemaker, pp. 96–133, who thinks that the exegesis of these Psalms determines the structure of Hebrews.

and structure for this argument, but legitimates and guarantees it. For the author of Hebrews regards the Scriptures as nothing less than God's word. This is probably why the scriptural quotations are so often attributed to God's own speaking, either directly or through Christ and the Spirit. Remarkable by their absence from the introductory formulas of Hebrews are the terms γράφω and γραφή, which appear so often in connection with Old Testament quotations elsewhere in the New Testament. For him the Old Testament, while God's word and therefore valid, along with the Jewish institutions it establishes, is nevertheless anticipatory, demanding completion. Yet its prophecies may continue to point to the future, even for the Christian, and even its anticipatory and incomplete aspects serve to illumine the perfect revelation that has come in Christ.[150] Perhaps more than any other figure the unknown author of Hebrews deserves the title of the Old Testament theologian of the New.

The Old Testament language of the Revelation to John is indicated by the bold face type in the Nestle text and even more fully by the marginal notes. Swete counts 278 verses with allusions to the Old Testament or some dependence upon it out of the 404 verses of the book.[151] Yet John never quotes extensively. Not even a full verse from the Old Testament is quoted in its entirety. Never does he give any indication that he is quoting, and therefore he has no introductory formulas. Not surprisingly, in view of the allusive character of the author's use of the Scriptures, the Old Testament text of Revelation presents a difficult problem. J. A. Montgomery is probably correct in thinking that the Old Testament material in Revelation comes out of the rich storehouse of the author's memory rather than from a single textual tradition or combination of traditions.[152] Yet recent research has turned up

150. See the excellent statement by C. K. Barrett, "The Eschatology of the Epistle to the Hebrews," in *The Background of the New Testament and its Eschatology: Studies in Honour of C. H. Dodd*, ed. W. D. Davies and David Daube (Cambridge: Cambridge University Press, 1956), p. 392.

151. Henry Barclay Swete, *The Apocalypse of St. John: The Greek Text with Introduction, Notes and Indices*, 3rd ed. (London: Macmillan, 1911), p. cxl. His count is actually based on the "quotations from the Old Testament" given in the appendix of B. F. Wescott and F. J. A. Hort, eds., *The New Testament in the Original Greek* (Cambridge and London: Macmillan, 1881).

152. "The Education of the Seer of the Apocalypse," *JBL*, 45 (1926), 70–80, esp. 71 f.

some rather striking affinities between the Old Testament references in Revelation and the Aramaic Targums.[153] The semitizing character of John's Greek suggests the likelihood of his knowledge of targumic tradition. That such tradition might turn up in material drawn from his memory is not at all unlikely. John's method of using the Old Testament may also explain why he shows relatively little contact with the primitive church's tradition of scriptural proof or apologetic.[154] His mind moves independently along new paths, producing only occasional testimonies from the common tradition (or memory) of the church (see for example Zech. 12:10 f., found in Rev. 1:7 and John 19:37).

Naturally John's reminiscences of the Old Testament are heavily weighted toward the prophetic side of the canon. References to Isaiah are fairly numerous as one might well expect, since Isaiah is the prophetic book most frequently quoted in the New Testament. On the other hand there are numerous allusions to Ezekiel, Daniel, and Jeremiah—more in Revelation than in other New Testament books.

It is virtually impossible to discover any purpose behind John's use of the Old Testament distinguishable from his purpose in the entire work. This is exactly what his way of employing the Old Testament would lead us to expect. The author's language and thought world is the Old Testament, as he understands it, particularly the prophetic writings. Without them he could not have written at all. Thus the document itself is, literally, quite inconceivable apart from the Old Testament. While Revelation is unique among New Testament books generally, as well as unique in its appropriation of the Old Testament, in two respects it is strikingly typical. First, the prophetic-eschatological dimension of the Old Testament is dominant in Revelation. Actually, the predominance of allusions to prophetic books is disproportionate. Nevertheless, the New Testament is marked by its tendency to read the Old Testament as prophecy rather than law (the rabbis) or reli-

153. L. P. Trudinger, "Some Observations concerning the Text of the Old Testament in the Book of Revelation," *Journal of Theological Studies*, n.s. 17 (1966), 82–88; McNamara, *The New Testament and the Palestinian Targum to the Pentateuch*, pp. 97–125.

154. Cf. the judgment of Lindars, *New Testament Apologetic*, p. 29: "The Epistle to the Hebrews . . . is a highly individual study in its own right, so that its scriptural interpretation witnesses more to the outlook of the author than to a previous apologetic tradition. The Book of Revelation, which also contains a wealth of scriptural quotations, is so poetical in its approach . . . that it could be used only rarely for confirmatory evidence of conclusions drawn from other parts of the New Testament."

gious philosophy (Philo). (Perhaps Revelation shares with Qumran an emphasis on the future rather than the past or present fulfillment of prophecy, whereas the New Testament generally places greater weight upon the latter aspect.) Second, the author of Revelation expresses himself in a vocabulary and phraseology drawn from the Old Testament. Here again he represents a kind of exaggeration of a phenomenon found elsewhere in the New Testament, for it is well known that the Old Testament scriptures, particularly in their septuagintal form, served as a rich mine of theological (and other) vocabulary and conceptuality for the early Christian writers.

THE IMPORTANCE OF THE OLD TESTAMENT FOR THE NEW

The principal importance of the Old Testament for the New inheres precisely in the two points just mentioned above. When due account is taken of the historic novelty or uniqueness of the New Testament message and the extent of its orientation toward the Hellenistic world, one must still reckon with its deep indebtedness to Judaism and the Old Testament, both with respect to its theological language and conceptuality and with respect to its prophetic-historical consciousness.[155]

Because of this rootage, which is intrinsic to the Christian message and not merely its historically conditioned husk, the Old Testament is the indispensable theological-historical background for reading and understanding the New. This does not mean that

155. The importance of the Old Testament for the New, and for the Christian faith, has in recent years been the subject of considerable scholarly theological discussion. Note especially B. W. Anderson, ed., *The Old Testament and Christian Faith: A Theological Discussion* (New York: Harper & Row, 1963); Claus Westermann, ed., *Essays on Old Testament Hermeneutics*, trans. J. L. Mays (Richmond: John Knox, 1963); James Barr, *Old and New in Interpretation: A Study of the Two Testaments* (New York: Harper & Row, 1966); John Bright, *The Authority of the Old Testament* (Nashville: Abingdon, 1967); Daniel Lys, *The Meaning of the Old Testament: An Essay on Hermeneutics* (Nashville: Abingdon, 1967); K. H. Miskotte, *When The Gods are Silent*, trans. J. W. Doberstein (New York: Harper & Row, 1967); F. F. Bruce, *The New Testament Development of Old Testament Themes* (Grand Rapids, Mich.: Eerdmans, 1968); Claus Westermann, *The Old Testament and Jesus Christ*, trans. O. Kaste (German ed., 1968; Minneapolis: Augsburg, n.d.); Norbert Lohfink, *The Christian Meaning of the Old Testament*, trans. R. A. Wilson (Milwaukee: Bruce, 1968); and, especially, Brevard S. Childs, *Biblical Theology in Crisis* (Philadelphia: Westminster, 1970), an important programmatic statement. See also the summation of earlier literature by Roland E. Murphy, "The Relationship Between the Testaments," *CBQ*, 26 (1964), 349–59, and his "Christian Understanding of the Old Testament," *Theology Digest*, 18 (1970), 321–32.

the contemporary Jewish and Hellenistic milieu can be left out of account, however, because it is only in and through that milieu that the Old Testament was read by the early Christians, including the New Testament writers. It does mean that those who first brought the Christian message to theological articulation—even in most primitive form—saw that message as the culmination of the saga of Israel's history and faith, and therefore of Scripture. Furthermore, New Testament writers and theologians from Paul to Luke, John, and the author of Hebrews carried out their work in conscious continuation of this perspective, in different ways elaborating it or enlarging upon it. Thus Luke sees the relationship between Old and New primarily in terms of continuity. John sees it in terms of polarity, but not a polarity in which the Old has a purely negative function. Rather the Old must be seen completely in light of the New, and the failure to do so constitutes the ground for condemnation whereby "Israel" becomes "the Jews," and the latter, in their obduracy, "the world." In Hebrews we see a point of view closer to John than to Luke, but without the visible animus toward the representatives of an old dispensation that will not change. Nevertheless, "He abolishes the first in order to establish the second" (10:9); thus the Old is fulfilled and displaced by the New no less thoroughly in Hebrews than in John.

In a very helpful way von Rad has shown that the reinterpretation of the old sagas and traditions in the light of a new salvation-event, either anticipated or accomplished, is a phenomenon quite common in the Old Testament from the Exodus onward.[156] In principle, or formally considered, the New Testament represents a continuation or extension of this process, although the reinterpretation is carried through in a quite radical way. Again, the closest historically contemporary analogy to this reinterpretation is probably to be found in Qumran. Although Qumran has no "New Testament" in the proper sense of the word, the impetus and the initial stages of another canonical corpus, or at least the extension of the inherited scriptures in consequence of the sect's unique experience and consciousness, can already be seen in the surviving documents.[157]

156. *Old Testament Theology*, vol. II: *The Theology of Israel's Prophetic Traditions*, trans. D. M. G. Stalker (New York: Harper & Row, 1965), pt. 3, esp. pp. 319–35.
157. Eybers may be right in contending that, strictly speaking, the canon of Qumran

Perhaps even more important than this traditional-historical connection of the Old Testament and the New, with all its theological implications, is their common language and conceptuality. By this is not meant merely common vocabulary and a common treasury of ideas, although those are present and significant. Rather, there exists a common way of talking and thinking about Man and God in their confrontation and interaction. Man can only be understood and defined over against God. Conversely God and talk about God can only have significance in so far as they bear upon man; not man in the abstract, but man as a concrete historical being whose life is characterized by decision-making, dependency, and dying. In this respect, Rudolf Bultmann, whose views on the Old Testament have been much criticized,[158] has quite rightly affirmed the indispensability of the Old Testament for the New. In his characteristic way of putting the matter, the Old Testament as law provides the indispensable existential presupposition for understanding the New. Man in Old Testament terms is the man to whom the Gospel is addressed, because that man understands himself as responsible for disposing of himself before God. Only such a man can receive grace, for apart from such a self-understanding grace is a meaningless concept. Whatever may be said by way of criticizing or questioning the adequacy of this view of the Old Testament's relevance, it can scarcely be gainsaid as far as it goes. For the irrelevance and impotence of the church is the inevitable result of failure to understand man as a creature responsible before God, whose creatureliness and responsibility are neither resolved nor negated, but redeemed, by the Gospel message of the New Testament. Where the Old Testament is ignored, such an understanding of man as creature, indeed as historical and societal creature, usually disappears, and the New Testament is wrongly regarded as only a handbook of personal piety and religion.

---

was very close to the Jamnian canon. But the criterion of use is also an important factor in establishing canonicity, and by this criterion Qumran would seem to have been in the process of expanding its canon. See, for example, the War Scroll, the Manual of Discipline, and the Damascus Document.

158. See especially the B. W. Anderson volume which consists of an interesting and important series of critical responses to Bultmann's opening essay, "The Significance of the Old Testament for the Christian Faith" (first published in 1933).

THE RAHAB SAGA (JOSHUA 2):
Some Form-Critical and Traditio-Historical Observations

GENE M. TUCKER

Two of the most problematic issues concerning the Old Testament conquest traditions are the closely-related questions of the history and the nature of the stories in Joshua 1–12. Recent discussions of the literary and preliterary history of this material have been strongly influenced by the work of Martin Noth, who has argued convincingly that the books of Deuteronomy, Joshua, Judges, I and II Samuel, and I and II Kings comprise a single literary unit, the Deuteronomistic history work (Dtr.), composed in the exilic period by a writer who used older sources and oral traditions.[1] Noth also has analyzed the "sources" and traditions which the Deuteronomistic historian used in his account of the taking of the land.[2] Primarily as a result of Noth's work, the older effort to parcel out the material in the book of Joshua among the pentateuchal sources has been abandoned by most scholars.[3] However, the question of the existence of those sources within the conquest traditions has been raised from a fresh perspective recently by Sigmund Mowinckel,[4] who has argued that the remnants of a J version of the conquest can be seen in Joshua 1–12 and Judges 1. His work prompts us to examine once again the question of the

1. Martin Noth, *Überlieferungsgeschichtliche Studien* (Tübingen: Max Niemeyer Verlag, 1943), especially pp. 10 ff.
2. Martin Noth, *Das Buch-Josua, Handbuch zum Alten Testament* (Tübingen: J. C. B. Mohr [Paul Siebeck], 1953), vol. 7, especially 11–13; and Noth, *Überlieferungsgeschichtliche Studien*, pp. 40–47.
3. Noteworthy exceptions are Otto Eissfeldt, *The Old Testament: An Introduction*, trans. P. R. Ackroyd (New York: Harper & Row, 1965), pp. 241–57; Eissfeldt, *Hexateuch-Synopse* (Leipzig: J. C. Hinrichs Verlag, 1922), pp. 66–84; and Georg Fohrer, *Introduction to the Old Testament*, initiated by Ernst Sellin, trans. David E. Green (New York: Abingdon Press, 1965), pp. 196–205.
4. Sigmund Mowinckel, *Tetrateuch—Pentateuch—Hexateuch*, BZAW, no. 90 (Berlin: A. Töplemann, 1964). See also Mowinckel, *Erwägungen zur Pentateuch Quellenfrage* (Trondheim: Universitetsforlaget, 1964), pp. 107–11.

literary and preliterary history of the conquest traditions, with particular attention to the pre-Deuteronomistic stages.

The second question, that of the nature of the material in Joshua 1–12, raises above all the problem of defining and interpreting etiological sagas. Noth, following Gressmann,[5] Alt,[6] and others, classified most of the individual stories in the first half of the book of Joshua as etiological sagas: Each arose as an answer to the child's question "Why?" concerning some existing phenomenon, such as the name of a place, a cultic practice or the ruin of a city. The debate which followed Noth's evaluation is well-known, and need not be reviewed in detail here. First Albright[7] and then Bright[8] argued that the etiological factor was never the primary motivating force in the creation of the tradition but was only secondarily attached to historical traditions.[9] Few have seriously questioned the presence of etiological concerns in the stories in Joshua 1–12 and elsewhere;[10] the argument has turned around whether these concerns were primary or secondary. The recent form-critical works of Childs[11] and Long[12] have tended to confirm the conclusion that the etiological formulas and conclusions are secondary, that is, either the formulas were secondarily added to received traditions[13] or these "marks" of the etiology "seldom can be used as a way of determining whether or not a given narrative served an etiological purpose."[14]

But questions remain. Both Childs and Long have directed their attention primarily to the etiological formulas which con-

5. Hugo Gressmann, *Die Schriften des Alten Testaments*, 2nd ed. (Göttingen: Vandenhoeck & Ruprecht, 1922), 1:136 ff.

6. Albrecht Alt, *Josua*, BZAW, no. 66 (1936), pp. 13–29; reprinted in *Kleine Schriften zur Geschichte des Volkes Israel* (Munich: C. H. Beck'sche Verlagsbuchhandlung, 1953), 1: 176–92.

7. W. F. Albright, "The Israelite Conquest of Canaan in the Light of Archaeology," *BASOR*, 74 (1939), 11–23.

8. John Bright, *Early Israel in Recent History Writing*, SBT, no. 19 (London: SCM Press, 1956).

9. *Ibid.*, p. 91.

10. For Noth's response to Bright, see *Der Beitrag der Archäologie zur Geschichte Israels*, SVT, no. 7 (Leiden: E. J. Brill, 1960), pp. 262–82, especially pp. 278 ff.

11. Brevard S. Childs, "A Study of the Formula, 'Until this Day,' " *JBL*, 82 (1963), 279–92.

12. Burke O. Long, *The Problem of Etiological Narrative in the Old Testament*, BZAW, no. 108 (Berlin: A. Töplemann, 1968).

13. Childs, p. 292.

14. Long, p. 3.

clude narrative units. However, the form-critical classification and evaluation of units must depend upon more than the analysis of formulas. They must include, among other matters, the examination of the structure of the unit for indications of its genre, setting, and intention. One must look now, as Long has suggested,[15] at the narratives themselves for evidence for or against etiological functions or intentions. And at the same time, since it has been argued that etiological conclusions usually are secondary to the basic traditions, one must combine the analysis of the formal elements of narratives with traditio-historical and *redactionsgeschichtliche* investigations. Only in such a way can one determine how a given story functioned through the various stages of its development and at which point the etiological conclusion was added, if indeed it did not exist in the original tradition.

So at this point our two questions coalesce. We cannot adequately deal with the issue of the genre of the stories in Joshua 1–12 (primarily the question of etiology) without examining the history of those stories. This paper is an attempt to raise these two questions in a limited way through an analysis of a single story, the account of Rahab and the Israelite spies (Josh. 2:1–24; 6:17, 22 25). Our primary focal point will be the story itself, but in the process of examining the story we hope to make a contribution to the broader questions.

The Deuteronomistic Context

Our point of departure is the final form of the story of Rahab, as we have received it in its Deuteronomistic context. The book of Joshua, as an account of a definite stage in the history of Israel, is framed into the Deuteronomistic history work by the historian's introductory and concluding summaries in Josh. 1:1–18, 21:43–22:6, and 23:1–16.[16] The introduction in 1:1–18 is a well-rounded unit consisting of (1) Yahweh's speech to Joshua (1:1–9) including instructions for taking the land, admonitions to obey the law, and promises of success; (2) Joshua's instructions to the "officers" to

15. *Ibid.*, pp. 2 ff., 94.
16. Noth, *Josua*, p. 9. Chapter 24, which has been edited by the Deuteronomistic redactor, poses some special problems.

prepare the people for the crossing of the Jordan to take the land (1:10–11); and (3) Joshua's special instructions to the east Jordanian tribes to aid in the taking of west Jordan and their response (1:12–18). The location of these events is not specified. The Deuteronomistic historian assumes the location which he specified in Deut. 1:1 ff., the final wilderness stopping-place and the site of the last words and events in the life of Moses. The Mount Nebo of Deut. 34:1 he assumes to be in the immediate vicinity, "opposite Jericho." Josh. 1:1–18 continues immediately where Deuteronomy 34 had ended: After the death of Moses a new era begins under a new leader.

Joshua 2 maintains the general thread of the story to the extent that further preparations for the taking of west Jordan are made from a camp beyond the Jordan. However, a number of factors indicate a break between chapters 1 and 2. In the first place, the distinctively Deuteronomistic prose of chapter 1 is missing in 2:1 ff. Second, 2:1 specifies that Joshua sent the spies "from Shittim," a place not mentioned in the Dtr. version of the wilderness wandering. Third, chapter 1 seems to lead up directly to the crossing of the Jordan, and would be followed more logically by the narrative in 3:1 ff. than by that in chapter 2. Fourth, the reference to a crossing "within three days" (בְּעוֹד שְׁלֹשֶׁת יָמִים) in 1:11 accommodates *either* the events in chapter 2 (cf. v. 22) *or* those at the beginning of chapter 3 (cf. v. 2), but not both. And fifth, while we cannot agree with Hertzberg that the situation in chapter 1 makes the reconnaissance of the land superfluous[17] (since the idea of the holy war and Yahweh's promises do not preclude the use of stratagems), we can recognize that the accent has shifted from the general parenetic speeches promising success to the detailed stories concerning specific places and events in the taking of the land. We conclude, therefore, with Noth[18] and others that chapter 2 presents us with the first of the pre-Deuteronomistic stories of the conquest of west Jordan.

The various contexts of the Rahab story, then, reflect the successive stages in the history of its growth and composition. It belongs first of all to the Deuteronomistic version of the taking of the

---

17. H. W. Hertzberg, *Die Bücher Josua, Richter, Ruth*, 2nd ed., ATD, no. 9 (Göttingen: Vandenhoeck & Ruprecht, 1959), p. 18.

18. Noth, *Josua*, pp. 11 ff., 21 ff.

land, Joshua 1–24. Second, it is the initial chapter in the account
of the older source, Joshua 2–11. (Josh. 12:1–24 is another Dtr.
summary.) Third, it is a part of the collection of stories of events
around Gilgal and Jericho in Joshua 2–6, almost all of which conclude etiologically. More specifically within that collection, as we
shall see, the Rahab story and chapter 6 belong together as the
two parts of the account of the taking of Jericho. And finally, a
Rahab story or stories once existed independently before becoming
a part of that collection.

The Deuteronomistic redactor has allowed the story to stand
virtually as it was when he received it, making only a few editorial
additions. Most of these additions are found in Rahab's first speech
to the spies, 2:9 ff., where she "is quoted as being rather well read
in the Deuteronomic traditions of the exodus and the wilderness."[19]
Distinctively Deuteronomistic language and point of view are seen
at least in 2:9b (cf. Deut. 11:25), 2:10b (which recalls the Dtr.
version of the Amorite wars, Deut. 2:30–3:7), and 2:11b (cf. Deut.
4:39).[20] It is possible that the entire unit 2:9b–11 stems from
Dtr.,[21] but the precise parallels to Deuteronomistic language are
not visible in verses 10a and 11a. The only other demonstrably
Dtr. addition in chapter 2 is verse 24b, which parallels verse 9b.

The question of the presence of Dtr. material in the story's conclusion in 6:17, 22 ff. is more problematic. Mowinckel has attributed verse 23b to Dtr., apparently on the basis of the attitude it
reflects toward the presence of foreigners within Israel;[22] Noth
considered verse 25b a late addition and verse 26 Deuteronomistic;[23] and Bright raised the possibility that verse 27 was also
Deuteronomistic.[24] However, in none of these instances can
Deuteronomistic language or perspective be demonstrated with
certainty. And at any rate only verses 23b and 25b bear directly
upon the Rahab story, since verse 26 is the conclusion to the story
of the destruction of Jericho (chapter 6), and verse 27 is a general
summary statement concerning Joshua.

19. John L. McKenzie, *The World of the Judges* (Englewood Cliffs: Prentice-Hall, 1966), p. 48.
20. Noth, *Josua*, pp. 29 ff.
21. Cf. John Bright, "The Book of Joshua: Introduction and Exegesis," *IB*, 2: 543.
22. Mowinckel, *Tetrateuch—Pentateuch—Hexateuch*, p. 33.
23. Noth, *Josua*, pp. 9, 36, 41.
24. Bright, *The Book of Joshua*, p. 543.

Beyond these few redactional additions, it is very likely that the original beginning of the old collection was dropped when it was incorporated into the historian's work. The present beginning of the collection in 2:1 is too abrupt, and וַיִּשְׁלַח יְהוֹשֻׁעַ is an unusual beginning for a literary work.[25] One would expect at least a specification of the place in Trans-Jordan and possibly a general chronological reference. Furthermore, the historian expresses himself above all in introductory and concluding summaries. It is likely, then, that chapter 1 has displaced an older beginning, but the shape and contents of that introduction no longer can be determined.

The Deuteronomistic historian has framed this story (and the others in the older collection) into his theological history of Israel, but he has made few changes in the story itself. His additions contributed little of significance, and hardly changed the story at all. He was satisfied to fill out slightly Rahab's recitation of the salvation history and to underscore Yahweh's activity in history on behalf of Israel. This indicates that he had before him a story which was already completed and already a part of a larger context which extended at least through chapter 6. It is to be emphasized that the etiological conclusion as well as the picture of a conquest (not a migration) from the east of the Jordan by all the tribes of Joshua existed in the tradition before his time.

We must, therefore, examine in greater detail the earlier stages of the tradition, since the structure, genre, and intention from an earlier setting of the story remain in this final (literary) setting within the Deuteronomistic history work.

THE PRE-DEUTERONOMISTIC REDACTION

Context and structure

We turn now to an investigation of the pre-Deuteronomistic history of the Rahab story. The first issue before us is that of the relationship of the saga to its context in the source which the Deuteronomistic redactor incorporated into his history.

We have seen that 2:1 stands now as the beginning of the older collection of stories used by the redactor and also that chapter 2

25. Cf. Mowinckel, *Tetrateuch—Pentateuch—Hexateuch*, p. 49.

interrupts somewhat the sequence of events which moves more logically from the end of chapter 1 directly to 3:1 ff. The impression that chapter 2 is out of place is confirmed by an examination of its relationship to 3:1–5:15. The latter unit contains the traditio-historically complex account of the crossing of the Jordan (3:1–5:1), and the report of the first events in the land of Canaan, including the circumcision of the people of Israel (5:2–9), the first passover in the promised land (5:10–12), and the enigmatic story of Joshua's encounter with "the commander of Yahweh's army" (5:13–15). There is no inner connection between the stories of the taking of Jericho (chapters 2 and 6) and the accounts of the crossing, the circumcision, and the passover.[26] The brief narrative concerning Joshua and "the commander of Yahweh's army" is more closely re-lated to the themes of chapters 2 and 6, but its brevity, terseness, and isolation indicate that it is an independent tradition. Furthermore, the mood and tone of chapters 3–5 are quite different from that of chapter 2. The cultic and theological concerns in chapters 3–5 stand in contrast to the more "secular" account of the scouting expe-dition.[27] The thread which holds together all the stories in chapters 2–6 is their common locality, the region of Gilgal and Jericho.

In the pre-Deuteronomistic source the story thread of chapter 2 is woven into that of chapter 6. The most obvious connections are drawn in 6:22–26 which concludes both the Rahab story and the account of the fall of Jericho. The other explicit link is in 6:17b which reports Joshua's instructions that only "Rahab and all who are with her in her house" are to be spared from the ban. But chapter 2 itself also contains links with the story of Jericho's de-struction. Whatever the precise mission of the spies was, it is clear that their expedition is in preparation for the overthrow of Jericho as the first step in taking the land. Furthermore, the spy story con-sistently assumes the imminent total destruction of Jericho (cf. especially 2:13–14, 18–19), an assumption which is pointless with-out a sequel. Our analysis supports the conclusions of Noth[28] and Mowinckel[29] that this combination of chapters 2 and 6 was a result of the literary efforts of a pre-Deuteronomistic redactor.

26. Cf. McKenzie, *World of the Judges*, p. 48.
27. Cf. Mowinckel, *Tetrateuch—Pentateuch—Hexateuch*, p. 13.
28. Noth, *Josua*, p. 29.
29. Mowinckel, *Tetrateuch—Pentateuch—Hexateuch*, pp. 14, 42.

There are, however, factors which show that the stories in 2 and 6 once existed independently of one another. An examination of the structure and genre of the Rahab story as it appeared in the pre-Deuteronomistic source will begin to make some of these factors clear while at the same time bringing out the intention or function of the account at that stage in its development.

The structure of the Rahab story in chapter 2 and its epilogue in 6:22–25 is as follows:

Chapter 2

I. Introductory report of Joshua's sending the spies and their arrival in Jericho (1)

II. Account of events in Jericho (2–21)

    A. First scene: Rahab hides the spies (2–7)

        1. The report to the king and his response (2–3)

        2. General report that Rahab hid the spies (4a)

        3. Rahab's response to the men sent by the king (4b–5)

        4. Specific report that Rahab hid the spies (6)

        5. The pursuit by the king's men (7)

    B. Second scene: the agreement between Rahab and the spies on the roof (8–14)

        1. Introduction (8)

        2. Rahab's speech to the spies (9–13)

        [9b, 10b, 11b, Dtr.]

          a. Recitation of the history of salvation and account of the fear of Israel (9–11)

          b. Covenant request (12–13)

            (1) Request for an oath and a sign (12)

            (2) Plea for herself and her family (13)

        3. Response of the spies: their oath (14)

    C. Third scene: oath at the window (15–21)

        1. Rahab lets the spies down through her window (15)

        2. Her instructions for the escape (16)

        3. The spies' oath and instructions to Rahab (17–20)

          a. Promise of faithfulness to the oath (17)

          b. Instructions (18)

          c. Conditions of the oath: promise and threat (19–20)

        4. Rahab's acceptance (21a)

> 5. Report of the departure of the spies and the tying of
>   the cord (21b)
> III. The escape and return of the spies (22–24) [24b Dtr.]
>   A. Their escape (22)
>   B. Return and report to Joshua (23)
>   C. The content of the report (24)

Epilogue (6:22–25)

> I. Joshua's instructions to the spies (22)
> II. Report of their saving Rahab and her family (23)
> III. Report of the burning of the city (24)
> IV. Etiological summary (25)
>   A. Rahab and her "father's household" saved
>   B. She dwelt in Israel "to this day"
>   C. Reason: because she saved the messengers

The two main features of the structure of chapter 2 are a narrative framework reporting the action and three little conversations.[30] The first conversation is between Rahab and (presumably) the men sent by the king of Jericho. In the second one Rahab requests a sworn agreement—a covenant—from the spies and they grant it. And in the third the spies detail their terms for the agreement and Rahab accepts.

In the pre-Deuteronomistic source, the unit which begins in 2:1 does not conclude until 6:26. Chapter 6:22–26 is the epilogue to both 2:1–24 and 6:1–21, and assumes both the Rahab story and the account of the destruction of Jericho. Most of it should be attributed to the editor of the pre-Deuteronomistic source as his effort to draw the two stories together.[31] But at this redactional stage in the development of the traditions, the links between chapters 2 and 6 are not merely superficial and not limited to the epilogue. Some of the dominant themes of chapter 2 are left hanging in the air without the content expressed in 6:22–26.

On the other hand, however, there is a sense in which chapter 2 can be considered a more or less complete unit. We have seen that 2:1 marks a distinct break from chapter 1 and a clear if incomplete

---

30. Cf. Noth, *Josua*, p. 29.
31. Cf. Mowinckel, *Tetrateuch—Pentateuch—Hexateuch*, pp. 14, 35, 42. Mowinckel sees 6:25 as the original conclusion to the Rahab saga which has been placed at the end of chapter 6 by the pre-Deuteronomistic redactor.

new beginning. Furthermore, in 2:24 a definite conclusion has been reached in the story: Spies were sent out; they have accomplished their mission and given their report. This observation suggests—but does not by itself prove—that a story of Rahab and the spies once circulated independently in the oral tradition, and that its present dependence upon the story of the miraculous capture of Jericho is a result of the work of a redactor.

The impression that a Rahab story once circulated independently in the oral tradition is strengthened as one looks at the structure and contents of the chapter for evidence of an earlier stage in its development. Most of this evidence is in the inconsistencies, repetitions and duplicates, and unevenness in the style which we take to be traces of an earlier form (or forms) of the story.

In the first place, the sequence of events in the story is somewhat inconsistent and confusing. The spies were sent out to view the land and they returned with a report concerning "the whole land," but the story concerns only their activities in Jericho. It is possible that the account of the events in Jericho has been combined with another tradition about Joshua's spies which paralleled the account of the spies sent by Moses (cf. especially Numbers 13–14). The order of events in the first scene is especially confusing, since there are two reports that Rahab hid the spies (vv. 4a and 6), both of which disrupt the sequence. The first (v. 4a) comes between the speech of the king's men and Rahab's response. This inconsistency usually is smoothed over in the translations by rendering the waw consecutive imperfects וַתִּקַּח and וַתִּצְפְּנוֹ in the past perfect: "But the woman had taken the two men and hidden them. . . ." The other more specific account of the hiding of the spies follows Rahab's speech to the king's men but precedes the report of their response to her speech. The problems of sequence and duplication in verses 2–7 are coupled with a distinctly terse style. We would expect, for example, some notice that Rahab knew of the danger to her guests before she took steps to protect them.

The problem of sequence arises again in the narrative framework of the third scene (vv. 15–21). We are told that Rahab let the spies down on a rope through her window which was in the wall, presumably in the wall of the city,[32] gave them instructions

---

32. The precise meaning of בְּקִיל הַחֹמָה in v. 15 is unclear.

for their escape, they responded with an extended speech, and she then sent them on their way. We are left with the picture of the spies pausing to complete their agreement with Rahab as they cling to the rope from her window. Moreover, one would have expected the spies to spell out the terms of their agreement as they acceded to Rahab's request for a sworn agreement, but the report of their escape through the window (vv. 15–16) stands between their acceptance and their conditions. Some of the inconsistencies in the story, then, turn around the relationship of the speeches to the narrative framework.[33]

Furthermore, the generally uneven style tends to indicate a complex prehistory. The smooth and almost verbose speech in verses 17–20, for example, stands in contrast to the terse and fragmentary account in verses 2–7. This unevenness is probably best explained as a result of the pre-Deuteronomistic redactor's efforts: He has taken over old traditions and supplemented them through his own editorial work. The exact identification of those editorial additions is, however, an almost impossible task.[34] Whether or not it is possible to discern the shape of the older traditions at all is a question to which we shall return.

Genre

We raise now the question of the genre of the Rahab story as it appeared in the pre-Deuteronomistic source. The attempt to classify this unit and to draw relevant conclusions from that classification makes it immediately clear that our formal categories are in need of greater clarification and precision. The narrative as a whole is an etiological saga. That is to say at least that its aim (or better, *one* of its aims) is to account for a phenomenon by giving the story of its origin.[35] As we have seen, the most obvious sign of the etiology, the formula in 6:25, is a part of the work of the redactor of the older traditions. However, the etiological features of the story are not limited to this conclusion, but occur throughout

33. Hertzberg has also seen a duplicate in the references to swearing an oath and to giving a sign in v. 12 (p. 21).

34. Cf. Noth, *Josua*, pp. 12–13, 21.

35. Cf. Hermann Gunkel, *Genesis*, 3rd ed. (Göttingen: Vandenhoeck & Ruprecht, 1910), pp. xx ff.

the central part of chapter 2 as anticipation of just such a conclusion. As the story stands, the major result of Rahab's actions on behalf of the spies and their agreement with her—the main themes of chapter 2—is the preservation of Rahab and her family. So whatever the shape and contents of the earlier tradition may have been, at this stage it has the distinctive marks of the etiological saga concerned with an ethnological question: It is a narrative account of heroic deeds of the past, some of which have a private rather than a public nature; and it explains the existence of a certain clan and that clan's special relationship with Israel. The various suggestions that the story was an etiology of cultic prostitution within Israel in general or at Jericho in particular[36] do not affect this conclusion but bear only on the question of the older oral tradition. The story emphasizes the relationship between Rahab and the spies and through them the relationship between her clan and Israel.

Whether or not the story actually owes its existence to the etiological question itself[37] is not determined by these observations alone, however. To pursue that question further we must examine the intention or purpose of the story.

Intention

We have argued that at least one intention of the story is etiological. The dominant, if not the original, motif is the fate of Rahab and her family. But there is at least one other major motif—and intention—in the story. The examination of the structure shows that the two main themes are (1) the mission of the spies, presented in the beginning and concluding sections of chapter 2, and (2) Rahab's actions on behalf of the spies and the etiological epilogue.

What is the purpose of the spies' expedition, and what point does the *report* of that expedition make in its context? The purpose of the expedition and its results have been interpreted variously by different commentators. Many have seen beneath the present story

36. G. Hölscher, "Zum Ursprung der Rahabsage," *ZAW*, 38 (1919–1920), 56 ff.; Mowinckel, *Tetrateuch—Pentateuch—Hexateuch*, pp. 13–14.

37. This is the question posed by Y. Kaufmann. Cf. *The Biblical Account of the Conquest of Palestine*, trans. M. Dagut (Jerusalem: The Magnes Press, 1953), p. 71.

an old tradition which told how the city of Jericho was captured through an act of treason by Rahab, but the redactor has subordinated this tradition to the story of the collapse of the city walls, leaving only vestiges of the story of her treason (such as the account of the red cord which originally served as a signal to the Israelites).[38] Whether or not this was in fact the case must remain a matter of conjecture. However, on the level of the written tradition the purpose and results of the expedition are quite clear. At this point we can agree with Kaufmann: "Rahab does not help the Israelites to conquer Jericho, she does not disclose secrets to them, she does not give them signals. She merely expresses the terror and dismay of the Canaanites before the might of Israel's God (2:9–11, 24)."[39] The men were sent as spies to "view the land," an obviously military enterprise; but, as their report to Joshua makes clear, the "military" institution is the holy war.

This brings us to the question of the function of the spy motif within the story. The intention of this motif was *not* to show the cunning or the military skill of Joshua and his army. As we look at the broader Old Testament context we soon realize that some of the phrases in this motif have a very familiar ring. There are other accounts of the use of spies (cf. especially Numbers 13–14), and also of the use of stratagems and trickery in the conquest stories (cf. especially Josh. 8:1–23 and Judg. 1:22–26). While our story to some extent echoes such themes, the nearest parallel to the spy motif in chapter 2 is Numbers 13–14. The spies sent by Moses return with answers to two questions: Is it a good land, and shall we be able to take it? The spy motif in Joshua 2 deals only with the second question, to which the spies give a positive answer: "Surely Yahweh has given the whole land into our hand!" (2:24a). They have answered with the formula which is used repeatedly in the accounts of holy wars.[40] The war cannot begin without the assurance that Yahweh is with the people to give them victory. In the

---

38. Hölscher, pp. 54 ff.; K. Möhlenbrink, "Die Landnahmesagen des Buches Josua," *ZAW*, n.s. 15, 56 (1938), 258 ff.; Noth, *Josua*, p. 22; Roland de Vaux, *Ancient Israel: Its Life and Institutions*, trans. J. McHugh (New York: McGraw-Hill, 1961), p. 236.

39. Kaufmann, pp. 75–76.

40. Cf. G. von Rad, *Der heilige Krieg im alten Israel* (Göttingen: Vandenhoeck & Ruprecht, 1958), pp. 6 ff., for the pattern of the holy war and texts in which the formulas recur.

more common pattern, the assurance is received through the consultation of the deity, but the formula and the results are the same in this case: Yahweh is with us; the war may begin.

The place of chapter 2 in its context is now comprehensible. Given the theory of the holy war, it was essential that it be absolutely clear that Yahweh had given the land into the hand of Israel even before she entered the land. So the function of the spy motif here is to show that the conquest did not begin until the will of Yahweh had been determined.

It appears clear, then, that the Rahab story does not owe its existence to the etiological question, but to a number of factors. Among these factors are the theological conception and cultic institution of the holy war. The fact that the etiological intention dominates the story in its present form by no means proves that this intention created it. It dominates the Rahab story primarily because of the work of the pre-Deuteronomistic editor who added the epilogue and no doubt turned the thread of the story more in the direction of his conclusion. The etiological character of the story is then secondary in the sense that it is basically—if not exclusively—the work of the redactor of the story. Furthermore, as Childs has shown, the expression "and she *lived* in the midst of Israel to this day" is not a pure etiological formula which clearly draws the inference from the story to the present day.[41]

Setting

We turn now to the question of the setting of the Rahab story at the level of the pre-Deuteronomistic redaction. Since that setting was a literary one, the questions become those of the date and authorship of the redaction, the character of the work, and the perspective of the writer. These questions cannot be treated fully without a close examination of Joshua 2–11 (and Judges 1) as a whole, but some conclusions are warranted on the basis of the Rahab story.

Noth attributes the pre-Deuteronomistic stage of Joshua 2–11 to a *Sammler* who assembled his story from old traditions, including the series of etiological sagas (Joshua 2–6) concerning events in

---

41. Childs, p. 286. Cf. also p. 284.

the region of Gilgal. On the basis of Josh. 11:1–15 and the point of view of the *Sammler*, he has dated this work to approximately 900 B.C., arguing that it assumes the separation of the two states Israel and Judah.[42] As a result of the work of this "collector" the originally independent, primarily Benjaminite traditions became the history of the all-Israelite conquest, and Joshua was introduced into the story. Joshua did not appear in the original Benjaminite traditions, Noth argues, for, as the report of his burial place indicates (Josh. 24:29, 30), he was an Ephraimite hero.[43] Noth is reluctant to specify in detail just which verses in the story should be attributed to the work of his *Sammler* and which elements were received from oral or earlier written tradition. He does suggest, however, that the *Sammler*'s work is visible in certain transitional passages and in the inclusion of the stories of events which took place outside of Benjaminite territory (5:1; 6:27; 9:3, 4a; 10:2, 5, 40–42; 11:1, 2, 16–20).[44] Primarily on the basis of Josh. 10; 11:2, 16, 19, Noth concludes that the *Sammler*'s range of vision was Judean,[45] but his work is not to be associated with the older sources of the Pentateuch. These sources (J and E) led up to an account of the conquest by all the tribes from the east, but that account was dropped in the final editing of the Pentateuch.[46]

Mowinckel, on the other hand, sets out to uncover any traces which may remain of the J version of the conquest, arguing that the Yahwist must have written such an account since both the promises to the patriarchs and the report of the conquest of Trans-Jordan in J lead up to the conquest of west Jordan.[47] He finds such traces above all in Judges 1 and in some fragments in Joshua 2–11 and 24 which can be connected with Num. 32:32–42(J).[48] Viewing these traces as a whole, he concludes that J did not present a history of the conquest as such but rather a report of the *results* of the taking of the land and some anecdotes about the taking of certain cities.[49] The author of the pre-Deuteronomistic

42. Noth, *Josua*, pp. 12–13.
43. Noth, *History*, p. 93, and *Josua*, p. 12.
44. Noth, *Josua*, pp. 12–13.
45. *Ibid.*, p. 13.
46. Noth, *History*, p. 73.
47. Mowinckel, *Tetrateuch—Pentateuch—Hexateuch*, pp. 9–16.
48. *Ibid.*, pp. 14–16, 49.
49. *Ibid.*, pp. 14–16, 50.

history of the conquest (Joshua 2–11, 24; Judges 1) therefore was not the Yahwist, but a later redactor who used the J account as well as other traditions. Mowinckel identifies this stage of the history of traditions as J^v. Its point of view is actually nearer that of Dtr. than that of J.[50] Noth's date (approximately 900 B.C.) for the pre-Deuteronomistic redaction can be considered at best a *terminus post quem*.[51] Mowinckel agrees with Noth that the individual stories within this work were the independent local etiological traditions of the various tribes and originally had nothing to do with the conquest or with Joshua but were only secondarily adapted to the idea of an all-Israelite conquest under Joshua.[52]

Mowinckel holds open the possibility that the Rahab story as one version of the taking of Jericho originally stemmed from J. But he does argue that Josh. 2:1 is an unlikely beginning for a literary work, and therefore assumed an earlier chapter. That earlier chapter is to be found in Numbers 32.[53] At this point we may add a further piece of evidence which may indicate connections between the pre-Deuteronomistic account of the conquest and the older pentateuchal sources. We observed that Josh. 2:1 gives as the point of departure for the conquest of west Jordan a location not mentioned in the Deuteronomistic account: Shittim. Shittim is specified as the last Trans-Jordanian stopping place in Num. 25:1, which is probably J. A variation of the name (Abel Shittim) also occurs as the last point in the later list of the wilderness stopping places in Num. 33:49. Josh. 2:1 therefore continues the story of the older sources or at least assumes that version of the wilderness wandering and conquest of Trans-Jordan.

In spite of this additional bit of evidence, however, the presence of J and therefore of a source J^v in the conquest traditions is yet to be established satisfactorily. In order to attribute given units to a particular document one must be able to show the precise literary affinities between those units and the document. Mowinckel's conclusions are based primarily on links between the *content* of the pentateuchal sources and certain parts of the conquest traditions. His evidence has at least shown that the oldest *traditions* of the

50. *Ibid.*, p. 51.
51. *Ibid.*, p. 34.
52. *Ibid.*, p. 35.
53. *Ibid.*, p. 49.

Pentateuch did not stop with the account of the taking of Trans-Jordan but also told of the conquest of east Jordan. Since the materials which Mowinckel attributes to the Yahwist are so fragmentary and lack the specific stylistic characteristics of that redactor they could just as well stem from the older traditions upon which J itself depended.

Furthermore, the evidence for dating the pre-Deuteronomistic redaction of the conquest traditions is meagre indeed, and that question is best left open. It is impossible to determine whether or not the figure of Joshua was first introduced into the account by this redactor. In some of the stories—including Joshua 2—Joshua does not appear to be an essential or necessarily original element. But it is highly unlikely that the name and the activities of Joshua would have been created by a writer who at other points depends so heavily upon traditional material. Further study of the individual stories may be able to establish more concerning the history of the Joshua tradition.

But some positive results have been achieved. It now appears clear that there was indeed a written version of the conquest of east Jordan which preceded the Deuteronomistic history. That work was a redaction of older traditions into a more-or-less consistent account of a military conquest by the united Israelite tribes acting under Joshua. It was based in part on the older history of salvation (pentateuchal) traditions, from which it derived the general sequence of events, and in part on individual tribal traditions, particularly those of the tribe of Benjamin. Above all, that redaction assumed the conception of the holy war, and lived on soil which supported the holy war traditions. This conception of the conquest was no doubt inherited along with many other traditions, since it is assumed in most of the individual stories, including the Rahab saga and the account of the Gibeonite deception (Josh. 9:3–27). It is pointless to explain why particular families or tribes were spared unless it is taken for granted—as in the idea of the holy war—that all the enemies were to be killed.

The point of view of this redactor is indeed, as Mowinckel has observed,[54] near that of the Deuteronomistic historian. This is so

54. *Ibid.*, p. 51.

because the historian has not basically altered the older account of the conquest but only emphasized certain points, framed that account into his work, and added some general remarks which had the effect of stressing the completeness of the action under Joshua. Another link is the conception of the holy war common to both the Deuteronomistic and the earlier redactors.

THE RAHAB STORY IN THE ORAL TRADITION

The question of the oral prehistory of the Rahab saga now lies before us. Is it possible to reconstruct the older oral traditions which the pre-Deuteronomistic redactor had at his disposal? A number of factors indicate that the story once existed in the oral tradition; however, that evidence allows us to draw only very general and tentative conclusions concerning the shape of the story before it became a part of our pre-Deuteronomistic redactor's history of the conquest.

The evidence indicates, first of all, that the Rahab story once existed independently of the story of the destruction of Jericho now preserved in Joshua 6. Some of that evidence has been mentioned above (pp. 74 ff.). In terms of genre, style, and mood, the two stories are quite different.[55] Chapter 2 is basically a more-or-less "profane" anecdotal saga. Except for the Deuteronomistic additions and the observations concerning the fear which has gripped the inhabitants of Canaan (vv. 9a, 10a, 11a, 24a), the story proceeds without theological or cultic overtones. It deals with ordinary human beings and ordinary events. Chapter 6, on the other hand, has distinctively legendary features. The miraculous destruction of the walls is accompanied by actions of a cultic nature, and Yahweh is the actor in the drama.

Furthermore, the two stories in their present context lead up to two different etiological conclusions: the explanation of the house of Rahab and the explanation of the ruins of Jericho. And in the combination of the two stories some incoherence has appeared. The Rahab saga states that the harlot lived in a house in the walls, but according to chapter 6 those same walls were destroyed. In

---

55. Möhlenbrink, pp. 258 ff.

addition, the motif of the cord in Rahab's window (2:18) is not resumed in the account of the fate of the harlot and her family.[56] There is, at the very least, a gap or an incomplete transition between the stories which indicates their original independence. The *specific* links between the two are confined to the epilogue in chapter 6.

Some commentators have gone further to suggest that chapters 2 and 6 preserve what originally were two different versions of the taking of Jericho. One account originally told how the city was taken through the treason of Rahab and the other reported the miracle.[57] Such explanations must posit a part of the Rahab saga which once told how Rahab let the Israelites in to destroy the city.[58] This interpretation rests upon the assumption that the mission of the spies was the enlistment of a fifth column. But such a mission is neither assumed nor implied in the present story. The spies were sent out to "view the land" and returned with the report that Yahweh had given it into Israel's hand. Whether or not the Rahab saga once told how the city of Jericho was taken through the harlot's treason must therefore remain a matter of conjecture.

Secondly, the analysis of the structure of chapter 2 itself has shown that the story originally circulated in the oral tradition, and perhaps in more than one form. The general unevenness of the style, the tensions between the narrative framework and the conversation scenes, and the inconsistencies of the narrative suggest both oral transmission and combination of traditions.

But it is one thing to conclude that an oral tradition or traditions lie behind the present story and another to reconstruct the oral stage or stages. However, several reconstructions have been offered, most of them describing the original story as an etiological tale of one kind or another. Hölscher argued that the old story concluded with the report that the family of Rahab was saved from the bloodbath and remained in Jericho as cultic prostitutes at a sanctuary there. The story was thus an etiology explaining how the Israelites took over a cultic institution from the Canaanites.[59] Hölscher's

---

56. Noth, *Josua*, p. 31.

57. Mowinckel, *Tetrateuch—Pentateuch—Hexateuch*, p. 42; Hertzberg, pp. 21–22; Möhlenbrink, p. 258; Hölscher, p. 54.

58. Cf. Möhlenbrink, p. 258; Noth, *Josua*, p. 22; and F.-M. Abel, "Les stratagèmes dans le livre de Josué," *RB*, 56 (1949), 322 ff.

59. Hölscher, pp. 56 ff. Cf. also Mowinckel, *Tetrateuch—Pentateuch—Hexateuch*, p. 13.

conclusions, however, depend upon some (late) Greek parallels and a number of dubious assumptions, namely, that Rahab helped the Israelites take the city, that there was a sanctuary at Jericho in Israelite times, and that Israelites in the region accepted cultic prostitution.

Others have argued that the original tradition explained the presence of a tribe or clan, "the house of Rahab," in Israel,[60] some suggesting that Rahab—and other Canaanites—were treated as proselytes.[61] Noth is among those who have argued that the original substratum of the stories in Joshua 2–6 is a series of originally Benjaminite etiological traditions.[62] In the combination of the story of Rahab with the story of the fall of the walls of Jericho, he suggests, several features of the original story have fallen out, including the report of Rahab's help in the taking of the city. The earliest tradition transmitted the story in order to explain the existence of the Canaanite clan within Israel.[63]

But these reconstructions—and even the conclusion that the original tradition was an etiology of one kind or another—must remain highly conjectural. Noth himself has observed concerning the Rahab story that how far the individual lines of this story were etiologically grounded is not to be determined with certainty.[64] The most obvious indication of the etiological saga is the concluding formula. But the formula which concludes this particular story (6:25) depends upon the combination of two traditions, the Rahab saga and the story of the miraculous fall of the walls of the city. This particular etiological formula therefore belongs at least to the stage at which the two traditions had been combined, and very likely even to the stage of the pre-Deuteronomistic redactor. Supporting these observations is Child's conclusion that Josh. 6:25 is not even a genuine etiological formula which clearly draws the relationship between cause and effect.[65] Therefore the etiological conclusion is secondarily attached to the combined traditions, and any reconstruction of the original independent Rahab story as etiological must posit yet another earlier version of the conclusion.

60. Hertzberg, pp. 20 ff.
61. Abel, pp. 327 ff.
62. Noth, *Josua*, pp. 11 ff., and *History*, p. 93.
63. Cf. Noth, *Josua*, pp. 22 ff.
64. *Ibid.*, p. 23.
65. Childs, p. 286.

The conclusions which Long has drawn from his study of etiological formulas, then, are sustained by our study of this particular story. The story has some obvious though secondary etiological features, but one must be cautious about generalizations concerning the motive which "created" the story. No doubt some stories did arise as popular answers to questions about existing phenomena. This one probably did not. The pre-Deuteronomistic editor used it because it was a part of the tradition which he received. It is likely that he interpreted it in part etiologically because he saw its bearing on a contemporary phenomenon.

SPIRITUAL OBDURACY AND
PARABLE PURPOSE

FRANK E. EAKIN, JR.

Ancient man was convinced that behind actions and events stood personal cause rather than impersonal or natural sequential occurrence. That this pattern of belief, so characteristic of the ancient Near Eastern man in general, was accepted by the Hebrew is evident throughout his scriptures.

Numerous examples of this personal element pervading the historical process illustrate the point. Our interest here, however, falls not on this personalism in general; rather, we are particularly interested to relate this understanding to a specific concept, spiritual obduracy.

Spiritual obduracy figures as a major theme of Israel's[1] history as depicted by the Old Testament writers and editors. Time and again her stubborn rejection of Yahweh's sovereignty prevented her fulfilling the responsibilities accompanying the covenant relationship. This theme pervaded not only Israel's actions vis-a-vis Yahweh; a like theme was also recognized among certain non-Israelites as a result of Yahweh's influence.

In the former case, examples abound: Israel's refusal to believe that the redeeming, liberating God could lead victoriously into Canaan (Numbers 13–14), or Ahaz' inability to place his reliance solely in the preserving power of Yahweh during the Syro-Ephraimitic crisis (Isa. 7:1–8:15). Among the non-Israelites, the most familiar presentation of spiritual obduracy would be Yahweh's hardening the heart of the Pharaoh (Exod. 4:21; 9:12; 10:1, 20, 27; etc.).

As our attention focuses on the Christian Scriptures, we recognize that the theme of spiritual obduracy has not been expurgated. Jesus grieved at the hardness of heart of those who witnessed his ministry (Mark 3:5); hardness of heart prevented even the closest followers from understanding the feeding of the five thousand

---

1. "Israel" is here used as a general designation for the Yahweh worshippers, not as a distinction between Israel and Judah.

(Mark 6:52; note the similar passage in Mark 8:17); the Fourth Evangelist grappled with the problem via the presentation of his sixth sign, Jesus' restoring sight to the man born blind (John 9); Paul wrestled with the problem of the Jewish refusal to hear the message of Jesus, whether proclaimed by Jesus or by a later spokesman such as Paul, concluding that this refusal was understandable only in terms of divinely inflicted and purposeful obduracy (Romans 9–11, especially 11:25).

The conclusion that obduracy was inflicted by Yahweh raises no insurmountable problems as long as the object of the infliction be non-Hebrew. For example, Yahweh's causing the Pharaoh's heart to be hardened presented the interpreter some rather logical hermeneutical maneuvers.[2] Again, the situation where stubbornness is depicted only as human volition rather than as divine instigation presents no major difficulty, as with the Numbers 13–14 incident. The situation is more difficult when it is his own that Yahweh afflicts, a clear presentation of the problem being found in the commissioning experience of the prophet Isaiah (Isa. 6:1–13). Verses 9–13 present major interpretative problems, but in spite of (or because of?) this difficulty the synoptic writers were particularly fond of this passage when attempting to explain the purpose of Jesus' parables. Mark (4:10–12) alluded to this Isaianic passage, while Luke (8:9–10) gave similar treatment; Matt. (13:10–15)[3] quoted Isa. 6:9–10, although from the Septuagint rather than from the Masoretic text.[4]

2. See, for example, Walther Eichrodt, *Theology of the Old Testament*, trans. J. A. Baker (London: SCM Press, 1961), 1: 262; and Exod. 9:16.

3. Some other synoptic passages which deal with this same theme are Mark 4:21–25, 33–34; Luke 8:16–18, 11:33; and Matt. 5:15, 13:34–35.

4. The Fourth Evangelist (12:36b–50) used the Isaianic reference when summarizing and drawing to a conclusion Jesus' public ministry, attempting to clarify why the Jews were so spiritually blinded to the Truth. Since the Fourth Evangelist did not relate any parables of Jesus (granting the questionable nomenclature to be assigned to passages such as 15:1–11), this usage of the Isaianic commission was quite logical and not really dissimilar to synoptic presentation. The theme of obduracy is also found in Acts 19:9 and 28:23–28, the latter being a Lucan narrative in which Luke placed on the lips of Paul the Isa. 6:9–10 passage as explanation for the Jewish rejection of his message and the resultant mission to the Gentiles, a type of microcosmic view of the Pauline macrocosm as set forth in Rom. 9–11.

It should be indicated that the present writer does not find ultimate answers in linguistic analysis of the differences in perspective according to whether Matthew derived his quotation from the Septuagint or the Masoretic text. At best this serves as means to the end and not as the end *per se*.

Given the importance for the early Christian community of this spiritual obduracy concept, especially as found in this Isaianic commission, we cannot set aside the idea simply as an ancient concept no longer important. Most particularly is understanding consequential as regards the purpose of Jesus' parables, especially since the parable is depicted as Jesus' favorite teaching mechanism.[5] This investigation, therefore, has two primary foci of attention: (1) to investigate the spiritual obduracy concept via a study of the commission to Isaiah as recorded in Isa. 6:9–13; and (2) to relate where possible this understanding to the problem of parable purpose as recorded in the synoptic Gospels.

ISAIAH'S COMMISSION

The commission to Isaiah appears to be a masterful study in contradiction. By his response, "Here am I! Send me" (6:8), Isaiah opened himself to be the receptive instrument of Yahweh to his people, a function patently absurd if only judgment could result. As J. Philip Hyatt states: "A summons to repentance from sin implies that God will forgive those who do repent."[6] Edward J. Kissane says: "It is implied that by repentance the people may yet avert the threatened ruin (cf. I. 18 ff.)."[7]

In spite of the absurdity, however, Isa. 6:9–13 apparently does postulate inevitable judgment, indeed a situation where the very word of the Prophet acts as the catalyst to assure Israel's inability to hear Yahweh's word or to recognize his manifestation! Let us note some of the possible hermeneutical approaches to these difficult verses, acknowledging that any interpretation must be judged on the basis of its acceptable approach to the two primary problems raised by the passage: (1) as regards verses 9–10, if the obduracy response of the people be already determined, why should Yahweh compel Isaiah to be his *nabi*? and (2) with respect to verses 11–13, did the Prophet envision total destruction?

---

5. A. M. Hunter, *Interpreting the Parables* (Philadelphia: Westminster Press, 1960), p. 7, notes "that the parables of Jesus comprise more than one-third of his recorded teaching.

6. J. Philip Hyatt, *Prophetic Religion* (New York: Abingdon Press, 1947), p. 171.

7. Edward J. Kissane, *The Book of Isaiah* (Dublin: Browne and Nolan, 1941), 1: 75.

It has been suggested often that 6:9–13 reflects a late Isaianic (or possibly even post-Isaianic) understanding colored by years of popular rejection of the Prophet's message. This assumes a post-event and perhaps a post-Prophet writing of the commission, the former almost assuredly true, the latter likely;[8] furthermore, this interpretation answers the first question raised above by assuming that the rejection response was recognized later rather than at the initiation of the ministry. It is true that in the initial primary political crisis during which Isaiah was Yahweh's spokesman, the Syro-Ephraimitic conflict (see Isa. 7:1–8:15), Isaiah's advice was not heeded, with the result that Judah was reduced to an Assyrian vassal state.[9] In two other primary political involvements, however, Isaiah's message was acknowledged, and Hezekiah seemingly acted according to the Prophet's directive (see Isaiah 20 and 36–37). Since Isaiah's word was not accepted in every instance, therefore, it seems questionable that the rejection of his message was so thoroughgoing as to influence such a later recording of his commissioning experience.

The issue as regards our second question above becomes: does what we know of the Prophet apart from Isaiah 6 confirm the opinion that a late Isaianic (or possibly post-Isaianic) understanding would have envisioned total destruction? According to von Ewald's judgment, neither Isaiah nor any other prophet would have envisioned final and ultimate devastation, "otherwise the prophets would despair of their own mission."[10] Must we not reckon with the Prophet's attitude toward Judah as seen in the crisis of 735 B.C., which attitude cannot be reconciled with a reading of the commission as prescribing absolute devastation? The Shear-jashub reference of 7:3, numerous other remnant references

---

8. As an early proponent, see G. H. A. von Ewald, *Prophets of the Old Testament*, trans. J. F. Smith (London: Williams and Norgate, 1876), 2: 62–64. George Adam Smith, *The Book of Isaiah* (New York: A. C. Armstrong and Son, 1903), 1: 57, 78–89, agrees basically with von Ewald. This view is supported by Curt Kuhl, *The Prophets of Israel*, trans. R. J. Ehrlich and J. P. Smith (Edinburgh: Oliver & Boyd, 1960), p. 79; and S. H. Blank, *Prophetic Faith in Israel* (New York: Harper, 1958), p. 4.

9. John Bright, *A History of Israel* (Philadelphia: Westminster Press, 1959), p. 259.

10. Von Ewald, p. 69. It is interesting, however, that von Ewald's only support for this conclusion as regards Isaiah's commission was the final phrase of v. 13. We should acknowledge, however, that a passage such as Isa. 5:1–7 cannot be read apart from the Prophet's larger message. See further references in R. B. Y. Scott, "The Book of Isaiah: Exegesis," *IB*, 5: 212.

found in Isa. (1:9; 10:21; 11:11, 16; 16:14; etc.), as well as the persistent hope expressed in chapter 37[11] call in question an interpretation which accepts either implicitly or explicitly the radical devastation seemingly indicated by 6:11–13 on the basis that this passage is a record of the later Isaianic (or post-Isaianic) view. This interpretation, therefore, fails to deal adequately with our second question.

George Buchanan Gray maintained that the "doom of the people is inevitably fixed."[12] There is nothing that anyone, Isaiah included, can do by word or deed to avert the inevitable and absolute doom. The people have lived in their insensitivity, now they are left to exult in it. The Prophet's preaching will serve only "to render them blinder, deafer, and more insensitive."[13] As Elmer A. Leslie expressed this concept: "It will often seem that the more earnestly, intensively, and pertinently the prophet speaks the less attentive or responsive his hearers become."[14] Again, Hyatt states:

> It is not necessary to take refuge in the theory that this chapter expresses the prophet's later disillusionment after many unhappy experiences in prophesying. Without taking these words too literally, we may see in them the great depths of Isaiah's conviction and his devotion to his prophetic mission. What he is attempting to say through verses 9–13 is that he is willing to go and preach to his people *even if* they do not pay any attention to him, and *if* the only result of his work is that the land will nevertheless be destroyed.[15]

This fixity of judgment finds support when the final phrase of verse 13 according to the Masoretic text is removed. In its context "The holy seed is its stump" (זרע קדש מצבתה) has often been interpreted to imply the hope of continuation, but this phrase is found

11. In terms of the chronological factor in Isaiah's ministry, this hope would be the more significant if associated with a 690 or 688 B.C. invasion by Sennacherib. Regardless, it relates at least to the 701 B.C. incident.

12. G. B. Gray, *The Book of Isaiah*, 2 vols., The International Critical Commentary, no. 20 (New York: Scribner's, 1912), 1: 109.

13. *Ibid.*

14. Elmer A. Leslie, *Isaiah* (Nashville: Abingdon Press, 1963), pp. 24–25. Thomas Henshaw, *The Latter Prophets* (New York: Macmillan, 1958), p. 112, also supports this view.

15. Hyatt, p. 34.

neither in the Septuagint nor in the Hebrew manuscript of the book of Isaiah recovered near Qumran.[16] This phrase should be reckoned as a marginal comment added by a post-septuagintal individual who wrestled with this problem even as have we. The issue remains, however, for if the Prophet's proclamation purposefully served only to enforce exultation in insensitivity, why should Yahweh insist on the Prophet's word to his people?

Closely aligned to the idea that the Prophet's word served to enforce insensitivity, Andrew F. Key suggests that Isaiah's message to Judah via his commissioning experience must be understood against a magical background. Recognizing the דבר in its ancient context, Key dismisses the possibility that the Prophet's word might be either a judgment derived from past experience or an intuition related to the future; rather, he judges the word of the Prophet to be essentially the word of Yahweh, which articulation once uttered has the inherent ability to effect its realization. Key states:

> All this does not mean that prophetic thought gave up the idea that repentance could lead to forgiveness. The prophet is simply saying that the time for repentance is past, the day of judgment has now come, and there is nothing anyone can do about it. The prophet becomes the divinely appointed executioner. . . . The speaking of the prophetic words is not a call for repentance, but a signal for the beginning of God's actions.[17]

Thus, this interpretation assumes that the Prophet stands at the conclusion of a long series of Yahweh's actions and Israel's reac-

16. See William H. Brownlee, "The Text of Isaiah VI:13 in the Light of DSIa," *Vetus Testamentum*, 1 (Oct., 1951), 296–98, who admits to the final clause being a late insertion but restructures a portion of the remaining verse so as to relate the verse to the destruction of cult objects. See also Samuel Iwry, "Maṣṣēbāh and Bāmāh in 1Q Isaiah^a 6 13," *JBL*, 77 (Sept., 1957), 225–37, who likewise attempts to preserve זרע קדש מצבתה by textual reconstruction. To the contrary, Ivan Engnell, *The Call of Isaiah*, Uppsala Universitets Arsskrift 1949:4 (Uppsala: A.-B. Lundequistska Bokhandeln, 1949), pp. 5–15, asserts in reference to these final three words that "there is no doubt that the MT represents the authentic and right reading."

17. Andrew F. Key, "The Magical Background of Isaiah 6:9–13," *JBL*, 86 (June, 1967), 204, but see pp. 198–204. Pagination references found in the next four paragraphs refer to Key's article.

tions; now Yahweh has deemed the time of judgment to be imminent and irreversible. While Key does not use this argument, it might have been an editorial reason for preceding the commission with chapters 1–5, as it recounts the recurring rejections of Yahweh's way by Judah.

While such a view of the Word is commendable in terms of ancient man's thought patterns, it is interpretatively unacceptable to reduce the eighth-century prophets to such an either-doom-or-hope categorization. Even Amos, who is often classified as an exclusive doom spokesman,[18] has certain elements in his message which point to hope.[19] Isaiah, more clearly than Amos, holds to a hope for the future of his people. When it is stated that "the speaking of the prophetic words is not a call for repentance, but a signal for the beginning of God's action," one questions whether the prophetic concern for upholding man's responsibility to respond to his God can and should be relegated to the past tense. If this be so, we are brought back to one of our primary questions: Why should the Prophet speak at all during the three political crises and, furthermore, why should he so constantly refer to the hope of the remnant?

The magical background approach, therefore, gives a reason for the Prophet's speaking, in that by uttering his message the Prophet becomes Yahweh's executioner. The present writer finds this difficult because it removes the responsibility for human response at the moment of hearing insofar as it makes Yahweh's judgmental action contingent on the Prophet's speaking (if he did not speak, the Word would not be uttered and therefore would not occur; see Key, p. 203), and really does not answer why the Prophet should continue to speak once the word of judgment has been set in motion.

In Professor Key's defense, it should be acknowledged that his

18. Julian Morgenstern, *Amos Studies* (Cincinnati: Hebrew Union College Press, 1941), 2: 36, portrays the usual doom-oriented picture of Amos.

19. The recurring "yet you did not return to me" (Amos 4:6–11) implies the possibility of forgiveness. The harshness of 3:12 yet upholds the hope of a remnant. Note that the authenticity of a passage such as Amos 5:3–6, 14–15 is supported by J. Lindblom, *Prophecy in Ancient Israel* (Philadelphia: Fortress Press, 1962), p. 316; and Gerhard von Rad, *Old Testament Theology*, trans. D. M. G. Stalker (New York: Harper & Row, 1965), 2: 138, argues for the authenticity of Amos 9:11–15, which passage is judged almost universally to emanate from later redactors.

article deals only with the mode of the Prophet's proclamation, our first question. He clearly states that he was not interested at the time in investigating the "presence or absence of a remnant theory in this passage" (p. 198). The question raised by verses 11–13, therefore, is simply not addressed.

Again, akin to Gray's suggestion is Walther Eichrodt's proposal that continual refusal to heed God's word leads to a moral deadening which makes impossible man's hearing that word. Eichrodt states: "Deliberate disregard of divine truth, habitual failure to listen to God's warning, inevitably lead to that deadness in regard to God's operations which at the decisive moment notices nothing, but in a stupor, asleep, or drunk, lurches irremediably toward the approaching disaster."[20] Israel had refused for so long to be attuned to the word of Yahweh that ultimately her "will not" became her "cannot."[21] This interpretation would suggest that Israel's commissioned proclamation emanated from numerous occasions when Yahweh's people had refused to hear the divine word—the consistent "will not" gradually but assuredly crystallized into a firm "cannot" from which there could be no retreat. This principle holds firmly to an important tenet within Yahwism, namely, man's election by Yahweh does not remove the individual's responsibility for personal response. Human responsibility is more clearly expressed by Eichrodt than by Gray.

Man's refusal has become his inability! We recall that for the theistically-oriented Hebraic mind there was no contradiction sensed in affirming the God of creation to be behind all actions while holding to human responsibility. Given the deity's Lordship over history, it was logical to assume that he used man's actions, whatever they be, in the fulfillment of his purposes. Consequently, it was not the purpose of Isaiah's proclamation to produce obduracy; rather, it was the inevitable result, not just of his preaching, but of prior proclamation as well. From the perspective of our first question, a possible answer emerges, therefore, for in this view the people's choice has determined their inability to respond, whether this proclamation as found in verses 9–10 be preserved as spoken

20. Walther Eichrodt, 2: 432.
21. This is Eichrodt's view as summarized by von Rad, 2: 152.

by the Prophet or as formulated by a later editor who drew on the wisdom of already enacted history.

In his *Theology* Eichrodt does not directly speak to our second question, would there be an absolute devastation of Judah? He does discuss, however, the prophetic attitude which tended to see judgment as corporate rather than individual and resulting in the suffering of both the righteous and the wicked.[22] Specifically, as regards the remnant concept in Isaiah, he states that "the fact that the reality of the remnant depends entirely on faith makes its use as a way of escape from the doom of judgment impossible."[23] Might we assume, therefore, that Eichrodt would sense no problem with the general tenor of Isa. 6:11–13? In fairness to Eichrodt, however, we must not ignore the covenantal orientation of his entire *Theology*. The obvious question, therefore, is whether the covenant God would effect so thorough a judgment as is indicated in verses 11–13? We can do no more than speculate on Eichrodt's judgment, however.

As noted above,[24] Ivan Engnell, utilizing his characteristic traditio-historical approach, defends the authenticity of the Masoretic text. Summarizing his extensive arguments for the text's authenticity does not concern us, but some of his conclusions are apropos our concern. We have asked of verses 9–10, if the response be already determined, why should the Prophet speak? Engnell judges the העם הזה, "this people," of verses 9–10 to refer to both Israel and Judah; but he maintains that "it is also clear that the Northern kingdom is the primary object of the prophet's message. . . ."[25] A reason for speaking, therefore, arises out of Isaiah's remnant concept: "It is his mission from the very beginning to foretell doom and misfortune against its apostate people, that is for its future—as far as it got one—wholly dependent on the Judaean remnant, centered around the Davidic Messiah."[26] Already Gray, in a slightly different context, has answered this speculation. The

22. Eichrodt, 2: 431–37.
23. *Ibid.*, p. 434.
24. See above, n. 16.
25. Engnell, p. 52. A. J. Heschel, *The Prophets* (New York: Harper & Row, 1962), pp. 89–90, avoids this problem also by asserting that this passage refers not to Judah but to Israel.
26. Engnell, p. 52.

people of verse 5 must refer to the same people as the reference in
verse 9, and "in v. 5 the people must *at least* include Judah."[27]
We should note further that Engnell does not seek to explain why
Isaiah geographically confined his message to Judah. If his message
were primarily for Israel, why did he not go, as did Amos, to the
North with his proclamation?

Regarding the question of total destruction, Engnell does not
state specifically his judgment concerning the North, which in his
view will bear the brunt of Yahweh's judgment. As regards the
South, his acceptance of the remnant concept would automatically
preclude total devastation. In his judgment it is a violation of tradition and text to make Isaiah "a monomaniacal doom-foreteller."[28]
He states: "*Punishment—a remnant—and a Messianic future*, that is
Isaiah's teaching as we know it, and as we must therefore believe
it to have been."[29] Our second question, therefore, would be resolved by maintaining the preservation of at least Judah's remnant
when Yahweh's judgment is delivered.

Gerhard von Rad insists that an understanding of *Heilsgeschichte*
elucidates the spiritual obduracy concept. He maintains that it is
insufficient to focus on a type of divine *lex talionis*, for Israel's relationship with Yahweh was more personalized than such an auto-
matic reaction concept implies.[30] Nor is a psychological or
devotional explanation adequate, for such views would focus on
the hardening as an end rather than as the means to an end.
"Absolutely everything in Isaiah points out into the future—even
the saying about the hardening of Israel's heart which is the action
of Jahweh himself."[31] It was Isaiah's conviction, according to
von Rad, that in the future "all that had fallen on completely deaf
ears in his own day and generation will be fulfilled."[32]

Isaiah's hope for his nation's future lends support to interpreting
this imposed obduracy in terms of the *Heilsgeschichte*. Isa. 9:2–7, a
messianic kingship hymn, anticipates the inauguration of the mes-

27. Gray, p. 110.
28. Engnell, p. 53.
29. *Ibid.*
30. See von Rad, p. 152.
31. *Ibid.*, p. 155.
32. *Ibid.*

sianic king for whose reign there will be no termination, the thoroughgoing establishment of Yahweh's reign.[33] Indeed the remnant concept as expressed in Isa. 7:1–17 assumes that even in the event of the most devastating disaster, Yahweh assures the preservation of his people.[34]

Von Rad's interpretation deals with both of the questions raised by the commissioning experience of Isaiah. The Prophet recognized the ineffectuality of his message, but this recognition struck no fatalistic overtones. The God of the Covenant was the God of judgment and love—his love (אהבה) had elected Israel as his people, his love (חסד) would also preserve Israel as his people.[35] Consistent with Isaiah's perspective was his proceeding with his proclamation in spite of almost assured immediate failure. He was convinced that Yahweh would bring out of his seeming failure a surer awareness of Himself. There is every reason for the Prophet to speak, therefore, for the hope of the future, while secured in Yahweh's unique relationship with his people, is in part predicated upon the Prophet's proclamation.

As regards the question of total destruction, von Rad's assumption that a limitation upon destruction is implied appears sound. Both the general understanding of *Heilsgeschichte*, of which the prophets in general and Isaiah in particular were cognizant, and the remnant concept so clearly maintained by Isaiah suggest that the preservation of at least a part of Judah is a necessity. Yahweh will not abandon his people!

Each of the hermeneutical approaches which has been mentioned has inherent strengths and weaknesses. In general, however, it is not unfair to affirm that failure to evaluate the entire presentation of Isaiah's message has often narrowed the obduracy concept to an incident too minutely defined. We must never lose sight of the

---

33. This would not be altered if this hymn were originally used in reference to Hezekiah.

34. It should be acknowledged that a comparison of Isa. 7:1–17 with 10:20–23 makes difficult an understanding of the remnant concept. Was it a sign of hope or of judgment? Was it viewed one way at the beginning of the ministry, another at the termination?

35. See especially Norman H. Snaith, *The Distinctive Ideas of the Old Testament* (London: The Epworth Press, 1944), pp. 94–95, but see also fuller treatments of chapters 5 and 6.

fact that Yahweh's people possess more than just a present; they also are a part of their past and because of the covenant-God have an assurance of a future.

It is imperative, therefore, that we interpret Isa. 6:9–13, not as an isolated logion, but rather as a means to an end, i. e. the more complete manifestation of the covenant-God and, concomitantly, as the fulfillment of his covenant purpose. Just as the Pharaoh's heart was hardened "to show you my power, so that my name may be declared throughout all the earth" (Exod. 9:16, RSV), so, we must conclude on the basis of Israel's past history, the covenant concept, and Isaiah's larger message, that Isaiah envisioned his nation's developing a stubbornness and refusal of hearing as a result of his preaching but with the end result that Judah's more complete understanding and acceptance of Yahweh might evolve. Such an evolution would assume action in accord with understanding!

According to *Gesenius' Hebrew Grammar*, Isa. 6:11 is cited as example of a Hebrew grammatical usage expressing "actions or facts, which are meant to be indicated as existing in the future in a completed state. . . ."[36] The completion idea conveyed by this passage implies a time limitation upon the obduracy, with the recognition that Yahweh will utilize impending destruction as the divine revelatory instrument. Isaiah, then, would proclaim a message much like Amos (see Amos 3:9–12; 5:3; 6:9–10). Like Amos, Isaiah recognized imminent but only partially defined danger for the nation; but we acknowledge that Judah's reduction to an Assyrian vassal state in 721 B.C. was only the earnest of his conviction. The full impact of this danger was recognized in 597/587 B.C.[37] when Judah fell to Babylonia. How long will Judah's stubbornness prevail? Until her cities lie waste! There is in this both the recognition of judgment and hope of restoration. This logion stands within the *Heilsgeschichte* tradition.

Thus we would see the most probable solution to the hermeneutical problems raised by Isaiah's commissioning experience to be derived as one relates that commission to both Isaiah's and Israel's total experience. The word of Yahweh must be recognized

36. Emil Friedrich Kautzsch, ed. and enlarger, *Gesenius' Hebrew Grammar*, 2nd ed. rev. by A. E. Cowley (Oxford: The Clarendon Press, 1910), p. 313.
37. And 582 B.C. according to Jer. 52:28–30.

as a two-edged sword, cutting both to preserve and to judge. That sword even in judgment, however, inevitably hopes for preservation. All of the long history of Yahweh's dealing with man supports this *Heilsgeschichte* conclusion.

PARABLE PURPOSE

As suggested by F. W. Beare, "There is hardly an area of New Testament study which has witnessed such far-reaching changes in this century as our understanding of the Parables of Jesus."[38] Beginning especially with the publication in 1899 of Adolf Jülicher's *Die Gleichnisreden Jesu*, the widely accepted allegorical approach to parable interpretation was refuted. C. H. Dodd followed in 1935 with *The Parables of the Kingdom*, in which he emphasized parable interpretation in the context of Jesus' Kingdom proclamation. In the spirit of Dodd's work, in 1947 Joachim Jeremias crystallized further the impact of Dodd's methodology with his *The Parables of Jesus*, while making an important contribution himself by emphasizing that the contextual setting of Jesus' parables had been lost in the process of transmission by the early church.[39]

We emphasize, therefore, that our efforts to discern Jesus' purpose in his usage of parables is neither predetermined by past critical contributions nor so obvious as to reduce the exercise to one of mental gymnastics. There may indeed be at hand a clue, if we can discern such, to the understanding of Jesus and the early church.

The synoptic witness to parable purpose (Mark 4:10–12;[40] Luke 8:9–10; Matt. 13:10–15) uniformly suggests by drawing on Isa. 6:9–10[41] (explicitly so in Matthew) that Jesus' purpose in relating parables was to make obscure his message so that those who were enlightened might recognize truth while those not so

---

38. *The Earliest Records of Jesus* (New York: Abingdon Press, 1962), p. 105.

39. See brief but helpful summaries in *ibid.*, pp. 105–8, and Hunter, pp. 35–41.

40. J. Coutts, " 'Those Outside' (Mark 4, 10–12)," *Studia Evangelica*, ed. F. L. Cross (Berlin: Akademie-Verlag, 1964), 2: 155–57, dismisses the problem by asserting that 4:10–12 is misplaced in Mark, that the passage should follow 3:20–35.

41. H. D. A. Major, in H. D. A. Major, T. W. Manson, and C. J. Wright, *The Mission and Message of Jesus* (New York: E. P. Dutton and Co., 1938), p. 70, suggests that parable purpose must be understood in relation to the remnant concept of Isa. 6.

gifted might remain in darkness.[42] Customarily interpreters have affirmed that such a teaching motivation would have been incompatible with the basic nature of a parable, i. e. a simple and easily comprehended narrative drawn from the commonplace elements of existence which attempted to make emphatic one central point.

Since many interpreters have judged the synoptic tradition to be either misleading or misinformed as regards parable purpose, various objections to the apparent intention of the text as presently formulated have been raised: (1) Jesus' parables were intended to make clear rather than to obscure his message to the crowds upon whom he had such manifest compassion;[43] (2) the veiled understanding of Jesus' parables exemplifies the imposed "messianic secret" motif found in Mark's Gospel;[44] (3) the enigmatic parable purpose arose as an explanation on the part of the church to clarify why the Jews accepted neither Jesus nor the church;[45] and (4) the difficulty arose as a result of the church's clothing Jesus' parables with an esoteric flavor or orienting Jesus as a teacher toward a type of gnostic perspective, i. e. understanding Jesus' message according to the Hellenistic religions of the day.[46] Numerous other objections to the apparent parables intention as preserved by the synoptic witness have also been stated.[47]

Joachim Jeremias's comment on this difficult logion is char-

42. "The reason which Matthew gives is that the parables hide the message from the unbelievers, but convey it to those who believe." J. C. Fenton, *The Gospel of St Matthew* (Baltimore: Penguin Books, 1963), p. 215. Usage of "Matthew" to designate the Gospel, even when used in parallel with Mark and Luke in terms of authorship, is not intended to indicate an acceptance of Matthean authorship.

43. See as example B. Harvie Branscomb, *The Gospel of Mark* (New York: Harper and Brothers, n.d.), p. 78.

44. See Frederick C. Grant, "The Gospel According to Mark: Introduction and Exegesis," *IB*, 7: 699–700.

45. Branscomb states: "It is plain that we have to do with a theological explanation which the early Church created" (p. 78). C. H. Dodd, however, states: "But that he desired not to be understood by the people in general, and therefore clothed His teaching in unintelligible forms, cannot be made credible on any reasonable reading of the Gospels." *The Parables of the Kingdom* (New York: Scribner's, 1961), p. 4.

46. Note Joachim Jeremias, *The Parables of Jesus*, trans. S. H. Hooke (London: SCM Press, 1954), pp. 10–11. See also Grant, p. 636.

47. See D. E. Nineham, *The Gospel of St Mark* (Baltimore: Penguin Books, 1963), pp. 135–37; also J. Arthur Baird, "A Pragmatic Approach to Parable Exegesis: Some New Evidence on Mark 4:11, 33–34," *JBL*, 76 (Sept., 1957), 201–7. It can be only conjecture, but one wonders if the Fourth Evangelist's avoidance of parables resulted from an erroneous understanding of the parables common in the early church, which understanding coincided not at all with this Evangelist's concept of the clearly revealed Christ. See above n. 4.

acteristic: "The secret of the present Kingdom is disclosed to the disciples, but to the outsiders the words of Jesus remain obscure because they do not recognize his mission nor repent."[48] This was apparently the synoptic impression: Is this concept totally erroneous or is there historical awareness embedded in this passage? There would appear to be at least three lines of argument which help to clarify the synoptic understanding of parable purpose.

In the first place, the synoptics possibly recorded Jesus' parable purpose from a later perspective of rejection and refusal, creating a situation analogous to that often suggested for Isaiah. It is this point that Branscomb emphasizes when he judges that "we have to do with a theological explanation which the early Church created."[49]

In our earlier discussion of the Isaianic passage, we rejected the idea that the Prophet's commission was anachronistically formulated on the basis of a rejection of the Prophet and his message which pervaded his ministry. For our synoptic passage, however, the same negative argument cannot be used. The Gospel tradition, which is supported by the fact of forcible death, witnesses to Jesus' rejection at least by the religious leadership. Questions of authorship, dating, and provenance are of no import for this issue.[50] So long as the writer was oriented post-crucifixion,[51] the fact of Jesus' rejection was evident. We acknowledge that early Christian recorders and interpreters of the Gospel could and perhaps did emphasize the fact of rejection (as was the case with Mark) in order to ensure the correlation of their accounts with personal perspectives. This does not preclude our accepting that Jesus was misunderstood and rejected both by the religious leaders and ultimately by the masses. From the perspective of the canonical evangelists' post-crucifixion vantage point, therefore, we can understand why Jesus' purpose in using parables has seemed so enigmatic.

48. Jeremias, p. 15.
49. Branscomb, p. 78.
50. See the still helpful study by Frederick C. Grant, *The Earliest Gospel* (New York: Abingdon-Cokesbury Press, 1943).
51. We note only that the essential unity of Mark is generally assumed, attempts to prove to the contrary having gained less than scholarly consensus. See, for example, Grant, "Gospel According to Mark," p. 636.

Second, the Marcan concept of imposed spiritual obduracy was not the earliest recorded such usage in the New Testament. Mark's understanding was not unique, therefore; he derived his explanation from a rather well developed ecclesiastical tradition.

The most important witness to this tradition stems from Romans 9–11, where Paul, as one involved existentially (Rom. 11:1), attempted to clarify why the Jews had so manifestly rejected both Jesus and early Christian preaching.[52] For one who judged preaching to be essential to man's understanding God and Jesus the Christ (Rom. 10:14), the Jewish rejection of the kerygma raised difficult questions.

In Rom. 11:25–32,[53] Paul sought to answer the questions raised by the Jewish spiritual obduracy via a threefold formulation: (1) Israel's rejection of the kerygma was both partial and temporary;[54] (2) Israel's rejection made possible the Gentile entrance into the Kingdom; and (3) Israel will ultimately accept the kerygma and will be reconciled with God through Christ. Experientially-oriented, Paul expressed the conviction that the Gentile entrance into the Kingdom was a direct result of divinely inflicted and purposeful Jewish spiritual obduracy; but ultimately the obdurate Jews also would accept the kerygma. As expressed by one commentator: "The 'mystery' is that the Gentiles are both the beneficiaries of the Israelites' lapse, and also the means of the salvation of those very Israelites. . . ."[55]

We cannot digress extensively into the divergent reactions to this Pauline affirmation. To indicate the diversity, however, we

52. Beare, p. 111, mentions explicitly the relationship noted here: "Mark has compounded the difficulty by combining with this theory of an esoteric revelation through parables a doctrine of the reprobation of Israel akin to that which is expounded by St. Paul in Romans ix–xi."

53. See the excellent study by Richard Batey, " 'So All Israel Will Be Saved,' An Interpretation of Romans 11:25–32," *Interpretation*, 20 (Apr., 1966), 218–28; and the more definitive study by Johannes Munck, *Christ and Israel*, trans. Ingeborg Nixon (Philadelphia: Fortress Press, 1967).

54. Paul actually dealt with three distinct categories. On the one hand, there was the Jew like himself who did believe; with this group there was no problem. There was also the Jew, however, who refused to believe; and it was with this group's continued relationship with God that he was so concerned. And finally, there was the Gentile, i. e. the non-Israelite.

55. D. W. B. Robinson, "The Salvation of Israel in Romans 9–11," *Reformed Theological Review*, 26 (Sept.–Dec., 1967), 93, but see entire presentation, pp. 81–96. See also W. D. Davies, *Paul and Rabbinic Judaism* (London: S.P.C.K., 1948), p. 76.

note the following: Was Paul a universalist?[56] Was he more governed by ideas of predestination?[57] Was he writing with reference to a future judgment?[58] Or does this passage exemplify merely national prejudice?[59]

No such theologically- or nationally-oriented reaction alone sufficiently probes the apostle's Israelite historical heritage. We stated initially: "Ancient man was convinced that behind actions and events stood personal cause rather than impersonal or natural sequential occurrence" (p. 87). Specifically, the Hebraic mind affirmed that behind all thought and action stood Yahweh; the דבר of God revealed to man acted as a continually cutting sword which served to divide the faithful from the faithless.[60] This thought pattern supported or evoked Paul's Romans exposition and the synoptic Evangelists' statements on parable purpose.[61]

For understanding parable purpose, a study by J. Arthur Baird[62] is helpful. Baird accepted as material with which to work sixty-three parables attributed to Jesus. He then sought to analyze each parable according to two criteria: (1) whether the audience to whom Jesus spoke was constituted of disciples or non-disciples; and (2) whether the parable was explained or unexplained. He

56. C. H. Dodd, *The Epistle of Paul to the Romans*, The Moffatt New Testament Commentary (London: Hodder and Stoughton, 1932), p. 184. See also Robinson, pp. 81–96; and E. C. Blackman, "Divine Sovereignty and Missionary Strategy in Romans 9–11," *Canadian Journal of Theology*, 11 (Apr., 1965), 133, supported by pp. 124–34.

57. John Calvin, *Epistle of Paul to the Romans*, trans. John Owens (Grand Rapids: William B. Eerdmans, 1947), p. 437.

58. John Knox, "The Epistle to the Romans: Exegesis," *IB*, 9: 576–77.

59. Dodd, *Epistle of Paul to the Romans*, p. 183, states: "We can well understand that his emotional interest in his own people, rather than strict logic, has determined his forecast."

60. See, for one example, Exod. 19:5–6, where it is stated that "if you will obey . . . keep . . . you shall be my own possession. . . ." Note also that the verb "to hear" (שמע) connotes not only "hearing" but also "doing." He who truly "hears" responds with "actions." See Snaith, p. 141.

61. James M. Robinson, *The Problem of History in Mark*, Studies in Biblical Theology, no. 21 (Naperville, Ill.: Alec R. Allenson, 1957), p. 77, asserts that the problem of understanding revolves around "two levels of 'hearing': one is 'hearing but not understanding' (4.12); the other is the 'hearing' for which the chapter repeatedly calls (vv. 3, 9, 23, 24; ch. 7.14)." The existentialist theologians, consequently, recognizing man's basic nature in terms of decision, focus on a central aspect of the Christian message. See, for example, Rudolf Bultmann, *Jesus and the Word* (New York: Scribner's, 1958), pp. 51–56, especially p. 52. See also Beare, p. 53.

62. The author acknowledges his indebtedness for the content of this paragraph to Baird's article (see n. 47) and pagination references are to same.

concluded that forty-one were explained while twenty-two were left unexplained (p. 206). To the disciples twenty-eight were explained, while thirteen were explained to non-disciples. Only seven were left unexplained to disciples, while fifteen were left unexplained to non-disciples. Graphically this becomes the clearer:

	Disciples	*Non-disciples*	*Totals*
Audience	35	28	63
Explanations	28	13	41
Non-explanations	7	15	22

Baird states that "we observe what is perhaps our survey's most striking feature, namely the rough arithmetic ratio of twice the number of parables explained to the disciples . . . as to the non-disciples, and twice the number of parables left unexplained to the non-disciples . . . as to the disciples . . ." (p. 206). It is thus possible for Baird to conclude: "Behind this inner consistency of the Synoptic sources lies not an artificial creation forced in some arbitrary manner upon the recollections of the early Church, but rather the inner consistency of the mind and purpose of Jesus, preserved for us in sufficiently accurate detail to be recognizable" (p. 207). Thus, according to Baird's judgment, the basic principle of Mark 4:11–12 and parallels presents an authentic record of Jesus' parable intention.

Our primary point is simply that Mark was not the first New Testament contributor to utilize the imposed spiritual obduracy concept as explanation for Jewish rejection of Jesus' message. Paul had already expressed similar conviction in a more developed form. Given the traditional association of the Marcan Gospel with Rome, Paul's Roman correspondence looms even larger as a possible influence upon Mark's understanding of Jesus' parable purpose.[63] We emphasize, however, that the Pauline viewpoint may recount history per se rather than theologized history. A study such as Baird's raises the possibility that Jesus did indeed give

---

63. Other places in the Pauline corpus have similar emphasis but without the ample explanation of Rom. 9–11. See, as examplé, II Cor. 3:12–18.

explanations of the parables to his disciples more readily than to non-disciples.

Third, our earlier Isaianic investigation encourages examination of the synoptic parable purpose in terms of the *Heilsgeschichte* concept. *Heilsgeschichte* assumes the interrelatedness of past, present, and future, with the confident expectation that history will ultimately reveal God's purpose. This expectancy of the consummation of divine purpose permeates the Marcan Gospel, as is true also of Matthew and Luke. Furthermore, for the latter two, the awareness of *Heilsgeschichte* is the more transparent by virtue of the nativity narratives encompassing the genealogical affirmations. As regards Mark, if it be true that this Gospel was an elaboration of the kerygma,[64] a more *Heilsgeschichte* format would be difficult to envision. What further evidences of *Heilsgeschichte* orientation relative to our investigation do we confront in the synoptics?

We noted earlier that the existentialist theologians[65] emphasize that Jesus' message forced his hearer to assume his full humanity, to be creature confronted by and participating in the processes of decision making. No aspect of Jesus' message more clearly depicts this than his parables. With whom will you align yourself? For what will you seek? Whenever the individual is confronted by such ultimate decisions, the mode of confrontation is essentially a means of judgment. Each person reacts, and as the parable of the sower (Mark 4:1-9, 13-20) illustrates, that reaction is already judgment. This view coalesces with the *Heilsgeschichte* concept in that characteristic of Yahwism-Judaism is the affirmation that the covenant-God perpetually seeks man, thereby forcing the creature ultimately to make the choice so aptly phrased in the Hebrew Scriptures: "Who is on Yahweh's side?" (Exod. 32:26); "Choose this day whom you will serve . . ." (Josh. 24:15). Jesus' parables as preserved characteristically confront man with the ultimate choice in life—reaction to God and the establishment of his Kingdom. Past, present, and future are necessarily bound together in this confrontation and choice.

64. C. H. Dodd, *The Apostolic Preaching and Its Development* (New York: Harper & Brothers, n.d.), pp. 46–52, especially pp. 46–47.
65. See above n. 61.

When investigating Isaiah's commission, we expressed the conviction that it would be sheer folly for Yahweh to compel Isaiah
to serve as *nabi* if the Prophet's function were fulfilled in the causing
of consternation and confusion. Viewing the history of Yahweh's
relationship with men would not permit so negative a conclusion
for the Prophet's role; Isaiah's commission must have conveyed
the possibility of rectifying the relationship, else the Prophet would
have had nothing to proclaim.

For Jesus and his usage of parables, the situation is analogous.
If the parables were intended only to confuse and confound, there
would have been no need to speak. Rather than being characteristically enigmatic, it would have been easier and more practical
to restrict his teaching to the chosen disciples. The fact that Jesus
did not choose this alternative indicates that he was interested in
and tried to make his message lucid for the masses.[66]

It is possible that Mark made an error in judgment with his
usage of this portion of the tradition. Vincent Taylor notes that
Jesus would have been cognizant of semitic idiom which often used
"a command to express a result. . . ."[67] Being aware of this, Jesus
would have been "impressed by the similarity between the results
of His ministry and the experience of Isaiah . . . after the failure of
the Mission of the Twelve and his own fruitless activity in Cho-
razim, Bethsaida, and Capernaum. . . ."[68] Jesus' usage of the
Isaianic passage, therefore, had a justifiable particular placement
in his own ministry, a placement which the synoptics have eradi-
cated completely by associating this logion with parable purpose
in general.

As indicated early in this study, we do not wish to become em-
broiled in semantic and linguistic arguments. It is apropos our
investigation, however, to recall that Matthew quoted the Isaianic
commission from the Septuagint rather than from the Masoretic
text. One could not rely solely on this point since Matthew usually

66. See above, n. 45, for Dodd's comment.
67. Vincent Taylor, *The Gospel According to St. Mark* (New York: St. Martin's Press,
1966), pp. 254–58. Possibly the problem resulted from difficulties in linguistic transmission, a position advocated early by C. C. Torrey, i. e. a confusion resulting from
the koine Greek's usage of *ἵνα* to translate the Aramaic *dî*, the latter of which had
greater purposive force than the former. See also Grant, "Gospel According to Mark,"
p. 699.
68. Taylor, p. 258.

quoted from the Septuagint, but the Septuagint in Isaiah 6 differs significantly from the Masoretic text in that the former indicates that the people will not be able to hear because their hearts are hardened, while the latter indicates that God commissioned Isaiah to harden the peoples' hearts. The difference lies in cause (Masoretic text) and effect (Septuagint). Is it possible that Matthew was trying to indicate proper perspective by his usage?[69] To use Taylor's concluding statement: "This suggestion cannot be proved, but it is in every way superior to the view that iv. 11 f. is a Marcan invention."[70]

CONCLUSION

We conclude that the synoptic writers understood Jesus' purpose in teaching by parables as the historical awareness of Jesus' ministry and their own existential situation dictated, namely, that (1) Jesus' mission and message had indeed been rejected by the Jews (Mark 4:10–12; cf. John 12:36b–50); (2) earlier interpreters such as Paul (Romans 9–11) had discerned properly the reasoning behind such rejection; (3) man's rejection or acceptance of God must be understood in terms of the *Heilsgeschichte* rather than being narrowly confined to man's limited view of history; (4) God's message to man inevitably cuts to redeem and to judge; and (5) the covenant-God must by his very nature be concerned with all men, not a nation or a people in isolation.

We find irresolvable a basic question, i. e. is the parable purpose as recorded by Mark, and especially as elaborated by Matthew, derived from the early church or from Jesus? This uncertainty is the case because logical placement in both Jesus' ministry[71] and that of the early church is discernible.

69. Matthew's Gospel was the only Gospel to incorporate certain sayings attributed to Jesus (10:5–6; 15:24) which apparently supported an exclusively Jewish mission for Jesus and his disciples. If these sayings be authentic, and we would judge this likely (see Beare, p. 81), it is significant that Matthew (28:19–20) has also included uniquely a logion attributed to the resurrected Christ which speaks of universal concern. These passages point to: (1) an ever-present problem for the expanding mission of the church, a problem inherited from Judaism; and (2) an understanding of covenant which is Israelite in its best expression (Exod. 19:5–6; Isa. 42:6).

70. Taylor, p. 258. We note that whether or not the *Heilsgeschichte* view be accepted, a passage such as Mark 4:22 assuredly indicates that Mark did not assume exclusively a negative posture.

71. As long as one assumes that some awareness of the Jesus of history can be garnered from the Gospels, this statement holds. If *Formgeschichte* be pushed to its logical

For Jesus, being a zealous Jew and being prophetically oriented, it was inevitable that his awareness of the past would impress upon him the necessity of man's decision when confronted by God's word. Furthermore, Jesus was aware that the prophets of his people had not been warmly received (Matt. 5:12; Luke 6:23). Their word from God had acted as a word of judgment for many individuals who heard what was expected of them but made no positive response. They "heard" without "hearing"; they "saw" without "seeing." Such was the case when the Prophet from Nazareth spoke. His message fell mainly on unreceptive ears. His contemporaries, like those of the earlier prophets, refused to hear and to do. Thus, it is possible to envision Jesus' having recognized the similarity between his message and the reaction to that message by the hearers when this was compared to the commissioning experience of Isaiah.

There is equally good argument for seeing the application of this logion within the context of the church. There was, on the one hand, the reality of history, a history punctuated by rejection and refusal to hear. This rejection was the dominant characteristic of Israel's reaction to the early church, even during that brief span from the crucifixion until the penning of Mark's Gospel, a more intense rejection than that directed toward Jesus. Johannes Munck states: "There can be no doubt that the early church's discussion of Israel's fate had an influence on the transmission of Jesus' words and deeds and on the final shaping of the tradition as found in our four Gospels." [72]

Second, we cannot ignore the influence of Pauline understanding on the thought structure of the church in general and on the expanding Gentile mission in particular. This influence is probably most clearly seen in the aforementioned Romans 9–11 passage. Paul's view of Jewish obduracy inevitably would have influenced other early Christians.

Third, the synoptic view of parable purpose accords with the *Heilsgeschichte* concept. Mark's concern for the ultimate clarification

---

extreme (it is impossible in any sense to move beyond the early church's Christ of faith to the Jesus of history) the statement would be acknowledged inappropriate at that point.

72. P. 20.

of the parables (4:22) agrees with the Matthean conviction that the resurrected Christ expanded the original, more narrowly confined Jewish mission of the historical Jesus. Both the parable purpose concept and the Matthean exclusive passages may be attempts to relate history as observed. It is the conviction of the essential vitality of the word of the resurrected Christ (as Matt. 28:19–20) which has bestowed upon the church a mobility and universality not characteristic of Yahwism-Judaism in the main stream of its expression.

We find, therefore, that an attempt to clarify Isa. 6:9–13 does offer some hermeneutical assistance in interpreting synoptic parable purpose. While one cannot make dogmatic affirmations either about Isaiah's commission or Jesus' parable purpose, certain similar presuppositions may be applied to both passages: (1) the Prophet of Jerusalem and the Prophet of Nazareth were concerned to speak meaningfully to their people; (2) both prophets were convinced of Yahweh's enduring and unalterable concern for his people; (3) both men emerged from a context that took history seriously and recognized man's meaningful place therein, i. e. a *Heilsgeschichte* perspective; (4) both spokesmen understood Yahweh to be the Lord of history, the covenant-God, who would not so thoroughly reject his people as to leave them without the hope of redemption; and (5) both prophets recognized that Yahweh placed upon man the burden of receptive hearing, relegating to man thereby both the bane and blessing of serving as personal judge!

THE ISRAELITE CULT AND CHRISTIAN WORSHIP

DONALD L. WILLIAMS

INTRODUCTION

The basic presupposition of this article is the author's growing awareness of and appreciation for the influence of the cultus upon every aspect of Israelite life. As a student of the Old Testament, this writer is convinced that the Israelite cultus, or worship pattern, is responsible primarily for the origin, preservation, and transmission of a large portion of the Old Testament.[1] However, the interest in Israel's cultic life, while a strict discipline of Old Testament studies, is no mere search into the history of Israel's religion to satisfy one's antiquarian interests. Although Old Testament scholars continue to stress Israel's contributions in such areas as monotheism and ethical prophecy, not enough emphasis has been placed upon what H. H. Rowley has designated "Israel's achievement in worship."[2] Thus, if we believe that the Old Testament is a part of our Christian heritage, if we affirm that the God of Abraham, Isaac, and Jacob is the God and Father of our Lord Jesus Christ, then we should not be amazed to discover that the worship forms of ancient Israel are relevant for the Christian church, that the primary forms of Israelite worship have not been negated by the Incarnation; rather the forms have been reinterpreted in the light of the Christ-event. Too often the church has neglected Israel's achievement in worship and the church's worship has bogged into sterility. Thus, the purpose of this article is to explore the major lines of Israel's worship and to suggest the areas in which the Israelite cult can continue to enrich Christian worship.

This article was delivered originally as the author's Faculty Address at The Southern Baptist Theological Seminary, Louisville, Kentucky, November 5, 1968.

1. The literature concerning Israel's cultus has become extensive. The original purpose of the article, the scope of the inquiry, and the present place of publication must necessarily limit complete documentation. The reader is directed to the notes and bibliographies of the works cited for full documentation.

2. *Worship in Ancient Israel* (Philadelphia: Fortress Press, 1967), p. 271.

At the outset, the nature of the Israelite cult must be defined. To be sure, a cultus may be both "good" and "bad," a fact which explains why the term often has assumed a distasteful connotation. Nevertheless, the term *cult* carries no value judgment; *cult* means simply "organized worship." The character and content of the cult are the basis for value judgment. One cannot gloss over the existence of inappropriate or bad cultic forms in the Old Testament. Thus, in this article, the term Israelite cult is used to convey those forms of worship which this writer finds at the main stream of Yahwism, not the modifications or the deviations which otherwise make up the history of Israelite religion.

Undoubtedly, the scholar who contributed most to the studies of the Israelite cult was Sigmund Mowinckel. Beginning with his monumental *Psalmenstudien*,[3] published in the 1920's, and culminating in the two-volume English translation of *The Psalms in Israel's Worship*[4] almost fifty years later, Mowinckel has significantly redirected Old Testament studies. He has written:

> It has been said that religion appears in three main aspects, as cult, as myth and as ethos. Or in other terms, as worship, doctrine, and as behaviour (morals). . . . The cult is thus a general phenomenon appearing in all religions, even in the most "anti-cultic" Protestant sects and groups. It is indeed an essential and constitutive feature of a religion, that in which the nature and spiritual structure of a religion is most clearly manifested. . . . Cult or ritual may be defined as the socially established and regulated holy acts and words in which the encounter and communion of the Deity with the congregation is established, developed, and brought to its ultimate goal. In other words: a relation in which a religion becomes a vitalizing function as a communion of God and congregation, and of the members of the congregation among themselves.[5]

More succinctly, Mowinckel defines cult as "the visible and audible expression of the relation between the congregation and the deity."[6]

---

3. *Psalmenstudien I-VI, Skrifter utgitt av Det Norske Videnskaps-Akademi i Oslo*, Hist.-Filos. Kl., 1921–1924 (Amsterdam: P. Schippers, 1961), vol. 2.
4. Trans. D. R. Ap-Thomas, 2 vols. (Oxford: Basil Blackwell, 1962).
5. *Ibid.*, 1: 15.
6. *Ibid.*, p. 16.

Note the words "visible and audible," for they adequately convey the concreteness and objectivity of Israelite worship.

James Muilenburg, noting this objective quality of the Israelite cult, writes:

> [Israelite worship] was not a flight to the "dim unknown," to timelessness, or to "a presence that disturbs me with the joy of elevated thoughts," or to a shoreless ocean of quietude and unperturbed peace. Everywhere there is movement, active and ardent speaking, and live response to the speaking and acting Lord.[7]

We would underscore this objectivity, this concreteness of Israel's cult. In the classical sense, Israel's worship made no attempt to offer a psychological salve to escape the realities of living, no other-worldly elevation to the Elysian fields of spiritual bliss; Israelite worship was at every point "existential." Again, from Mowinckel: "In the cult, something happens: a relationship is established and developed which is of vital importance to the congregation, and the acts and words express what happens."[8] So, the purpose of the Israelite cult is, in Mowinckel's words, "to create life,"[9] that is, to maintain the ordered course of the world of nature and the world of man as it was created by God and as it is sustained by God. Encounter with God through worship sustains the world order, reaffirms man's relationship with his creation, and maintains man's relationship with his neighbor. The cult sustains, creates, and recreates a relationship—not magically, but sacramentally,—a relationship initiated, sustained, and continually renewed by God himself.

In the Israelite cult, the overriding purpose was the "representation of history," the contemporizing of those creative historical acts of salvation which had formed, nourished, and sustained Israelite existence. None will deny that the faith of Israel was historically oriented, based upon the fact that God redeemed a people from Egyptian bondage, welded them into a covenant people through the Torah, and confirmed that salvation by the gift of the land. Whatever tribes or clans actually experienced the Egyptian Exodus-

---

7. *The Way of Israel* (New York: Harper and Brothers, 1961), p. 108.
8. *Psalms*, 1: 17.
9. *Ibid.*

event, all Israel affirmed that God had acted in her behalf, that Yahweh had served Israel, and that this salvation was a continuing process in her existence. To be sure, the Exodus-event happened only once, at a particular point in human history, a unique and unrepeatable act. But, Israel, uniquely conscious of history, could not allow this formative event to recede into timeless myth as her Near Eastern neighbors would have done. In no sense could the Exodus-event be subject to annual repetition in the same way that Marduk in Babylon annually defeated the chaotical Tiamat—the uniqueness of the Exodus-event precluded annual cyclic recurrence. Nevertheless, Israel's cult sustained the faith that because God had acted once, he would continue to act for her salvation. Brevard Childs has written:

> The Old Testament witnesses to a series of historical events by which God brought the people of Israel into existence. . . . These redemptive events of the Old Testament shared a genuine chronology. . . . There is a once-for-all character to these events in the sense that they never repeated themselves in the same fashion. Yet this does not exhaust the biblical concept. These determinative events are by no means static; they function merely as beginning. . . . Redemptive history continues . . . the influence of a past event continued to be felt in successive generations, which obvious fact no one could deny. Rather, there was an immediate encounter, an actual participation in the great acts of redemption. The Old Testament maintained the dynamic, continuing character of past events without sacrificing their historical character as did myth.[10]

Thus, Israel, freed from the reduction of her past to myth and assured of the continuation of redemptive history, "re-presented" in the cult those historical acts which were determinative for her life. This "re-presentation," in the words of Martin Noth, is

> inseparably linked [with] the subject of . . . God acting, and indeed acting in history. . . . "Re-presentation" is founded on this—that God and his action are always present, while man in his inevitable temporality cannot grasp this presentness ex-

10. *Memory and Tradition in Israel*, Studies in Biblical Theology, no. 37 (Naperville, Ill.: Alec R. Allenson, 1962), pp. 83–84.

cept by "re-presenting" the action of God over and over again in his worship. . . . If Christian proclamation means to take its biblical basis seriously, it will have to follow the biblical witness also in the question of the "re-presentation."[11]

These functions are primary to the Israelite cult: to actualize, to re-present unrepeatable historical events, to bring the worshipper into an existential identification with these events, to bridge the time and space gap and to participate in the original history. In the Israelite cult, each generation vicariously entered into that original, and nonrepeatable, history through two patterns: 1) historical recital and 2) dramatic representation.

CULTIC ACTUALIZATION BY HISTORICAL RECITATION

Gerhard von Rad has isolated several creedal statements in the Old Testament which he has argued stand at the level of primary tradition.[12] Among these confessions is Deut. 26:5–9:

A wandering Aramean was my father; and he went down into Egypt and sojourned there, few in number; and there he became a nation, great, mighty, and populous. And the Egyptians treated us harshly, and afflicted us, and laid upon us hard bondage. Then we cried to Yahweh, the God of our Fathers, and Yahweh heard our voice, and saw our affliction, our toil, and our oppression; and Yahweh brought us out of Egypt with a mighty hand and an outstretched arm, with great terror, with signs and wonders; and he brought us into this place and gave us this land, a land flowing with milk and honey.

To be sure, von Rad has overstated his position by asserting that these creedal statements represent the "hexateuch in miniature";[13]

11. "The 'Re-presentation' of the O.T. in Proclamation," trans. James Luther Mays, in *Essays on Old Testament Hermeneutics*, ed. Claus Westermann (Richmond: John Knox Press, 1963), pp. 85–86. This article was written in 1952.

12. "The Form Critical Problem of the Hexateuch," *The Problem of the Hexateuch and Other Essays*, trans. E. W. Trueman Dicken (Edinburgh and London: Oliver and Boyd, 1966), pp. 3–8. This article was written in 1938. See also von Rad, *Old Testament Theology*, trans. D. M. G. Stalker, 2 vols. (New York: Harper and Brothers, 1962), 1: 121 ff.

13. Von Rad employed the term "Hexateuch *in nuce*," in his *Genesis*, trans. John H. Marks, The Old Testament Library (Philadelphia: Westminster Press, 1961), p. 16.

nevertheless, for this writer the creedal character of these verses cannot be denied. The emphasis of these creedal statements is historical: Egyptian bondage, salvation from that bondage by Yahweh, the occupation of the land. Moreover, one cannot escape the fact that these affirmations are in plural address—"we" were in Egyptian bondage, "we" were redeemed by Yahweh, "we" were given this fertile land. Each time this affirmation was recited in the cult, the worshipper bridged the time and space gap and became identified with that never-to-be-repeated salvation, he actualized, he contemporized, he re-presented history.

Another example of historical recitation is found in the antiphonal liturgies in Josh. 4:6–7 and 24:14–28. Although the liturgical form has been clouded by the context of historical narration, the liturgy may be easily reconstructed:

The priest:	What do these stones mean?
The congregation:	They mean that the waters of the Jordan were cut off before the Ark of the Covenant of Yahweh; when it passed over the Jordan, the waters were cut off.
The priest:	So these stones shall be to the people of Israel a memorial forever.

These liturgical formulations emanate from the cult at Gilgal, a center of worship which carefully preserved the Jordan crossing and the conquest traditions.[14] In these liturgies the reader is in touch with historical recital of the re-creation of history, a means of allowing the existential involvement of later generations in those acts of Yahweh which effected salvation and which continued to effect salvation.

Or, one may cite a central thrust of the Jerusalem cultus, namely the liturgical affirmation of the Psalter, "Yahweh has become / is king."[15] Despite the discussion which this affirmation has evoked,[16] no thought of a dying-rising Yahweh is intended; nor was the kingship of Yahweh predicated upon an annual cultic renewal cere-

14. So, Hans-Joachim Kraus, *Worship in Israel*, trans. Geoffrey Buswell (Richmond: John Knox Press, 1965), pp. 152–65.

15. יהוה מָלָךְ' in Psalms 93, 96, 97, 99 and related themes in the "royal" and/or "enthronement" Psalms. Mowinckel, *Psalms*, 1: 107–16.

16. See Kraus, pp. 205–8.

mony. Nevertheless, in the Jerusalem Temple, this liturgical affirmation brought the worshipper face to face with the reality of Yahweh's kingship, not a theological abstraction, but an experiential and existential encounter which demanded a response. Indeed, one may posit that just such a worship encounter underlies the Temple sequence in Isaiah 6, an encounter with the cultic reaffirmation of Yahweh's kingship which redirected the Prophet's life. Thus, in some sense, in the Jerusalem cultus, Yahweh's kingship was reactivated in worship and he "became king" for those who entered into the experience.[17] Cultic recital provokes existential identification.

To be sure, Israel's cult was not limited to creedal and liturgical confessions—a flexibility developed within the cult, as witnessed by the book of Deuteronomy. In fact, Deuteronomy is one gigantic cultic actualization. Deut. 5:3 reads: "Not with our fathers did Yahweh make this covenant, but with us, who are all of us here alive this day." This passage originated between the eighth and the sixth centuries,[18] a time far distant from the Sinai-event; nevertheless, centuries later Israel could corporately and cticly confess that the present generation stood anew at the foot of the holy mountain. Moreover, historical recitation and re-presentation gives way to preaching, a fact which explains Deuteronomy's homiletic or parenetic character.[19] The creed is expanded into

17. Although often misinterpreted, Mowinckel's position has merit:
"To the interpretation that the enthronement psalms on a special festival state that Yahweh has become king, it is not a valid objection to say that Yahweh had, according to the Israelite view, always been king. The latter statement is correct enough. . . . But this did not prevent the view that Yahweh at a certain point of time *became* the king of Israel, i. e. at the election at the Exodus from Egypt (Ps. 114:1 f.), or at the making of the covenant on Mount Sinai (Deut. 33:5). That Yahweh *became* king is bound up with the fundmental fact of salvation in the life of the people. . . . But in the cult the fact of salvation is re-experienced as a new and actual reality. . . . And in the cultic experience the whole attention is concentrated on that which is again witnessed as something actual; it is there conceived as something happening at that moment. The Lord, Yahweh, becomes king, he shows himself as king, and performs kingly deeds, and in the graphic conception and presentation of the cult this is all gathered up in the definite picture of his royal entry and arrival, invisibly mounted on the cherub-borne throne" (*Psalms*, 1: 114–15).
18. This writer places the origin of Deuteronomy earlier than von Rad, *Studies in Deuteronomy*, Studies in Biblical Theology, 1st ser., no. 9 (Chicago: Henry Regnery, 1953). More cogent is the view of E. W. Nicholson, *Deuteronomy and Tradition* (Philadelphia: Fortress Press, 1967).
19. Nicholson.

injunction and call for obedience as each generation is recalled to affirm Israel's ancient faith, to bridge the time and space gap, to participate existentially and creatively with those events which culminated in the covenant. Thus, Deuteronomy, with its pattern of creedal recitation and homiletical expansion, sets the pattern for Christian preaching.

These examples of Israelite historical recitation will serve to illustrate the means by which Israel sought to re-create her history by liturgical re-presentation.[20] Small wonder that the early church also presented its message by historical re-presentation. The early Christian hymns and creeds contained in the Pauline corpus (I Cor. 15:3–7 and Phil. 2:6–11) are harmonious with the Israelite pattern of historical recitation and re-presentation, for their emphases are upon the historical, concrete memories of our Lord's life and death. Even more illustrative is the creed in I Tim. 3:16:

> He was manifested in the flesh,
>> vindicated in the spirit,
>>> seen by angels,
>> preached among the nations,
>> believed on in the world,
>>> taken up into glory.

The death and Resurrection of our Lord was a once-for-all, unique, unrepeatable historical event, and the early church, following the pattern of its spiritual ancestor, constructed similar historical recitations by which in the cult they stood again at the foot of the cross, by which they bridged the time and space gap, by which the Christ-event continued in contemporaneity through cultic re-presentation.

And the church continued to formulate her creeds. To be sure, such classic creeds as the so-called Apostles and Nicene were formulated to preserve dogmatic integrity; nevertheless, the basic character of these creeds is rightly historical. Of course, Israel would not have opened her creeds with the theological abstraction of God's "almightiness," nor would she have spoken at the outset of creation; nevertheless, when the Apostles Creed begins the article

---

20. This position goes beyond and to some extent modifies the conception of "theology as recital." G. Ernest Wright, *God Who Acts*, Studies in Biblical Theology, 1st ser., no. 8 (Chicago: Alec R. Allenson, 1952).

on Jesus Christ, the Hebraic cultic pattern is maintained: "born
of the virgin Mary," "crucified under Pontius Pilate," "died,
buried, raised on the third day." To give audible expression to the
Apostles Creed in worship is not an intellectual exercise in dogmatic assertion; in this audible expression something should happen, the worshipper should encounter anew the historical elements
of our faith, and, in some sense, experience the sacramental contemporaneity of our Lord with the worshipper. If we are to take
the Israelite cult seriously, then we are confronted with the demand
to reactivate the purpose of re-presentation by historical recital, to
view creedal affirmations not as tests of theological soundness, but
as a means of existential identification with the past, as a means
of bridging the time and space gap, as a means of re-creating the
original event and existentially participating in those events which
have accomplished our salvation.

Undoubtedly, many protestant evangelicals have eschewed
creedal statements primarily because the basic purpose has been
lost; nevertheless, this writer would plead from the example of
Israel's cultus that such creedal re-presentations be restored to
Christian worship in order that the church may possess a more
vital sense of its history, that it may become more aware of its
corporate relationship with the church of all ages, that it may
participate in God's saving act in Jesus Christ and recognize the
demands that Event makes on the individual. The loss of historical
identification undercuts the dynamism of the Christian faith;
Israel's cultic pattern has pointed the way to a recovery of that
historical involvement in Christian worship.

HISTORICAL RE-PRESENTATION BY DRAMATIC PRESENTATION

Recent studies of the history of Israel's religion have demonstrated convincingly that the formative events of Israel's faith were
dramatically acted out in the cult. In fact, some of the Old Testament narratives have reached their present form as a result of the
historicizing of cultic dramatic re-presentation. We would note
three prime examples of this thesis.

First, Johannes Pedersen has drawn attention to the fact that
the Exodus narrative in Exodus 1–19 is a reclothed festal liturgy

from which something of the ritual may be recovered.[21] In Exod. 12:42, the "watch night" drama appears, a re-creating and a re-presenting of the drama in which the Hebrews anxiously awaited the intervention of Yahweh in Egypt, a repeated cultic drama which bridged the gap of space and time and reestablished the saving relationship for each generation with Yahweh. In close connection is Exod. 12:1 ff., the instructions for the Passover Feast, said to be observed as "a memorial to all generations." The re-creation of the watch night, the blood on the doorposts and the lintel, the eating of unleavened bread and bitter herbs—these acts were re-created annually and physically in the active cult. For Israel, no sterile symbolism is present, no mere lifeless memory—by re-creating history through dramatic presentation, Israel re-presented her saving history, actualized her salvation, renewed her relationship to her God. Thus, historical recital has given way to historical re-creation.

Further, Hans-Joachim Kraus has proposed that the narratives of Joshua 2–6 are rehistoricized festal liturgies from the Gilgal cult.[22] At Gilgal, through dramatic presentation, the crossing of the Jordan was re-created, the march around the ruins of Jericho reenacted, not in mere historical memory, but in contemporary actualization. The close connection of dramatic re-presentation with liturgical re-presentation as noted earlier is clearly evidenced in these passages from Joshua. Thus, the Gilgal cult, annually or periodically, re-presented the conquest story, dramatizing its history and making it sacramental.

But, the greatest example of re-presentation of dramatic form is the Jerusalem cultus. Much has been written about the royal ritual in Jerusalem with its interlocked themes of David and Zion.[23]

21. *Israel III–IV* (London: Oxford University Press, 1940), pp. 728–37. Although Pedersen would end the "Passover legend" with Exodus 15, the limits may be extended to Exodus 19 with ease.

22. Pp. 152–65.

23. The terminology here is woefully inconsistent, reflecting the viewpoint of the proposed content of the festival, e. g., "Enthronement Festival," "Covenant Festival," "New Year's Festival." The author prefers the title "Royal Zion Festival" and is more inclined to the mediating position of Aubrey Johnson, *Sacral Kingship in Ancient Israel* (Cardiff: University of Wales Press, 1955). See also Mowinckel, *Psalms*, 1: 106–92; Kraus, pp. 205–18; Artur Weiser, *The Psalms*, trans. Herbert Hartwell, The Old Testament Library (Philadelphia: Westminster Press, 1962), pp. 35–52; Keith R. Crim, *The Royal Psalms* (Richmond: John Knox Press, 1962).

Despite those who find minimal cultic influence, one has little basis for doubting that the Royal Psalms have their setting in life in a Royal Zion Festival during which those events surrounding the Davidic dynasty were dramatically enacted at Jerusalem. The Psalms speak of the "night watch" at Gihon, of the procession through the streets of Jerusalem which preceded the entrance of the Ark into the Temple, and finally of the reactualization of the Davidic king as Yahweh's servant. The Psalms are primary testimony to historical re-presentation by dramatic actualization.

These three examples are more fully illuminated by this incisive quotation from Mowinckel:

> The cult is not only by its origin, but in all places and at all times, drama. The cult is sacred art. But at the same time it is sacred reality, not merely an acted drama or a play, but a real drama and one that manifests reality, a drama which realizes the dramatic event with real power, a reality from which real forces emanate, in other words it is a sacrament. . . . The basic idea is this: that through the dramatic, "symbolic" presentation, realization and reanimation of the particular event this event is actually and really repeated; it repeats itself, happens all over again and exercises afresh the same mighty, redemptive effect that it exercised for our salvation on the first occasion at the dawn of time or in the far distant past.[24]

Precisely at this point Christian worship has departed from the pattern of the Israelite cult, with particular reference to the Lord's Supper. If one will view the history of the Lord's Supper, one will find few periods when the real drama of this cultic presentation has been preserved. The theology of the Lord's Supper has moved from the extreme of the Roman church with its doctrine of transubstantiation to the barren symbolism of nonliturgical congregations. Both positions, this writer submits, are in error. If the Old Testament cult is correctly viewed, then an idea of the actual recreation of the body and blood of our Lord in the mass is incorrect. The suffering and death of Jesus were once-for-all, nonrepeatable, unique events in history—in no sense can the event be literally and physically re-created in worship. But, on the other hand, the

24. *Psalmstudien*, 2: 21. Quoted by Kraus, p. 9.

elements of the Lord's Supper transcend barren symbolism. In the celebration of the Lord's Supper, something happens—not with the elements themselves—but in a dramatic re-presentation of history. To borrow the pattern of the Deuteronomic preachers, "not with the disciples did our Lord institute the new covenant, but with us, all of us, we who are here alive today." The Lord's Supper is sacred art, a drama which manifests reality; it allows the worshipper to span the time and space gap of history and stand again with those who first experienced our Lord's death. In the mystery of dramatic presentation, the worshipper reenters original history, not as festal myth, but as actualization. "This is my body broken for you," a brokenness which continues over and over again, a presentness of contemporary encounter. Thus, as one partakes of the elements, one becomes part of the original event which was accomplished for our salvation.

The demand is to recover the true meaning of the Lord's Supper in Christian worship, a meaning which will be patterned from the Israelite cult with its motif of dramatic re-presentation. If the study of the Israelite cult is taken seriously, the Lord's Supper must be rescued from its place as addendum in many congregations and restored to the central place of worship. The Lord's Supper is the reenactment of the Christian Exodus-event, the historical beginning which continues to give the church life. Jesus said, "This do in remembrance of me." Yet, to remember is not an intellectual discipline, "to re-member" is to re-create, "to re-member" is to become involved, "to re-member" is to actualize, "to re-member" is to re-present, "to re-member" is to respond.[25] In Deut. 16:3, the feast of the Passover is said to be observed, "so that you may remember the day when you came out of the land of Egypt." Here is the annual re-presentation of history. Thus, "This do in remembrance of me" must mean, "so that you may participate in the sufferings and death of our Lord and respond to them." For as Israel was redeemed from Egyptian bondage in the exodus and annually actualized that redemption in the cult, the Christian church finds itself released from a similar bondage and must actualize that redemption by dramatic re-presentation. The Lord's

25. See further, Edward P. Blair, "An Appeal to Remembrance," *Interpretation*, 15 (Jan., 1961), 41–47.

Supper is truly sacramental in that by participating in the drama of our redemption, God himself reestablishes, maintains, and renews his relationship with us and we respond in obedience.

The Cult in Contemporary Worship

To this point, the attempt has been made to present the primary purpose of Israel's cult as a re-presentation of history through the use of audible and visual means. Beyond the two basic ideas of historical recitation and dramatic presentation and their application in Christian worship, four other areas may be noted briefly in which the Israelite cult has relevance for Christian worship.

First, in worship, evangelicals in particular have tended to overemphasize the audible aspects of worship to the exclusion of the visible aspects. Primarily in the Lord's Supper the vitality of tangible and visible presentation has been retained. The Israelite cult is "sacred art." Only recently has the church begun to grasp the power of acted-out faith and worship in drama. Contemporary worship patterns need a new awareness of the impact of the visible which often is more effective than the audible. Dramatic presentation of our faith offers a new and creative channel through which the re-presentation of history may be accomplished, through which the dynamism of the Christian faith may be preserved, through which we may bridge the time and space gap of two thousand years.

Second, and closely related to the first, is the area of symbolism. The temple in Jerusalem was filled with symbolism, not merely as decorative art, but as a means of re-creating history. The Ark of the Covenant, the central cult object, stood in its semidarkness as the throne of the invisible King Yahweh.[26] The altar of incense, standing before the "Holy of Holies," continually emitted sweet-smelling smoke to recreate the theophany of Sinai where Yahweh appeared "in a thick cloud."[27] The great free-standing pillars outside the temple, at least according to one interpretation, served as mammoth incense burners by which the whole temple came to

26. Walther Eichrodt, *Theology of the Old Testament*, trans. J. A. Baker, The Old Testament Library (Philadelphia: Westminster Press, 1961), 1: 107–9.

27. J. Kenneth Kuntz, *The Self-revelation of God* (Philadelphia: Westminster Press, 1967), pp. 226–77.

represent Sinai.[28] The trumpets sounded in the liturgy were more than musical instruments, their sound re-created the thunder of the Sinaitic theophany.[29] To be sure, the author is not pleading for the installation of incense burners in sanctuaries; he is pleading for an increased realization that cultic symbolism re-creates, re-presents, actualizes, and activates history. With the renewed emphasis upon liturgy and worship, the church can learn much about the place and purpose of creative symbolism from the Israelite cult.

Third, the Israelite cult was, as Mowinckel stated, a place where something happened, a fact which is beginning to dramatize renovations in church architecture. Renewed emphasis upon worship as action and participation by the whole congregation has brought about circular buildings with the communion table at their centers. Startingly, a Northfield, Minnesota, architect has proposed that except for its size, the best analogy for church architecture is the Japanese tea room. The architect, Edward Anders Sovik, said: "Like a church, the tea room is not a place for private meditation, but for dialogue and certain actions in which human relationships are established."[30] This statement is reminiscent of Mowinckel who spoke of the cult as the "visible and audible expression of the relation between congregation and deity." Thus, the recovery of the dynamism of Israel's cult may well influence our traditional conceptions of sacral architecture with renewed emphasis upon the worship as visible and audible, as expressions of relationships, as an event in which "something happens."

Finally, insight into the Israelite cult will grant Christian worship increased flexibility. Every Old Testament student knows that many of Israel's worship patterns were adapted along the lines of Near Eastern culture and even the Jerusalem cultus is a compromise between Yahwistic and Jebusite cultic patterns. Israel could and did adopt forms from her contemporary culture, introduce them into her ancient patterns of worship, and baptize them into her distinctive Yahwism. This freedom to employ non-Christian elements in Christian worship must be recovered. While some have viewed attempts to introduce jazz and modern dance into

28. William Foxwell Albright, *Archaeology and the Religion of Israel* (Baltimore: Johns Hopkins Press, 1956), pp. 144–48.
29. Kuntz, pp. 82–86, 227.
30. *Louisville Courier-Journal and Times*, July 14, 1968.

worship as anathema, this writer would suggest that these experiments are harmonious with the Israelite point of view. The increased use of and adaptation of twentieth-century art and music forms offers new and exciting challenges for creative revitalization of Christian worship.

Conclusion

In conclusion, the original thesis of this article is reaffirmed. If the God of Israel is the God and Father of our Lord Jesus Christ, as the church claims he is, then to contend that he chooses to be worshipped in similar patterns is not difficult to affirm. The central purpose of both Israelite and Christian worship is to re-present creative history by means of audible and visible expression, a re-presentation which culminates in active response. Perhaps one reason the Christian church has lost much of its vitality in the twentieth century is that it has lost the art of worship because it has divorced itself from the sense of the history which effected its salvation. Recovering that historical status is part and parcel with the revitalizing of the drama of worship. Edward Blair has written provocatively:

> By remembering, the God of the past becomes *our* God, the covenants made at Horeb and Calvary *our* covenants, and the promises given to the fathers *our* promises. In the biblical kind of memory time recedes. The patriarchs and the prophets become our contemporaries. We all tarry behind the bloody lintel, loins girded, staff in hand, the smell of roasted lamb in our nostrils, and wild fear in our hearts while the angel of death passes. We all stand before the holy mountains, dark and quaking, where God is speaking his eternal word. And we all wait for the glorious day when promise will become fulfillment.[31]

31. Blair, p. 47.

THE CONDEMNATION OF EDOM IN
POSTEXILIC JUDAISM

BRUCE C. CRESSON

Professor Stinespring, with charismatic ability for expressing ideas in remembrable statements, has explained to several decades of students that one of the characteristics of postexilic prophecy is a "Damn-Edom" theology. This volume provides an appropriate occasion for consideration of this oft-noticed but seldom pursued aspect of Old Testament prophetic thought.

Edom and the Edomites are frequently spoken of in the Old Testament. Such bitterness, hatred, and contempt characterize these references that it is scarcely hyperbolic to say that never a kind word is spoken about Edom in the Old Testament.

There are four significant relationships in which Edom is mentioned in the Old Testament: (1) the stories concerning the nation's origin and kinship with Israel; (2) the Israelite-Edomite contact in the wilderness after the Exodus; (3) the accounts of periodic subjugation and control of Edom by Israel or Judah during the period of the Hebrew monarchies; and (4) the hatred and condemnation of Edom and the Edomites, primarily in the prophetic writings. There are other brief references to Edom in the Old Testament, but they give little help in our understanding of relationships and attitudes between these nations. The fourth of the above enumerated relations is of major concern in this study. However, the first three demand some initial consideration. The intense hatred of Edom by the Jews must have had some historical background.

The stories of conflict between Jacob and Esau, the patriarchs of the nations Israel and Edom, are well known. The relationship between these stories and the later hatred between nations is not clear and is rarely explored. To attempt to explain the hatred between Israel and Edom by saying that Esau (and his descendants) refused to forgive Jacob (and his descendants) for the bowl of pottage withheld from Esau is hopelessly naive, but evidently such an explanation for this hostility is uncritically accepted by some students of the Old Testament.

The Esau-Jacob stories in Genesis testify to an insistent and unbroken tradition of ill feeling between Israel and Edom. The prominent place these stories occupy in the Old Testament, but not their origin, can be understood in the light of Damn-Edom theology. One place to look in search of an understanding of the hatred between Edom and Israel is to the history of Edom.

I

The references to Edom, especially historical, in the Old Testament, though not extensive, are not altogether insignificant. The territory of Edom was located south of the Dead Sea reaching to the northern tip of the Gulf of Aqabah. The only boundary in question is the western boundary. There is some evidence limiting Edomite territory to the region east of the Wadi Arabah, but there is evidence, however, pointing to Edomite occupation and control of territory on both sides of the Wadi Arabah. It is nevertheless very clear that the most important part of Edom lies to the east of the Arabah. The home territories of the kings and chieftains of Edom mentioned in Genesis 36 and I Chronicles 1 appear to be in this eastern area, as do the sites of conflict with Edom in the wilderness period and the Hebrew kingdoms period.

Little of certainty can be known concerning Edomite history during patriarchal Old Testament times. Nelson Glueck reports evidence that there was a civilization of high achievement in Edom and nearby areas between the twenty-first and nineteenth centuries B.C. Then, about 1900 B.C. there was a thoroughgoing destruction visited upon the land, marking the end of this particular civilization. Several centuries followed, according to Glueck's analysis, with the territory of Edom occupied by no more than nomadic clans. He posits the founding of the Kingdom of Edom in the thirteenth century.[1]

1. Nelson Glueck, *Rivers in the Desert* (New York: The Jewish Publication Society of America, 5719–1959), p. 11; Glueck, *The Other Side of the Jordan* (New Haven: American Schools of Oriental Research, 1940), p. 114. G. Lankester Harding has raised questions about these conclusions. The evidence at present suggests that Glueck is probably correct. See Harding, *The Antiquities of Jordan*, rev. ed. (New York: Frederick A. Praeger, 1967), pp. 32–33.

That the Edomites were present in the twelfth century B.C. is clearly evident from biblical references and archaeological evidence. The view of Glueck is that near the beginning of the thirteenth century B.C., with both Egypt and Assyria weak, there came an influx of Bedouin or seminomadic peoples from the desert areas to the south and east absorbing or dispossessing the seminomadic inhabitants who had developed no sedentary civilization while having held the land since around 1900 B.C. This movement encompassed the Trans-Jordan area from Lake Huleh to the Gulf of Aqabah. The subsequent division of the land into five kingdoms was influenced probably by both the separate tribal groups of invaders and the topographical divisions of the land. Edom, the southernmost of the five kingdoms, developed rapidly during this late Bronze–early Iron Age into a highly advanced, strongly organized, and well-integrated kingdom. The agricultural potential of the territory was used to good advantage.[2]

The value of the land of Edom, besides its agricultural potential when the strictest methods of water conservation and use were employed, lay in the presence of copper and in the strategic position of the land with the "King's Highway" traversing the length of its territory. The extent of copper mining activity in Edom during the thirteenth to the fourth centuries is unknown. It is a logical guess that the Edomites carried on some mining operations in this time.[3] The location of Edom on the King's Highway gave opportunity for control of, enrichment from, and participation in ancient commerce, particularly that between Egypt, Arabia, and India (by way of Arabia) and the regions to the north. The kingdom of Edom must have become strong and relatively wealthy. The presence of strong and well-situated border fortresses and a significant decrease in the thickness of protecting walls of individual cities suggest that this was a kingdom with protected borders, strong central authority and national unity.[4] The account in Numbers 20 indicates that the kingdom of Edom was sufficiently strong to admit or refuse entry to other peoples into its borders.

Concerning the history of Edom beginning with the thirteenth

---

2. Glueck, *Other Side*, pp. 127–28; M. E. Kirk, "An Outline of the Ancient Cultural History of Transjordan," *Palestine Exploration Quarterly*, 76 (1944), 187, 188.

3. Kirk, p. 185; Glueck, *Other Side*, p. 83.

4. Kirk, p. 187.

century B.C., after the accounts of the contact with the Hebrews
in the wilderness, there is silence in the biblical account for a considerable period of time. Down to the time of Saul there is no
evidence to Edom's history except the listing of the king-chiefs in
Genesis 36. Eight kings are listed who ruled Edom before the
establishment of a monarchy in Israel (vv. 31–39); then eleven
chiefs of Edom are enumerated (vv. 40–43). No chronology of any
sort is supplied. Little of historical value can be gathered from the
lists.

From the period of the Hebrew monarchy relatively little evidence concerning the history of Edom comes from extrabiblical
sources. There are questionable references to excursions from
Egypt into Edom in the period of nineteenth and twentieth dynas-
ties.[5] Shishak's expedition that took him into Jerusalem in the time
of Rehoboam took him also into Edom, which he claims in an
inscription at Karnak to have overrun.[6] These evidences are interesting but cast little, if any, light upon the history of Edom. From
the records of the Assyrian king, Adad-Nirari III (810–783 B.C.),
is the claim that he made expeditions to the west in 806, 805, and
797 B.C. in which tribute was received from, among other places,
Edom. Edom is named by this monarch as a new conquest for the
Kingdom of Assyria.[7] Tiglath-pileser III (744–727 B.C.), in an
extant building inscription, relates that he received tribute from
"Kaushmalaku (Qaushmalaku) of Edom" as well as from many
other rulers and nations.[8] The Broken Prism of Sargon II (721–
705 B.C.) records an attempted revolt in which Edom was involved.[9]
According to the Oriental Institute Prism of Sennacherib (704–
681 B.C.), in the same campaign (701 B.C.) in which he besieged
Jerusalem, Aiarammu of Edom, among other rulers, offered
gifts and obeisance to Sargon.[10] Esarhaddon (680–669 B.C.) claims
to have forced Qaushgabri, King of Edom, with twenty-one other
kings from Hatti, to transport building materials to Nineveh.[11]

5. G. A. Frank Knight, *Nile and Jordan* (London: James Clark and Company,
1921), pp. 233–41, 250, 254, 257.

6. *Ibid.*, pp. 279, 280.

7. James B. Pritchard, ed., *Ancient Near Eastern Texts Relating to The Old Testament*
(Princeton: Princeton University Press, 1950), p. 281, col. 2.

8. *Ibid.*, p. 282, col. 1. In the same list Jehoahaz of Judah is mentioned.

9. *Ibid.*, p. 287, col. 1.

10. *Ibid.*, p. 287, col. 2.

11. *Ibid.*, p. 291, cols. 1, 2. Manasseh of Judah is one of the kings listed.

Ashurbanipal (668–633 B.C.) records that he received tribute from Qaushgabri, King of Edom, who, with other kings, accompanied him (probably with their armies) in his attack on Egypt.[12]

Shortly after the beginning of the sixth century B.C. Edom was a participant in a revolt against Nebuchadrezzar, the Babylonian Empire having then succeeded the Assyrian in world dominance. This rebellion of western states led to the 587 B.C. destruction of Jerusalem. Details of what befell Edom for its participation are lacking. G. L. Robinson assumes that Edom's power was dealt a severe blow but that consequences were not as severe for Edom as for Judah in the way of destruction and deportation. He argues also that this fatal weakening of Edom set the stage for the Nabataean encroachment.[13]

The biblical evidence concerning Edom in the period of the Hebrew monarchy relates that Saul fought against Edom, but there is no evidence that this was more than a brief expedition against a harassing enemy neighbor (I Sam. 14:47). David conquered the Kingdom of Edom, but details of the conquest are almost completely lacking. It is simply reported that "he [David] slew eighteen thousand Edomites in the Valley of Salt. And he put garrisons in Edom; throughout all Edom he put garrisons, and all the Edomites became David's servants" (II Sam. 8:13, 14).[14] For a period of six months after this initial battle, Joab and his army were engaged in establishing Israelite control of Edom; "for Joab and all Israel remained there six months, until he had cut off every male in Edom" (I Kings 11:15, 16). Although there may have been a great slaughter, this is obviously a hyperbolic statement. Upon the deaths of David and Joab, Hadad, a royal prince who had escaped to Egypt in the time of David's conquest of Edom, returned, evidently seeking to raise the standard of revolt against Solomon. He probably harassed Solomon but never succeeded in throwing off Israelite domination. That Solomon retained control of Edom during the entirety of his reign is evident from the account of his establishment of naval operations centered at

---

12. *Ibid.*, p. 294, cols. 1, 2. Manasseh is again listed.

13. G. L. Robinson, *Sarcophagus of an Ancient Civilization* (New York: The Macmillan Company, 1930), pp. 364–65. Such an assumption seems to go beyond the evidence. Edom may well have escaped the wrath of Nebuchadrezzar's army. Concerning this period of Edom's history additional archaeological evidence would be most valuable.

14. Emending the text with the Greek, אדם for ארם; cf. I Chron. 18:12, 13.

Ezion-geber (I Kings 9–10), and from recognition that the first account of Edomite independence came in the time of Jehoram of Judah, when a successful revolt was carried out.[15]

For a considerable period of time after David's conquest of Edom, perhaps 200 years, the struggle continued between Edom and Israel-Judah for control of the land of Seir. The Hebrews held the upper hand from David to Jehoram, but there were continual attempts at rebellion by the Edomites. Glueck has set forth the idea that the fierceness of this struggle, which was mutually exhausting on both sides, was one of the contributing factors in the Edomite weakness that resulted in the subsequent disappearance of the Edomites as a separate ethnic and political group.[16] The desire of the Hebrews to control Edom may be traced to three important assets possessed by Edom: the trade routes it controlled, the Gulf of Aqabah seaport, and the natural resources, especially copper and iron, found in Edom but lacking in Palestine proper.

During the reign of Jehoram of Judah the Edomites successfully revolted[17] but were again subdued by Amaziah of Judah, who captured Sela and changed its name to Joktheel.[18] Amaziah's son, Uzziah, pursued to a successful conclusion the attack upon Edom, even capturing Elath.[19] Glueck equates the marked rise in prosperity and peace in Uzziah's time with the control of Edom and the wealth received therefrom.[20] It was in the time of Ahaz that Judah's control of Edom was permanently broken.[21] A weakened Edom was never again to regain her former splendor, and, although forced later to change homelands, she probably retained some measure of independence until the Maccabaean period. While Ahaz was king the Edomites were making raids upon Judah for

15. See II Kings 8:20–22; II Chron. 21:9, 10. Intervening references indicate that this was not the first revolt attempted (cf. II Chronicles 20). Other references relate that in the time of Jehoshaphat, "There was no king in Edom; a deputy was king." (I Kings 22:47), that Jehoshaphat controlled Ezion-Geber, the site of the disaster to his navy (I Kings 22:48), and that Edom aided Jehoshaphat of Judah and Jehoram of Israel in a campaign against Moab (II Kings 3:9).
16. Glueck, *Other Side*, pp. 53, 54. If this is true, the exhaustion incurred by Judah in the same struggle may well have contributed to its downfall under the Babylonians.
17. II Kings 8:20–22.
18. II Kings 14:7; II Chron. 25:11, 12.
19. II Kings 14:22; II Chron. 26:1, 2.
20. Glueck, *Other Side*, p. 87.
21. II Kings 16:5, 6, accepting emendations in v. 6, omitting "Rezin" and changing "Aram" to "Edom."

the acquisition of slaves, with the result that Ahaz appealed to Assyria.[22] The appearance of Tiglath-pileser III restored the precarious situation: the Assyrian monarch conquered Syria and received recognition of Assyrian dominance from the regions to the south.[23] Heavy tribute was burdensome; and Edom, along with other states (but not Judah at this time), was encouraged into revolt by Egypt. This revolt was easily subdued by Sargon II.[24]

The biblical records, as well as secular records, maintain almost complete silence concerning the role of Edom following the decline of the Assyrian Empire. Concerning what was happening with regard to Edom in the time of the fall of Nineveh, the death of Josiah at Megiddo, and the defeat of Necho at Carchemish by Nebuchadrezzar, nothing is recorded. Jehoiakim had, meanwhile, begun to reign in Judah about 608 B.C., placed on the throne by Necho of Egypt. He became a vassal of Nebuchadrezzar about the year 601 B.C. It seems that Nebuchadrezzar was busy elsewhere when, after three years of vassalage, Jehoiakim rebelled. But Nebuchadrezzar employed Edomites,[25] Ammonites, and Moabites along with Chaldaean troops, perhaps his own garrisons in Syria, to harass the city of Jerusalem. Jehoiachin, who had succeeded his father as king of Judah when Nebuchadrezzar arrived on the scene to lay siege to the city, surrendered in 597 B.C., and the first deportation from Jerusalem-Judah followed. Peace and subjection to Babylon followed for a brief time. But tribute was tiresome and chafing, and soon trouble was brewing again. Edom along with Ammon, Moab, Tyre, Sidon, and Judah plotted a revolt against their Babylonian overlord. This revolt failed to materialize, perhaps because of the influence of Jeremiah,[26] or because of the discovery that Egypt would not join them, or because Nebuchadrezzar heard of their plans and took prompt measures to forestall the revolt,[27] or perhaps because the conspirators could not agree among themselves.

22. II Chron. 28:16, 17.

23. G. L. Robinson, pp. 360, 361. Robinson mistakenly calls the ruler Tiglath-pileser IV.

24. *Ibid.*, p. 364.

25. II Kings 24:2, accepting the reading of the Syriac, "Edom" for "Aram."

26. Jer. 27:4–11.

27. W. O. E. Oesterley and Theodore H. Robinson, *A History of Israel*, 2 vols. (Oxford: The Clarendon Press, 1932), 1: 438.

As to the part played by Edom and the effect of the circumstances in Palestine on Edom in the 587 B.C. destruction of Jerusalem, the historical records—biblical and nonbiblical—are silent. Assumptions are recorded ranging from one extreme to the other. G. L. Robinson says that the effective end of Edom as a national kingdom came as a result of the sixth century B.C. alliance with Judah and other neighboring nations against Nebuchadrezzar of Babylon. He argues that Edom was conquered in 587 B.C. and that some Edomites were deported from their homeland, but most remained in Edom.[28] On the other hand, W. F. Lofthouse contends that Edomites were among the troops used by Nebuchadrezzar in this destruction of Jerusalem and that the callous attitude of these Edomites brought forth the undying hatred of their beleaguered kinsmen.[29] Whatever the involvement (or lack of it) of Edom in the events of 587 B.C., she remained not strong enough to resist effectively the surging desert tribes on the move from Arabia. In the years after the destruction of Jerusalem, with Edom in a weakened state, Nabataean nomads moved in and took over the land of Edom.[30] The Nabataean invasion and consequent move of the Edomites into the Negeb of Judah are especially relevant to the development of Damn-Edom theology, because this may have been one of the causes for the emergence of vehement hatred of the Edomites. Evidence from Aramaic-inscribed vessels found at Tell el-Maskhuta in Lower Egypt suggests that a late sixth- or early fifth-century B.C. date may be assigned to the Nabataean invasion of Edom.[31]

Some of the Edomites in the time of this invasion were absorbed

28. G. L. Robinson, p. 364.

29. W. F. Lofthouse, *Israel After The Exile*, The Clarendon Bible, Old Testament, vol. 4 (Oxford: The Clarendon Press, 1928), p. 100.

30. There is little evidence upon which to base conclusions relative to the Edomite settlement of the Negeb. Josephus (*Antiquities* x.9,181 f.) relates that in 582 B.C., Nebuchadrezzar made war on and subjugated Ammon and Moab; no mention is made of Edom, cf. Martin Noth, *History of Israel*, trans. P. R. Ackroyd (London: A. and C. Black, 1960), pp. 293, 294. At the time of the writing of Ezekiel 35 the Edomites were in part of Judah. The only conclusive evidence is that this Edomite migration into the Negeb took place between 587 B.C. and 312 B.C., for in this latter year the Nabataeans were in control of Petra. (Diodorus Siculus, *Bibliotheca Historica*, xix, 94.)

31. The argument in brief is that these Qedarite Arabs, friends of the Persians pushed the Nabataeans who in turn pushed the Edomites. See Isaac Rabinowitz, "Aramaic Inscriptions of the Fifth Century B.C.E. from a North-Arab Shrine in Egypt," *Journal of Near Eastern Studies*, 15 (1956), 2, 3.

by the Nabataeans; others emigrated to southern Judah and the Negeb south of Judah. The Nabataeans built a remarkable civilization of their own in Edom, higher and grander than that of the Edomites. The displaced Edomites, now in southern Judah, are known as Idumaeans, at least from the time of Alexander the Great.

Idumaea is mentioned in the texts of several classical authors[32] but with little detail useful in the reconstruction of its history. The Old Testament apocryphal books, especially I Maccabees and Josephus, are the major sources for this period. In the absence of evidence indicating otherwise, it is assumed that the Jews and Idumaeans existed side by side without major provocation until the time of the Maccabaean Revolt. Josephus and I Maccabees relate the exploits of Judas Maccabaeus against the Idumaeans; John Hyrcanus I later conquered the Idumaeans, and henceforth they were technically a part of the Jewish people. Well known is the story of the rise of the Idumaeans, Antipater and his family, to power over the Jews under the Roman Empire. The end of Idumaea probably came with the 70 A.D. destruction of Judaea and Jerusalem by Vespasian and Titus.

This brief summary has presented the known historical contacts and relationships between Hebrews and Edomites relevant to this study in hatred between the two nations. It will provide a background against which to examine the Damn-Edom passages.

II

Within the Old Testament prophetic literature there are several expressions of the anti-Edom bias of the Hebrews. These are found both encompassed in and separate from the collections of the anti-foreign-nation oracles. These passages fall generally within the cursing or judgment type oracles, but there is great variation in the developed literary expressions voicing this cursing of the Edomites.

The most obvious and vehement expression of Damn-Edom theology in the Old Testament is found in the book of Obadiah. This, the shortest book in the Old Testament, has received more

---

32. Diodorus Siculus, *Bibliotheca Historica* xix: 95, 98; Pliny the Elder, *Natural History*, V. xiv; Strabo, *Geography* XVI.ii.2; Claudius Ptolemaeus, *Geography* v.16.10.

attention from exegetes seeking to justify its place in the canon
and attempting to glean some moral or spiritual lesson from its
verses than from those trying to understand its message and background. Among critical scholars the problem of relationship between Obadiah and Jeremiah 49 has claimed most attention. The
message of the book has been pushed aside and ignored. It gives
unmistakeably and clearly the message: "May Yahweh damn
Edom" as the theme of verses 1–14; and "May all the nations—and
especially Edom—be damned while Judah is blessed," in verses
15–21.

The unity of the book has been frequently questioned.[33] The
most likely division occurs between verses 14 and 15. The references
in verses 19–21 argue quite conclusively for a postexilic date for
the completed book. The vigor of the condemnation of Edom in
verses 1–14, the white heat of hatred, the freshness of wounds revealed demand a date for the composition of this passage near the
calamitous event that provoked it. When the possible dates—disasters to Jerusalem[34] in which the Edomites could have so behaved
—are considered, the date must be placed within a generation of
587 B.C. The latter portion of the book, verses 15–21, contains
nothing indicating an exact date. The tenor of the poetic message
points rather clearly to postexilic times. With some arbitrariness
confessed, an approximate date of 400 B.C. is assigned to verses
15–21.

The oracle of Obadiah contains a prediction of the punishment
that either is to befall or is befalling Edom, a description of the
hostility of Edom toward Judah in the day of her distress, and a
prediction of the coming of the Day of Yahweh upon all nations,
especially on Edom, coupled with the restoration and exaltation

33. The most radical analysis is that found in Theodore H. Robinson and F. Horst,
Die zwölf kleinen Propheten, Handbuch zum Alten Testament, ed. by Eissfeldt (Tübingen:
J. C. B. Mohr [Paul Siebeck], 1938), pp. 109–16.

34. Recorded disasters to Jerusalem are: (1) Shishak's invasion (I Kings 14:25; 16;
II Chron. 12:1–12); (2) an invasion of Judah and presumably Jerusalem by Philistines
and Arabs (II Chron. 21:16, 17); (3) an invasion by Jehoash of Israel when Amaziah
was King of Judah (II Kings 14:8–14; II Chron. 25:17–24); (4) Nebuchadrezzar's
invasion in 597 (II Kings 24:10–17); (5) Nebuchadrezzar's second invasion in 587
(II Kings 25:3–21; II Chron. 36:17–21). Julian Morgenstern's fascinating hypothesis
of a 485 B.C. disaster to Jerusalem has insufficient historical evidence to support it.
See Julian Morgenstern, "Jerusalem—485 B.C.," *Hebrew Union College Annual,* 27 (1956),
101–79; 28 (1957), 15–47; 31 (1960), 1–29.

of the house of Judah. The concept of Jewish nationalism is seen in the various parts of the oracles, in the cry for revenge upon the hated Edomites as well as in the restoration and glorification of the Jewish nation. Obadiah gives the most forthright expression of Damn-Edom theology. This, while undoubtedly expressive of bitter hatred, is far more than a fanatical national hatred. The damnation of Edom is based upon the writer's idea of divine retributive justice: supposed blood-kin and neighbors who behave in such a way are certainly in line for terrible punishment. The narrow particularism of the viewpoint set forth must also be recognized. Judah-Israel is Yahweh's chosen people, and the covenant necessitates their restoration as surely as divine justice decrees the punishment of Edom. The faith Obadiah holds expresses itself in a conception of the eschatological reign of Yahweh as king (v. 21). With Weiser, "We may perhaps think of Obadiah as a prophet of salvation in the circles faithful to Yahweh. . . . His oracles give us a supplementary insight into the sufferings and hopes after the collapse of Judah and reveal the association of religion with national aspirations which was one of the characteristics of the prophecies of salvation in Israel."[35]

The oracle attributed traditionally to Jeremiah in his prophecy, 49:7–22, is closely related to Obadiah. That there was some literary relationship is evident. The Jeremianic Damn-Edom oracle stands as one in a series of ten oracles against foreign nations, comprising chapters 46–51.

An outline of Jer. 49:7–22 reveals the content of this expression of Damn-Edom theology:

1. The traditional wisdom is gone from Edom. (7)
2. Calamity will befall Edom. (8)
3. The degree of destruction will be total annihilation. (9, 10)
4. A later addition to the oracle. (11)
5. The coming destruction is certain. (12, 13)
6. Edom's present pride is contrasted with her coming fall. (14–16)

35. Artur Weiser, *The Old Testament, Its Formation and Development*, trans. Dorothea M. Barton (New York: Association Press, 1961), p. 249. More generally on this theme see Gerhard von Rad, *The Message of the Prophets*, trans. D. M. G. Stalker (London: SCM Press, 1968), pp. 89–99.

7. The coming destruction is with Yahweh's purpose and plan. (19–21)

8. The coming terror will render Edom's warriors ineffective. (22)

This passage in Jeremiah has close parallels with Obadiah. Verse 9 parallels Obadiah 5 and verses 14–16 parallel Obadiah 1–4. There are thought parallels with no significant new element in Jeremiah between verse 7 and Obadiah 8, verse 10a and Obadiah 6, and verse 22b and Obadiah 9a. Verse 8 contains no specific new element. It speaks in general terms of coming calamity. Verse 10 relates how complete will be the exposure and destruction of Edom and adds to previously noted thoughts that the brothers and neighbors of Edom will share its fate. Verse 11 is an intrusion of "sweetness and light" in the midst of a picture of doom, suggesting that the widows and fatherless children of the Edomites will be cared for by Yahweh. In contrast, total destruction is elsewhere the theme of Damn-Edom theology.

The oracle on Edom in Ezek. 25:12–14 is brief, similar in form to the preceding oracles in chapter 25 on Ammon (1–7) and Moab (8–11), and the following oracle on the Philistines (15–17). The denunciation of Edom is stated briefly and in very general terms. The accusation directed against her is that she "acted revengefully against the house of Judah" (v. 12). The punishment decreed is complete destruction and desolation which, significantly, is to be effected by Israel as the instrument of Yahweh's wrath (v. 14).

Chapter 35 of the book of Ezekiel denounces Edom more vehemently and with much more exactness. This oracle precedes a general denunciation of the "rest of the nations" in chapter 36 in which Edom alone is singled out by name. One question that demands consideration in a study of this chapter is, why a second oracle on Edom and not on other nations? The answer lies in the singularly intense hatred of the Jews for the Edomites, especially in the exilic and postexilic periods—a hatred far exceeding their hatred of other nations. Another facet of the answer lies in the fact that "Edom" became a symbolic representation of the enemies of the restored community in general. From Ezekiel comes additional evidence that a Damn-Edom theology was a real and lively part of the life and thought of Judaism in the sixth and following centuries B.C. There is no unanimity on the solutions to problems of date and authenticity of chapter 35. The chapter is probably a later addition to the text of Ezekiel, but perhaps is built around a genuine nucleus of thought if not of words. Three possibilities are recognized as reason for the presence of the oracle as a reiterative and specific denunciation of Edom: the continuing bitterness and unbounded hatred of Edom for her actions against Judah; the new aggravation of old wounds by the Edomites since the oracle in chapter 25 was composed; and the developing tendency to use *Edom* as a designation of the enemies of the Jews.

The elements included in Ezek. 25:12–14 and 35:1–15 which have not presented themselves in Obadiah and Jeremiah are significant additions to Damn-Edom theology. The attempt of Edom to take possession of Judah's territory, seemingly in the time of the Exile, is brought forward as a reason for the condemnation of Edom. This did come, probably not in the time of the Exile except for scattered Edomite settlements, but soon thereafter as a result of the Nabataean invasion of the old homeland of Edom. The concept that the destruction which is to befall Edom is designed in part to bring the Edomites to a recognition of Yahweh as Lord has been discerned, but doubtfully, in Obadiah. It may occur there in verse 21: "Deliverers shall go up from Mount Zion to rule Mount Esau; and the kingdom shall be Yahweh's." This verse has been noted earlier as a late addition to Obadiah, and it probably refers to territorial expansion and control. Thus the concept of a "missionary" purpose in Edom's doom is to be considered as addition to Damn-Edom theology by the writer of Ezekiel 35.

The book of Lamentations, the dirge over the fallen city, Jerusalem, contains the assurance that the same or at least a similar destruction as that which befell Jerusalem lay in store for the Edomites. The passage that contains this assurance, 4:21–22, probably comes from the late exilic (or possibly the early postexilic) period. The rejoicing of Edom over the misfortune of Jerusalem is indicated as the reason for her doom. It is quite noticeable that in verse 22 the concepts of the punishment of Edom and the restoration of Judah are tied together. This passage from Lamentations makes no significant contribution of new ideas to Damn-Edom theology but does contain vehement expression of the characteristic thought of previously noted oracles.

The book of the prophet Joel contains only a brief mention of Edom, and that along with Egypt, for having done violence to the people of Judah and for having shed innocent blood in their land. The passage 2:30–3:21 tells of coming doom and divine judgment upon all the nations, including Edom. Eschatologically, again, judgment on Edom is associated with the restoration of Judah-Israel.

The best-known of the prophetic collections of oracles condemning the nations is that in the book of Amos. The fourth of the oracles on the nations in chapters 1 and 2 is devoted to Edom. In the familiar formula of denunciation in Amos, Edom is "damned" for ill will toward brothers, for pursuing them with the sword, and for retention of anger. The predicted punishment is quite typical of Amos, devouring fire upon Teman and Bozrah. Serious question has been raised concerning the authenticity of this oracle. It is probably to be assigned to the postexilic period in agreement with most other Damn-Edom material. The charges against and punishment of Edom are general and are in line with charges made elsewhere in the anti-Edom oracles in prophetic literature.

The doom and destruction of Edom are spoken of in Mal. 1:2–5. This passage is generally accepted as genuine and is dated with the book of Malachi about 450 B.C. The doom predicted on Edom by Malachi is not of the same vividness and fervor as that of other prophets. In contrast to the love Yahweh has for Jacob, he hates Esau. Esau's country is laid waste, and, if he tries to rebuild it, it will be destroyed again. The Edomites will be known as the people with whom Yahweh was angry unto hidden ages. The evidence that the reference of Malachi is to the Nabataean encroachment is found in: "I have . . . left his heritage to jackals of the desert." Seir is usually referred to as hill country; the Nabataean invaders would be desert people. Verse 5 indicates the rejoicing of the Jews upon their vindication in this revenge-satisfying blow which fell upon Edom.

The book of the prophet Isaiah presents many problems to the interpreter in general. One of the specific instances of such problems is the material on Edom. In Proto-Isaiah references are first found to Edom in 21:11, 12. This passage does not belong to Damn-Edom literature.

Chapter 34 of Proto-Isaiah requires treatment as a part of

Damn-Edom theology, although there is no unanimity among scholars in so identifying the chapter. Widely varying dates, views of authorship, and interpretations have been given this poem.

Chapters 34 and 35 are a logical unity in which the doom and destruction of the nations, especially Edom, are contrasted with the blessedness and fertility of Judah. These poems were probably one single oracle not composed by Isaiah of Jerusalem and probably belong to the very early postexilic period, but are pre-Maccabean.

Both Muilenburg and R. B. Y. Scott (who follows Muilenburg) interpret Isaiah 34 as an eschatological poem, of uncertain but late date. Serious questions are raised by them as to whether this oracle spoke of condemnation for historical Edom. Perhaps, they would suggest, condemnation is decreed here for the enemies of Judah, "all the nations" of verse 2, for which the name *Edom* is only a symbol.[36]

That there are mythological elements in abundance in this poem is obvious, and that it belongs in the general classification of eschatological literature is not argued. The form of the poem itself suggests that doom to the nations is the theme and that the mention of Edom in verses 5 and 6 is a device of parallelism: Edom is representative of the nations. How, then, does this relate to Damn-Edom theology? The author wrote at a time when the Damn-Edom oracles were an accepted part of Jewish literature. He wrote an eschatological poem about the catastrophic end of the nations in the Day of Yahweh, and he used the figure of Edom and her destruction, so well known from Damn-Edom theology, to depict what was to happen on that day to the nations of the world.[37] The chapter is not Damn-Edom theology in a historical sense. Damn-Edom theology has taken on the garments of eschatological and, to a small degree, apocalyptic thought. The usage of Edom as a symbol for "the enemy" continues, being used in postbiblical Jewish writings as a designation for Rome, the current enemy.[38]

36. James Muilenburg, "The Literary Character of Isaiah 34," *JBL*, 59 (1940), 339–65; R. B. Y. Scott, "The Book of Isaiah: Introduction and Exegesis," *IB*, 5: 354–58.

37. C. C. Torrey, *The Second Isaiah, A New Interpretation* (Edinburgh: T. & T. Clark, 1928), pp. 122–24.

38. C. G. Montefiore and H. Loewe, *A Rabbinic Anthology* (Greenwich Editions, Meridian Books, n.d.), p. 562. Yigael Yadin, *The Scroll of the War of the Sons of Light Against the Sons of Darkness*, trans. by Batya and Chaim Rabin (Oxford: Oxford University Press, 1962), pp. 24, 25. For the Talmudic use of Edom as a designation for

The doom, destruction, and desolation which are ascribed to Edom in this magnificent poem show that, while there were new developments, Damn-Edom theology was not losing its intensity by the time of this writing. The description of the slaughter of the inhabitants is blood-curdling and vengeful in its picturesque expressions. The devastation and resultant emptiness of the land are portrayed in vivid striking pictures, for instance, "They shall name it 'No Kingdom There.' " Isaiah shows an interesting and significant development in Damn-Edom theology, dating probably from the end of the sixth century B.C. or a little later.

Isaiah 63:1-6 has much in common with chapter 34. In it Yahweh is pictured as coming from Edom,[39] where he has completed a mighty destruction and slaughter, with his garments red with blood-stains. This dramatic poem also belongs to Jewish eschatological literature. It depicts the judgment of Yahweh upon those who incur his wrath, i. e., the enemies of his people. Perhaps Edom here is thought of as the place of the eschatological judgment of Yahweh. This passage belongs to a later time but to the same general thought as does chapter 34.

The expression of Damn-Edom theology was not the exclusive property of the prophets. Psalm 137 gives one of the most repulsive expressions of condemnation of Edom found anywhere. The Psalm is obviously represented in verse 1 as exilic in date, and there is no good reason to remove it far from that time. It is either exilic or early postexilic. The Psalm belongs among the Imprecatory Psalms[40] or the Psalms of National Lament.[41] Mowinckel says that such a regularly repeated psalm of lamentation as this borders on the ordinary psalm of prayer.[42]

Rome see especially in the Babylonian Talmud: Sanhedrin, 12a, 94a, Pesahim, 87b. In many other places in the Talmud "Edom" is similarly used. *The Babylonian Talmud* edited by Isidore Epstein, 35 vols. (London: The Soncino Press, 1935-1952); see especially the index volume.

39. Attempts have been made to emend "Edom" and "Bozrah" to "red" and "vintager." These are conjectural and should be rejected. See James Muilenberg, "Isaiah: Introduction and Exegesis, Chs. 40–66," *IB*, 5:726.

40. Hardly the only one in the Psalter as claimed by William R. Taylor, "The Book of Psalms: Exegesis," *IB* 4: 638, 639. See A. R. Johnson, "The Psalms," in *The Old Testament and Modern Study* (Oxford: The Clarendon Press, 1951), p. 180. The Psalm is classed as *Mischungen* in Gunkel's analysis.

41. Sigmund Mowinckel, *The Psalms in Israel's Worship*, translated by D. R. Ap-Thomas, 2 vols. (New York: The Abingdon Press, 1962), 1: 221.

42. *Ibid.*

Strophe 1 (1–3) is a lament on conditions in the Exile. Strophe 2 (4–6) is a combination of a lament and curse called upon the writer if he should forget Jerusalem. Strophe 3 (7–9)[43] is a curse pronounced upon Edom for its glee in and encouragement of the destruction of Jerusalem (and upon Babylon, as the text stands, the destroyer of the city), as well as a call for vengeance: happy is the one who repays her foul deeds, such as by taking the Edomite or Babylonian children (sucklings) and smashing their heads against the rock. Mowinckel says that these last three verses show Psalm 137 to be also a cursing psalm, a prayer for Edom,

> whom the Jews hated with all their hearts—to be overtaken by all sorts of disasters. The prayer arises out of the background of the bitter memory of the fall of Jerusalem, when the Edomites seized the opportunity of settling in southern Judea. The prayer finally passes into a direct curse in particularly refined form, namely as a word of blessing on the person who shall inflict the most cruel revenge on Edom.[44]

This passage is accepted as referring to Edom rather than to Babylon. The reference of the final thought in the Psalm is to extermination, especially of the male offspring, thus wiping out the line forever.

There are other brief references to Edom in words of deprecation in the Psalter: 60:8, 9 (identical with 108:9, 10) and 83:6. These brief notices add nothing significant to the understanding of Damn-Edom theology except to witness to its ubiquitous presence in Judaic thought of the exilic and postexilic periods.

The broad concept of the peculiar position of Israel-Judah in the postexilic period: that Israel-Judah is to be blessed while the

---

43. Verse 8a is probably a later gloss. The omission of the verse will leave three pentrametric tetrastichs. The verse intrudes on the theme that condemns the offender, Edom. Charles Augustus Briggs and Emilie Grace Briggs, *A Critical and Exegetical Commentary on the Book of Psalms*, 2 vols., International Critical Commentary, eds. Driver, Briggs, and Plummer (Edinburgh: T. & T. Clark, 1906), 2: 485. Artur Weiser, *Psalms*, trans. Herbert Hartwell, The Old Testament Library (Philadelphia: The Westminster Press, 1962), p. 796, interprets the entire Psalm as "Damn-Babylon" thought. W. O. E. Oesterley, *The Psalms* (1939; London: S.P.C.K., 1953), pp. 547–48, accepts the presence of condemnation of both nations since both were involved in the 587 B.C. catastrophe. He interprets the babes dashed against the rock as referring to Babylonians, contending that here the author has reverted to his main theme.

44. Mowinckel, *Psalms*, 2: 52.

rest of the nations are doomed, is of the same theological pattern as is the damning of Edom. But the anti-Edom bias in Old Testament religion stands apart from the broad concept by virtue of its numerous expressions, its vehemence, and its particular emphasis upon one nation. Its presence, vehemence, and emphasis is found in most every type of Hebrew canonical literature, its absence in the wisdom literature being noticeable. This concept was primarily prophetic, at least in origin, but came to encompass Jewish life and thought to the extent that it became the ready expression for the enemy of God's people.

The presence of denunciations of Edom is evident from this rapid survey of oracular material. The question considered now is that of how to interpret this expression of hatred. Just as Old Testament theology is in general related to history; so Damn-Edom theology is rooted in history.

The existence of animosity in varying, but usually intense, degrees between Israel-Judah and Edom in the Old Testament is amply evident. About the only kind word spoken for the Edomites is concerning their admission into the "congregation of Yahweh" and may well be a late addition to the Old Testament text.[45] Traditionally there was hatred between Hebrew and Edomite, as reflected in the Old Testament text. The Jacob-Esau tradition in Genesis gives clear indication that from time immemorial there had been ill feelings between the people who became the Edomites and those who were the Hebrews. The refusal of the Edomites to give passage to the Hebrews on their way to Canaan from Egypt was, perhaps, instrumental in the development of this tradition. The conquest of Edom by David and its control and exploitation by Solomon and some of his successors was fuel for the fires of ill feeling already kindled. The see-saw struggle between Edomites and Judaeans in the period of the divided monarchies was the sort of situation that makes bitter enemies who take every opportunity to inflict damage and destruction each upon the other. The Edomites and Judaeans appear briefly as potential allies against a common enemy in the period between 597 B.C. and 587 B.C. But this anti-Babylonian alliance never materialized.

The exact role played by Edom in 587 B.C. is nowhere clearly

45. Deut. 23:8, 9.

evident. It seems indicated by available evidence that the Edomites were involved in the siege and destruction of Jerusalem. Whether they volunteered to aid Nebuchadrezzar or were drafted for this service is not known. The possibility must also be acknowledged that the Edomites may have simply stood by and taken no action to aid the Judaeans in their day of disaster. The Old Testament evidence is that, whether draftees or volunteers, these Edomites exceeded what the Judaeans considered the call of normal duty in their vindictiveness and cruelty in the action against Jerusalem. The suggestion is made (although it is not provable) that the Edomites volunteered for this duty as a result of a combination of circumstances.

Nebuchadrezzar knew that the Edomites had been involved in a plot with these Hebrews to revolt against his imperial control. Volunteering for service in this siege of Jerusalem would afford an excellent opportunity to convince Nebuchadrezzar of their loyalty to him and to gain his support, and they did not really care for these Hebrews, anyway. Perhaps the cause of the Edomite alliances, first with Judah and others, then with Nebuchadrezzar, was that Edom needed help. Pressure was already being felt at home from Arab tribes and perhaps, even at this time, from the precursors of the Nabataean invasions from the Hejaz.[46] That the Edomites did participate, and with a fury and a vindicative spirit, in the 587 B.C. destruction of Jerusalem is clearly evident from the biblical references; and it is to this event and to this participation that most of the Damn-Edom passages ultimately are to be related. Further animosity arose, no doubt, as a result of the Edomite settlement of the Negeb, as far north as Hebron, in the territory that the small postexilic Jewish community hoped and planned to control. The Edomites, now known as the Idumaeans, were probably in southern Palestine as early as the fifth century B.C., posing a threat to the small Jewish community.

Historical evidence makes it difficult to explain the intense hatred of the Jews for Edom unless the Edomites did actively participate in the destruction of the Temple in 587 B.C. Efforts to find another disaster caused by or participated in by Edom have

---

46. John Gray, *Archaeology and the Old Testament World* (London: Thomas Nelson and Sons, 1962), p. 102.

failed. The best evidence relating Edom to the 587 B.C. disaster is I Esdras 4:45: "Thou shalt also vow to build up the Temple, which the Edomites burned when Judaea was made desolate by the Chaldaeans." Verse 50 of the same chapter refers to Edomite occupancy of Jewish territory.

In view of existing evidence it is suggested that the prominence of Damn-Edom theology in early postexilic Judaism came historically as a result of two factors: 1) Edomite participation and cruelty in the destruction of Jerusalem; and 2) the Idumaean grasping of traditionally Jewish territory in the south. This Idumaean settlement of the south land was probably quite gradual and may have covered a long period of time. Exact dates are impossible to ascertain; the process began in the sixth century B.C. and continued for a century and a half or two centuries. It is possible that some Idumaeans were already in southern Palestine upon the return of the Jews from the captivity in Babylon. If there was open hostility between Jews and Idumaeans prior to the Maccabaean period it is not recorded. Friendly relations, however, were not likely.

The development of a Damn-Edom theology in the Jewish community after 587 B.C. was a part of their confrontation with the world in which they lived—characterized as a hostile world. Significantly related to this was their sense of "calling" to be Yahweh's chosen nation. The struggle for self understanding and expression in the postexilic world may be expressed best in terms of the struggle between the "nationalists" and the "universalists." An oversimplification (for such neat compartmentalization of life or thought is *almost always* in error) is: "Do we accomplish our purpose as Yahweh's chosen people by becoming an outgoing part of the world community, teaching them what we know of Yahweh?" or "Do we better fulfill our divinely appointed purpose by trying to be an island of isolated purity in a sea of sin and false religion?" The anti-Edom thought of the Old Testament was the product of the narrow nationalists who labelled the world about them as hostile to Yahweh and his purpose.

Damn-Edom theology is, as already set forth, both a part of a tendency of the Hebrews to hate and condemn their neighbors and a separate phenomenon. Moab, Ammon, Tyre, Philistia,

Egypt, and others are condemned in the Old Testament with some regularity; but none of these approaches the position of Edom in this respect. The literary attestation of the Old Testament is that Edom was the most hated of all Israel's neighbors and, indeed, became a symbol for the enemies of God's people.

It is impossible to set Damn-Edom theology in a pattern of ancient Near Eastern thought. There are insufficient materials upon which to base conclusions that xenophobia was common to other countries of the ancient Near East. Perhaps the nearest parallel to the attitude of Israel toward Edom is found in the Egyptian attitudes toward the Nubians and the Asiatics.[47] These groups were condemned with regularity by the Egyptians. Probably similar attitudes existed at times in the thought and literary expressions of other nations, but such is not probable at the present time. Such literary expressions, especially in their intensity and frequency, were peculiar to Israel-Judah in the ancient Near East, especially in the thought behind them. The hatred of the Egyptians for the Nubians and the Asiatics stemmed from the fact that these two groups presented more or less constant threats to the autonomy of Egypt, to her peaceful and prosperous existence, and to her imperial designs. Israel considered herself a distinctively different nation. More so than nations about her she considered herself called by the one Universal World God as his peculiar people. In the context of the Abrahamic and Mosaic covenants, Israel understood herself to be a special people, enjoying a special relationship with Yahweh. Other nations who did not understand these matters, particularly those who interfered with her attempts to fulfill her divinely appointed purpose, were to be condemned. H. H. Rowley[48] convincingly contends that Israel's view of her election was vastly different from the attitudes of ancient Near Eastern kings who considered themselves the chosen ones of the

47. Pritchard, *ANET*, pp. 230, 238, 374, 445. E. A. Wallis Budge, *A History of Ethiopia, Nubia, and Abyssinia*, 2 vols. (London: Methuen and Company, 1928), 1: 23, 24, says of the kings of the 19th dynasty (1321–1215): "In the bas-reliefs painted and sculptured during the reigns, these kings are represented as slaying the 'chiefs of the abominable Kesh [Nubia],' but this every king, from the time of the 1st Dynasty downwards, was supposed to do, and such representations formed part of the stock-scenes which every court painter and sculptor was expected to use."

48. H. H. Rowley, *The Biblical Doctrine of Election* (London: Lutterworth Press, 1950), esp. pp. 16–19.

gods. It is granted that at many times the Israelites did not correctly interpret their election as an election to service rather than to privilege, but they were constantly aware that they were the Chosen People.

A compartmentalization of elements in Old Testament thought will not provide the solutions needed for an understanding of Damn-Edom theology. Such an approach has been expressed by Rolland Emerson Wolfe in "The Editing of the Book of the Twelve." In Wolfe's interpretation of the Minor Prophets there were some thirteen editors or redactors who left their particular imprint on this collection. He has determined that the "Anti-Neighbor Editor" was the fifth of the thirteen. This editor's work came in the early part of the fifth century B.C. when the returned exiles attempted to regain Palestine, found harassment at the hands of their neighbors, and resultantly had their jubilant hopes frustrated. Wolfe says:

> Some fiery hearted Jew, who felt impelled to give literary expression to this new movement of thought, set himself to the task of composing oracles, which for the most part may be called massas (משא), against Judah's hated neighbors. While, in the absence of more definite information, it may be assumed that Amos, in the authentic portions of chapters 1 and 2, originated that type of prophecy, it was this Anti-Neighbor Editor who made most use of the massa style of writing and popularized it. While his writings are also found in Jeremiah and Ezekiel, the major deposit is found in parts of chapters 13–24 of Isaiah.[49]

Wolfe further points out that this editor was particularly bitter against Edom and the inhabitants of the Mediterranean coast.

It must be granted that the anti-Edom bias in Old Testament religion is an aspect of the more general antiforeign nation feeling of postexilic Judaism, but it is obvious that the anti-Edom element was, or at least became, more than simply a part of the general attitude. The wide distribution of antiforeign oracles and especially of anti-Edom oracles indicates that this attitude was held by more than some fiery-hearted Jewish editor or school of editors.

49. Rolland E. Wolfe, "The Editing of the Book of the Twelve," *Zeitschrift für die attestamentliche Wissenschaft*, 12, n.s. (1935), 90–129, esp. 96.

That there was within postexilic Judaism both universalistic and particularistic thought, tendencies, and perhaps even parties has long been obvious to interpreters of the Old Testament. The dating of these tendencies, or movements, is very difficult, if not impossible, in the light of present knowledge of postexilic Old Testament history. It is probable that in the exilic and early postexilic periods the destruction of Edom was a part of the hope of restoration. The destruction of Edom was considered a necessity: the Edomites occupied part of their land. It is fairly obvious that both universalism and particularism existed concurrently, with first one and then the other surging to the fore. Judging from the literature of the period, the narrow, particularistic or nationalistic school of thought was the predominant one; and it was this type of thought that fathered Damn-Edom theology. The complete separation of the two types of thought may be impossible, for, as expressed in the Old Testament, universalism is the reverse of the coin of which nationalism is the obverse. "Hope of judgment upon the pagan world and of vengeance on Israel's enemies is only one side of the attitude of the post-Exilic prophets towards foreign nations. The other is the possibility of their conversion to Yahweh, the God of Israel,"[50] The books of Ruth and Jonah, as well as Isaiah 40–55, with their kinder attitudes towards foreign nations were products of this universalist element in Judaism. It is, perhaps, significant that Edom is not condemned, nor even mentioned in these books.

That the anti-Edom bias in Old Testament religion was a part of this ambivalent postexilic thought cannot be denied. The ready and frequent condemnation of Edom went beyond this, however, and became more than the expression of hatred for Edom. The Edomites had exhibited the ultimate, or near-ultimate, in inimical action against the Jews. They, and their nation, became the exemplification of a nation and a people opposed to the Jews and their nationalistic desires and endeavors as well as what they interpreted to be their divinely appointed mission. Thus *Edom* came to equal the enemy of the Jews. Probably first (although such development cannot be traced with exactness) *Edom* was used as an expression for the neighboring opponents of the Jewish

50. J. Lindblom, *Prophecy in Ancient Israel* (Oxford: Basil Blackwell, 1962), p. 417.

state and later became a symbol for "the enemy," and so was
used for Rome in postbiblical Jewish literature.

For these doubtless sincere and devout religious leaders and
writers of the postexilic period, Edom became the classic example
of the enemy of God's people. Probably there is a complex background to this thought: a very ancient tradition and history of
hostility, the culmination of this hostility in the despicable behavior of the Edomites in the day of Jerusalem's fall and destruction, and the encroachment of Edom into traditional Jewish
territory. To the historical background must be added the postexilic theological struggles concerning how best to express their
role as a chosen nation in a hostile world. Edom becomes the
type of the hostile nation and symbolizes the hostile world. This
designation of "the enemy" remains in the transition from prophetic to apocalyptic literature and with rich historical overtones
graphically expresses to the discerning student of Old Testament
thought the abundant hatred of whoever might be, at any moment
of history, the accursed "Edomites."

H. WHEELER ROBINSON AND THE PROBLEM OF ORGANIZING AN OLD TESTAMENT THEOLOGY

MAX E. POLLEY

Old Testament theology is an historical discipline which arose from the need to show the relationship between history and revelation in the religion of Israel. Before the rise of historical criticism there was no biblical theology; the use of the Bible in precritical times was as a "proof-text" for orthodox doctrines. The study of biblical content was a part of the discipline called systematic theology rather than one aspect of biblical studies as it is today. The material of the Bible was therefore arranged under the headings that best suited the needs of the systematic theologian: God, man, and redemption. The Bible was seldom allowed to speak for itself; the theologian simply listened to the echo of his own voice.[1]

With the rise of biblical criticism that was dedicated to a study of literary and historical problems of the Bible, there arose also the desire to study the religious thought of the Old Testament independent of dogmatic interests. The actual beginning of biblical theology is attributed to John Philipp Gabler in a lecture published in 1787 entitled "Oratio de iusto discrimine theologiae biblicae et dogmaticae regundisque recte utruisque finisbus."[2] In this lecture

I wish to express my gratitude to Dr. William F. Stinespring for his continuous guidance in helping me analyze the contributions of H. Wheeler Robinson to Old Testament studies. My initial contact with Robinson's thought was in Dr. Stinespring's course in prophecy at the Duke Divinity School in 1953. My dissertation entitled "The Contribution of H. Wheeler Robinson to the Contemporary Rebirth of Old Testament Theology" (Duke University, 1957) was directed by him and with his aid and encouragement I have had two occasions (summer of 1959 and the academic year of 1964–65) to examine the private notes of Robinson while studying at Regent's Park College, Oxford University.

1. Robert C. Dentan, "The History, Nature and Method of Old Testament Theology" (Ph.D. diss., Yale University, 1946), pp. 6–7. A condensed form of this dissertation was published in a monograph entitled *Preface to Old Testament Theology* (New Haven: Yale University Press, 1950). In 1963 a revised edition of this monograph was published in book form by The Seabury Press.
2. See C. T. Craig, "Biblical Theology and the Rise of Historicism," *JBL*, 62 (Dec., 1943), 281; Norman W. Porteous, "Old Testament Theology," *The Old Testament and Modern Study: A Generation of Discovery and Research*, ed. H. H. Rowley (Oxford:

Gabler made a distinction between dogmatic theology and biblical
theology. Biblical theology, he maintained, is simply the religion
of the Bible as held by its authors and as presented in their writings,
while dogmatic theology proceeds to formulate the religion of the
Bible in terms of Western philosophical concepts and ideas. Dogmatic theology always reflects the character and time of the theologian, while biblical theology reflects the ideas and age of the
biblical personages themselves. Because biblical theology is concerned with what the sacred writers thought about divine matters,
it is, necessarily, a historical discipline. If the thought of the biblical
writer is to be understood, the historical environment of the writer
must be carefully examined. The biblical theologian, therefore,
must take three steps in the study of the biblical material: first, he
must interpret each passage grammatically and historically; second,
he must compare each passage with other biblical passages; third,
with the use of the material he now possesses, he will formulate an
Old Testament theology based upon certain recurring themes in
the biblical passages.[3]

Gabler's analysis is astute. At the birth of a new discipline, he
had focused the attention of scholars upon the major issue in
writing an Old Testament theology, i. e., how to relate history
and theology. Every biblical scholar who undertakes the task of
writing an Old Testament theology must decide what organization
of the material best relates theology and history. It is not surprising that throughout the history of the discipline there have
been two basic ways of organizing the material: systematically
(theology providing the categories of organization) and chronologically (the history of Israel being the basis of organization).

The vast majority of scholars have chosen to arrange the material
topically, arguing that a theology requires systematic schematiza-
tion. In most cases the organization was borrowed from systematic
theology, the three most popular topics being theology, anthropology, and soteriology.[4] Other scholars selected one basic theme

---

At the Clarendon Press, 1956), p. 312; Emil G. Kraeling, *The Old Testament Since the
Reformation* (London: Lutterworth Press, 1955), p. 56.

3. See Dentan, *Preface to Old Testament Theology*, pp. 7–8.

4. Cf. J. C. F. Steudel's *Vorlesungen über die Theologie des alten Testamentes* (1840)
uses the themes God, man, and salvation; Heinrich Ewald's *Die Lehre der Bibel von
Gott oder Theologie des alten und neuen Bundes* (1871–1876), is a four-volume work organ-

and attempted, through this theme, to give unity to the entire Old Testament.[5] This latter group of scholars has defended this approach on the ground that the unifying principle they adopted was based not upon the categories of systematic theology but upon the biblical material itself.

Because Old Testament religion is an historical religion, another smaller group of scholars used history as the only basis of organization. The history of Israel is seen as *Heilsgeschichte*; Old Testament theology consists of a confessional recital of this history.[6] Von Rad states the case for the confessional approach to an historical revelation most forcefully when he writes:

A theology which attempts to grasp the content of the Old Testament under the heading of various doctrines (the doctrine of God, the doctrine of man, etc.) cannot do justice to these credal statements which are completely tied up with history, or to this grounding of Israel's faith upon a few divine acts of salvation and the effort to gain an ever new understanding of them.[7]

But in fact, both methods of organization have produced results that show that they are of value. The value of the systematic

---

ized around the themes: doctrine of the Word of God, doctrine of God and the universe, and doctrine of the life of man and the kingdom of God; A. B. Davidson's *The Theology of the Old Testament* (1904) is systematized around the headings God, man and salvation; Ernst Sellin's *Alttestamentliche Theologie auf religionsgeschichtlicher Grundlage*, vol. 2 (1933) uses the dogmatic categories of God, man, judgment and salvation; Paul Heinisch's *Theologie des Alten Testamentes* (1940) is arranged into the divisions God, creation, the conduct of life, the world beyond and salvation; Theodorus Christian Vriezen's *Hoofdlijnen der Theologie van het Oude Testament* (1949) adopts the themes God, man, intercourse between God and man, intercourse between man and man (ethics), and God, man, and the world in the present and the future. English trans. by S. Neuijen, *An Outline of Old Testament Theology* (Oxford: Basil Blackwell, 1960).

5. Cf. G. F. Oehler's *Prolegomena zur Theologie des alten Testaments* (1845) has its emphasis upon the Spirit of Christ; Hermann Schultz's *Alttestamentliche Theologie* (1869–1896) finds the unity of the Old Testament in the doctrine of the Kingdom of God on earth; the covenant concept is central in Walter Eichrodt's *Theologie des Alten Testaments* (1933–1939); in Ludwig Köhler's *Theologie des Alten Testaments* (1936) the unifying theme is God as Lord and man as servant. English trans. by A. S. Todd, *Old Testament Theology* (Philadelphia: The Westminster Press, 1957).

6. Cf. J. C. K. von Hofmann's *Weissagung und Erfüllung im alten und im neuen Testamente* (1841); Eduard Riehm's *Alttestamentliche Theologie* (1889); Gerhard von Rad's *Theologie des Alten Testaments* (1957–1960); G. Ernest Wright's *God Who Acts: Biblical Theology as Recital* (London: SCM Press, 1952).

7. Gerhard von Rad, *Old Testament Theology*, trans. D. M. G. Stalker (Edinburgh: Oliver and Boyd, 1962), vol. 1: *The Theology of Israel's Historical Traditions*, p. vi.

approach is that it is able to free itself from the rigidly developmental method of the *Religionsgeschichtlicheschule*, enabling the Old Testament scholar to find mature religious conceptions in what was formerly regarded as primitive material. Furthermore, this approach also makes readily available to the systematic theologian the wealth of the biblical material in terms that he can understand and appreciate. The great weakness of such a topical arrangement is its artificiality, since the Old Testament, being a record of historical revelation, is not easily organized around doctrinal categories. On the other hand, this full awareness of the nature of historical revelation is the great virtue of the *Heilsgeschichte* method of exposition. The question is whether it can justifiably be called an Old Testament theology if: (1) it lacks topical arrangement and (2) it fails to include in its organization all the biblical material (e. g., the wisdom literature is difficult to include under this principle of organization). This approach also suffers because it is extremely difficult for the nonbiblical scholar to comprehend the position being expounded.

H. Wheeler Robinson[8] throughout his scholarly career was concerned with the problem of the relationship between history and theology in organizing an Old Testament theology. The direction in which his thought was moving near the close of his life was an outgrowth from his intensive study of the nature of revelation. An analysis of Robinson's struggle with this problem and the extreme difficulty he had arriving at an acceptable solution will help direct us to the basic issues involved.

Early in his career Robinson raised objections to a systematic organization of the Old Testament. In discussing the nature of sin in *The Christian Doctrine of Man*, he avoided such categories as "universality of sin," "inborn sinfulness," and "origin of sin," "not only because of the undogmatic character of the Old Testament in general, but because incidental discussion of these points would have blurred the historical perspective of the development."[9] In discussing the nature of man in the New Testament, he wrote:

8. H. Wheeler Robinson (1872–1945) was a Baptist Old Testament scholar and principal of Regent's Park College, Oxford University. He is most noted for his work on prophetic symbolism and corporate personality.
9. H. Wheeler Robinson, *The Christian Doctrine of Man* (Edinburgh: T. & T. Clark, 1911), p. 56.

In the New Testament we do not find dogmatic discussions of human nature and its problems, any more than in the Old; nor ought we to expect the unity and consistency rightly demanded of a formal system. What we do find is a new centre, around which the ideas of the Old Testament, as modified by the later Judaism, can arrange themselves in all their fluidity, the time of dogmatic crystalization not yet having come. This new centre is the personality of Jesus, around whom all the problems of God and man ultimately gather.[10]

In biblical studies he called for freedom from the systematic collecting and combining of the biblical content in favor of the historical approach.[11] It is only after a study of the history itself that any religious ideas will emerge.

According to Rabbinic legend, Moses saw from Pisgah not only Israel's future land, but also Israel's future history, unrolled in swift panorama before his eyes. Some such outline of events is necessary for us, in order that the characteristic features of the history may appear. The most remarkable of them all is the issue from that history of the religious ideas which will claim our attention.[12]

Thus, sin and suffering in Hebrew thought are not abstract problems upon which one speculates; they are part of the living and dynamic experience of the people.[13] The use of abstract thinking and organization is foreign to the Hebrew people, for they always think and write in concrete and picturesque terms. "Fortunately, for us, they could not discuss sociological or historical or religious problems with our own wealth—or poverty—of long words; to utter a general truth at all, they had to use the particular image."[14] The Bible is therefore not a system of doctrine but a divine drama acted out upon the arena of history.

To write an Old Testament theology one must be fully aware of historical development in Israel's religion. To abstract the ideas

10. *Ibid.*, p. 75.
11. H. Wheeler Robinson, *The Religious Ideas of the Old Testament* (London: Gerald Duckworth & Co., 1952), p. 3.
12. *Ibid.*, p. 6.
13. *Ibid.*, p. 178.
14. H. Wheeler Robinson, "The Cross of the Servant," *The Cross in the Old Testament* (London: SCM Press, 1955), p. 71.

from their historical setting is to make them lifeless. "It cannot too often be asserted that the revelation of Israel's living God is in the dynamic movement of history; from the beginning and throughout most of the course of that history the written record held a quite subsidiary place."[15] History is the primary medium through which revelation comes and therefore must be an essential part of any Old Testament theology. It is revelation that makes history meaningful; it is history that makes revelation actual.

It is probable, judging from Robinson's writings, that had he written an Old Testament theology it would have been historically oriented. In 1913 his *Religious Ideas of the Old Testament* was published. In the first chapter Robinson consciously accepted the historical approach. He looked to history as the source of the basic ideas of the Old Testament. "For it is a history progressively creative of the great ideas which are the foundation of the Christian faith."[16] Again, in the last chapter, in a discussion of "The Permanent Value of the Old Testament," he reemphasized history as divine revelation. "The Old Testament, interpreted in the light it throws on its own origin, testifies to the reality of a divine revelation in the *life* of Israel. God was revealed not simply in words, but in a series of acts extending over a thousand years."[17] It was when Robinson pressed through this history to the ideas which it creates that the difficulty arose. He found four basic ideas emerging: the idea of God, the idea of man, the idea of suffering, and the idea of the kingdom. Each of these concepts was examined through its historical development. But because he chose to organize the material around these central concepts, he was not able to present the history as a true development. There are historical units interspersed throughout the book, but no sense of the dynamic movement of the history. Furthermore, the selection of these four ideas comes dangerously close to the organization he desired to avoid: theology, anthropology, and soteriology. What Robinson had done was to take the results of historical study and to arrange them systematically. Something much more than this was needed. That he had not actually united history and theology is apparent when,

15. H. Wheeler Robinson, *The Old Testament: Its Making and Meaning* (London: University of London Press, 1953), p. 19.

16. H. Wheeler Robinson, *Religious Ideas of the Old Testament*, p. 24.

17. *Ibid.*, p. 217.

in dealing with the idea of God, he mentioned the Exodus event only in passing.[18] But this event, as he argued in subsequent works, is primary in revealing the nature of God in the history of Israel. Nor was Robinson able to cover all the biblical material in this way; the wisdom literature was scarcely mentioned.[19]

In 1932 Robinson's short essay entitled "The Religious Ideas of the Old Testament" was published in *The Teachers' Commentary*, and he used virtually the same organization as he had in his earlier work by the same title: God, man, sin, suffering, and death. In understanding the nature of God, Robinson referred once again to the history of Israel:

> God is to be loved because he has shown himself to be so lovable. The great redeeming act to which prophets and psalmists point (as do the apostles and evangelists to the cross of Christ) is the deliverance of Israel from Egypt. This began (for the nation) the series of saving deeds which are the essence of Israel's religious history. The God of Israel is a living God; he does things, and he is known by what he does. Prophecy, on its higher levels, is the interpretation of Israel's history as controlled by God.[20]

Robinson also included a section on the mediation of revelation through prophet, priest, and book, which eventually resulted in a separate work, *Inspiration and Revelation in the Old Testament*. But this essay, like the earlier writing, lacked the real dynamic of history so vital to an Old Testament theology. History was acknowledged as important, but it was never actually united with theology.

By 1937, however, it would appear that Robinson's position as to the relation between history and theology in the organization of an Old Testament theology was beginning to take shape. In the concluding paragraph of an article, after surveying the best books on the Old Testament, he commented that there was no contem-

18. *Ibid.*, p. 107. The Exodus is also discussed in the section on history and the covenant.

19. *Ibid.*, p. 43. It should be noted, however, that Robinson did not intend this small book to be a complete Old Testament theology. The reason it is mentioned here is to analyze his earliest attempt to unite history and theology.

20. H. Wheeler Robinson, "The Theology of the Old Testament," *The Teachers' Commentary*, ed. G. Henton Davies and Alan Richardson (London: SCM Press, 1955), p. 93.

porary English book that could be called a competent Old Testament theology. As to the nature of such a book, he wrote:

> Such a book would be concerned with the history of the religion only so far as was necessary to bring out its true nature and permanent values. It would show the religion of Israel as the matrix of both Judaism and Christianity, but would distinguish it from both. It would penetrate beneath the naturally propagandist exegesis of the O. T. in the N. T., and those beliefs of the contemporary Judaism which have helped to shape the present form of the O. T. itself, such as the priority and extent of the Law given on Sinai. The enlightened Christian student would not need to fear the results of such an impartial study of the theology of the O. T., for it would surely reveal a spiritual continuity which is the true modern form of the old and now discredited 'argument from prophecy.'[21]

It is obvious that Robinson regarded the history of the religion of Israel of importance for the writing of an Old Testament theology. Yet just how important history is to be the words "only as far as was necessary" do not reveal. It is obvious, however, that he believed an Old Testament theology must penetrate through the history to the true nature of the religion. What form this theology would eventually take he did not make clear.

The following year Robinson stated his views on a theology of the Old Testament in two essays in *Record and Revelation*. It is significant that in the first essay he dealt with "The Philosophy of Revelation," which he believed formed a necessary introduction to an Old Testament theology. Here, through the category of revelation, was presented for the first time in Robinson's thought a synthesis of the historical approach with theological interpretation. Some years earlier, Otto Eissfeldt in an article entitled "Israelitisch-jüdische Religionsgeschichte und alttestamentliche Theologie," had registered his alarm at the increasing desire to unite theological and historical studies.[22] He believed that both disci-

---

21. H. Wheeler Robinson, "The Best Books on the Old Testament," *The Expository Times*, 48 (Jan., 1937), 154.

22. Otto Eissfeldt, "Israelitisch-jüdische Religionsgeschichte und alttestamentliche Theologie," *Zeitschrift für die alttestamentliche Wissenschaft*, n.s., 3 (1926), 1–12.

plines were necessary, but they were not to be confused by blending them. There should continue to be histories of the religion of Israel in which all scholars could objectively participate, but at the same time, there should be Old Testament theologies written by the confessional group with religious faith as a special instrument by which divine revelation could be comprehended. For Eissfeldt the contrast between faith and reason was to be carried over into a contrast between theology and history. A history of religion, approached by the faculty of knowledge which deals with the world of space and time, is not concerned with revelation; an Old Testament theology, approached through faith which deals with eternal truths, is not concerned with history. Robinson saw this as a false dichotomy and insisted that the uniqueness of Israel's religion rests upon the paradoxical fact that it is an "historical revelation." "The Philosophy of revelation is, for the Hebrews, primarily the philosophy of history."[23] Such a concept of revelation is not, however, without its difficulties.

> We can gather them [the difficulties] up by saying that the very phrase 'a historical revelation' is a paradox, according to conventional ideas of revelation. History implies dynamic movement of some kind, whether or not it can be called progress; revelation implies static and permanent truth. How can absolute truth be relative to each of a series of generations? How can human transiency serve divine eternity? How can free human activity be made to serve fixed divine purpose? All such questions are different forms of the perennial problem of the philosophy of history, viz., the relation of time and eternity, of which perhaps, the only solution is a *solvitur vivendo*.[24]

The solution to the intellectual paradox of the relationship of timeless revelation to changing history is found in the "actuality of living" where revelation and history form a blended unity. If revelation is historical, there was a time when revelation and history were united. What is called for is a reliving of the initial experience. Robinson believed that the proper approach to the

23. H. Wheeler Robinson, "The Theology of the Old Testament," *Record and Revelation: Essays on the Old Testament by Members of the Society of Old Testament Study*, ed. H. Wheeler Robinson (Oxford: At the Clarendon Press, 1938), p. 304.
24. *Ibid.*, p. 305.

Old Testament was to interpret it from within, being sensitive to its claim to be God's Word to man. He believed that this "subjective" approach can be realized best through a study of revelation as it occurs in the biblical material, taking seriously its claim to be God's encounter with man. It was partly with this in mind that he wrote *Inspiration and Revelation in the Old Testament*. While the major purpose of this volume was to provide an understanding of the form that revelation takes in the Old Testament, nevertheless a secondary purpose mentioned in the closing paragraphs of the book was to enable the reader to approach the biblical material from within. "Let us constantly remind ourselves that this religion, like any other, can be understood only from within, or through a sympathy that makes us its 'resident aliens' (*gerim*)."[25] Only by sharing the faith of biblical writers can one hope to unite again eternal revelation and temporal history.

Robinson proceeded to ground the possibility of revelation in the belief in an active God who takes the initiative in disclosing himself to man and in the kinship between God and man which makes such revelation possible. This led him to examine the variety of the media of revelation found in the Old Testament with special emphasis upon the prophetic consciousness through which history is interpreted as revelatory. Robinson concluded this first essay with a discussion of revelation as mediated through legal ordinances (the priestly material) and moral teachings (the wisdom literature). The central emphasis throughout the essay was upon God's activity and man's response, a union of the human and the divine.

Building upon this foundation of an analysis of historical revelation, Robinson proceeded in his second essay to discuss certain characteristic doctrines of the Old Testament under the four categories of God, man, sin and grace, and the judgment of history. Robinson apparently believed that an Old Testament theology necessitated the organization of the material topically, yet he continued to be acutely aware of the fact that revelation comes to Israel through history. In his discussion of the doctrine of God, for example, he does not present a lifeless analysis of the attributes of God, but rather allows the concept of God to emerge from the history through which it developed:

25. H. Wheeler Robinson, *Inspiration and Revelation in the Old Testament*, ed. L. H. Brockington and Ernest A. Payne (Oxford: At the Clarendon Press, 1953), pp. 281–82.

God, as we have seen, is taken for granted in the Old Testament, though this is far from meaning that the conception of Him is a fixed quantity. The *growth* of the idea, bound up as it is with the history of the people, is a most significant feature of the revelation. But when we try to systematize the idea, this feature of it renders our task very difficult. At the beginning we see the emergence of Yahweh of Israel, as one god among other gods (for other peoples). He is localized at Sinai as a storm-god, and accompanies His people as a war-god in their desert-wanderings, whilst already He is concerned with the social life of His people. His jealousy (Exod. xx.5, xxxiv.14) is aroused only by the invasion of Israel's loyalty by other gods. At the end the God of the Psalmists is the only God of all the earth, all other gods being reduced to shadow-names, or absorbed into His angelic court, whilst the highest moral and spiritual attributes are now assigned to Him. It is the result of this development which chiefly concerns us, though we must remember throughout that any attempt to fix it in static form contradicts the essentially dynamic character of the God of Israel.[26]

In the analysis of the various names of God which follows, Robinson was careful to point out the periods when these names were used and the significance of their development. This was also true of his discussion of God as "holy," "righteous," and "gracious," where these divine attributes are seen through the encounter between God and his people. "It will be seen that the divine righteousness is not abstract quality; it is the essence of His personal character as seen in the concrete experience of life under His control."[27] Robinson concluded his analysis of the doctrine of God with a discussion of the relation of God to Israel and the world, where his examination of election, the covenant, and miracles lent themselves naturally to a blending of theology and history.

While the doctrine of man is not so easily tied to historical development, still Robinson's discussion of both corporate personality and the future life was based upon the emergence of these concepts within the history of Israel. This emphasis upon

26. H. Wheeler Robinson, "The Theology of the Old Testament," p. 321.
27. *Ibid.*, p. 325.

historical development is even more obvious in the section on sin and grace, for after a brief discussion of the etymology of certain key Hebrew words, Robinson proceeded to trace the growth of the ideas of sin and grace from their primitive origins, through the period of prophetic moralization, to their postexilic interpretation by the cult.

It is significant that Robinson concluded this discussion of the characteristic doctrines of an Old Testament theology with a unit on "The Judgement of History." Here the intimate relationship between theology and history is disclosed in Israel's appeal to history for the vindication of her faith in a just and gracious God. The introductory paragraph to this section is worth quoting in full.

> Emphasis on the fact and interrelation of sin and grace is, second only to monotheism, the outstanding theological contribution of Israel's religion. But this contribution is not made in the abstract terms of doctrine; it is evolved within the framework of a changing history, and it is largely derived from the interpretation of that history, in its social or individual features. Israel appealed unto history, and to this Caesar she had to go for the fuller vindication of her faith. It is always needful to remember that derivation of a doctrine from historical experience implies confidence that the judgement given by history will be the last and vindicating word. We can too easily forget that the familiar words of the religion of the Old Testament are the analysis or interpretation of an experience, by which they ultimately stand or fall. If we feel, on the one hand, the ceaseless marvel of this appeal to history by a politically insignificant people, often made in their periods of lowest depression, we must also recognize that, for such a faith as theirs, the world's history must at last be the world's judgement.[28]

While the Hebrew is painfully aware that in the course of history God uses the nations of the world to punish his rebellious people, he also has an indestructible faith that ultimately God will redeem Israel. Robinson found that historical revelation reaches its culmination in the expectations of the apocalyptists "based on the super-

28. *Ibid.*, pp. 341–42.

natural intervention of God in human history, as a necessary intervention to bring it to its goal, since man had failed, even from the beginning, to actualize the divine purpose."[29]

James Smart raises questions about this essay on the grounds that it is a "presentation in systematic form of the same materials which formerly were set in a historical continuity. It does not seem to be realized that the problem is much too complex for such a simple solution and that Old Testament theology must achieve something far beyond a mere rearrangement of the materials."[30] It is obvious that Robinson's two brief essays do not go far enough in presenting an Old Testament theology, a fact which he would have been the first to acknowledge; still what is presented is far more than a simple rearrangement of the materials. Robinson attempted in both essays to show the relationship between history and revelation; in the first essay the nature of historical revelation is analyzed, while in the second essay certain basic concepts that emerge from within this redemptive history are discussed. It was Robinson's mature position that only by such a synthesis could an Old Testament theology which is both fully historical and fully theological be written.

What Robinson presented in this short essay in *Record and Revelation* he was later to develop into the Speaker's Lectures of 1942–1945. To this work he devoted his last energy, and his death in 1945 occurred before the lectures could be published. Owing to the interest of two colleagues, the Reverend L. A. Brockington and the Reverend E. A. Payne, the work appeared posthumously under the title *Inspiration and Revelation in the Old Testament* as the first volume of an Old Testament theology. According to the editorial note, the volume "would have constituted the prolegomena, setting out in detail the *form* of the revelation whose *content* would have supplied the material for the theology."[31] The main thesis of this volume is that the form which revelation takes in Israel's religion is determined by two factors, viz., the media through which God acts and the interpretative response of those who receive this revelation. Without an understanding of this two-fold

29. *Ibid.*, p. 346.
30. James Smart, "The Death and Rebirth of Old Testament Theology," *The Journal of Religion*, 23 (Apr., 1943), 133.
31. H. Wheeler Robinson, *Inspiration and Revelation*, editorial note.

aspect of revelation, with all its diversity, the Old Testament will remain a mystery to the reader. The book consists of seven parts. The first three parts deal with the media through which revelation takes place, nature, man, and history. But in each case, revelation is not possible until there is a response on the part of man. "The divine revelation in Nature, Man, and History is through *acts*, which need to be interpreted through human agency to make them *words* in our ordinary sense."[32] The last four parts deal with man's response to God's activity as seen in the faith of prophet, priest, sage, and psalmist. Revelation is found in the union of God's activity and man's response. Here theology and history are brought into a dynamic relationship; it is in the encounter between God and man that God reveals himself in the totality of life as man interprets the experiences of life as revelatory. A final chapter was to have been written on the growth of the canon and the nature of its authority, but death prevented its completion. It would appear, as Norman W. Porteous pointed out,[33] that this organization of an Old Testament theology was anticipated by A. B. Davidson in his *Theology of the Old Testament*. With respect to the division of an Old Testament theology, Davidson wrote:

> In point of fact, the threefold theological division—Theology, or doctrine of God; Anthropology, or doctrine of man; and Soteriology, or doctrine of salvation— is somewhat too abstract for a subject like ours. What we meet with in the Old Testament are two concrete subjects and their relation. The two are: Jehovah, God of Israel, on the one hand, and Israel, the people of Jehovah, on the other; and the third point, which is given in the other two, is their relation to one another. And it is obvious that the dominating or creative factor in the relation is Jehovah.[34]

Davidson then proceeded to discuss four avenues by which revelation is mediated to Israel, through prophets, priests, psalmists, and wisdom writers. However, Davidson did not follow these divisions

32. *Ibid.*, p. 159.
33. Norman W. Porteous, "Old Testament Theology," *The Old Testament and Modern Study*, pp. 315–16, 336.
34. A. B. Davidson, *The Theology of the Old Testament*, ed. from the author's manuscripts by Seward D. F. Salmond (Edinburgh: T. & T. Clark, 1904), pp. 12–15.

in writing his Old Testament theology but rather returned to the use of the traditional threefold categories of God, man, and salvation.[35] It was by Robinson that this division of the material was fully developed.

Robinson had presented in considerable detail the *form* revelation takes in Israel's history, that is God's acts and man's response. Certainly in this first volume of what was to be his Old Testament theology, he had successfully united history and theology. At every point in his analysis he was forced back to history itself as it was interpreted by the man of faith. It is in the last two paragraphs of this volume that Robinson suggested the way he would organize the second volume of his Old Testament theology which would constitute the *content* of the revelation.

As for the content of the revelation (in distinction from its form), it is inevitable that we should state this in a series of propositions to constitute a 'Theology of the Old Testament', even if they are arranged in historical order, and called a 'History of the Religion of Israel'. If they are stated topically, and not chronologically, as a 'theology' requires, they become still more abstract and remote from the once-living, vibrating, and dynamic religion of Israel. Let us constantly remind ourselves that this religion, like any other, can be understood only from within, or through a sympathy that makes us its 'resident aliens' (*gerim*).

Such a theology naturally requires a volume to itself. It will have to be rewritten in each generation, for each has different needs and each will interpret the past in its own characteristic way. But it will have its inevitable poles around which all else turns. Over against each other are God and man, and all that lies between can be conceived as belonging

35. A. B. Davidson's *The Theology of the Old Testament* is a collection of his papers posthumously edited by Seward D. F. Salmond. It would seem that had Davidson written the book himself he would have written an Old Testament theology along the lines of a history of Israel's religion, in which case the emphasis would have been upon historical development rather than theological categories. On page 11 he wrote: "We do not find a *theology* in the Old Testament; we find a *religion*—religious conceptions and religious hopes and aspirations. It is we ourselves that create the theology when we give to these religious ideas and convictions a systematic or orderly form. Hence our subject really is the History of the Religion of Israel as presented in the Old Testament."

to the Kingdom—the active kingly rule—of God. The Jew will find the beginning of that Kingdom in the increasing obedience of man to the divine Torah. The Christian sees it as already begun in the life, death, and resurrection of Jesus the Messiah. But both, in their different ways, depend on that religion of Israel which is neither Judaism nor Christianity but the mother of them both.[36]

It is unfortunate that these paragraphs are so difficult to interpret. C. R. North, in a presidential address delivered to the Society of Old Testament Study in 1949, confessed that he found that the concluding paragraphs of Robinson's last book lacked clarity.[37] He thought Robinson was calling for an Old Testament theology organized around a series of propositions arranged in historical order and called a history of the religion of Israel, but he could not conceive how this would be accomplished. He noted, however, that Robinson finally adopted the traditional topical method of organizing the material, but not without an awareness that by so doing he was running the risk of separating theology from the dynamic of history.

On the other hand, Norman W. Porteous, in a review of Robinson's book written in 1947, maintained that Robinson thought the content of an Old Testament theology should be stated in a series of propositions arranged topically.[38] However, in an article on Old Testament theology Porteous held that Robinson could not decide whether the content of an Old Testament theology should be arranged historically as a history of the religion of Israel or topically in the form of a series of propositions.[39]

It is clear that the paragraph under consideration is susceptible to variant interpretations. The present writer favors the view that Robinson conceived of organizing the content of an Old Testament theology around a series of propositions arranged topically. Such a position he fully realized is in danger of divorcing revelation and history, but he believed that none other than a topical ap-

36. H. Wheeler Robinson, *Inspiration and Revelation*, pp. 281–82.
37. C. R. North, "Old Testament Theology and the History of Hebrew Religion" *Scottish Journal of Theology*, 2 (June, 1949), 114–15.
38. Norman W. Porteous, review of Robinson's *Inspiration and Revelation* in *The Journal of Theological Studies*, 48 (1947), 77.
39. Norman W. Porteous, "Old Testament Theology," pp. 336–37.

proach could be properly called an Old Testament theology. This method he believed to be "inevitable" and "required." The phrase "even if they [the propositions] are arranged in historical order, and called a 'History of the Religion of Israel' " reveals Robinson's awareness of the close relationship between theology and history. But in fact, he believed these propositions must be stated not chronologically but topically, for this is the arrangement a "theology" requires.

Has Robinson, therefore, failed to unite history and theology? Has he decided in favor of a systematic approach and abandoned the attempt to relate these topics to history? It is true that he could not conceive of a strictly chronological approach doing justice to the subject of an Old Testament theology. On the other hand, it is unjustified to regard the topical arrangement as necessarily divorced from the history of Israel. As we have already seen in his two essays on Old Testament theology in *Record and Revelation*, both the first essay on "The Philosophy of Revelation" and the second essay on "Characteristic Doctrines" are rooted in history. The same thing would have applied to his two-volume Old Testament theology. The first volume, *Inspiration and Revelation in the Old Testament*, is a fully developed statement of the nature of historical revelation. The second volume would undoubtedly have contained a series of doctrines such as God, man, sin and grace, etc. so developed that they would have been wedded to the history from which they emerged. The "inevitable poles around which all else turns" would appear to be the activity of God and the response of man; all else could be related to these two major poles of God and man and their relationship to one another (cf. A. B. Davidson). We shall never know whether Robinson would have succeeded in relating these doctrines to history, but that this was his mature position on the organization of an Old Testament theology seems certain.

Robinson's statement that each generation will need to rewrite its own Old Testament theology is of interest. It reveals his own belief in the relevance of Old Testament theology to modern problems and shows that he believed man's needs will determine how he views God's Word in Scripture. But it also reveals his awareness that each generation has its own contribution to make to the writing of an Old Testament theology. The one prior to his own was concerned with the historical development of Israel's religion, a necessary and important contribution. Robinson believed the present generation's concern with psychology would provide new light for the understanding of the Old Testament and consequently for the writing of an Old Testament theology.[40]

Perhaps even more important than the actual organization of the material of an Old Testament theology, Robinson believed the content of the revelation must be approached through fellowship with God. In an earlier chapter in *Inspiration and Revelation in the Old Testament*, Robinson, commenting on the faith of the Psalmist, wrote:

> It will be seen that all these illustrations of response are equally illustrations of personal trust (*baṭaḥ*). It is this trust which is able (with the pioneer guidance of the prophets) to interpret the revelation of God in these various ways and to respond to it. Because of this comprehensive variety the book of Psalms is not only the living and passionate utterance of Israel's piety at its highest, but also supplies the data for an epitome of Old Testament theology.[41]

By regarding the Psalms as an epitome of Old Testament theology, it appears Robinson had two things in mind. First, that the Book of Psalms presents the results of the psalmists' response to God's revelation in nature, man, and history, thus offering the reader a comprehensive survey of the entire faith of Israel. But second, and equally important, through a study of the Book of Psalms the faith of the psalmists can become our faith so that we enter with them into the temple and there, before the divine presence, we are recreated. If Scripture is approached through such a living fellowship with God, then the actual writing of an Old Testament theology, regardless of the method of organization, will come close to conveying the dynamic faith of Israel which rested in the living God. This function of the Psalms was aptly expressed by Porteous

40. H. Wheeler Robinson, "Hebrew Psychology," *The People and the Book*, ed. A. S. Peake (Oxford: At the Clarendon Press, 1925), pp. 353–82; unpublished personal notes " 'The psychological terms of the Hebrews,' material collected and studies of special points for the Senior Kennicott Scholarship, October, 1901; The Hebrew Idea of Personality, vol. 1," in The Angus Library at Regent's Park College, Oxford University.

41. H. Wheeler Robinson, *Inspiration and Revelation*, p. 269.

when he concluded his review of Robinson's book with these words:

> In the Psalms we are brought closer than anywhere else in Scripture to the piety of the ordinary Israelite to whom the prophet looked for a response to revelation like his own. The ideal theology of the Old Testament would not take us far from the concreteness of a community which, in obedience to the God who called it into being, embodied, however imperfectly, the human relationships, and made the response of spiritual worship, which we associate with the name Israel.[42]

In conclusion, it might be helpful to clarify the exact relationship in Robinson's thought between Old Testament theology and the other biblical disciplines, viz., a literary introduction to the Old Testament, a history of Israel, and a history of the religion of Israel. For Robinson, an introduction to the Old Testament was primarily a critical literary analysis of the Old Testament, dealing with such subjects as literary sources, composition, literary style, authorship, date, and so on. A history of Israel was a thorough reconstruction of the history of the Hebrew people from the patriarchal period to the Roman destruction of Jerusalem, based upon all available sources, such as the literature of Israel, the literature and history of surrounding nations, and archaeological discoveries. If the literature of Israel is interpreted from within, then the divine factor will be a part of the history. A history of the religion of Israel concentrates upon the religious development and the emergence of religious institutions in that history. All those historical facts which had a direct influence on the religion of Israel would be surveyed, while those facts which did not influence Israel's religion, even if they had international significance, would be omitted.[43] An Old Testament theology would be based upon all three disciplines. Literary criticism would be necessary to recover from the canonical literature the essence of Israel's faith in its proper chronological order. A history of Israel and a history of the religion of Israel would provide the basic historical framework through which revelation was mediated. The method

42. Norman W. Porteous, review of Robinson's *Inspiration and Revelation*, pp. 77–78.
43. H. Wheeler Robinson, "The Place of the Old Testament in Christian Education," *Religion in Education*, 2 (Apr., 1935), 75.

of approach to all these disciplines, however, was identical. Regardless of what aspect of biblical studies is investigated, the critic must approach the materials sympathetically, as one who has dwelt in their midst and shared their faith. No distinction was made between the method of approach used in historical-critical studies and in Old Testament theology. The literature and the history must be approached both critically and from within.[44] One must remain aware of the religious message of the literature while analyzing it; one must be open to the divine factor operative in the history while recording the data. In like manner, an Old Testament theology must embody the results of the literary and the historical approach while remaining sympathetic toward the biblical faith. The real distinction between these biblical disciplines is not in the method of approach but in the function they fulfill and in the arrangement of the material. A literary introduction provides a knowledge of the making and the essential meaning of the books of the Old Testament. A historical study provides the reader with a knowledge of the facts and the factors in the history of the Hebrew people. An Old Testament theology would reorganize the great religious truths of Scripture, as they are mediated through history, setting them forth in the form of a series of propositions arranged topically. But the main function

---

44. Compare and contrast Krister Stendahl, "Biblical Theology, Contemporary," *IDB*, 1: 418–32 where he advocates the use of a descriptive approach in writing an Old Testament theology. However, it should be noted that description includes, for Stendahl, a viewing of the faith and practice of the Old and New Testaments from within its original presuppositions. He writes:

> This descriptive task can be carried out by believer and agnostic alike. The believer has the advantage of automatic empathy with the believers in the text—but his faith constantly threatens to have him modernize the material, if he does not exercise the canons of descriptive scholarship rigorously. The agnostic has the advantage of feeling no such temptations, but his power of empathy must be considerable if he is to identify himself sufficiently with the believer of the first century. Yet both can work side by side, since no other tools are called for than those of description *in the terms indicated by the texts themselves*. (p. 422, italics mine)

While Robinson advocated a faith approach to Scripture, he also denied the validity of reading into the texts one's own religious beliefs and practices. To carry out the task of an accurate description of biblical revelation requires, for both Stendahl and Robinson, becoming a "resident alien" in this foreign land. However, Robinson did believe that a person's interpretation of the Old Testament was affected by the age in which he lived; this was inevitable if the Old Testament was to speak to the needs of men in every age. He also held that an Old Testament theology written by a Jew would differ from one written by a Christian. On these two points Robinson contrasts sharply with Stendahl (see above, p. 164).

of all biblical studies is to bring the reader into a living contact
with the God of Israel, who is seen in the record of the history of
Israel but who must be encountered anew by each successive
generation.[45]

45. Robinson also used Old Testament theology as a basis for his writings in the
field of Christian systematic theology. In the field of systematic theology he produced
three memorable volumes: *The Christian Doctrine of Man*, *The Christian Experience of the
Holy Spirit*, and *Redemption and Revelation: In the Actuality of History*. In each case he
used his understanding of the Old and New Testaments as a basis upon which his
systematic theology was constructed and as a norm by which to judge whether or not
his theological formulation was Christian. *The Christian Doctrine of Man* is the clearest
example of his conception of the relationship of biblical theology to systematic theology.
In the first chapter he discussed the Old Testament doctrine of man, including Hebrew
psychology, the place of the individual in Hebrew thought, the conception of sin, and
the relation of man to nature and God. The second chapter continues the development
of the biblical view of man by presenting the New Testament doctrine of man. Here
the positions of Jesus (as contained in the synoptic Gospels), Paul, and the Johannine
literature are presented. Only after a sound biblical position had been expounded did
Robinson turn to the field of systematic theology proper.

A DIVINE BANQUET AT UGARIT

MARVIN H. POPE

Among the Ugaritic texts recovered at Ras Shamra in the twenty-fourth campaign of excavations in 1961 is an especially interesting document, RS 24.258, which deals with a feast given by El, the father of the gods. The gods eat and drink to satiety and inebriation, but El goes beyond this to a state of delirium in which he is confronted by an apparition with horns and tail, is stricken with diarrhea and enuresis, and collapses as in death. There is loss of some lines at the bottom of the obverse of the tablet and again at the top of the reverse, but enough is preserved to suggest that the final concern is with medication to relieve the aftereffects of alcoholic excess.

Preliminary reports[1] on this provocative text were given by the late lamented Charles Virolleaud who for four decades prepared the masterly copies of the alphabetic texts from Ugarit, and by the distinguished excavator of Ras Shamra, C. F. A. Schaeffer. Now that the full text has been published in autograph, transliteration, translation, and with brief commentary by Virolleaud,[2] others may assay to contribute to the elucidation of this intriguing text. The following notes are a purely provisional attempt to supplement the brief, preliminary observations of Virolleaud. Many obscurities remain.

The text is given here in transliteration with presumed stichom-

1. *Comptes Rendus de l'Académie des Inscriptions et Belles Lettres* (1962), pp. 105 ff.; *Comptes Rendus du Groupe Linguistique d'Études Chamito-Sémitiques,* 9 (1962), 41, 51 f.; *Bulletin de la Société Ernest Renan,* extract of *Revue de l'Histoire des Religions* (1962), p. 25; "El als Gastgeber," *Archiv für Orientforschung,* 20 (1963), 214.

2. Charles Virolleaud, "Les nouveaux textes mythologiques et liturgiques de Ras Shamra (XXIVe Campagne, 1961)," in J. Nougayrol, E. Laroche, Charles Virolleaud, and C. F. A. Schaeffer, eds., *Ugaritica V, Mission de Ras Shamra XVI,* Institut Français d'Archéologie de Beyrouth, Bibliothèque Archéologique et Historique, vol. 80 (Paris: Imprimerie Nationale, 1968), pp. 545–606. RS 24.258 is treated as text 1, pp. 545–51.

The first issue of the annual *Ugarit Forschungen* (1969), included three articles on text 24.258: S. E. Loewenstamm, "Eine lehrhaftige ugaritische Trinkburleske," pp. 71–78; J. C. de Moor, "Studies in the New Alphabetic Texts from Ras Shamra," pp. 167–75; Hans-Peter Rüger, "Zu RS 24.258," pp. 203–6. Unfortunately these studies came too late to be utilized in the present treatment.

etry indicated by the caesuras. The translation is arranged
according to the stichometry. The parenthetical numbers in the
translation correspond roughly to the beginnings of the lines of
the transliterated text so that the reader may quickly correlate the
translation and the text. Philological notes and commentary follow
the translation.

RS 24.258

OBVERSE

(1) *il dbḥ.bbth.mṣd.* ‖ *ṣd.bqrb*
(2) *hkl[h].* ‖ *ṣḥ.lqṣ.ilm.* ‖ *tlḥmn*
(3) *ilm.wtštn.* ‖ *tštn y(n)* *ʿd šbʿ* ‖
(4) *trt.ʿd.škr.* ‖ *yʿdb.yrḥ*
(5) *gbh.* ‖ *km [. . . .] yqtqt.tht*
(6) *tlḥnt* ‖ *il.dydʿnn*
(7) *yʿdb.lḥm.lh.* ‖ *wdlydʿnn*
        d mṣd
(8) *ylmn.ḥtm.tht.tlḥn* ‖
        bqrʿ
(9) *ʿttrt.wʿnt.ymǧy* ‖
(10) *ʿttrt.tʿdb.nšb.lh* ‖
(11) *wʿnt.ktp.* ‖ *bhm.ygʿr.tǧr*
(12) *bt.il.* ‖ *h!n lm! k!lb tʿdbn*
(13) *nšb.* ‖ *linr tʿdbn ktp* ‖
(14) *b il abh.gʿr.* ‖ *ytb.il.[b(?)]*
(15) *at[rh]* ‖ *il.ytb.bmrzḥḥ* ‖
(16) *yšt[.il y]n.ʿd šbʿ.* ‖ *trt.ʿd škr* ‖
(17) *il.hlk.lbth.* ‖ *yštql.*
(18) *lhṭrh.* ‖ *yʿmsn.nn.tkmn*
(19) *w šnm.* ‖ *wngšnn.ḥby.* ‖
(20) *bʿl.qrnm w ḏnb.* ‖ *ylšn*
(21) *b ḥrih.w tnth.* ‖ *ql.il.*
(22) *il.k yrdm.arṣ.* ‖ *ʿnt*
(23) *w ʿttrt.tṣdn.* ‖
        . . *b* . . . .
        . . . .

REVERSE

. . . .

(1) ᶜ*ṯ*]*trt w*ᶜ*nt*[

(2) *w*(?)*bhm.tṯṯb*[   ]*dh*[?]

(3) *kmtrpa.h / in n*ᶜ*r*

---

(4) *d yšt.llṣbh ḫš*ᶜ*r klb*

(5) [*w*] *riš.pqq.w šrh*

(6) *yšt.aḥdh.dm zt.ḫrpnt*

TRANSLATION

OBVERSE

I	(1) El offered game in his house,
II	Venison in the midst (2) of his palace.
III	He invited the gods to mess.
IV	(3) The gods ate and drank,
V	Drank wine till sated,
VI	(4) Must till inebriated.
VII	He prepared and mixed (5) his *tripe*(?).
VIII	Like [ ] they tapped under (6) the tables.
IX	The god who knew (7) prepared food (venison) for him;
X	He who knew not (8) knocked with staff under the table (on the ground).
XI	(9) ᶜAštart and ᶜAnat arrived.
XII	(10) ᶜAštart prepared a *brisket* for him,
XIII	(11) And ᶜAnat a shoulder.
XIV	The porter of (12) El's house chided them:
XV	"Lo, for the dog prepare (13) a *brisket*,
XVI	For the cur prepare a shoulder."
XVII	(14) El his father he chided.
XVIII	El sat [in] (15) [his pl]ace.
XIX	El sat in his *mrzḥ*
XX	(16) [El] drank [wi]ne till sated,
XXI	Must till inebriated.
XXII	(17) El went to his house,

XXIII		Descended (18) to his court.
XXIV		Ṭkmn(19)-w-Šnm carried him.
XXV		There accosted him a *creeper*
XXVI	(20)	With two horns and a tail.
XXVII		He floundered (21) in his excrement and urine.
XXVIII		El collapsed, (22) El like those who descend into Earth.
XXIX		ʿAnat (23) and ʿAštart went roaming.
XXX		. . . .
XXXI		. . . .

REVERSE

XXXII		. . . .
XXXIII	(1)	[ʿAš]tart and ʿAnat [ ]
XXXIV	(2)	And with them they brought back [ ]
XXXV	(3)	As one healed, lo, a lad(?) no dysentery(?)

XXXVI	(4)	[ ] one puts to his gullet ḫšʿr
XXXVII	(5)	So that heart and head recover (?) *klb* and *pqq* tops (?)
XXXVIII	(6)	Let one administer (it) together with green olive juice.

Line 1

Virolleaud observes that since the subject of the verb *dbḥ*, "sacrifice," is a deity, it can only be translated as the offering of a banquet or feast. In amplification of this appropriate comment, it should be noted that the noun *dbḥ* is applied to a divine banquet in which some sort of obscene conduct by the female servants so scandalized Baal that he rose and spat in the midst of the assembled gods, saying:

> Two banquets Baal hates,
> Three the Cloud Rider:
> A banquet of shame,

> A banquet of baseness,
> And a banquet of maidservants' lewdness;
> For therein shame is seen,
> And therein is maidservants' lewdness.[3]

Just what the divine serving wenches did that so disgusted Baal we are not told. The terms, however, with which Baal characterized the offensive feasts suggest sexual license and are reminiscent of the biblical strictures against the Israelites' lapses into orgiastic pagan rites. In the present text, however, in spite of the drunkenness, there is, unless we miss the meanings of some of the words, no suggestion of sexual activity, apart from the suggestion below with respect to the role of the dog in the festivities.

Anthropologists have long appreciated that a fundamental aspect of the idea of sacrifice is communion with the divine through a sacramental meal. That the meals of the gods are also termed sacrifices reflects the ancient notion that man can and should supply the gods with food and share it with them. The application of the term *sacrifice* to the Christian Eucharist, first attested in the Didaché (14:2–3), was not merely a development from Paul's concept of spiritual sacrifice (Rom. 12:1), but had a very ancient background in pre-Israelite paganism, as illustrated by the Ugaritic use of the term with reference to the gods' eating and drinking among themselves.

Line II

The stichometry of the first bicolon is uncertain. Virolleaud placed the caesura between the words *mṣd* and *ṣd*, construing both as nouns: "(Le Dieu) Il offre dans sa maison un *mṣd*, un *ṣd* dans l'enceinte (2) de son palais." Since there are elsewhere in the Ugaritic mythological texts several bicola that end with the parallel "in his house" ‖ "in the midst of his palace," it might seem preferable to divide the lines thus. Such a division, however, would

---

3. From the Ugaritic text see A. Herdner, *Corpus des Tablettes en Cunéiformes Alphabetiques: Découvertes à Ras Shamra-Ugarit de 1929 à 1939* (Paris: Imprimerie Nationale, 1963), text No. 4, Col. III, lines 17–22; hereafter cited as *CTCA*. On the argument for citing the texts according to *CTCA*, cf. M. Pope, "Marginalia to M. Dahood's *Ugaritic-Hebrew Philology*," *JBL*, 85 (1966), 455.

require that *ṣd* be construed as a verb parallel to *dbḥ* and with the cognate noun *mṣd* as its object. The requisite meaning "provide," "supply," or the like, could be supported by the reflexive form *hiṣṭayyaḍnû*, "we provided | supplied ourselves" (Josh. 9:12). This sense, however, is not otherwise attested for the verb in Ugaritic or Akkadian where the word occurs frequently as a verb of motion, "prowl," "roam," "hunt." Accordingly, we follow Virolleaud's stichometry and construe *ṣd* as a noun. Even if this is mistaken, it does not change the sense of the line in any significant degree.

Although Virolleaud did not translate the words *mṣd* and *ṣd*, he noted in his commentary the parallelism of *mṣd* and *dbḥ* in the Keret Epic[4] and the glossing of the word *lḥm*, "food," by *mṣd* in line 7, of the present text. The food in question, as Virolleaud noted, is the product of the hunt, "game," or "venison." The savory quality of wild game or venison is emphasized in the story of the patriarch Isaac's partiality to this delicacy (cf. Gen. 27:4, 9, 14). The Aramaic cognate *ṣûdnîṭāʾ* is applied in rabbinic usage to the tasty dish served to mourners as the funeral meal. This dish was considered so delectable that any opportunity to eat it was seized. It is reported (BT, Šabbat 136a) that Rabbi Dimi ben Joseph had a child who died within thirty days of birth and when he sat and mourned for it—which was not obligatory—his father said, "Do you wish to eat *ṣûdnîṭāʾ*?" Similarly (BT, Moed Qatan 20b) when Mar Uqba's father-in-law's son died, he thought of sitting seven [days of mourning] for him and [continuing to] thirty days, but Rabbi Huna went to his house and found him [in formal mourning]. "Do you desire," he said, "to eat *ṣûdnîṭāʾ*?" (The reading of *r* for *d* by Jastrow[5] who proposes to connect the word with *ṣawwāʾr*, "throat," in the sense of [throat tickling] dainties, is mistaken. The connection with game or venison gives the taste.) The mess of pottage which Jacob prepared and for which Esau traded his birthright (Gen. 25:29), according to the Midrash Rabbah,[6] was a mourning meal to comfort Isaac at the death of Abraham.

4. *CTCA*, 17, 78–79, IV, 170–71.
5. Marcus Jastrow, *Dictionary of Talmud Babli, Yerushalmi, Midrashic Literature and Targumin* (New York: G. P. Putnam's Sons, 1903) 2: 1265b.
6. Soncino ed. LXIII 11, p. 566.

Line III

The third colon *ṣḥ lqṣ ilm* Virolleaud rendered "Il crie pour réveiller les dieux," connecting *qṣ* with Hebrew *q(y)ṣ*. A broken line in the ʿAnat Text[7] *gm ṣḥ lq[. . . .]* appears to be nearly identical with the present line and Gordon[8] accepts the sense suggested by Virolleaud, "aloud he shouts to wake up the gods." The gods of Ugarit regularly shout even in ordinary conversation and there is no intimation that they are given to somnolence or need to be aroused to eat and drink. Moreover, *qṣ* cannot be connected with either of the Hebrew roots *q(y)ṣ* or *yqṣ* meaning "to wake" since the original sibilant in both instances is *ẓ* which is distinguished in Ugaritic orthography. The *ṣ* of *qṣ* may represent either original *ṣ* or *ḍ*, but not *ẓ*. The several occurrences of *qṣ* in Ugaritic appear to be related to the root *qṣṣ*, "cut." The word occurs at least three times in the cliché descriptive of divine feasting, *bḥrb mlḥt qṣ mri*, in which it is manifestly a noun in construct relation with *mri* which is in the genitive case. Yasin[9] related the word to Arabic *qaṣṣ* which designates a cut of meat, the breast or outer front part of the thorax. This fits beautifully the parallelism with *ṯd*, "breast," in the ʿAnat Text:[10]

> *ybrd ṯd lpnwh*, He profferred a breast before him,
> *bḥrb mlḥt qṣ mri*, with sharp(?) knife a cutlet of fatling.

But in other instances[11] *ṯd* is not in parallelism with *qṣ* but a component of the term "breast suckers," *mrǵtm ṯd*, a designation of the gods,

> *tlḥm tšty ilm*   The gods ate and drank,
> *wtpq mrǵtm ṯd*   Supplied were the breast suckers,
> *bḥrb mlḥt qṣ mri*   With sharp knife a cutlet of fatling.
> *tšty krpnm yn*   They drank from the jars wine,
> *bks ḫrṣ dm ʿṣm*   From cups of gold blood of the vine.

---

7. *CTCA*, 1 IV, 2.
8. C. H. Gordon, *Ugaritic Textbook*, Analecta Orientalia, no. 38 (Rome: Pontifical Biblical Institute, 1965), 19.2162, p. 474 a. Cited hereafter as *UT*.
9. Izz-al-Din Al-Yasin, *The Lexical Relation Between Ugaritic and Arabic*, Shelton Semitic Monograph Series, vol. 1 (New York: Shelton College, 1952), p. 69, No. 543.
10. *CTCA*, 3 I 6–8.
11. *CTCA*, 4 III 40–45, VI 55–59.

It is not clear whether *qṣ* in the present line *ṣḥ lqṣ ilm* is to be construed as a verb or a noun. Taken as an infinitive, it would mean "to partake" (of a meal), or the like; as a noun it would be a technical term for a sacral or ritual meal. The rendering "to mess" is intended to reflect the ambiguity of the original.

The consonants *qṣ* have interesting connections with ritual meals in other Semitic dialects. In Syriac the final weak root *qĕṣā* is used of the breaking of bread, especially in the celebration of the Christian Eucharist, or Holy Communion (cf. the Peshitta of Isa. 58:7, Jer. 16:7, Luke 24:35, Acts 2:46, I Cor. 11:24). The rare use of the geminated root *qṣṣ* in this connection is presumed to be an error, but one may wonder whether this is actually the case. Syriac *qĕṣāṣā* may be related to the identical form in rabbinic terminology which designates a sort of ritual meal. The rabbinic ruling that a child may be believed who testifies that he ate at someone's *qĕṣāṣā* (BT, Ketubot 28b) called for elucidation of the obsolete term. If a man sold a field, it was explained, his relatives brought vessels and filled them with parched grain and nuts and broke them before the children who collected the tidbits and said: "So and So is cut off from his possession." If, however, the man took back his possession, the same procedure was repeated and the children cried, "So and So has taken back his possession." The same was done in the case of a man who took a wife whom his relatives regarded as unworthy. The children gathered the goodies and said, "So and So is cut off from his family." If later the man forsook the objectionable wife, the ceremony was repeated and the children said, "So and So has returned to his family." The breaking of the vessel full of sweetmeats for the children is strikingly similar to the Mexican custom of breaking the piñata. In Syriac the (pointed) end of a storage jar is termed *qeṣ*. In the rabbinic illustrations of *qĕṣāṣā* there is intentional play on *qṣṣ*, "cut," as a severing of relations, *niqṣaṣ pĕlônî*, "So and So is cut off." This, however, cannot be the proper sense of the term since the same procedure is used for the restoration of the one who was cut off. Thus, *qĕṣāṣā*, in spite of the rabbinic explanation, appears to be a designation of a ceremonial meal for occasions both sad and joyful. The term applies to the meal and not simply to the special treat for the children who were allowed to participate and who later

may be believed if they testify, "We ate at the *qĕṣāṣā* | *qĕṣîṣā* of
So and So."

Lines IV–VI

The gods of Ugarit eat and drink at every opportunity, in accordance with ancient oriental hospitality, but it is not elsewhere
explicitly stated that they indulge to the point of inebriation. This
must be an extraordinary occasion reflecting a human affair in
which it was deemed proper or obligatory to drink to excess.
Mourning was such an occasion which allowed for the submerging
of sorrow in wine. Ten cups were allowed by the rabbis to be
drunk in the house of mourning. Four extra cups were added as
toasts to various notables, the religious and civic leaders, and one
in honor of Rabban Gamaliel. But when the religious authorities
observed that some became intoxicated, the rule was restored to
the original ten cups (BT, *Ketubot* 8b; *Soṭah* 14a). At the festival
of Purim it was permissible to drink until one could not tell the
difference between accursed Haman and blessed Mordecai (BT,
Megillah 7b). The orgiastic character of pagan rites to which the
Israelites were not infrequently seduced is attested by the prophetic
protests.

Line VI

Whether the word *trt*, OT *tîrôš*, is related to Hittite *tuwarsā*,
"vine," is uncertain. The derivation commonly proposed, from
the root **yrt*, is enhanced by the word play in Mic. 6:15:

You will tread olives, but not anoint yourselves with oil;
You will tread (*tîrôš*), but not drink wine.

The Jerusalem Targum to Deut. 29:5 renders the Hebrew *šēkār*
with *mērat* which presumably is merely another nominal pattern
from *yrt* with the same meaning as Hebrew *tîrôš*. The form *mrt* is
now attested in Ugaritic and Gordon's definition[12] as "perhaps
a wine product" seems overcautious since it is associated with
wine and is potable as indicated by a line in an epistle to the
Queen Mother which refers to *mrt.d.štt*, "the *mrt* which I | thou

12. *UT*, 19 . 1558.

did | st drink." The rendering "must," rather than the traditional "new wine," is chosen purely on poetic grounds since a single word for a parallel to "wine" is hard to find. It is clear from the Ugaritic use and from the OT (e. g., Hos. 4:11) that the stuff was intoxicating, as was Old English *must*:

> Butt thei are drounken, all thes menze,
> Of *muste* or wyne, I wolle warande[13]

Line VII

Virolleaud did not translate *yrḫ gb*, but in his notes suggested *mois complet* as perhaps the name of the festival the beginning of which is marked by this feast. The word *gb*, as Virolleaud noted, occurs in a fragment of the ᶜAnat Text,[14] but the context is broken and what is intelligible gives no hint that a feast is in progress. Gordon[15] took *yrḫ* as the name of the lunar deity Yariḫ, "(Il) makes Y. his Gb." Although the sense of the line is uncertain, we incline to take *yrḫ* as a verb coordinate with *yᶜdb*. The few Semitic roots with the consonants *rḫ*, Arabic *wariḫ* and *raḫḫ*, Akkadian *reḫū*, are related to moisture and liquids and this seems appropriate for the object *gb* which in Akkadian designates a moist or semi-liquid part of human and animal bodies. Passages from neo-Babylonian texts indicate that the *gabbu* of cattle or sheep was an edible internal part.[16]

The drinking of juices from the body of a deceased relative or friend is an ancient and widespread custom[17] and appears to be attested also at Ugarit. In a brief mythological vignette inscribed on the back of a lexical text, the goddess ᶜAnat is depicted as consuming the flesh and blood of her brother-consort (Baal) without benefit of knife or cup, because he was beautiful.

---

13. Cf. *Century Dictionary and Cyclopedia* (New York: Century Co., 1897), 6: 3911, s.v. "must 2."

14. *CTCA*, 1 V 13; cf. *UT*, 19 . 548a.

15. *UT*, 19 . 1151.

16. Cf. A. L. Oppenheim, ed., *The Assyrian Dictionary of the Oriental Institute of the University of Chicago* (Chicago: The Oriental Institute, 1956), 5: 5b, s.v. *qabbu* B. Cited hereafter as *CAD*.

17. Cf. James Hastings, John A. Selbie, *et al.*, eds., *Encyclopaedia of Religion and Ethics*, 13 vols. (New York: Scribner's, 1910–27), vol. 5, s.v. "Drinks, Drinking," p. 79b (cited hereafter as *ERE*).

ᶜAnat went mad (at) the beauty of her brother,
And (at) the handsomeness of her brother, for he was fair.
She ate his flesh without a knife,
She drank his blood without a cup.[18]

We are not told whether her handsome "brother" was dead or
alive when she consumed his flesh and blood, but it seems probable
that he was presumed dead and that ᶜAnat's act was a mourning rite.

Line VIII

The missing word after the comparative particle k (with enclitic
emphatic -m) was, presumably, the noun to which the comparison
applied. If the item compared were preserved, we might more
easily divine the meaning of the verb *yqtqt* which Virolleaud
rendered conjecturally "il cache(?)," but in his comments suggested comparison with Arabic *qatta*, "draw, pull toward oneself."
In Syriac *qtt* in the simple stem means "to remain fixed, stuck,
motionless" and one might think that the inebriated gods were
stiff under the table, but the clue to the meaning of *yqtqt* is supplied
by line 8, *ylmn ḥtm tḥt tlḥn*, "he | they knocked with staff under the
table." Taking the cue from *ḥlm*, "beat, strike," *yqtqt* could be
related to Mishnaic and Talmudic *qišqēš*, "knock, strike, clap,"
or the like, which is used of various beating or striking operations
such as ringing a bell, kneading dough, plumping one's feet into
the water, slapping a person, hoeing the ground, and in the re-
flexive stem it is applied to the rattling of a nut in the shell, liquid
shaken in a bottle, the brain in the skull, or the motion of breasts.

The correlation of lines 5, 6, and 7, 8, suggests a striking explanation of the action under the tables which interpretation is
enhanced and confirmed by the gloss of line 9 no matter whether
one reads *bqr*. "against the wall" (taking the final wedge as the
word divider), or *bqrᶜ* (taking the wedge as representing the consonant ᶜ*ayin*). With the reading *bqrᶜ* one could appeal to *qrᶜ* used
for rending the garments in mourning, or to the Arabic noun *qarᶜ*

---

18. For the text and differing interpretations, cf. M. Astour, *Hellenosemitica* (1965),
p. 180; E. Lipinski, *Syria*, 42 (1965), pp. 45–73. Cf. W. F. Albright, *Yahweh and the
Gods of Canaan* (London: Athlone Press, 1968), pp. 131 f., and Arvid S. Kapelrud,
The Violent Goddess (1969), p. 44.

used for knocking or rapping and also meaning "bottom" or "ground." Beating on the ground, or on floors and walls is a common practice in death rites, usually explained as a means of driving away ghosts. The Russian Lapps, for example, beat on the walls with branches after a death and some New Guinea tribes beat on the floor, throw sticks against the wall, or knock on the wall with loud shouts supposedly to drive away the ghosts.[19]

Beating on the ground may also be a fertility rite. In the Eleusinian mysteries, according to Pausanias (VIII 15.3), the priest donned a mask of Demeter Cidaria and beat with rods those underground (τοὺς ὑποχθονίους) for reasons unknown to Pausanias. J. G. Frazer[20] compares this with a ritual of the Guarayos of Bolivia who beat the ground with bamboo and pray for genial rains and plentiful crops and with the ritual beating of the ground with willow-withs and palm branches during the Jewish festival of Sukkot (cf. Mishnah Sukkah III.9 and especially IV.6, "they used to bring in palm branches and beat them on the ground beside the altar, and that day was called 'the Day of the Beating of Branches' "). The prayers for rain and the water-pouring rites of the festival Sukkot suggest that the beating on the ground (*qarqa*ᶜ) was also intended to produce rain.

Line IX

It is not clear whether *il* is bound to the preceding word *ṭlḥnt*, "tables," or is the subject of the verb which follows. In either case, it appears that *il* is here the appelative "god" rather than the proper name of the chief god. If the word is connected with *ṭlḥnt*, it may be taken as superlative. We incline to Virolleaud's interpretation, "Le dieu qui sait prepare un mets de gibier pour lui," except that *dmṣd*, written in smaller characters below the line is taken as an explanatory gloss to *lḥm*. If *il* is taken as the proper name, it seems necessary to take it as a *casus pendens*, "As for El, etc." The fact that El holds the affair in his house and invites the gods to partake does not militate against the likelihood that he is

19. Uno Holmberg, *Finno-Ugric, Siberian Mythology, Mythology of All Races* (Boston: Archaeological Institute of America, Marshal Jones Co., 1927), 4: 23; J. G. Frazer, *The Golden Bough*, 3rd ed. (London: Macmillan, 1927), 3: 168, 170.

20. *Pausanias' Description of Greece* (New York: Macmillan, 1898), 7: 239.

also the central figure for whom the meal of savory venison is prepared. As in Jewish mourning the consolation meal, *sĕ'ûdat habbĕrā'āh*, is prepared for the mourner by a neighbor, so here one or more of the gods who had skill prepared the meal while the unskilled beat with staff on the wall or ground.

Lines XI–XIII

The goddesses ʿAštart and ʿAnat come and prepare special cuts of meat for "him," presumably for El since there is no other antecedent for the singular pronoun. The word *nšb* which stands here in parallelism with *ktp*, "shoulder," designates some sort of edible meat, presumably a choice cut. It occurs in a list of cuts of beef, geese and goose grease(?).[21] No etymology or cognate is immediately apparent and the rendering "brisket" is conjectural. Arabic *naṣf* in the sense of morsel or bite is a remote possibility as a cognate.

Line XIV

The expression *gʿr b-*, "cry out against," "rebuke," is identical with the Hebrew usage, as in Gen. 37:10 and Jer. 29:27. The masculine pronominal suffix *-hm* leaves us in doubt whether its antecedent is the two goddesses who have just arrived or the whole divine company. In line 14 we see that the rebuke also applied to Father El and this may explain the gender of the suffix pronoun which could refer to the two goddesses and to Father El, as well as to the other gods in the company.

Line XV

Virolleaud's copy and reading, *pn.lmgr lb*, presented considerable difficulty. Akkadian *migir libbi*, "satisfaction of heart," offers a variety of meanings, such as "obedience," "free will," and "propriety." The latter sense would be suitable here, "Look to propriety." The porter of El's house would thus rebuke the goddesses for impropriety in neglecting to provide for the dog the same cuts

---

21. Cf. *UT* text 1128 line 18 and the glossary, *UT*, 19 . 1710.

of meat prepared for their father. Instead of the dubious *mgr lb* one would expect the common Semitic term for dog in view of the occurrence of another word for dog in the following parallel line. The non-Semitic word *inr* (line 13) occurs three times in the Keret Epic (*UT* 125:2–3, 15–17, 100–1) in parallelism with the common Semitic term for dog, *kalb*. It occurred to the writer that the parallelism in the present passage also calls for similar apposition, *klb* ‖ *inr*, but it did not occur to him to question Virolleaud's copy. The solution was offered by Delbert R. Hillers[22] who pointed out that Virolleaud had apparently mistaken similar signs and that instead of *pn.lmgr lb* the reading should be *hn.lm klb*. Perfect parallelism is thus restored:

> Lo, for the dog you should prepare a *brisket*,
> For the cur you should prepare a shoulder.

Line XVI

The dog was generally despised as a scavenger, and as impudent in sexual activity. C. H. Gordon's assertion[23] that dogs were especially favored at Ugarit and even allowed in the palace, as in the Homeric world, cannot be supported by the Krt text where the barking dog is mentioned along with other boisterous beasts that disturb men's morning sleep, the neighing stallion, the braying ass, and the lowing ox, and there is no indication that any of these were palace pets. The dog as a companion of young Tobias (Tob. 5:17; 11:4) has been assumed to be a foreign feature, but it is likely that the dog was appreciated for its friendly qualities and loyalty, in spite of its lack of modesty and fastidiousness.

Dogs figure in cultic symbolism in many cultures. Among the Hittites the dog had an important role in religious rites[24] and in the Vedas (Rig Veda X.xiv 10–12; Atharva Veda viii 1, 9) dogs guarded the entrance to the other world. In Persia the dog was thought to guard the Chinvat Bridge over which the dead had to pass. In Parsee funerary rites the corpse is exposed to the dog gaze

---

22. *Bulletin of the American Schools of Oriental Research*, 198 (Apr., 1970), 46.
23. C. H. Gordon, *Before the Bible* (New York: Harper & Row, 1962), p. 140.
24. Cf. Friedrich Blome, *Die Opfermaterie in Babylonien und Israel* (Rome: Apud Pontifical Institutum Biblicum, 1934), 1: 125.

(*sagdid*). A "four-eyed" dog, one with spots resembling an extra set of eyes, is brought near the corpse to frighten away the corpse-demon with his gaze. In Yezd the ordinary street dog is used and morsels of food are strewn around the body, or in older usage placed on the corpse's bosom, for the dog.[25] There are rabbinic references to food for dogs at weddings and funerals (cf. BT, Moed Qatan 28a, Erubin 81a, Midrash Lev. Rabbah xxviii 6) and a particularly provocative story about dogs at David's death. According to Midrash Rabbah Qohelet V. 10, David died on a sabbath and was left lying in the sun with hungry dogs nearby while Solomon inquired of the scholars at the House of Study what he should do. He was instructed to cut up the carcass of an animal and place it before the dogs and set a loaf of bread or a child upon his father and then the body could be moved. The devious logic of this stratagem, presumably, was that it would be permissible to move the child (or the loaf?) and along with it the corpse. But how could the cutting of the carcass of an animal be condoned on the Sabbath? It may be that we have in this story the echo of a rite older and more urgent than Sabbath taboos. The matter of a choice cut of meat for the dog was of sufficient import to embolden the divine porter in the Ugaritic text under consideration to rebuke the great goddesses and even the head of the pantheon. In the story of David's demise it may be that the Sabbath motif was introduced to supply a rationale for the custom of placing food on or near the corpse and giving the dog(s) choice cuts of meat.

The role of the dog in the divine banquet may be illuminated by a usage attributed to early Christians in their love-feasts. I am indebted to my colleague, Dr. Ian Siggins, who called my attention to the following item.

Tertullian in his *Apology* (chapters 7 and 8) mentions the accusations against the Christians that in their reprobate feasts they murdered and ate babies and after the repast engaged in adulterous and incestuous orgies. Dogs, "the pimps of darkness," allegedly procured license for their impious lusts by putting out the lights in a manner which is of particular interest in connection with the

---

25. Cf. *ERE*, 1: 512a, 4: 502a, 6: 738b; Jivani Jamshedji Modi, *The Religious Ceremonies and Customs of the Parsees*, 2nd ed. (Bombay: J. B. Karani's Sons, 1937), pp. 56–58.

present passage. In ridiculing the idea that Christians could do such things, Tertullian gives further details of the alleged proceedings: "Yet, I suppose, it is customary for those who wish to be initiated to approach first the father of the sacred rites to arrange what must be prepared." Then he says, "Now, you need a baby, still tender, one who does not know what death means, and one who will smile under your knife. You need bread, too, with which to gather up his juicy blood; besides that, candlesticks, lamps, some dogs and bits of meat which will draw them on to overturn the lamps. Most important of all, you must come with your mother and sister." As a reward for such crimes, the Christians allegedly promised eternal life and Tertullian retorted: "For the time being, believe it! On this point I have a question to ask: If you believed it, would you consider the acquisition of eternal life worth attaining with such a [troubled] conscience? Come, bury your sword in this baby, enemy though he be of no one, guilty of no crime, everybody's son; or, if that is the other fellow's job, stand here beside this [bit of] humanity dying before he has lived; wait for the young soul to take flight; receive his fresh blood; saturate your bread with it; partake freely! Meanwhile, as you recline at table, note the place where your mother is, and your sister; note it carefully, so that, when the dogs cause darkness to fall, you may make no mistake—for you will be guilty of a crime unless you commit incest."[26]

Marcus Minucius Felix (*Octavius*, chap. 9) tells us more about the alleged initiation of Christian novices, stories as detestable as they were notorious. "An infant covered with a dough crust to deceive the unsuspecting is placed beside the person to be initiated into the sacred rites. This infant is killed at the hands of the novice by wounds inflicted unintentionally and hidden from his eyes, since he has been urged on as if to harmless blows upon the surface of the dough. The infant's blood—oh, horrible—they sip up eagerly; its limbs they tear to pieces, trying to outdo each other; by this victim they are leagued together; by being privy to this crime they pledge themselves to mutual silence. These sacred rites are more shocking than any sacrilege."

26. Tertullian, *Apology*, trans. Sister Emily Joseph Daly, in *The Fathers of the Church, A New Translation* (New York, 1950), 10: 25–29.

Minucius Felix continues: "On the appointed day, they assemble for their banquets with all their children, sisters, and mothers— people of both sexes and every age. After many sumptuous dishes, when the company at table has grown warm and the passion of incestuous lust has been fired by drunkenness, a dog which has been tied to a lamp stand is tempted by throwing a morsel beyond the length of the leash by which it is bound. It makes a dash, and jumps for the catch. Thus, when the witnessing light has been overturned and extinguished, in the ensuing darkness which favors shamelessness, they unite in whatever revoltingly lustful embraces the hazard of chance will permit. Thus, they are all equally guilty of incest, if not in deed, yet by privity, since whatever can happen in the actions of individuals is sought for by the general desire of all."[27]

The testimony of Tertullian and Minucius Felix regarding the use of dogs in the incestuous orgies which were alleged to take place in Christian love-feasts is of considerable interest for our present text, particularly in view of the association of dogs with sacral sexual rites and funeral feasts in glyptic art of the Near East. From the Early Dynastic III period of Mesopotamia (ca. 2500 B.C.), we have a representation (fig. 1) of sexual rites showing a copulating pair on a couch and under the couch is a dog. Behind the dog is some object difficult to identify. At the foot of the couch is another couple standing back to front, the forward figure (presumably female) extends the hand backwards grasping the prodigiously long and slender phallus of the figure behind her. It looks as if the member is needle pointed and extends the width of the female's hips on her right side. This could, however, be a matter of crude perspective and the intent may have been to show the female as assisting intromission, as in a plainer representation of a scene in which the female reaches back and similarly grasps or guides the inserted member. The present scene has been characterized as a ritual marriage,[28] but the involvement of more

27. Minucius Felix, *Octavius*, trans. Rudolph Arbesmann, in *Fathers of the Church*, 10: 337–38.

28. Cf. Henri Frankfort, *Stratified Cylinder Seals from the Diyala Region*, University of Chicago Oriental Institute Publications, vol. 72 (Chicago, 1955), pp. 34, 38, and pl. 34, no. 340. The dog, according to Frankfort, refers to Gula, as the scorpion under the couch in No. 559 refers to Ishara. "Both are aspects of that great goddess of fertility whose union with a male god, consummated at the New Year's festival, insured the

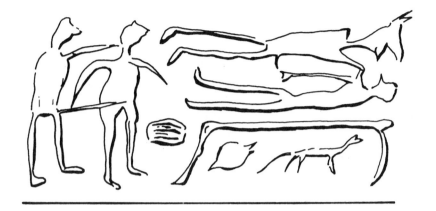

Fig. 1.   Dog in Early Mesopotamian "sacred marriage" scene; after
P. Amiet, *La glyptique mesopotamienne archaique*, pl. 91, no. 1202. Cf. n. 28.

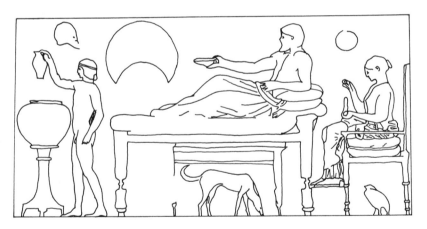

Fig. 2.   Anatolian tomb relief; cf. n. 29.

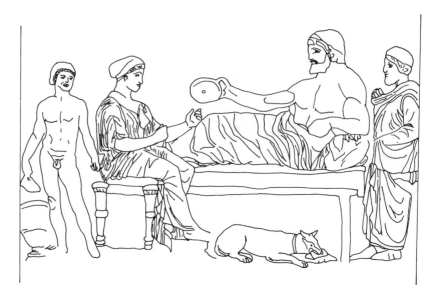

Fig. 3.   Funerary relief from Piraeus; cf. n. 30.

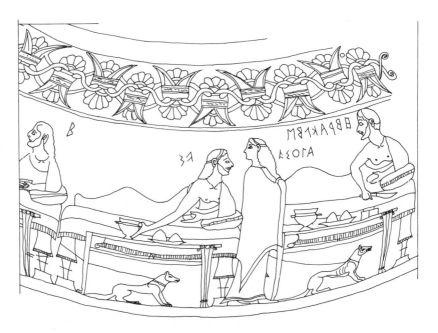

Fig. 4.   Early Corinthian crater; cf. n. 31.

than a single pair suggests a communal affair. A canine beneath the couch is commonplace in funerary sculptures. A marble relief (fig. 2) from Thasos dating to the middle of the fifth century B.C., shows under the drinker's couch a dog standing with muzzle to the ground as if eating.[29] Another fifth-century B.C. funerary relief (fig. 3) from Piraeus shows the dog reclining under the couch and gnawing at a hefty hunk of meat.[30] An early Corinthian crater (fig. 4) exhibits underneath the drinkers' couches dogs leashed to the couch legs.[31] Tertullian's explanation of the bizarre function of the dogs as the "pimps of darkness" at orgiastic love feasts taxes our credulity, since the mode of extinguishing the lights, apart from the fire hazard, rivals the ingenuity of a Rube Goldberg. Nevertheless, textual evidence coupled with the representations in art indicate that the dog played an important role in such celebrations calling for pieces of meat, either as provocation, pacification, or reward. It is possible that more than one purpose was served by the cur. At any rate, the dog continued to appear on funeral reliefs down to late antiquity, as on the urn of Iulia Eleutheris in the Thermen Museum in Rome which depicts the mourners around the body carrying on the *conclamatio mortis* while beneath the bier reposes the persistent canine.[32] The association of the dog with sacral sexual rites and funeral feasts attested over a wide area of the Near East for more than two millennia presents a fascinating problem that calls for further investigation which cannot be undertaken here.

Line XVIII

Virolleaud restored at the beginning of line 15 *at*[*rt*] and rendered "(Alors) le Dieu s'assied . . . à côté de (15) Aše[rat]." RS 24.252, line 2 *ytb il b*ᶜ*ttrt* appears to favor Virolleaud's restoration, but see

---

prosperity of the community; for the fertility of nature depended upon this act" (p. 38). Frankfort, however, admits in advance the possibility that the two figures on the couch in Nos. 340 and 559 represent humans and that no ritual significance attaches to the scene.

29. Cf. Ekrem Akurgal, *Die Kunst Anatoliens* (Berlin: deGruyter, 1961), pp. 272 f., fig. 240.

30. E. R. Goodenough, *Jewish Symbols* (New York: Pantheon Books, 1953), vol. 11, fig. 224.

31. Humfry Payne, *Necrocorinthia, A Study of Corinthian Art in the Archaic Period* (Oxford: The Clarendon Press, 1931), p. 302, pl. 27, no. 780.

32. Cf. A. C. Rush, *Death and Burial in Christian Antiquity* (Ph.D. Diss., The Catholic University of America, 1941), pl. III and pp. 108 f.

the suggestion of B. Margulis.[33] In the present passage, however, the broken word stands in parallelism with *bmrzhh*, "in his *marzih*" which suggests that the restoration might be *batrh*, "in his place / shrine." There is no objection to El sitting with his sometime consort and mother of his numerous progeny, but she is not mentioned elsewhere in the text and the parallelism suggests a place rather than a person. Further ground for the restoration of *atrh* rather than *atrt* is given in the comments on the next line of our text, in connection with the use of *atr* in the Rephaim Texts.

Line XIX

The word *marzēah*[34] occurs twice in the OT, in Amos 6:7 and Jer. 16:5. The RSV renderings, "revelry" in one instance and "mourning" in the other, suit the respective contexts but reflect the long standing puzzlement as to the precise meaning of the term. The Septuagint in Jer. 16:5 rendered *marzēah* as θίασος, i. e. a company assembled to celebrate a festival in honor of a deity. Rabbinic references connect the term with the funeral feast which was often characterized by excessive drinking (see comment on lines IV–VI above) and also with pagan sexual orgies, particularly the Israelite apostasy to Baal Peor when the people began to whore with Moabite girls who invited them to the sacrifices of their gods and the people ate and worshiped their gods (Num. 25:1–2) with sacral sexual intercourse (Num. 2, 5:6–8). The Sifre (Num. 131) identified these banquets or sacrifices as *marzĕhîm* and Midrashic comment further relates the *marzēah* to the Mayumas festivals (cf. Midrash Leviticus Rabbah 5:3, Numbers Rabbah 10:3, 7); the latter reference informs us that wife-swapping characterized the festivals and that each tribe had its own celebration. Mayumas festivals, we know from Greek and Roman sources, were observed along the Mediterranean, especially in port cities like Alexandria, Gaza, Ashkelon and Antioch, with such licentiousness that Roman

---

33. "A Ugaritic Psalm (RŠ 24.2525)," *JBL*, 89 (1970), 293 f.
34. Several scholars have recently discussed the term in considerable detail. Cf. Y. Kutscher, *Words and their Histories* (in Hebrew) 1965, pp. 167–71; Otto Eissfeldt, "Etymologische und archäologische Erklärung alttestamentlicher Wörter," *Oriens Antiquus* 5 (1966), 167–71; "Kultvereine in Ugarit," *Ugaritica VI* (Paris, 1969), pp. 187–95.

rulers felt constrained to ban them. Rabbi Hanan apparently alluded to these rites in his comment that "it was done in the cities of the Sea what was not done in the generation of the Flood" (Midrash Genesis Rabbah 20:8). The equation of *marzēaḥ* and Mayumas is also made by the mosaic map of the sixth-century church at Madeba which labels the Trans-Jordanian area in which the Baal-Peor apostasy occurred as "Betomarseas [i. e. Beth Marzeaḥ] alias Maioumas."[35]

Considerable data on the *marzēaḥ* comes from Palmyra[36] whence we have dedicatory inscriptions by principals in such affairs and numerous tessarae decorated with a banquet scene and bearing an inscription mentioning a *marzēaḥ*. The participants were termed "members [lit. sons] of the *marzēaḥ*," *bny-mrzḥ²*, and a specific deity was usually designated, for example, *bny mrzḥ Nbw*, "members of the *marzēaḥ* of Nabu." The most popular *marzēaḥ* at Palmyra was apparently that of Bel (Baal), to judge from the numerous tessarae which mention "the priests of Bel." Each *marzēaḥ* had a chief, *rb mrzḥ²*, who served for an unspecified term, although one inscription erected "on the occasion of the leadership of the *marzēaḥ* (of / by) Yarḥai Agrippa" indicates that he served for a whole year and provided the priests with old wine for a whole year.

In the Greek of some of the bilingual inscriptions from Palmyra, the leader of the *marzēaḥ* is called the symposiarch and we know something of the Greek symposia and the role of the symposiarch as king of the feast. The symposiarch was usually chosen by lot and he decided the mixture of the wine, the number of drinks and the general rules of the affair. The portions were small at the beginning but grew larger as the drinking progressed, and each had to be downed without breathing between swallows, ἀπνευστί. The feasts were often held at the houses of celebrated *hetairai* and served by beautiful girls as waitresses and musicians; the affair, understandably, often ended in sacrifices to Aphrodite Pandemos.[37]

35. V. R. Gold, "The Mosaic Map of Madeba," *The Biblical Archaeologist*, 21, no. 3: 50–71, does not treat "Betomarseas alias Maioumas," on which see the literature cited by Eissfeldt, pp. 167 ff.

36. Cf. Eissfeldt, pp. 172 f., and Porten, pp. 167 ff.

37. Cf. E. Guhl and W. Koner, *The Life of the Greeks and Romans*, trans. from 3rd German edition F. Hueffer (New York: Appleton, 1876), pp. 266–69 and fig. 304, p. 268.

We may assume at least rough similarities between the *marzēaḥ* and the symposia.

The Akkadian documents from Ras Shamra[38] which mention *marzēaḥ* indicate that it was an important institution. The king Niqmepa bequeathed "a house of the *marzēaḥ*-men" to the *marzēaḥ*-men and their children. A house of the *marzēaḥ*-men of (the god) Šatran was taken over for official use, but another house was given in its place. A vineyard of Ištar was divided between the *marzēaḥ*-men of the city of Ari and those of the city of Siyanni. In a fragmentary Ugaritic alphabetic text[39] in five of the six lines there is the phrase *mrzḥ⁽n*[. . .], but in the second line occurs *šd kr*[*m*. . .], "field vineyard." Eissfeldt proposes the restoration *mrzḥ ᶜn*[*t*] and suggests that the text may deal with the bequest of several vineyards to the *marzēaḥ* (Kultverein) of ᶜAnat.[40] This suggestion could have been strengthened by appeal to the phrase *šd ilm šd aṭrt wrḥm⟨y⟩* in lines 13 and 28 of the Birth of the Beautiful Gods[41] where *rḥm⟨y⟩* is an epithet of ᶜAnat. Viticulture is manifestly vitally connected with the *marzēaḥ* as a bacchanalian celebration.

The so-called Rephaim Texts,[42] fragments apparently belonging to the Aqht Epic, also deal with a *marzēaḥ*, but in this instance with the variant spelling *mrzᶜ*.[43] In spite of the numerous lacunae and lexical and grammatical difficulties, the burden of the fragments is that Danel, presumably in mourning for his murdered son Aqht, invites the Rephaim, the deified dead, to a *mrzᶜ*. The word *aṭr*, "place," occurs several times apparently in the sense of "shrine" and presumably as a designation of the locale of the feast; see comment on line XV above. In the last of the Rephaim fragments, the phrase *bn bn aṭrk*,[44] "among the sons of your place," may refer to the participants in the cult feast. The puzzling term "your little hand," *ydk ṣg̊r* (with masculine adjective),[45] occurs in the next line

---

38. Eissfeldt, pp. 174 f., Porten, p. 180.
39. *UT*, text 2032.
40. P. 174.
41. *CTCA*, 23, the original editors' designation SS, and text 52 in Gordon's system.
42. *CTCA*, 20, 21, 22, *UT*, texts 121–124.
43. Cf. *UT*, 19 . 2313.
44. *CTCA*, 22, Col. B. 3, *UT*, text 124: 3.
45. As a paired bodily member, *yad*, "hand," is regularly feminine in grammatical gender. It is apparent, however, that both in Hebrew and Ugaritic the word is sometimes a circumlocution for "phallus" (e. g. Isa. 57:8 and Song of Songs 5:4 and in

following a slight lacuna, and then come several words that make sense together, *tnšq šptk ṯm* (5). *ṯkm bm ṯkm*, "she / they will kiss your lips there, shoulder to shoulder." A love-fest of some sort seems to be envisaged. After several lines which are almost perfectly preserved but quite enigmatic, ʿAnat[46] prepares fowl, beef, veal, pours several different kinds of wine, the Rephaim eat and drink for six days, and then just at the climactic "Behold on the seventh [day]" the text again breaks off.

From the various strands of information, we gather that the *marzēaḥ* was a social and religious institution which included families, owned property, houses for meetings and vineyards for wine supply, was associated with specific deities, and met periodically, perhaps monthly, to celebrate for several days at a stretch with food and drink and sometimes, if not regularly, with sacral sexual orgies. The biblical and rabbinic correlation of the *marzēaḥ* with both mourning and licentious pagan revelry may seem incongruous and even contradictory from our puritan and Victorian perspective, but not from the viewpoint of a fertility religion which recognized life and death as integral natural process and confronted death with the assertion and reaffirmation of life.

The etymology of *marzēaḥ* remains uncertain. Joseph Qimḥi, followed by his son David, connected it with Arabic *mirzīḥ* which is alleged to signify a vehement voice, sound, or noise and thus *marzēaḥ* would designate a loud cry whether of mourning or revelry. This etymology, however, is questionable. There is no sure basis for positing a root *rzḥ*, "to cry," and still less for a second homonymous root with the meaning "unite oneself" to support a presumed meaning *Kultverein*.[47] The basic meaning of *rzḥ* in Arabic is to fall down from fatigue (or other weakness) and remain prostrate without power to rise; it may be used of a man, a camel, or a grapevine. A *marzaḥ* is a place where a camel collapses from fatigue and a

---

the poem called the "Birth of the Beautiful Gods" on which cf. Marvin Pope, *El in the Ugaritic Texts* [Leiden: E. J. Brill, 1955], pp. 39 f.), and as such would presumably, have masculine grammatical gender. We cannot, however, be too confident of this logic because of striking reversals such as the masculinity of the word for "breasts."

46. *CTCA*, 22, Col. B. 11–25.

47. Cf. Otto Eissfeldt, "Sohnespflichten im Alten Orient," *Syria*, 43 (1966), 45 f., and "Etymologische und archäologische Erklärung," pp. 176 f. Porten, p. 186 n. 147, also considers Eissfeldt's distinction between the two supposed homonyms *rzḥ*, "shout," and *rzḥ* "unite," to be arbitrary.

mirzaḥ is a prop for a fallen grapevine.[48] The assured meaning of Arabic *rzḥ* thus seems highly appropriate to the aim and end of a marathon bacchanal and suits the state in which we find El at the end of his *marziḥ* in the text under consideration. Nouns of the pattern of *maqtil* may designate either the locale or the nature of the action, or both, as seems to be the case with **marziḥ>marzēaḥ*.

Lines XVII–XXIII

These lines are puzzling. The banquet began in El's house and there is no mention of a move to another locale unless the statement that "El sat in his *marzēaḥ*" presumes that everyone knows that a *marzēaḥ* is separate from one's house. Unless the clear statement that "El went to his house / descended to his palace" has some metaphorical or hidden meaning that eludes us, we have to conclude that El's *marzēaḥ* was not in his house where the banquet began and to which El returned after toping in his *marzēaḥ*.

The spelling *ḥṭr* for *ḥẓr* is exceptional and puzzling. In the Nikkal Poem original *ṭ* is represented by *ẓ*, perhaps under Hurrian influence. The use of *ṭ* for original *ẓ* here corresponds to later Aramaic practice, as in *ḥūṭrā*, "enclosure."

Line XXIV

Tkmn and Snm are the Kassite deities Sukamuna and Sumaliya who also found their way into the Babylonian pantheon where Suqamuna is equated with Nergal or Nusku, but Sumaliya is associated with the equally obscure Kassite deities Sibarru and Sugurru.[49] The position and role of Tkmn and Snm in the Ugaritic pantheon remain obscure.[50]

---

48. Cf. E. W. Lane, *Arabic-English Lexicon*, pp. 1075 f., s.v. *rzḥ*.

49. Cf. D. O. Edzard, s.v. "Kassitischer Götter," *Wörterbuch der Mythologie*, ed. H. W. Haussig (Stuttgart: E. Klett, 1965–), 1: 1. H. Gese, "Die mythische epische Überlieferung Ugarits," in *Die Religionen der Menscheit*, ed. Christel Matthias Schroder (Stuttgart: W. Kohlhammer, 1960–), vol. 10, pt. 2: 97 f., suggests that the compound name means "Träger und Gipfel" and corresponds to Atlas in Greek myth. That lifting of the drunken father seems scant support for attributing to *ṭkmn wšnm* the function of Atlas as bearer of the world.

50. Cf. Pope, *El in the Ugaritic Texts*, p. 90.

Lines XXIV–XXVI

Virolleaud rendered "et il rencontre le *ḥby* (20) du Baˤal à deux cornes et la queue," simply transliterating *ḥby* for which he could find no acceptable sense. The citation of Dan. 8:6 should have prevented the mistaking of *bˤl* as the proper name of the great Storm God rather than the common noun *owner* which could have been otherwise expressed simply with the particle *ḏ*, as in the Arabic epithet of Alexander the Great, *dū ʾl- qarnain*, "He of the two horns." Gordon[51] properly renders "possessor of horns and tail" but takes *ḥby* as a proper name. Virolleaud suggests that we have here a prefiguration of Satan, perhaps the god Ršp, the Nergal of the Babylonians, who afflicts humanity with all kinds of evils, and he notes that in Hab. 3:5–6 the Vulgate translates *rešep* by *diabolus*. Ršp was an important deity and we have a representation of him wearing a helmet with small cervine head and horns,[52] but he is never depicted with a tail. Many deities were horned or wore horned headdresses. The word *ḥby* may be connected with the meaning "hide," as in Hebrew, or with Arabic *ḥbw / ḥby*, "crawl, creep"; a Hider, or a Hidden-One might be an appropriate designation for a sudden or furtive apparition, and a creepy creature, especially one with horns and tail, is suitably bizarre for a fit of alcoholic *delirium tremens* (cf. Prov. 23:33). It is not clear whether the subject of the verb *ngš* (*wngšnn* is presumably an error for *wyngšnn*) is El or the *ḥby*, but it does not matter greatly who confronted whom in this instance since the interest is in El's state rather than in the phantom of his delirium. Considering El's condition, that he is being carried or supported by Tkmn and Snm, it seems more likely that the *ḥby* is the subject of the verb and that the *-nn*, "energic," ending hides the object suffix referring to El, as the translation indicates.

Line XXVII

Again it is uncertain whether the subject of the verb is El or the *ḥby*. It seems more likely that the line concerns El's reaction to the

---

51. *UT*, 19 . 831a.
52. Cf. J. B. Pritchard, *The Ancient Near East in Pictures* (Princeton: Princeton University Press, 1958), fig. 476.

encounter rather than the action of the creature with horns and
tail, imaginary or otherwise. It is improbable that the verb *ylšn* is
denominative from the word for tongue since it is hard to see how
any of the attested meanings would relate to excreta. Virolleaud
rendered "il pautage," from *l(u)š*, "knead." Arabic, as usual, offers
several possibilities: *l(w)s*, "taste food by turning it about in the
mouth"; *l(w)š*, "be excessively tired, out of breath, and unable to
move on"; *lss*, "lick, pluck (grass) with the lips"; and *lšš* which in
the reduplicated form *lašlaš* means to be seized with fear so as to
drop excrement," "run to and fro in fear." The latter possibility
seems most plausible in view of the explicit involvement with excreta and the common association of involuntary defecation and
urination with sudden and intense fear as well as with excessive
alcoholic intoxication.

The sad plight of the father of the gods prostrate in his own filth
is reminiscent of Isaiah's description of the sacral feasts of the religious leaders of the Northern Kingdom, in Isa. 28:7–8.

> These too with wine stagger;
> With drink they totter.
> Priest and prophet stagger with drink,
> Befuddled with wine.
> They stagger in ——————,
> Reel in ——————,
> For all the tables are full
> Of vomit (and) excrement,
> Without a place . . . .

One may suspect that this text has been doctored to eliminate
offensive words. The meaningless *brʾh* vocalized *bārôʾeh*, "in the
seer," in verse 7h could be easily restored to read "in excrement,"
bḥrʾ. The following stich 7i is also confused but more difficult to
reconstitute. In any case, enough is preserved to set a scene similar
to that in which we find El at the end of our Ugaritic document.

The reference to excrement is interesting in the light of the rabbinic derision of the depravity associated with the cult of Baal Peor
who was allegedly worshiped with ceremonial defecation (BT,
Abodah Zarah 44b). A Jew was forbidden to relieve himself before
Baal Peor since this was the regular mode of worshiping the idol

(BT, *Sanhedrin* 60b, Mishnah Sanhedrin VII, 6). There is a story about a certain Jew who hired his ass to a gentile woman and accompanied her. When they came to Peor, she asked him to wait while she went in. When she came out, he asked the same of her: "But are you not a Jew?" she asked. He replied: "What is it to you?" and he entered and defecated before the idol and wiped himself on the idol's nose while the acolytes praised him saying, "No man ever served this idol thus." The sage opinion on this resort was that although the intent was to degrade the idol, the act constituted worship (BT, *Sanhedrin* 64a). It is difficult to assay how much of this story may derive from direct knowledge of the pagan cult and how much from play on one of the meanings of the word $p^c r$.

Line XXVIII

El is down[53] and, at least temporarily, out, "like those who descend into Earth," i.e. into the netherworld.

Lines XXIX–XXXIV

In spite of the losses at the bottom of the obverse and the top of the reverse of the text, it seems clear that ʿAštart and ʿAnat went roaming and brought back something with them. What they fetched presumably was the material mentioned in the following lines which appears to be medicine for El to bring him out of his comatose state and relieve his acute distress.

Line XXXV

Whether one takes *kmtrpa* as composed of the particle *k-* and the reflexive-passive participle *mtrpa* or as *k-* with enclitic, emphatic *-mā* before a finite verbal form *trpa*, it is at least certain that the matter involves healing and concerns El who needs it.

Virolleaud read *hn n^c r* and translated "Voici l'enfant." In support of this reading and interpretation one might adduce the reference to recovery from illness in Job 33:25,

---

53. On the meanings of *qll*, cf. Gordon, *UT*, 19 . 2231.

> His flesh becomes plump as a boy's,
> He returns to the days of his youth.[54]

The reading *hn*, however, is not certain and could as well be seen as the negation *in*. The vocable *nᶜr* in this context might also suggest something other than a boy or young man. Among various meanings of *nᶜr* as a verb we find "stir," or "rouse," used in connection with rising from sickness or from death, and "empty," "evacuate," used of emptying a dish or pot, or of making a flock discharge excrement on the area one wishes to have manured. Thus *nᶜr* in the present context, whether construed as a noun or verb, might have reference either to El's ailment or to the recovery therefrom.

Lines XXXVI–XXXVIII

The remainder of the text below the colophon line is a medical prescription similar in form to those in the hippiatric texts[55] which give the medication and the mode of administering it. Here we have a sick god rather than a horse and the medicine is given orally instead of through the nose. The materials here prescribed for the god are those regarded as beneficial to humans in similar state.

Line XXXVII

The verb *yšt* here is probably from *š(y)t*, "put, place" rather than *šty*, "drink." The word *lṣb* occurs sometimes in the cliché *yprq lṣb wyṣhq*, "he parted the jaw and laughed"; thus it designated the mouth, oral cavity, or throat. In Arabic the word is connected with the notion of narrowness, used for example, of a sword sticking tight in the scabbard, while the noun *liṣb* applies to a cleft in mountains, a narrow pass or valley. Accordingly, it has been suggested that the precise reference is to the narrow opening between the upper and lower dentition.[56] It is not clear, however, how much depth is envisaged for the narrowing opening. In any case, medicine administered by way of the *lṣb* will get to the seat of the trouble.

---

54. Cf. Marvin Pope, trans., *Anchor Bible* (Garden City: Doubleday and Co., 1965), vol. 15, *Job*.
55. *CTCA*, 160 and 161.
56. Cf. E. Ullendorff, "Ugaritic Marginalia," *Orientalia* 20 (1951), pp. 271 f.

For *ẖš⁽ᶜ⁾r* there are several possibilities. Akkadian *ḫašurru*, Sumerian GIŠ.ḪA.ŠUR, denotes a kind of cedar used for perfume, but the oil also served as a vehicle for crushed herbs to be drunk on an empty stomach.[57] Sumero-Akkadian *ḫašḫur*, "apple," might be the original of our word *ẖšᶜr*, the second *ẖ* being altered to ᶜ. In Mesopotamian magic and medicine *ḫašḫūru*, with various modifiers, such as *ḫašḫūr-abi / api*, "swamp apple," was prescribed for gastric and urinary troubles, for instance for a disease called picturesquely "red water."[58]

Line XXXVII

It is not clear whether *klb* is the word for "dog" or the particle *k* plus *lb*, "heart." There is in Akkadian a medicinal plant called *šêr kalbi* which was mixed with oil and taken internally for intestinal and urinary problems.[59] The transformation of *ḫašḫur* to *šêr* might be explained, if there were need, but the matter is not urgent in view of the uncertainty. If *klb* is analyzed as *k-lb* then the restoration of the symbol before *riš*, "head" at the beginning of the line might well be the conjunction *w-*, "and," *klb* [*w*]*riš* perhaps meaning "so that heart and head. . . ." The following word *pqq* might be taken as the name of some pharmaceutical. Akkadian *piqū*, *piqqūtu* is a plant identified as colocynth, the tops of which plant were used as a cathartic, while the seeds were boiled in oil and taken as a remedy for debility.[60] (Colocynth is still used as an ingredient, along with other substances, such as calomel and rhubarb, in pink, pleasant purgative pellets). There is, however, a consideration which excludes the equation of *pqq* in the present text with Akkadian *piqū* or *piqūtu*, "colocynth," viz. that the word had originally a final ᶜ, *pqᶜ*, which would be preserved in the Ugaritic cognate, as it is in Hebrew and Arabic. It is unlikely that the Akkadian form of the word with loss of the laryngal would be borrowed by Western Semites among whom the word must have been in common use with the laryngal intact. It is possible that *pqq* is a verb. The hollow

57. *CAD*, 6: 147b.
58. *CAD*, 6: 140 a (1) (b).
59. R. C. Thompson, *A Dictionary of Assyrian Botany* (London: British Academy, 1949), p. 23.
60. *Ibid.*, p. 85.

root $p(w)q$ has several interesting connections with drunkenness and the recovery from the same; it is used of drunken reeling and collapse, as in the passage Isa. 28:7 cited above. At the end of a long section in the Talmud dealing with the effects of intoxication and the cure (BT, ʿErubin 65a), Rabbi Hanina made a multiple word play on Job 41:7 and the roots $p(w)q$, ʾpq, and npq in connection with the action of a man who in a state of drunkenness still has enough consciousness, reverence and sense of unworthiness to stand up during the Prayer of Benedictions. Without going into the complicated puns,[61] it appears that $p(w)q$ in the causative stem may denote recovery from intoxication. This sense is confirmed by Arabic usage where the verb in the factitive (D or II) stem may mean "recover one's senses" and in the causative (IV) stem "recover (from illness or a swoon)." In the Vth stem there is further evidence of connection both with drinking and recovery from its effects, in the meanings "to drink from time to time one after another" and to "remember or try to remember." It is hard to see how meanings could be found more suitable to the present context. The form pqq may be explained as the L form, $pôqēq$, like $qômēm$ and $rômēm$, used in Hebrew and Ugaritic for the D stem of "hollow" verbs.[62]

If one seeks for $šrh$ as a noun a botanical or pharmaceutical meaning, there is Sumerian ŠE.RU.A (Akkadian $šerʾu?$), "licorice," the tops of which were used as medicine for gastric and urinary problems.[63] It seems more likely, however, that $šrh$ is a verb coordinate with pqq, for which there are some plausible possibilities. Elsewhere in Ugaritic[64] $šrh$ occurs as a verb meaning to "flash" (lightning), as in Job 37:3, but this sense is unsuitable to the present context. Arabic $šrh$, "be greedy for food or drink," is a possibility despite the deviation from the usual permutation of $š$ and $š$. In the Krt Epic,[65] when $Š^ctqt$ healed the ailing monarch "she washed him of sweat / his appetite for food she opened / his yen for meat." Arabic srw, meaning in the II stem "to rid someone of worry, grief, fear, or the like, to regain one's composure and feel again at peace

61. Jastrow, *Dictionary*, p. 1154b. s.v.
62. Cf *UT*, 9 . 32, 26, pp. 81 f.
63. Thompson, pp. 133 f.
64. *CTCA*, 4, V, 71.
65. *CTCA*, 16, VI, 10–12.

after a period of disquiet," offers sense appropriate to the present context. The final -*h* of *šrh* might be the suffixed object pronoun referring to El as the recipient of the healing. Akkadian *šurrū* and Hebrew and Aramaic *šarā* in the sense "begin, loosen, set free, etc.," also offers a suitable range for the passage in question.

Line XXXVIII

Here also, as above, *yšt* must be from *š(y)t*, "put," rather than *šty*, "drink," because of the similarity to the formulas in the hippiatric texts which direct that the materials be mixed together and poured in the horse's nose, *ydk aḥdh wyṣq baph*.[66] The final -*h* of *aḥdh* is the adverbial ending which has directive force with words like *šmmh*, "heavenward," and perhaps here too since the meaning may be "into a unit." The Ugaritic *aḥdh* is analogous to Akkadian *ištēniš*.

Olive juice, *dm zt*, is literally "blood of the olive," as wine is termed *dm ʿṣm* "blood of trees." The adjective *ḥrpnt* which modifies the olive juice is from a common Semitic root which seems to have the basic sense of "early," as applied to fruit, harvest, rains, and so on. Early olives would be green or unripe.

The life situation of our text we can roughly divine, although many puzzling questions remain. El's experience in his *marzēaḥ* mirrors that of his worshipers in theirs. "Wine which cheers gods and men" (Judg. 9:13), after a certain point brings also woes. The creepy creature with horns and tail encountered by El and the bizarre images reported by delirious drunks confirm the warning of the biblical moralist (Prov. 23:33), "Your eyes will see strange things." The father of gods and men floundering in excrement and urine was emulated by princes and people, priests and prophets, even among the Israelites, who reeled and tottered among tables full of vomit and fecal matter (Isa. 28:7). Dignity was scarcely a concern here and those who have admitted El's otiose character but compensated by emphasizing his dignity, *otium cum dignitate*, will have difficulty maintaining the dignity of a deity smutched with ordure. The crapulent deity's worshipers, in their devotional drinking, shared the god's distress and the medicine which was

---

66. *CTCA*, 160, 161, *et passim*.

prescribed for the god was doubtless what had been found helpful
for restoring mortals to consciousness and relieving the lingering
distemper. The worshipers must have been sympathetic with their
god whose plight they understood and shared. There is no hint of
moralizing or disapproval of the divine deportment since it was
human behavior projected to the realm of the gods.

The drinking of intoxicating liquors by gods and men is common
in myth and cult. The Vedic gods attained their immortality by
drinking the soma and the Homeric deities by drinking nectar and
eating ambrosia. Intoxicating liquors were used in earliest Brah-
manism and the modern Saktas still include as prime components
of proper worship intoxicating beverages and sacral sexual intercourse. Liquor drinking continues to be a part of most Parsee ceremonies. In the early Christian love-feasts and in the Eucharist the
drunkenness which St. Paul tried to curb was doubtless a survival
of oldtime religion which always dies hard. The Cup of Blessing
in the Jewish Qiddush has much the same background as the Christian Eucharist and both are chastened and purified transformations
of ancient communal feasts. Sacral drinking in connection with
funeral celebrations is attested among many peoples in different
parts of the world. The Irish wake has analogues in the funeral
celebrations of many societies of Africa, Asia, Australia, and the
Americas. To bring the random comparative comments up to date,
a Texas tycoon has recently announced plans to create a multi-
million-dollar fund to provide in perpetuity free cocktail parties as
a memorial to himself. This philanthropist is probably not aware
of the historical antecedents of his idea, seeing that he left school in
the third grade, but certain aspects of his plan comport with vener-
able custom and tradition.

The Ugaritic text here discussed is nearly a millennium older
than the earliest data on the *marzēaḥ* previously available to us and
approximately two millennia older than the remarks of the rabbis
on the subject. In spite of the great gap in time, the evidences,
early and late, conform to clarify our understanding of the puzzling
term *marzēaḥ*.

A note of apology may be in order for the unedifying features of
the text here treated. A more salubrious subject might have been
selected, but it happened that this was the text that engaged my

attention at the time of the invitation to contribute to this volume in honor of my beloved teacher. In dealing with some of the documents from Ugarit one may feel constrained to explain that he did not compose the text but seeks only to understand it. Among the many valuable lessons taught me by Professor Stinespring was the importance of honesty in dealing with a text. Candor dictates the confession that many of the suggestions here offered are highly uncertain and tentative, but it is hoped that some may prove helpful in the ongoing effort to understand this puzzling text.

I am happy for the opportunity to express to Professor William F. Stinespring my profound gratitude for the lively introduction he gave me to the Hebrew language and the study of the Bible and its background, for his encouragement and help in the pursuit of this interest, my respect for him as a scholar, and above all my admiration and affection for him as a man. *yîšar kōḥô.*

"OF CABBAGES AND KINGS"—OR QUEANS
Notes on Ben Sira 36:18–21

JOHN STRUGNELL

In Ben Sira 36:18–37:15[1] we find four roughly analogous sections on the subject of foods (36:18–20), women (36:21–26), friends (37:1–6), and advisers (37:7–15). These sections are now of very different lengths and degrees of development, perhaps because of the accretion of other proverbial material on these themes, which elsewhere too have excited the sages of Israel to eloquence; but it can be seen that each started with a thematic statement of either pattern A, for example,

> Every meat doth the belly eat
>> yet is one meat more pleasant than another (36:18)

or pattern B, for example,

> Every friend sayeth: I am a friend;
>> But there is a friend who is (only) friend
>>> in name (37:1, cf. 37:7),

i.e. schematically:

> There are all sorts of X
>> but one X is better than others utterly bad.

The introductory verse to the section on women, 36:21, is formally and verbally close to pattern A:

> A woman will receive any man,
>> yet is one woman more pleasant than another.

The Greek presents this verse in its correct position, at the start of the section on women, and in a form roughly equivalent to the above translation:

1. There are many systems of numbering verses in Ben Sira; to avoid giving a chaotic series of alternative numbers for each verse we cite only according to the enumeration of G. H. Box and W. O. E. Oesterley *apud* R. H. Charles, *The Apocrypha and Pseudepigrapha of the Old Testament* (Oxford, 1913), vol. 1. Unless otherwise stated, the translations given also come from the same work.

πάντα ἄρρενα ἐπιδέξεται γυνή,
ἔστιν δὲ θυγάτηρ θυγατρὸς κρεισσῶν.

The Syriac has omitted the whole verse, for reasons that will become understandable later. The mediaeval Hebrew MS B, which recent studies have proved to be a faithful descendant of a Hebrew text of the first century B.C.,[2] gives this verse in a different place (in the middle of the section on foods, after 36:18) but in a form which essentially coincides with that of the LXX:

כל זכר תקבל אשה
אך יש אשה מאשה תנעם

Despite the formal accord between this verse and other verses of the A pattern, such as 36:18,

כל זכר תקבל אשה   [=כל אוכל אוכל כרש]
אך יש אשה מאשה תנעם [=אך יש אוכל מאוכל נעים]

36:21 does not give us the sense that we require. Here we have a first hemistich that tells us that there are all sorts of *men* that a *woman* can marry (or whatever the odd term תקבל would mean); and yet the second hemistich (which also agrees formally with the pattern of the surrounding verses) shows us that such a first hemistich, though making an intellectually conceivable statement, is incoherent with its context. To contrast properly with the second hemistich we need rather, as the French commentator Lévi saw[3]—

2. The objections raised against the substantial authenticity of these Cairo Geniza MSS of Ben Sira were already laid to rest by A. A. Di Lella in his *Hebrew Text of Sirach: a Text-Critical and Historical Study*, Studies in Classical Literature, 1 (The Hague: Mouton and Co., 1966); see also my review in *CBQ*, 30 (1968), 88–91. The Ben Sira MS subsequently discovered by Yigael Yadin at Masada and edited by him in *The Ben Sira Scroll from Masada* (Jerusalem: Israel Exploration Society, 1965) and in *Eretz-Israel*, 8 (1967), 1–45, shows that the whole dispute was one of the aberrations of scholarship.

3. I. Lévi, *L'Ecclésiastique, ou la Sagesse de Jésus, Fils de Sira*, Bibliothèque de l'École des Hautes Études: Sciences Religieuses, vol. 10, nos. 1–11 (Paris: Leroux, 1898–1901) 2: 172–73. The difficulty was also sensed by earlier commentators. Typical of their suggestions is that of J. Knabenbauer's commentary on Ecclesiasticus in *Cursus Scripturae Sacrae* (Paris: Lethielleux, 1902). He glosses "omnem masculum excipiet mulier" by "debet nubere quicumque demum ei assignatur, cf. L(esêtre) Fr(itzsche) R(yssel)"; and explains "ipsa itaque mulier non potest discernere; at aliter res se habet ex parte viri; ille potest et debet discernere quam in matrimonium ducturus est." Although such a thought would restore coherence to the distich, the words crucial for making the contrast are unfortunately not in the text but only in Knabenbauer's exegesis.

they see these things clearly in France—a statement on the many types of *women* that a *man* can choose to marry.

Either one of two very simple corrections to the Hebrew can, however, restore this needed sense.

כל זכר דובק לאשה
[כל זכר ינקף לאשה]
אך יש אשה מאשה תנעם

> Every male cleaveth unto a woman[4]
> yet is one woman more pleasant than another.

By altering the word division (transferring the final ל from the end of the verb to the start of the word אשה) and by correcting what remains of the verb, either into דובק[5] or into ינקף,[6] we get the statement about the many types of women which we need, and which contrasts properly with the second hemistich; and we gain in the process a statement which conforms to the facts of life—a criterion not to be neglected in editing the shrewd sages of the ancient East. We all get married, but not everyone gets a Helen of Troy.

That the above emendation does not strain the material and palaeographical possibilities of textual corruption in the second century B.C. will be readily granted. The wrong word division, and the consequent changes of the verb, will have occurred very early in the textual tradition, because the error—surely a *conjunctive* error—affected at a very early date the common archetype of LXX and of the Geniza MS.[7] It will have taken place under the influence of the form of verses like 36:18, where כל אוכל is the object of the

---

4. Cf. Gen. 2:24 with זכר instead of איש and אשה instead of אשתו (cf. perhaps LXX Mss a d p d₂): does the modified form of the verse no longer imply a reference to marriage? The reader can supply for himself modern proverbial parallels.

5. If both the form and the preposition be allowable, the דו will have been misread as ח, and the remaining consonants will have suffered metathesis after the erroneous word division.

6. In this case the יע will have been misread as ח and the פ will have become ב. A *piel* would be unexpected but ינקף could be a further Aramaism, in orthography also, for a *qal*. נקף ל׳ is the standard Syriac equivalent of דבק ב׳, cf. Gen. 2:24. The sense of the verb in Jewish Aramaic is analogous, though it is not, to my knowledge, used about matrimony. Hopefully we show good taste in refusing to speculate about a possible reading with √נקב.

7. For another conjunctive error that has affected the tradition of Ben Sira at a similarly high date, see my "Notes and Queries on 'The Ben Sira Scroll from Masada,' " in the festschrift for W. F. Albright, *Eretz-Israel*, 9 (1969), 116–17.

verb and not, as here, its subject—corruptions naturally have their own mechanical reasons which should not be construed as arguments for the good quality of the resultant text—but against nonsense, however well attested, the Bentleian canon of *ratio et res ipsa* must prevail.

In both the Hebrew and the Syriac versions, 36:18 is followed immediately by 36:19. In the Hebrew MS B, however, 36:21 is placed between 36:18 and the remaining verses on foods (36:19–20). It is clearly misplaced here. Moreover, in the place where it should come, after 36:20, we find a peculiar verse which occurs in none of the other versions.

This verse is transcribed by the editors in various ways. All agree in reading

כל ??? תאכל חיה

אך יש מכה ממכה תנעם

The second word is transcribed נכה by Peters,[8] נבר by Lévi,[9] נכד by Smend,[10] and נכס by Segal.[11] Peters translates נכה with "Jeden Erschlagenen frisst das Getier, aber die eine Zuchtigung ist angenehmerer als die andere," a translation that lacks something in coherence (!) and could perhaps be improved by giving מכה the sense of "corpse / thing slain." Segal's text is similar in meaning: "a wild beast eats all animals that it has killed (= טרף), but not all the meats are of equal quality." Smend saves himself from the duty of translating his text by maintaining that the verse is a senseless variant conflated from 36:18 and 36:21. Lévi suggests no translation of his נבר, asking whether it might be a mistake for נברה (from the verb ברה, "nourish oneself"), and observing furthermore that the sense of מכה is far from certain.

Two words then are causing our difficulties, מכה and נ°°. The readings נכה and נכס must be rejected on palaeographical grounds. Of the materially possible readings נכד, נכר, נבד, and נבר, the first three are lexicographically or materially of dubious digestibility, even for wild animals. נבר, however, and this is perhaps the easiest

8. N. Peters, *Der juengst wiederaufgefundene hebraeische Text des Buches Ecclesiasticus* (Freiburg i. Br: Herder, 1902).

9. Lévi, 2: 174.

10. Rudolph Smend, *Die Weisheit des Jesus Sirach hebraeisch und deutsch* (Berlin: Reimer, 1906), p. 31.

11. M. S. Segal, ספר בן סירא השלם[2] (Jerusalem: Bialik, 1958).

reading of all from a material point of view, gives us a perfectly acceptable meaning. The verb נבר means in rabbinic Hebrew "to dig up with the snout." It has the same meaning in Jewish Aramaic, and Syriac; in Syriac we find also *nbwr*ʾ, "a snout," and *nbr*ʾ, "the claws of a cock." [12] נבר (*néber* or *nibbār*) will then naturally mean "a thing dug up by the snout."

"An animal will eat all that can be rooted up by its snout" is a perfectly plausible sense for the first hemistich; but what of the second? Like our predecessors, we find מכה unpromising. However, our restoration of "digging up with the snout" in the first hemistich points us to a very specific domain, that of the finding of truffles; and the Hebrew word for "truffles" is, not מכה, but כמה! [13] By metathesis of the consonants, the rare word כמה has been corrupted into the common מכה—this is the easiest of corruptions to admit—and the resultant sense harmonizes perfectly with the best material reading of the first hemistich, and with the form of the surrounding aphorisms. The verse (?36:18c–d) should then be translated:

> An animal will eat all that can be rooted up by
> his snout,
> but some truffles taste better than others, [14]

12. For Hebrew see *b* Baba Kamma 17b, and see E. Ben Yehuda, *Thesaurus totius Hebraitatis* (Berlin and Jerusalem: Langensheit, 1908–59), p. 3493 *sub verbo*. For Jewish Aramaic see Marcus Jastrow, *A Dictionary of the Targumim* . . . . (N. Y.: Pardes, 1950), p. 870 *sub verbo*. For Syriac see R. Payne Smith, *Thesaurus Syriacus* (Oxford: Clarendon Press, 1879–1901), 2: 2273 and T. Audo, *Dictionnaire de la langue Chaldéenne* (Mosul: PP. Dominicains, 1897), 2: 81, each *sub verbo*. I find also in J.-B. Belot, *Vocabulaire Arabe-Francais* (Beirut: Imprimerie Catholique, 1898), p. 798, a meaning "Fouiller, chercher" given for the Arabic *nabara*.

13. The word is common Semitic; cf. Wolfram von Soden, *Akkadisches Handwörterbuch* (Wiesbaden: Harrassowitz, 1965–69), 1: 432, on *kamʾatu*; E. W. Lane, *An Arabic English Lexicon* (London: Williams and Norgate, 1863–1893), p. 2629, on *kmʾ* (the precise form is disputed); Payne Smith, 1: 1723, on *kymʾ*; Audo, 1: 468, on *kmtʾ*; Ben Yehuda, p. 2416, on כמה. The Hebrew lexicographers hesitate on the proper form and gender of the singular; the plural is indifferently כמהים and כמהות. If we merely make the minimum correction to Ben Sira we will have here a feminine noun כמה (cf. the verb) and there is nothing impossible in this; however it could be that the gender of the verb was subsequently changed to the feminine in consequence of the corruption to מכה.

14. On truffles we have little to add of substance to the treatise given by I. Loew, *Die Flora der Juden* (Vienna and Leipzig: R. Loewit, 1926), 1: 26–44, where one finds multifarious details; the truth of our second hemistich is amply demonstrated there. For the medicinal uses of truffles see Ibn el Beïthar, *Traité des Simples*, Notices et extraits des MSS de la Bibliotheque Nationale, Vols. 23, 25, 26 (Paris: Imprimerie

and the words נבר and כמה should be restored to our dictionaries of early Hebrew.

Does this proverb form an original part of Ben Sira's book? Nothing in the contents or the attestation of the verse is irreconcilable with its genuineness,[15] even though it is not clear whether it stood originally after 36:18 or after 36:20. A discoverer has a natural tendency to favor his own discoveries; but we hope that other scholars will share our taste for Ben Sira's truffles.

Nationale, 1877–1883), 3: 192–94, to which R. P. B. Couroyer O.P. kindly drew my attention. They grow in the southern desert of Palestine as well as the Syrian Desert: Prof. M. Zohary of the Botanical Department of the Hebrew University informs me that he does not know of any specimens found in the more settled wooded parts of Palestine. The truffle of the Syrian Desert, the best reputed species, can be found by men, because it causes a slight elevation in the level of the soil; see R. Montagne, *La civilisation du désert* (Paris: Hachette, 1947), p. 24 (a reference for which I thank R. P. R. de Vaux O.P.). I can find no ancient reference from the Near East to the use of pigs or dogs for finding and digging up truffles; however, Prof. Zohary tells me that he has seen the Beduin in Syria use dogs (though not pigs) to locate them. Even this verse does not necessarily imply that animals were employed to dig up truffles for their masters, but only that they have a tendency to dig them up on their own account; it is indeed for this reason that pigs have, as indirectly attested by Prov. 11:22, rings in their noses.

15. Its formal closeness to 36:18, 21, could be used to argue either for its authenticity (it will even have belonged, with them, to Ben Sira's source) or alternatively for its being an early marginal gloss (being added because of its formal similarity, it will have been inserted in various copies after different verses). The aberrant positions of this verse and of verse 21 are not satisfactorily explained by saying that only *one* of them is a gloss, for we would still have to explain the odd position of 36:21 in MS B. One could equally well explain the evidence of the Hebrew MSS by postulating that the two formally similar verses simply swapped places; or alternatively one could assume that, in one of the MSS that preceded MS B, the verse on truffles once came directly before 21 and subsequently (by homoeoarchton and homoeoteleuton) has swallowed that verse up in MS B; in another of its sources the two verses will have stood together after 36:18, and after a similar haplography (this time of the former of the two verses) 36:21 now stands alone in its surprising position in MS B. If the verse is a genuine part of Ben Sira we must grant that the haplography of the whole verse in the Greek and the Syriac is a *non-conjunctive* error, committed independently by the translators of those versions. This is not so implausible as it might seem; the Syriac has in fact omitted not only this verse but the probably adjacent 36:21 as well; this version is characterized by the frequent omission of whole verses and especially of verses whose sense was obscure or corrupt; and the corrupt מכה would probably have stood in the text that the Syriac translator used.

ANTHROPOLOGY AND SOTERIOLOGY IN THE DEAD SEA SCROLLS AND IN THE NEW TESTAMENT

WILLIAM HUGH BROWNLEE

The ancient Psalmist, standing beneath the Palestinian sky at night, exclaimed:

When I look at Thy heavens,
> the work of Thy fingers,
the moon and the stars
> which Thou established,
what is man that Thou rememberest him,
> a human that Thou carest for him?

(Ps. 8:4–5 [=8:3–4])

This is still a relevant question; for every scientific advance in the knowledge of the cosmos leads all the more poignantly to the question: "What is man?"[1] Biblical answers are also still relevant. Ancient Jews languishing in exile at Babylon were assured by God's prophet that He had not forgotten them, although all nations are but as "a drop from a bucket" in His sight, by appealing to the might of Yahweh who created and sustains each star. Puny humans should not think that God disregards them.

25 To whom would you compare Me,
> that I be equal? asks the Holy One.
26 Set your eyes toward the sky
> and see Who created these:

It is a heartfelt privilege to contribute this article to the honor of Dr. William F. Stinespring who was both my former teacher and colleague at Duke University. His own scholarship and enthusiasm in all that relates to biblical studies and the biblical languages have served to guide and to inspire me through the intervening years since I first came to know him. His prophetic concern for righteousness and justice in society and in the world at large, together with his cordial and sympathetic spirit, elicit admiration and esteem. Above all, he is my friend.

1. Albert Einstein is reported to have said, approximately: "If there is a God, He is the great Mathematician, preoccupied with the whole universe. If so, He has no time for me." As yet I have not been able to verify this quotation; but it sounds very much like him. In any case, this expresses well the mood of many in our day.

Who marshals their army by number,
    mustering them all by name!
By His multiple powers
    and mighty strength
    not one is missing!
27 Why do you say, O Jacob,
    and complain, O Israel:
"My way is hidden from Yahweh,
    my cause has no standing with my God!"
28 Have you not known
    or even heard?
"The God of eternity is Yahweh,
    Creator of earth's far reaches.
Inexhaustible and untiring is He;
    unsearchable are the insights of Him
29 Who gives[2] strength to the exhausted
    and multiplies the vigor of the powerless.

(Isa. 40:25–29)

Deutero-Isaiah indulges in verbal play when he asserts that Yahweh
with "His multiple powers" "multiplies the vigor of the powerless."
This same intimate care of the Almighty for impotent man is paralleled in the teaching of Jesus (Matt. 10:29): "Are not two sparrows
sold for a penny? And not one of them will fall to the ground without your Father's will. . . . Fear not, therefore; you are of more
value than many sparrows."

For the people of Qumran, the question of "What is man?"
was one of moral perplexity arising quite as much from man's sinfulness as from his apparent insignificance.[3] The answers given to
this question by these ancient Jews are the subject to be taken up
here. Correlated with the nature of man is the nature of God's
saving work, so that anthropology and soteriology stand together.
The ideas of the people of the Dead Sea Scrolls will be discussed
also in relation to the New Testament.

---

2. The presence of the article with the participle in the text of 1Q Isaᵃ requires
the translation "Who gives" rather than "He gives." The Massoretic Text can be
translated either way.

3. For the question "What is man?" see 1Q S xi, 20–22; 1Q H iv, 29 ff.; ix, 29;
xiii, 13 ff.; xv, 21; xviii, 21.

God Created Man within a Context of Dualism

It is the dualistic context of life which explains both the angelic heights and the demonic depths of which human nature is capable. The basic passage dealing with the nature and destiny of man is found in the Qumran Society Manual (1Q S iii, 13–iv, 26).[4] In my translation of 1951, I entitled this section "The Instruction of the Community Concerning the Moral Nature of Man, or the Divisions of Mankind and the Spirits by Which They Walk." Others have referred to this simply as the passage concerning the Two Ways. Man's creation took place in a context of dualism; for not only are there two classes of men, righteous and wicked, children of light and children of darkness; but also the character of man is determined by two angels (or spirits) which the God of knowledge created. The good angel is referred to variously as the "angel of light" or "the spirit of truth," and as the "prince of lights." The evil angel is designated variously as the "spirit of perversity" and the "angel of darkness." The good angel leads men forward in holiness and to eternal life in everlasting light. The evil angel leads men ever more deeply into sin, to their perpetual ruin in the realms of everlasting darkness. Although some of this dualistic language comes from the Old Testament, the overall presentation and terminology remind one much more of Zoroastrianism.[5] Hebrew monotheism is safeguarded not merely by asserting that God is the source of everything, but also by designating this God as "the God of Israel" (iii, 24). This merging of Zoroastrian dualism with the ethical dualism of the Old Testament was undoubtedly accomplished by interpreting the Old Testament in peculiar ways. Indeed

4. This document has also been called "The Sectarian Document," "The Manual of Discipline," and "The Community Rule," etc. See "Scroll Nomenclature and Abbreviations," in W. H. Brownlee, *The Meaning of the Qumran Scrolls for the Bible* (New York: Oxford University Press, 1964), pp. xix–xxi. Hereafter this will be cited as *Meaning*. H. Farley has employed my nomenclature which is designed to fit the technical symbols, in his translation of Marcel Simon, *Jewish Sects at the Time of Jesus* (Philadelphia: Fortress Press, 1967).

5. The Zoroastrian influence was noted briefly in *The Dead Sea Manual of Discipline, Translation and Notes*, Bulletin of the American Schools of Oriental Research, Supplementary Studies, Nos. 10–12 (1951), p. 13, n. 21, p. 15, n. 30. K. G. Kuhn and André Dupont-Sommer have in their studies (cited in *Meaning*, p. 96, n. 76) presented detailed comparisons. See also David Winston, "The Iranian Component in the Bible, Apocrypha, and Qumran: a Review of the Evidence," *History of Religions*, 5 (1966), 183–216.

the idea of the two angels could be readily derived from Zech.
3:1 f., in which the prophet describes a scene in which Satan appears as an accuser before the throne of God and the angel of the
Lord as the champion of the accused. Similarly in the Book of
Job, Satan is Job's accuser, and despite his general mood of despair,
Job at times rises to the idea of a heavenly redeemer, or intercessor
on his behalf.[6] In the dualistic passage of the Society Manual, the
roles of accuser and intercessor are entirely passed over, and the
two angels appear rather as enticing, or seductive powers. The one
allures men into the way of truth and righteousness. The other
seduces men into the way of error and sin. This view of the two
angels was not without precedent in the Old Testament; for already
in I Chron. 21:1 Satan is said to have incited David to sin, and
Elihu in Job 33:23 entertains the idea of an angelic mediator who
is also man's moral guide. Under the influence of Zoroastrianism,
it seems, the two angels (or spirits) both came to be regarded as
tempters: the one tempting men to be good, and the other tempting
men to be evil. The idea that God had created these two angels
was probably read into Isa. 45:7, which in the Massoretic text
reads:

> I form light and create darkness;
> I make weal [שלום] and create woe [רע].

The intention of this verse was to assert that the Lord is the creator
of both fortune and misfortune, which are symbolized by light and
darkness respectively. The Qumran sect, however, probably interpreted the creation of light and darkness as referring to the creation
of the angels of light and darkness; and a peculiar reading in
1Q Isaᵃ increases this probability. There one reads no longer "I
make שלום and create evil," but "I make טוב and create evil." The
substitution of טוב ("good") for שלום ("weal") probably arose as an
interchange of synonyms; but the result is the presence of two anti-
thetical terms capable also of an ethical interpretation: "I make
good and create evil." The midrashic explication of this would be
that God made the mediating powers through which good and
evil come to man. This is quite unlike gnosticism in which with
greater pessimism all the mediating powers become evil, with the

---

6. See *Meaning*, pp. 96 f.

human spirit being but a spark of light immersed in a sea of darkness and evil.[7]

According to the Society Manual it would appear there is only darkness, and not light, in the children of darkness; for we are told: "In the hand of the angel of darkness is *all the rule* over the sons of perversion." On the other hand, though "the rule over *all the sons* of righteousness is in the hand of the prince of lights," the text does not say that this is "*all* the rule" over them. The different placement of the qualification "all" indicates that the "sons of righteousness" (children of light) are at times under the sway of the angel of darkness. In fact, we are explicitly told: "It is because of the angel of darkness that all the sons of righteousness go astray, so that all their sin and their iniquities and their guilt and the transgressions of their deeds are under his dominion (according to God's mysteries), until his end." Although "all the spirits allotted" the angel of darkness strive "to trip the sons of light, yet the God of Israel and His angel of truth have helped all the sons of light." One finds then a hopeless situation for the damned and an ambiguous, though hopeful, situation for God's elect. The demarcation between the two parties is complete, even though moral perfection is not within the reach of the righteous "during the dominion of Belial" which precedes the messianic kingdom.[8]

Not all Qumran thought can be so harmoniously systematized; for the horoscopes found at Qumran do not draw such a sharp demarcation between the good and the evil. One man, born under the constellation of Taurus, is declared to possess "six (parts) spirit in the House of Light and three in the Pit of Darkness." Another fragmentary description tells of a man who has "eight (parts) spirit in the House of [Darkness] and one (part) from the House of Light."[9] Thus, it would seem, there are gradations of light and

7. Yet cf. the various proportions of light and darkness in the Qumran horoscopes, cited at n. 9.

8. 1Q S i, 18. The defeat of the forces of Belial figures prominently in the Military Manual (1Q M) and in the Melchizedek *Pesher* (11Q Mel.).

9. J. M. Allegro, "An Astrological Cryptic Document from Qumran," *Journal of Semitic Studies*, 9 (1964), 291–94, with improved readings by J. Carmignac, "Les Horoscopes de Qumrân," *Revue de Qumran*, 5 (1965), 199–217. According to P. Wernberg-Møller, "A Reconsideration of the Two Spirits in the Rule of the Community (IQ Serek iii, 13–iv, 26)," *Revue de Qumran*, 3 (1961), 433, each person according to 1Q S iv, 16, 25 has received the two spirits in equal proportions. A. A. Anderson, "The Use of 'Ruaḥ' in 1Q S, 1Q H, and 1Q M," *Journal of Semitic Studies*, 7 (1962),

darkness in the make-up of every person. Such a view does not logically follow from the usual dualism of Qumran; and therefore these horoscopes may be late intrusions into the community from the outside. Their point of appeal to the sectaries of Qumran would be their common dualistic analysis between light and darkness, also their preoccupation with human destiny. It could also be that delayed messianic fulfillment according to their interpretations of the Scriptures was a contributing factor. Thus in their vain efforts to predict the future, they may have increasingly turned to astrology during their last decades.

Qumran dualism with its good and evil spirits which motivate human conduct is closer to New Testament thought than to Old Testament thought; for in the New Testament we find a fully personal Devil, or Satan, and a fully personal Holy Spirit. The former tempts men to follow the ways of wickedness and the latter leads men in the way of righteousness. The Devil is a fallen angel and therefore a creature of God. The Holy Spirit is no creature, but rather a hypostasis of the one true God. The only place where one may question this is in the Johannine literature where we find the Qumran terminology "Spirit of truth" and "Spirit of error."[10] The "Spirit of truth" figures both in the Gospel according to John and in the First Epistle; but the "Spirit of error" figures only in I John. Identity of terminology does not prove identity of meaning, and nothing is said in this literature which would indicate that the Spirit of Truth is to be thought of as an angel and therefore as a creature.

In the Epistle (I John 4:1–6) it is evident that "the Spirit of truth" is the same as the "Spirit of God." In the Gospel (John 14:16 f., 26) it is clear that "the Spirit of truth" and "the Holy Spirit" are the same; but an ambiguity appears in a key passage

---

300, finds rather that according to 1Q S the spirits are received in various proportions in accord with the horoscopes. Unless there is an inconsistency within this Two-Ways passage, no parts light could be allotted to the sons of perversion, for otherwise they would not be wholly under the power of the "angel of darkness." Only the children of light would have various proportions of light and darkness, and presumably always more light than darkness. The struggle between right and wrong within the human heart would in that case be wholly the experience of the children of light.

10. "The spirits of truth and perversion [or error]" (1Q S iii, 18 f.) may be compared with I John 4:6 and the Testament of Judah 20:1. The "Spirit of truth" alone figures in John 14:16 f.; 16:13.

of the Society Manual (IQ S iv, 21), where "a [or the] spirit of holiness" is parallel with "a [or the] spirit of truth." The context is one of spiritual cleansing from sin in which the description of the Spirit of Truth as holy is apt. This does not necessarily mean that the Spirit of Truth in the scrolls is the same as God's Holy Spirit of other passages.[11] Yet it does introduce an element of uncertainty affecting also the Fourth Gospel, unless we accept the evidence of I John for the Spirit of Truth as God's own Spirit.[12] Although there are a few passages in the Old Testament which personify God's Spirit and hence prepare for hypostatization of the Spirit in the New Testament,[13] it is John's synthesis of Qumran's Spirit of Truth with the Holy Spirit which gives us the strongest evidence of all for the Holy Spirit as a personal distinction within the one God, as a person within the Godhead.

God Created Man to Lord It Over the Creatures, But Not Over His Fellow Man

The Manual of Discipline declared (iii, 17 f.) that God "created man for dominion over the world." This statement rested upon Gen. 1:26–28 and Ps. 8:6–9. The former passage reads as follows:

11. For studies on רוח in Qumran usage, see George Johnston, " 'Spirit' and 'Holy Spirit' in Qumran Literature," in *New Testament Sidelights: Essays in Honor of A. C. Purdy*, ed. H. K. McArthur (Hartford: Hartford Seminary Foundation Press, 1960), pp. 27–42; W. Foerster, "Der heilige Geist im spät Judentum," *NTS*, 8 (1962), 117–34; Joseph Schreiner, "Geistbegabung in der Gemeinde von Qumran," *Biblische Zeitschrift*, n.s. 9 (1965), 161–80; A. A. Anderson, "Use of '*Ruaḥ*' in 1Q S, 1Q H, and 1Q M," *Journal of Semitic Studies*, 7 (1962), 293–303; F. Nötscher, "Heiligkeit in den Qumranschriften," *Revue de Qumran*, 2 (1960), 163–81, 315–44; J. Pryke, " 'Spirit' and 'Flesh' in the Qumran Documents and Some New Testament Texts," *Revue de Qumran*, 5 (1965), 345–60.

12. See here Jean Paul Audet, "Affinités litteraires et doctrinales du Manuel de Discipline," *Revue Biblique*, 60 (1953), 41–82.

13. Although a few have argued that the "spirits of truth and perversity" at Qumran are only personifications of the good and evil tendencies within man, a concept current in rabbinic thought, yet the representation of these spirits as angels engaged in a cosmic struggle indicates that the term "spirit" is here more than a psychological term according to Helmer Ringgren, *The Faith of Qumrân: Theology of the Dead Sea Scrolls* (Philadelphia: Fortress Press, 1963), pp. 68–80.

Many references to God's Spirit in both the Old and the New Testaments allow for the Holy Spirit as simply a manifestation of God's own power and presence, without any clear personification at all. However, sometimes the Spirit possesses personal attributes. Thus the Spirit is grieved by human sin. (Isa. 63:10, Eph. 4:30) and intercedes for Christ's followers (Rom. 8:26 f.). See A. H. Strong, *Systematic Theology* (Philadelphia and Toronto: The Judson Press, 1907), pp. 323–26; Louis Berkhof, *Systematic Theology*, 3rd ed. (Grand Rapids: W. B. Eerdmans, 1946), pp. 95–99.

And God said, "I will make man in My image, after My likeness. They shall *rule* the fish of the sea, the birds of the sky, the cattle, the whole earth and all the creeping things that creep on the earth." God said to them, "Be fertile and increase, fill the earth and *master* it; and rule the fish of the sea, the birds of the sky, and all the living things that creep on the earth." (Jewish Publication Society)

The same idea is eloquently expressed in Ps. 8:5–8:

For Thou hast made him little less than a god;
    with glory and honor hast Thou crowned him.
Thou hast installed him over the works of thine hands
    and put all things beneath his feet:
sheep and cattle, all,
    even beasts of the wild,
birds of the air, fish of the lakes,[14]
    every swimmer of the currents of the seas.

The first clause is rendered in the Revised Standard Version, "Yet Thou hast made him little less than God." The older versions which took אלהים as "angels" rather than "God" were better. A number of Old Testament passages refer to subordinate members of the divine assembly as "gods" or "sons of God." The Septuagint often translates these terms as referring to the angels.[15] Even the texts of Qumran distinguish between God and angels by calling the former אל and the latter אלים, with no fear that the latter would call into question Jewish monotheism. That man is infinitely less than God all ancient Jews knew right well; but the Psalmist declares man to be but little less than the angels, little short of supernatural.

In our day man's dominion over the world is vastly extended through modern technology, so that he has begun to harness the atom and to explore space. All this is fine and is a legitimate expression of man's God-given dignity, but he must beware lest he feel self-sufficient and independent of the Almighty Creator and all-

14. Or "fish of the sea," but ים includes all large bodies of water. The shift from the singular to the plural in the parallelism is purely stylistic.

15. Pss. 8:6 (=8:5, English); 96:7 (=97:7, Hebrew and English); 137:1 (=138:1, Hebrew and English). Cf. also Deut. 32:43 according to the LXX and one manuscript of 4Q (Brownlee, *Meaning*, pp. 9–12).

gracious Redeemer. To dispense with God is to deify oneself and to become guilty of the gravest offense to God; and, in the end, self-deified man tyrannizes his fellowmen. In his lament to Yahweh, Habakkuk complained:

Thou hast made man as fish of the sea,
    as gliding things *over which is no ruler*

                         (Hab. 1:14)

If this reading of the Massoretic Text is correct, the prophet is remonstrating that by subjecting the Kingdom of Judah to Babylonia, Yahweh is making His people subject to exploitation like subhuman creatures which have no governmental protection. In this case, the language of Habakkuk stands related to the descriptions of creatures like the ant and the locust in Proverbs (6:6–8; 30:27), which are there declared to have no ruler. This text is reshaped, however, in the ancient Habakkuk Commentary from Qumran so as to read:

Thou hast made man as the fish of the sea,
    as gliding things *over which to rule.*

"The fish of the sea" and the "gliding things" reminded the commentator of Gen. 1:26–28 and Ps. 8:5–8. Even the verb *rule* (or participle *ruling one, ruler*) seemed reminiscent of these passages where man is assigned the role of ruling, or mastering, the lower creatures.[16] Consequently the author of the commentary altered "over which is no ruler" to "over which to rule." According to this wording, Habakkuk's remonstrance protests the fact that God has reduced man to the status of animals in making him subject to exploitation by the Chaldeans. Yet the Almighty had never intended man either to exploit, or to be exploited by, his fellowman; but He made him to have dominion over the works of His hands. The author of the Habakkuk Commentary applied the text to the Kittim (probably the Romans),[17] whom he charges with harsh

16. Cf. here 1Q H i, 15 f. as restored by André Dupont-Sommer, *The Essene Writings from Qumrân* (Cleveland and New York: The World Publishing Company, 1962), p. 202.

17. The best study on this is still Roger Goosens, "Les Kittim du Commentaire d'Habacuc," *La Nouvelle Clio* (1952), pp. 137–70. 4Q p Nahum i, 3 now confirms this identification by distinguishing a period "from the time of Antiochus until the coming of the rulers of the Kittim."

rule and exploitation. It is they who in their worldwide conquest and vast empire tyrannize men, treating them as if they were mere fish of the sea, which man has the right to take for his own use.

How often has man tyrannized his fellowman in human history. Whenever man exploits his fellowman, he reduces him to the status of a mere animal. In seeking to lord it over men, he assumes the role of God, who alone has absolute sovereignty over humanity;[18] but in so doing he makes a beast of himself and treats others as beasts. Accordingly the commentary declares that the Kittim have deified their instruments of war:

> And as for what it says, "Therefore they will sacrifice to their net and burn incense to their seine," its interpretation is that they sacrifice to their military standards and that their weapons of war are their objects of veneration.

In this interpretation of Hab. 1:16, the commentary has followed an interpretation which was found already in an ancient targum; but what it says fits admirably the ruthless Romans who a century later than the Qumran text actually erected their military standards in the Jewish temple and performed sacrifice to them.[19] This was their crowning act of contempt to the God of Israel after they had conquered his holy city Jerusalem and gained control of his temple.

TO WALK HUMBLY WITH GOD IS TO
WALK HUMBLY WITH GOD'S PEOPLE

The Society Manual contains at least six allusions to Mic. 6:8,[20] which is the grandest epitome of what is involved in godly living to be found in the prophets. The grammatical constructions of the document show that אהבת חסד was understood as a nominal phrase with the meaning "ḥesed-type love." 1Q S v, 3 f. illustrates this:

18. Yahweh says to the oppressor: "Let my people go, that they may serve *Me*." Cf. Jer. 5:19.

19. Josephus, *Jewish Wars*, VI, vi, 1 (§316). This was probably a unique event in so far as the Jewish temple is concerned; but the assured earlier dating of 1Q p Hab indicates that the practice must not have been unknown elsewhere. Contrast G. R. Driver, *The Judaean Scrolls: The Problem and a Solution* (New York: Schocken Books, 1965), pp. 213 f.

20. 1Q S ii, 24 f.; v, 4, 25; vi, 5; viii, 2; x, 26.

According to their judgment [i. e., that of the priests], the divinely guided decision is reached with regard to every matter, whether Torah, or property, or laws, *to practice* truth, unity and humility, righteousness and *justice*, and *devoted love and humble walking in all their ways.*

Notice in the italicized words that all the virtues of Mic. 6:8 are presented as the object of the infinitive "to practice" which also derives from that verse. The meaning of the verse as understood at Qumran was:

He has told you, O man, what is good,
    and what does the LORD require of you,
but to practice: justice
    and devoted love
    and humble walking with your God?

The treatment of the infinitive phrase והצנע לכת ("to walk humbly") as nominal is as much supported by the parallelism with *ᵃhavat ḥesed* as the opposite conclusion that the latter is to be interpreted as containing a verbal idea: "love for *ḥesed*" = "to love *ḥesed.*" It could therefore be, as Philip Hyatt has argued, that the Qumran construction is correct.[21] The point one wishes to make here is Qumran's interpretation of the "humble walking":

They shall all live in true community and good *humility*, and *devoted love* and righteous purpose, *each toward his fellow* in the holy Council, and as members of the eternal assembly.
(1Q S ii, 24 f.)

In the Council of the Community, there shall be twelve laymen and three priests who are perfect in all that is revealed of the whole Law, through *practicing* truth and righteousness and *justice and devoted love and humble walking each with his fellow.*
(1Q S viii, 1 f.)

Notice that all the virtues, including "the humble walking," are "each with his fellow." This interpretation may be partly due to a

21. "On the Meaning and Origin of Micah 6:8," *Anglican Theological Review*, 34 (1952), 232–39. I do not agree, however, that this verse is nongenuine, on the basis of a supposed universalism in the use of the word *man* (אדם). If there was a special reason for using this Hebrew word, it may allude to the time of Adam's walking with God in Eden. The simplicity of God's requirement upon Israel is like that placed on Adam.

reverential avoidance of too intimate language in connection with one's relationship to God, but it is more than this. It is founded upon the theological proposition that fellowship with God and his angels is to be found only within the society of God's people.[22] Fellowship with the divine is conditioned upon a person's right relations with his fellow religionist. One has moved far in the direction of I John 4:20: "for he who does not love his brother whom he has seen cannot love God whom he has not seen."

However Helpful a Life of Discipline, True Righteousness Must Come as a Gift of God

The sect of Qumran placed such great emphasis upon discipline and good deeds that one of its self-designations is "the doers of the Law."[23] Neophytes were not admitted to full membership until after two years probation during which they were tested annually according to their progress in understanding and deeds. These annual examinations continued even after this so that members could be promoted or demoted according to their accomplishments. Failure to conform with the regulations of the society led to the imposition of fines, such as a deprivation of one-fourth of one's food for thirty days. The more severe infractions were punished by expulsion. In a society governed by such strict discipline, salvation would logically be due largely to human effort; but whenever referring to the subject of human righteousness in prayer or praise, the people of Qumran discard this logic and declare their sole dependence upon God's righteousness and grace. Their philosophical outlook may be described in terms of the popular Sunday school aphorism of our day: "Work as though everything depends upon you; but pray as if everything depends upon God." It is because these people worked so hard at being good and were as much concerned with the inner man as with the outer man that they quickly realized their human limitations and confessed their sole dependence upon the grace of God. The hymnic material of the last column of the Society Manual is replete with language emphasizing

22. See Menahem Mansoor, *The Thanksgiving Hymns*, Studies on the Texts of the Desert of Judah (Leiden: E. J. Brill, 1969), 3: 77–84; Ringren, pp. 81–93.
23. 1Q p Hab vii, 11; viii, 1; xii, 4 f.

man's sinfulness and his dependence upon God's righteousness and mercy for justification.

xi, 2   As for me, my justification belongs to God;
                and in His hand is the perfection of my way,
                together with the uprightness of my heart. /
     3   Through His righteousness my transgression shall be
                blotted out . . .
     9   But I belong to wicked humanity,
                to the assembly of perverse flesh.
         My iniquities, my transgressions, my sins
                (together with the perversities of my heart) /
     10 Belong to the assembly of worms
                and of things that move in darkness.
         For a man's way is [not] his own;
                a man does not direct his steps;
         For to God belongs the decision,
     11   and His counsel / is perfection of way . . .

Here the worshipper confesses his own sinful nature and due mention is made not only of overt "sins" but also of the "perversities of the heart." Although the worshipper despairs of having any righteousness of his own, his prayer is no cry of despair to God, but it is a confession of glad confidence that God's righteousness and grace are sufficient for all his sin:

xi, 12 And I, if I totter,
                God's dependable mercy is my salvation forever;
         And if I stumble in the guilt of flesh,
                My justification through God's righteousness
                will stand everlastingly.
     13 And if He begin my affliction,
                even from the pit He will draw out my soul,
                and He will direct my steps in the way.
         In His compassion He has brought me near,
     14   and in His dependable mercy He will bring my
                justification.
         In His steadfast righteousness He has justified me
                and in His great goodness He will pardon all
                        my iniquities;

15 And in His righteousness, He will cleanse me from
impurity,
and from the sin of the children of men.

The last lines are particularly remarkable in stressing that not only
is "God's righteousness" (צדקת אל) the source of man's justification
(משפט) and the ground by which God will pardon (יכפר), but it is
also the source of man's moral and spiritual cleansing, so that "in
His righteousness *He will cleanse me* [יטהרני] from . . . impurity and
from sin." God's righteousness is not primarily forensic, but a force
of divine goodness which purges away all sin and fills the justified
with inner righteousness.

So strikingly similar are these ideas with those of Paul that one
stands in amazement of them. Although some scholars would seek
to minimize the correspondence by translating משפט as "judgment"
and שפטני as "he has judged me," poetic parallelism strongly rein-
forces the above translations.[24] "My salvation" in line 12 finds its
parallel in "my justification." So also in line 14, "In His steadfast
righteousness He has justified me" receives as its parallel: "In His
great goodness He will pardon all my iniquities." Sometimes in
the Old Testament itself, צדק ("righteousness") and its cognates
are connected with God's vindication and deliverance, and the
same is true even of שפט,[25] but nothing goes quite this far, despite
Isa. 53:11:

After his mortal suffering, he shall see light
and shall be satisfied in knowing himself *vindicated*.
My servant shall *vindicate* many,
since it is their iniquities that he bears.[26]

24. So P. Wernberg-Møller, *The Manual of Discipline*, Studies on the Texts of the
Desert of Judah (Leiden: E. J. Brill, ·1957), 1: 38 f.; A. R. C. Leaney, *The Rule of
Qumran and Its Meaning* (Philadelphia: Westminster, 1966), pp. 235 f. A real connection
of these passages with justification is found in the authors surveyed by Herbert Braun,
Qumran und das Neue Testament (Tübingen: J. C. B. Mohr, 1966), 1: 173 f., on Rom.
3:21–26. See also Walter Grundmann, "The Teacher of Righteousness of Qumran
and the Question of Justification by Faith in the Theology of Apostle Paul," in *Paul
and Qumran*, ed. Jerome Murphy-O'Connor (Chicago: Priory Press, 1968), pp. 85–114.
25. See *Meaning*, pp. 180–82 and n. 43, p. 182. Matthew Black, *The Scrolls and
Christian Origins* (New York: Scribner's, 1961), pp. 125–28, finds here a continuation
of the piety of the prophets and psalmists.
26. On this verse, see *Meaning*, pp. 226–33.

The vindication of the Suffering Servant corresponds with the early Christian hymn quoted in I Tim. 3:16: "He was vindicated in the spirit."[27] Here is more than agreement of language, for in both passages there is a vindication which is a triumph through and beyond death.

Paul goes beyond all these passages by making the "righteousness of God" identical with the salvation wrought by God's Suffering Servant Jesus. The Qumran Community did not identify this "righteousness of God" with any messianic figure. Yet Paul was able to do so, perhaps under the influence of Isaiah 53. It is this interpretation which explains the larger place he gives to forensic righteousness. In this, Paul is far in advance of Qumran; but in so far as δικαιοσύνη is for Paul an infused righteousness imparted by the Spirit of Christ, he is very close to Qumran thought. It is Christ and his work of atonement which marks the difference in Paul's understanding of justifying righteousness. The folk of Qumran seem not to have pondered much the problem of how a just God can pardon unjust men. Although they believed, like other Jews, that the suffering of all good men, or saints, atones,[28] this belief was left out of consideration when justification by God's righteousness was being discussed.

Despite partial Old Testament anticipations, the people of Qumran appear to be distinctive among pre-Christian Jews in basing their salvation upon a righteousness which God alone possesses and imparts. This remarkable fact may justify positing at least an indirect influence of Qumran upon Paul; for these semimonastic Jews were probably not able to keep all their ideas wholly to themselves, so other Palestinians may have been influenced by them at least indirectly.[29] Yet the suggestion that Paul's long stay in "Arabia" (Nabatea) brought him into direct contact with the Covenanters

27. On the contrastive earthly and heavenly spheres of this hymn, Eduard Schweizer compares Phil. 2:6–11 in his *Gemeinde und Gemeindeordnung im Neuen Testament*, Abhandlungen zur Theologie des Alten und Neuen Testaments, no. 35 (Zürich: Zwingli Verlag, 1959), p. 150, n. 592; p. 202, n. 877.

28. See Brownlee, "The Servant of the Lord in the Qumran Scrolls, II," *Bulletin of the American Schools of Oriental Research*, no. 135 (Oct., 1954), 33–38, esp. 34 f. On p. 34, please alter the misprint of "external planting" to "eternal planting." See also *Meaning*, p. 149, n. 59; Robin Scroggs, "Romans vi. 7," *NTS*, 10 (1963–1964), 104–8.

29. For four methods whereby New Testament authors could become familiar with language and ideas found in the Qumran Scrolls, see my comments in Brownlee, *et al.*, "The Dead Sea Scrolls: Their Significance to Religious Thought: A Symposium," *The New Republic* (Apr. 9, 1956), p. 22b.

of Judea (Qumranites) is a reasonable (though unprovable) speculation.[30] In either case, there is nothing here to undermine Paul's
originality in understanding "God's righteousness" messianically.
The partial parallels of Qumran, far from undermining Christian
faith, reinforce the conviction that God was still working through
his people, the Jews, for through them he prepared a theological
perspective by means of which the work of redemption could be
more adequately viewed. Contrariwise, if Apostolic revelation be
taken as a standard for religious truth, then Paul's epistles to the
Galatians and the Romans prove the validity of the Qumran conviction that despite man's striving after righteousness, its attain-
ment is ultimately only as God's gracious gift.

HUMAN FRAILTY AND INHERITED SIN MAKE MAN ENTIRELY DEPENDENT UPON GOD'S DELIVERANCE

The reason for man's sole dependence upon God's righteousness
is his innate weakness and proclivity to sin. This is spelled out most
specifically in the Hymn Scroll:

iv, 29   What sort of flesh is this?
        and what creature of clay
        to extoll [such] wonders?

    30   For he is [steeped] in iniquity / from the womb;
        and unto old age is in guilty rebellion;

    For I know for myself
        that no man has righteousness,

    31   nor a son of man perfection of / way.

    To God Most High all deeds of righteousness are
        credited;
    and a man's conduct is not established,

    Except through the spirit God fashioned for him, /

---

30. Cf. W. F. Albright, *New Horizons in Biblical Research* (London: Oxford Univer-
sity Press, 1966), p. 48: "In any case, Paul was probably in close association with the
Essenes during those years of his life which he spent in Arabia, that is the Jordan
Valley, Transjordan and the general area between the Arabian Desert and Palestine-
Syria, the home of the Essenes." I doubt that "Arabia" was ever extended to the
west part of the Jordan Valley; but Josephus interprets Gilead and Moab as "Arabia"
(*Jewish Antiquities*, I, iii, 5 (§89). Note that the designation "land of Damascus" in
the Cairo Fragments of a Damascus Covenant (CDC) is not "the city of Damascus,"
and it may therefore be the equivalent of what Paul calls "Arabia." Cf. Vermès, p.
103.

32   to perfect a way for the sons of men,
So that they may know all His works
          through His Mighty power,
And that His abundant mercy may rest
33   upon all the sons of / His favor.
But, as for me, trembling and shivering seized me
          and all my bones were about to break,
and my heart melted
          as wax before fire,
and my knees flowed [uncontrollably][31] /
34   as water plunging down a precipice!
For I remembered my own guilty deeds,
          together with the treachery of my fathers,
when the wicked rose against Thy covenant, /
35   and the impious against Thy word.
Then said I, while in my transgression,
          "I am forsaken, outside of Thy covenant."
But when I remembered the strength of Thy hand,
36   as well as the abundance of Thy compassion,
I regained my footing and stood erect,
          and my spirit held its stand
          in face of the scourge;
37   For [I] leaned / on Thy dependable mercy,
          and on the abundance of Thy compassion;
For Thou dost purge iniquity away[32]
          and dost c[leanse] man from guilt through
               Thy righteousness.
38   It is not for man's sake,
          [but for Thy glory] that Thou hast done [this];
For Thou hast created the righteous and the
               wicked . . .[33]

---

31. Cf. Ezek. 7:17; 21:12 [English, 21:7], "All knees will flow with water [= urine]."
In the Septuagint this is rendered: "All knees will be defiled with water." Under
conditions of fright, one may lose bladder control.

32. The meaning "purge" is especially appropriate for כפר when it receives a
direct object, as in Ps. 65:3; Ezek. 43:20, 26. Cf. Isa. 6:7. The verb is often rendered
in the Septuagint by verbs meaning "to purify." See C. H. Dodd, *The Bible and the
Greeks* (London: Hodder and Stoughton, 1935), pp. 82–95.

33. For the restorations, see Jacob Licht, *The Thanksgiving Scroll* (Jerusalem: The
Bialik Institute, 1957), p. 97, and Mansoor, p. 131.

In this lengthy excerpt man is declared to be steeped "in iniquity from the womb; and unto old age, in guilty rebellion." This appalling diagnosis of man's condition reminds one of Ps. 51:5 (or 6):

Behold, I was brought forth in iniquity,
      and in sin did my mother conceive me.

This verse is an exceptional Old Testament statement and the grounds for its conviction are not explained. It appears, however, in the context of deep remorse and repentance, in which the Psalmist expresses his need for divine cleansing by acknowledging that his sin is congenital and permeates his whole being. He must therefore call upon God, who desires "truth in the inward being," to "create" in him "a clean heart" and to "put a new spirit within" him. The same sense of sin reinforced by this ancient penitential psalm of the Bible might be regarded as sufficient explanation for the words of the Qumran Hymn.

Some have seen in the Hymn Scroll a reference to man's guilt and sinful nature inherited from Adam and Eve. Even the technical expression "Original Sin" has been used by Meir Wallenstein and André Dupont-Sommer to translate פשע ראשון in 1Q H ix, 13, whereas others translate "former transgression."[34] The passage reads:

For Thou hast established my spirit
      and knowest my intention.
Thou hast comforted me in my anguish,
      and in pardon I delight,
            being comforted concerning *former transgression.*

Menahem Mansoor translates the final phrase as "the first transgression." Yet concerning this he comments: "It is doubtful whether the 'Original Sin' [i. e., the sin of Adam and Eve] as such is meant here but rather the fact that sin . . . has been cleaving unto mortal man since his creation."[35] In either case, "Original Sin" would be

---

34. Wallenstein is cited by Mansoor, p. 159. Dupont-Sommer, *The Essene Writings from Qumran,* trans. Géza Vermès (Cleveland and New York: The World Publishing Co., 1962), p. 231, explains this as "the sin of the first parents in Eden, the cause of man's corruption." For the translation "former transgression," see Géza Vermès, *The Dead Sea Scrolls in English* (Baltimore: Penguin Books, 1962), p. 180; cf. "former iniquities" in Ps. 79:8 (KJV) which means "the iniquities of our forefathers" (RSV).

35. P. 159, n. 8.

the theological term used by modern theologians to describe this condition. If this is indeed an expression designating inherited sin, no matter how defined, it is quite remarkable; for, although in the writings of Paul there is a doctrine of Original Sin, there is no technical expression meaning this.[36]

What then is the source of man's inherited sinfulness according to the Hymn writer? At least three possibilities may be explored. The first is that man is made from such dishonorable materials that he is prone to sin. In the hymn just cited, one may note the following line (ix, 29):

> What sort of flesh is this?
>> and what creature of clay
>> to extoll [such] wonders?

Other hymns stress the same theme. One of these is i, 13 ff., which in the translation of Géza Vermès runs:[37]

> And yet I, a shape of clay
>> kneaded in water,
> a ground of shame
>> and a source of pollution,
> a melting-pot of wickedness
>> and an edifice of sin,
> a straying and perverted spirit
>> of no understanding,
>> fearful of righteous judgments,
> what can I say that is not foreknown,
>> what can I utter that is not foretold?

Such language strongly suggests an almost Gnostic notion of a taint of evil clinging to the material substance out of which man was made.[38]

---

36. Naturally, "the first transgression" as an expression would be as intelligible as "the first Adam," provided there were supporting context, which is not the case. The classical arguments for Paul's doctrine of original sin appear in the exegesis of Rom. 5:12–21 in Charles Hodge, *Commentary on the Epistle to the Romans*, new ed. (New York: A. C. Armstrong and Son, 1909), pp. 221–98. On recent disputation as to the presence of this doctrine in Paul, see Robin Scroggs, *The Last Adam* (Philadelphia: Fortress Press, 1966), pp. 78 f., and the literature cited there in n. 8.

37. Pp. 151 f.

38. See here Herbert Braun, *Gesammelte Studien zum Neuen Testament und seiner Umwelt* (Tübingen: J. C. B. Mohr, 1967), pp. 100–19.

Other passages, however, seem to indicate that man's physical nature is not so much a direct source of evil, as it is the ground of weakness which leaves him open to attack by evil spirits. This then is the second possible explanation of man's being steeped in iniquity from the womb. One passage supporting this idea is 1Q H xiii, 13–16:[39]

> [But what is] the spirit of flesh
>> that it should understand all this,
> and that it should comprehend
>> the great [design of Thy wisdom]?
> What is he that is born of woman
>> in the midst of all Thy terrible [works]?
> He is but an edifice of dust,
>> and a thing kneaded with water
> whose beginning [is sinful iniquity],
>> and shameful nakedness,
>> [and a fount of uncleanness],
> and over whom a spirit of straying rules.

This "spirit of straying" may well be the "angel of darkness," or "spirit of perversity" mentioned in the Manual of Discipline. In any case, it is said to rule man's physical nature. The helplessness of the flesh in the presence of evil spirits comes out even more plainly in another passage (1Q H xvii, 23–25):[40]

> Strengthen the [loins of Thy servant
>> that he may] resist the spirits [of falsehood,
> that] he may walk in all that Thou lovest,
>> and despise all that Thou loathest,
>> [that he may do] that which is good in Thine eyes.
> [Destroy] their [domin]ion in my bowels,
>> for [within] Thy servant is a spirit of fl[esh].

---

39. Translation that of Vermès, pp. 191 f. On the Pauline doctrine of the body, see John A. T. Robinson, *The Body: A Study in Pauline Theology*, Studies in Biblical Theology (Chicago: Alec R. Allenson, 1952); W. D. Davies, *Paul and Rabbinic Judaism*, 2nd ed. (London: S.P.C.K., 1958), pp. 17–35; Davies, "Paul and the Dead Sea Scrolls: Flesh and Spirit," in *The Scrolls and the New Testament*, ed. Krister Stendahl (New York: Harper, 1957), pp. 157–82; W. D. Stacey, *The Pauline View of Man in Relation to its Judaic and Hellenistic Background* (London: Macmillan, 1956).

40. Translation and text that of Vermès, p. 199.

If I understand this passage correctly, man's physical nature and even his very soul are unable to resist unaided the evil spirits which take up their abode in him. "Flesh" is not evil *per se*; but it is weak and dominated by evil spirits. The expression רוח בשר ("spirit of flesh") is not equivalent to the Pauline phrase τὸ φρόνημα τῆς σαρκός ("Mind of the flesh") in Rom. 8:6;[41] but it means rather "the spirit of frail humanity." According to this understanding, the last petition quoted above may be paraphrased:

> Destroy *Thou* the reign of evil spirits in my body;
>> for within Thy servant is only a frail human spirit
>> which is unable to cope with them.

This understanding of the phrase "spirit of flesh" fits well also the earlier quotation, "But what is the spirit of flesh," i. e.:

> What is the spirit of frail humanity
>> that it should understand all this,
> and that it should comprehend
>> the great design of Thy wisdom?

The "spirit of flesh" is finite and weak in the presence of the divine, and without God's help it is also impotent in the face of evil spirits.

There is still a third possible explanation of man's involvement in sin from birth. It is to be found in the first lengthy quotation from the Hymns, iv, 34:

> For I remembered my own guilty deeds,
>> together with the treachery of my fathers,
> When the wicked rose against Thy covenant,
>> and the impious against Thy word.

Here man's guilt is declared to be twofold: "his own guilty deeds" and the "treachery" of his forefathers. The idea of being held accountable for the "sins of the fathers" is a very old Hebrew notion. It is imbedded even in the Ten Commandments (Exod. 20:5):

> I, the LORD your God am a jealous [or zealous] God, visiting the iniquity of the fathers upon the children to the third and fourth generation of those who hate Me.

41. Cf. also τοῦ νοὸς τῆς σαρκὸς αὐτοῦ (Col. 2: 18).

Despite Ezekiel's denial of the proposition that "the fathers have eaten sour grapes and the children's teeth are set on edge" (18:1 ff.), this doctrine held a prominent place in postexilic Judaism. Ezekiel, however, may be interpreted to mean simply that the force of paternal guilt is broken whenever a man repents, that repentance avails both for personal and for inherited sin. In fact, confessing the sins of the fathers received a prominent place in postexilic prayers of repentance.[42]

The annual ritual of entering the covenant at Qumran contained certain traditional elements, such as blessings and curses, preceded by the rehearsal of the saving acts of God (1Q S i, 16–ii, 18). In view of man's sinfulness, a new element is given prominence, the confession of sin. The ceremony began with a blessing of "the God of saving acts and all His deeds of faithfulness" recited by the priests and the Levites, with the people responding "Amen! Amen!" Next followed two rehearsals. First the priests give a traditional recital of God's righteousness, might, and gracious deeds toward Israel. Following this the Levites narrate Israel's sins. To this the people respond, confessing:

> We have perverted ourselves! [We have transgressed, we have sinned], we have done wickedly—both we [and our fathers] before us—because we have walked [contrary to] true [ordinances]. And [God] is righte[ous who has executed] His justice upon us and upon [our] fathers; but the abundance of His grace He has [be]stowed upon us from everlasting to everlasting. (1Q S i, 25–26)

Note how the confession of sin leads to an acknowledgment of God's justice and then returns to the theme of God's graciousness. The confession is thus a response not merely to the Levitical rehearsal of Israel's sins but also a response to the priestly recounting of God's mighty and gracious deeds (1Q S i, 21–23). The covenant which one enters is not simply a promise of obedience as the covenant at Sinai, but it is a "covenant of repentance" whereby one

---

42. Cf. Ezra 9:7; Neh. 9:33 f.; Dan. 9:8; CDC xx, 29 (=9:51); also the "Words of the Heavenly Lights," Vermès, pp. 202–5, first published by M. Baillet, "Un recueil liturgique de Qumrân, Grotte 4: 'Les paroles des luminaires,' " *Revue Biblique* (1961), pp. 195–250.

turns from sin to the Law of Moses.[43] Associated with it were lustral rites and a stern warning that without sincere repentance one could not through these receive cleansing or forgiveness. This last appears to be an admonition, almost a sermon, on baptisms and repentance.[44] The occasion for this ceremony was the admission of new members and a renewal of the covenant each year on the part of the old members, at the Feast of Weeks (Pentecost).[45]

One would like to dwell on this passage and point out the importance of this and other material at Qumran for the account of Pentecost in the Acts of the Apostles;[46] but this would divert us

43. CDC xix, 16 (=9:15). Cf. 1Q S vi, 14 f.: "And if he grasps instructions, he shall bring him into the covenant to turn to the truth and to turn away from all perversity"; v, 8 f.: "Then he shall take a binding oath to return to the Torah of Moses according to all that he commanded, with wholeness of heart and wholeness of soul toward all that is revealed of it to the sons of Zadok." Cf. CDC xv, 11 f. (=19:11 f.). Cf. Herbert Braun, " 'Umkehr' in spät jüdisch-häretischer und in frühchristlicher Sicht," in Braun, pp. 70–85.

44. 1Q S ii, 25b–iii, 12. It may be that this belongs solely to the instruction concerning the significance of the covenant, for no speaker is specified. Although i, 1–iii, 12 does have imbedded within it a liturgy, it seems probable that in the present form of the material we have instruction given by the $maśkil$, the instructor of the community. In any case, the prescriptions for the covenant terminate in warning, promise, and exhortation as to the real significance of the covenant. This may be compared with the function of the prophetic oracle in the covenant festival as shown by Ps. 50:5–23; 8:7–17 (=81:6–16). Note similarly in Deuteronomy that following the curses and blessings, Moses presents a sermon on the significance of the covenant (Deuteronomy 29–30). A form-critical study on the Society Manual will appear in the forthcoming dissertation of Eugene F. Roop.

45. See Brownlee, "Light on the Manual of Discipline (DSD) from the Book of Jubilees," Bulletin of the American Schools of Oriental Research, no. 123 (Oct., 1951), 32. Millar Burrows, The Dead Sea Scrolls (New York: The Viking Press, 1965), p. 236; J. T. Milik, Ten Years of Discovery in the Wilderness of Judea, trans. John Strugnell, Studies in Biblical Theology, no. 26 (Naperville, Ill.: Alec R. Allenson, 1959), pp. 116 f.; Roland de Vaux, Ancient Israel: Its Life and Institutions (New York: McGraw-Hill Book Co., 1966), p. 494. The rival view that the covenant renewal was on the Day of Atonement is presented by Manfred Weise, Kultzeiten und kultischer Bundesschluss in der "Ordensregel" vom Toten Meer, Studia Post-Biblica, vol. 3 (Leiden: E. J. Brill, 1961), pp. 79 f.

46. The similarities may be briefly outlined as follows: (1) "They were all together in one place" (Acts 2:1). Cf. Kenneth Carroll cited in Appendix C of The Dead Sea Manual of Discipline, p. 53. (2) Theophany, as in Yahweh's manifestation at Sinai (Exod. 19:16–19; Deut. 5:2–5; Psalm 50; Jub. 1:1). The manifestations of the Holy Spirit through Moses is referred to in Neh. 9:20; Isa. 63:10 f. Cf. 1Q 34 ii, 6 f.: "And Thou wilt renew [or, didst renew] Thy covenant with them with a manifestation of glory and words of Thy Holy Spirit." Yahweh's "Holy Spirit" is interpreted in the Targum of Jonathan (Isa. 63:10 f.) as "the word of His holy prophets." Hence note the next point. (3) Peter's sermon is an example of prophetic preaching. Note that in Deut. 5:4 f., the Ten Commandments were mediated through Moses (Deut. 5:4 f.). 1Q 34 ii, 8 refers to Moses (or the new Moses) as "the faithful shepherd." Note the place of the prophetic oracle in the covenant psalms (Psalms 50 and 81). (4) The

ANTHROPOLOGY AND SOTERIOLOGY 233

from our present thrust, confession of the sins of the fathers. Nothing in these annual covenantal rites suggests that Adam is included among the "fathers" whose sins are confessed. Nor is anything said which would suggest that the sway of evil spirits over man's flesh is a consequence of the guilt of the fathers. In other words, these varied explanations of man's involvement in sin from birth are neither correlated with each other nor in any way connected with the rebellion of Adam and Eve. The idea of the Fall at Qumran, as for most Jews at that time, was probably more connected with fallen angels mentioned in Gen. 6:1–4, than with the story of Adam and Eve in the Garden of Eden.[47] It was because Paul saw in Jesus Christ the New Adam that antithetically he developed so fully his doctrine of the First Adam. The old humanity weighed down with sin finds its representative in Adam and must now give way to the new humanity which is Christ.

PERSONAL SALVATION IS THROUGH DIVINE ELECTION

In so far as creation plays a role in explaining human wickedness, it is not concerned simply with the first human pair but with God's continuing creation of each new person. The lengthy excerpt from 1Q H iv already quoted above concludes with the words: "For Thou hast created the righteous and the wicked. . . ." This refers to a doctrine of determinism, whereby some are predestined to righteousness and others are foredoomed to wickedness. Those who are "chosen for righteousness" (1Q H i, 13) become righteous only through the gift of grace bestowed by God. This doctrine is correctly discussed by Menahem Mansoor under the title "Salvation through Election."[48] The break in the text at iv, 38 does not shed any light on how, or for what reason, God "created the righteous

---

specification of the terms of covenant in Acts 2:38 as consisting of (a) repentance, (b) baptism, (c) forgiveness of sins, and (d) the gift of the Holy Spirit—all of which motifs stand related to the exhortation of 1Q S ii, 25b–iii, 12. Cf. Julian Morgenstern, *Some Significant Antecedents of Christianity* (Leiden: E. J. Brill, 1966), p. 25, n. 1.

47. This is the emphasis of Jubilees 5 or I Enoch 6–10, both of which works were held in honor at Qumran. See also 4Q 180, fragment 1, 4Q 181, frag. 2, appearing in John M. Allegro, *Qumrân Cave 4 I (4Q 158–4Q 186)*, Discoveries in the Judaean Desert of Jordan, vol. 5 (Oxford: Clarendon, 1968), pp. 78, 80. See the significant application of this material by J. A. Sanders, "Dissenting Deities and Philippians 2:1–11," *JBL*, 88 (1969), 279–90.

48. *The Thanksgiving Hymns*, pp. 62–65.

and the wicked"; but fortunately in column xv, we have a detailed
discussion in which the righteous and the wicked receive separate
treatment. Beginning at the close of the fourteenth line we read of
the righteous; then in line seventeen the discussion of the wicked
begins. Note first of all what is said concerning the righteous:

> xv, 14–15 Thou alone hast [created] / the righteous;
> and from the womb hast ordained him
> for the time of divine favor,
> That he may give heed to Thy covenant
> and walk [in it] wholly,
> And that Thou mayest be sparing toward him /
> 16   through Thy abundant mercy
> And relieve his soul from all that constricts it
> opening up eternal salvation
> and perpetual well-being with nothing lacking,
> 17   as Thou exaltest / his glory over flesh.

One notes that as truly as man is elsewhere described as steeped
"in iniquity from the womb," it is here asserted of the righteous
that "from the womb" he is ordained to heed God's covenant and
to be the recipient of His mercy and salvation. One line is translated
freely, since this more clearly conveys the sense of the Hebrew.
Mansoor gives a literal translation: "And to open all the straitness
of his soul unto an everlasting salvation." "Straitness" is seldom
used today and is readily confused with "straightness." Here it
renders the Hebrew noun ṣarah, which refers to that which presses
in upon and oppresses the human spirit, restricting life to narrow
limits. The etymological meaning of "salvation" (ישועה), in contrast, refers to spaciousness, an idea which belongs to the present
passage. When one is delivered by God, the restrictive pressures
upon his soul are lifted and he has room to move about freely and
to achieve fullness of life. hence one translates:

> And relieve [Thou] his soul from all that constricts it,
> opening up eternal salvation
> and perpetual well-being with nothing lacking.

In an age which stresses self-fulfillment, we need to help people to
see that true release and true self-fulfillment are only through
God's deliverance from all that would impress our lives into some

evil and unworthy mold. This way of interpreting salvation may seem indebted to contemporary psychology, but it really goes back to the Old Testament itself.[49] Here, however, the oppressive element may well be thought of as the body, for the concluding clause reads "as Thou exaltest his glory over flesh." This refers to the spiritual triumph of the righteous over his sin-ridden flesh, "his glory" meaning "his soul."[50] It is even possible that the reference here is to eternal life in the world beyond, in which the human spirit comes into fullness of life unhampered by the body. If so, this is a hellenistic element unlike the prevalent view of the New Testament which regards man's salvation and immortality as incomplete without the resurrection of the body.[51]

In the same hymn, one turns now to a discussion of the reprobate:[52]

xv, 17 But the wicked hast Thou created
   [for the time of] Thy [wra]th,
  and from the womb hast consigned them
   to the day of slaughter,

 18 BECAUSE they have walked in the way not good
   and have rejected [Thy] co[venant],
  and their soul has abhorred Thy [Law],

 19 And they have not delighted in all/Thou commandest,
   but have chosen that which Thou hatest.

---

49. Cf. Ps. 4:2 (=4:1): "Thou hast given me room when I was pressed in," and Ps. 18:18 f. (=18:19 f. and II Sam. 22:19 f.): "They constricted me, on my day of repression. . . . He brought me forth into a broad place. . . ."

50. Note the parallelism of נפש with כבודי (Gen. 49:6), of נפשי and חיי with כבודי in Ps. 7:6 (=7:5), of לבי with כבודי in Pss. 16:9 and 108:2 (=108:1).

51. Josephus seems to attribute to the Essenes belief in immortality of the soul alone (*Jewish Antiquities*, XVIII, i, 3, 5); but his description of their attitude under martyrdom may imply resurrection (*Jewish Wars*, II, viii, 10, §153): "Smiling in their agonies and mildly deriding their tormentors, they cheerfully resigned their souls, confident that they would receive them back again." Avoidance of resurrection in any explicit way may be accounted for by Josephus' accommodation to Greek ideas. Hippolytus, *Heresies*, xxvii, states: "The Doctrine of Resurrection, however, is very firm among them, for they teach both that the flesh will rise again, and that it will become immortal in the same manner as the soul is already immortal." On Hippolytus, cf. Matthew Black, "The Account of the Essenes in Hippolytus and Josephus," in W. D. Davies and D. Daube, *The Background of the New Testament and Its Eschatology* (Cambridge: Cambridge University Press, 1964), pp. 172–75. On the belief of the people of Qumran in the resurrection, see Mansoor, pp. 54, 84, 87–90, and n. 5 on p. 147. The resurrection of the wicked for judgment is referred to in 1Q p Hab x, 4 f.

52. For the restorations, see Mansoor, p. 184.

> *Yet*, in Thy [mysterious wisdom], Thou hast ordained
>   them,
>   in order to wreak great judgments upon them /
> 20   in the sight of all Thy creatures,
>   That they may become a sign
>   and a por[tent for] perpetual [generations],
>   That all may know Thy glory
> 21   and Thy strength / so great.

That God should create the wicked in order to make his justice known in their final punishment sounds like a rather harsh and severe determinism. Yet careful exegesis must be given the first word כי of line 18. It is "BECAUSE" these people "have walked in the way not good / and have rejected" God's "covenant," that they are consigned at birth "to the day of slaughter." What this means, I believe, is that God has foreseen that they would behave in this way and has therefore foreordained them for punishment. This doctrine of reprobation is predestination based upon foreknowledge. One cannot have foreknowledge without determinism, not simply because God's control of history is necessary to his foreknowledge, but rather for the opposite reason. If God foresees that certain people will turn out wicked and yet he proceeds to create them, he is thereby foreordaining their wicked lives. That is the meaning of the conjunction כי ("because") at line 18. It is also the significance of the next occurrence of the same word in line 19, which contextually in this case means "yet." God has foreseen the evil deeds of the wicked, and *yet* he has ordained them.[53] Thus the Hebrew particle *kî* is doubly the *key* to the theological interpretation of predestination of the wicked. God has foredoomed them to punishment *because* he has foreseen their wickedness, and *yet* he has foreordained their existence.

This doctrine of predestination finds a remarkable parallel in Paul's Epistle to the Romans (9:21 f.):

> Has not the potter no right over the clay, to make out of the same lump one vessel for beauty and another for menial use? What if God, desiring to show His wrath and to make known His power, has endured with much patience the vessels of wrath

53. For כי in the sense of כי אם, see my discussion of 11Q Pssᵃ xxviii, 4 in *Revue de Qumran*, p. 383, n. 6. See also the Hebrew lexicons.

made for destruction, in order to make known the riches of His glory for the vessels of mercy, which He has prepared beforehand for glory. . . . (RSV)

This passage in Paul shares with the Qumran hymn the idea of double predestination. Some people God has foreordained as recipients of his mercy, and others as recipients of his wrath. Both authors relieve God of direct responsibility for the wickedness of the wicked. Paul expresses this by saying that God "has endured with much patience the vessels of wrath made for destruction." His endurance of them *with patience* indicates that God is displeased with their wickedness and is giving them an opportunity to repent.[54] Still the fact that they are described as "vessels of wrath made for destruction" indicates that in foreordaining their existence God has also foreseen their unrepentance and has foredoomed them to be recipients of his wrath, precisely as in this Qumran hymn. Neither in this letter of Paul, nor in this Qumran hymn, is there any special word for foreknowledge; but this is implied in both passages by the logic and the sequence of thought.

Although some have attributed the determinism of Qumran to Zoroastrian influence, it may well owe far more to predictive prophecy with its implication that God knows and foreordains the future. In apocalyptic literature of postexilic times we find examples of long-range prediction, such as Daniel's prediction of three empires which will succeed in turn the Babylonian Empire under which he was living, with all these to be succeeded in turn by the kingdom of the saints of the most high, seventy weeks of years after the Babylonian Exile. Such formally scheduled history, foretold hundreds of years in advance, receives as its natural corollary a doctrine of determinism.

THE FINAL SALVATION WILL BE ACHIEVED THROUGH JUDGMENT

Salvation in Qumran thought is not simply of the individual, but of the people of God as a community on earth. The messianic

54. See Charles Hodge, pp. 502 f.; Franz J. Leenhardt, *The Epistle to the Romans* (Cleveland and New York: World Publishing Co., 1961), p. 258. See also David Flusser, "The Dead Sea Sect and Pre-Pauline Christianity," *Scripta Hierosolymitana* (Jerusalem, Magnes Press, 1958), 4: 215–66, who discusses Paul's predestination beliefs in relation to Qumran thought on pp. 220–22.

age will be established through the definitive struggle between the forces of good and evil, in which the latter will be forever banished from the earth. The Military Manual (1Q M) can portray this as a war between the sons of light and the sons of darkness, in which the holy and elect angels under the command of Michael defeat the evil angels under the authority of Belial. Before this triumph is achieved, God himself appears in a luminous theophany of judgment. The house of Israel is then illumined with joy, for the authority of Michael is established over the gods and the dominion of Israel over all flesh.[55]

A commentary (or *pesher*) upon an assorted group of biblical passages was found in the eleventh Qumran cave which gives a prominent place to Melchizedek as commander of the heavenly forces which will defeat the hordes of Belial. When this victory is achieved, the "anointed of the Spirit" will proclaim the "good news" that "your God [or, god] has become king."[56]

The Society Manual can present the struggle between good and evil as an internal struggle within the heart of man. In keeping with this internalization of the conflict, the final eschatological judgment can be thought of as beginning with the suffering and purgation of the righteous, during which God will refine by his truth one man more than other sons of men. From this man's flesh every evil spirit will be purged away; and, through the sprinkling of the Spirit of Truth, he will be purified in order to become a fit instrument to make known to God's elect sons of the covenant the undefiled truth and knowledge of the sons of heaven. All evil will then be destroyed and the righteous will be endued with all the glory of Adam. This new age is anticipated as "the time of the decree and the making of the new," with apparent allusion to the New Heavens and the New Earth.[57]

---

55. See Brownlee, "Jesus and Qumran," in *Jesus and the Historian*, ed. F. Thomas Trotter (Philadelphia: Westminster Press, 1968), p. 68; also *Meaning*, pp. 124 f.

56. See my discussion in Trotter, pp. 64–70 (the reference in note 34 of p. 79 requiring correction to "*New Testament Studies*, Vol. III, p. 205"). See also Merrill P. Miller, "The Function of Isa. 61:1–2 in 11 Q Melchizedek," *JBL*, 88 (1969), 467–69. On the rabbinic understanding of Isa. 52:7 (which along with Isa. 61:1 was interpreted messianically at Qumran) see Joseph Klausner, *The Messianic Idea in Israel*, trans. W. F. Stinespring (New York: Macmillan, 1955), p. 468.

57. 1Q S iv, 15–26, noting the revised translation in the *Bulletin of the American Schools of Oriental Research*, no. 135, pp. 35–38; *Meaning*, pp. 261–70 and discussion on

The Book of Mysteries (1Q 27) speaks of those enthralled with the "mysteries of iniquity" but who "do not know the Mystery to come, nor understand former things, nor understand what it is which will come upon them, and so they do not deliver their soul from the mystery to come." This "mystery to come" is apparently the last judgment overtaking the wicked; but it is portrayed as light banishing darkness:[58]

> And this will be the sign to you when it comes. When the off-spring of perversity are imprisoned, wickedness will be banished before righteousness, as darkness is banished before light. As smoke vanishes and is no more, so will wickedness vanish for ever. Then will righteousness be revealed like the sun to govern the world and all who support the bewitching mysteries will be no more for ever, but knowledge will fill the world and no folly will be there for ever.

This imprisonment of "the offspring of perversity" apparently refers to the confinement of the wicked to Hell,[59] but there is no hint here as to how this will be achieved. In the Habakkuk *pesher* the universal knowledge of the Lord will be preceded by a theophany of judgment.[60] The revelation of this knowledge, according to the Testament of Levi 18, will be the work of the messianic priest.[61]

"The Man" in *Jesus and the Historian*, pp. 59–64. According to Numbers Rabbah xiii, 12, the radiance of Adam's face is to be regained in the messianic age.

58. In the citation below, the expression "bewitching mysteries" translates רזי פלא of i, 7 as read by J. T. Milik in *Discoveries in the Judaean Desert*, 1955, 1: 103. G. Vermès, *The Dead Sea Scrolls in English*, rev. ed. (Baltimore: Penguin Books, 1965), p. 210, translates "the mysteries of sin," reading רזי פשע as at i, 2. On this passage, see also Brownlee, "Jesus and Qumran," p. 69.

59. See Dupont-Sommer, p. 327, n. 2.

60. Note that "the knowledge" is discussed separately at 1Q p Hab xi, 1 after the destruction of "[the man (or prophet) of] lies." It is evident that the text of the missing lines of x, 16 f. should be reconstructed from CDC xx, 10 f., 14 ff., 25 f. (=9:36, 39 f., 49) somewhat as follows: "When they turn aside [with the Man of Lies, the wrath of Go]d [will be kindled against them; for His glory will shine out to Israel and all those who turned aside with the Man of] Lies [will be cut off]. Then afterward, the knowledge will be revealed. . . ." That the "glory" of Hab. 2:14 really does refer to a theophany of judgment is indicated by form-critical considerations, for in each pronouncement of woe, the word כי introduces the reason for the impending judgment (as at vv. 8, 11, 17). At v. 18b it introduces the reason for the futility in turning to an idol in order to avert the woe.

61. Unpublished fragments of the Testament of Levi from 4Q may or may not contain this chapter. The concern for a priestly messiah in chap. 18 correlates well

What all these passages have in common is the belief that messianic salvation must come from above, through God himself, his angels, the Spirit of Truth, or somehow mysteriously through Truth itself banishing all evil and error. It is not enough that God by elective love redeem individuals for a life which transcends this world; but God must redeem this world itself by defeating evil here. All this has much in common both with Jewish apocalyptic literature generally and with fulfillment and expectation in the New Testament. To draw out the similarities and contrasts with primitive Christian thought would be a study too lengthy for the present chapter. It is enough here to point out that Christianity in keeping with its Jewish antecedents holds that the Kingdom of God must certainly come on earth, and that his will be realized here as it is in Heaven.[62] The most fundamental differences are the fulfillments by Jesus the Christ which validate the messianic expectation of Judaism and assure us of the final victory of the Kingdom.

---

with Qumran expectation, so that this passage should in no case be attributed in its entirety to Christian composition, though it may in the form we know it have undergone Christian editing.

62. Matt. 6:10; 13:36–43; 28:16–20; Acts 1:6; 3:19–21; Rom. 8:18–21; 11:12; I Cor. 15:24–28; Phil. 2:9–11; Heb. 2:5–9; James 1:18; 5:1–11; II Pet. 1:19; 3:13; I John 2:8; Rev. 11:15. Although Christ's kingship is not from this world (John 18:36), his kingdom will prevail upon earth in the world to come. Cf. Ethelbert Stauffer, *New Testament Theology*, trans. John Marsh (New York: Macmillan, 1955), chaps. 58–59, pp. 225–31.

Moreover, the Jewish Scriptures are still the Scriptures of the church, so that God's saving purpose for all mankind and his goal of universal peace depicted there still remain authentically within the Christian hope. This seems not to be considered by Joseph Klausner in his contrast between "The Jewish and the Christian Messiah," pp. 519–31. Elsewhere he states: "So it was clear to the Jews that if all 'the seventy nations' of the pagans should accept the teaching of Paul, monotheism would be assimilated by polytheism, and not the reverse; a drop of wine cannot flavor a bucket of water." *From Jesus to Paul*, trans. W. F. Stinespring (New York: Macmillan, 1944), p. 534. To the contrary, the Kingdom of Heaven is like a handful of yeast, which leavens a whole tub full of dough (Matt. 13:33; Luke 13:30 f.). Already, despite manifestations of the demonic in human society, foregleams of the final victory of God's kingdom are to be seen in human history.

A STUDY OF GNOSTIC EXEGESIS
OF THE OLD TESTAMENT

ORVAL WINTERMUTE

Professor W. F. Stinespring has spent over thirty years at Duke University in a program of research and teaching which has provided many a student with knowledge of the necessary linguistic, historical and theological background for serious, scholarly exegesis of the Old Testament. Professor Stinespring would be the first to charge us with the "all fallacy" if we were to claim that all of his students became thoroughly skilled in the art of exegesis. Nevertheless, his success with the vast majority of students has contributed significantly to the present-day respect for serious biblical and theological studies in this region and elsewhere. Therefore it is a great privilege to dedicate this footnote on the history of Old Testament exegesis to my friend and patron, Professor Stinespring.

The library of Coptic texts discovered in the region of Nag⁾ Hammadi in 1945 contains among its treasures an untitled work by an unknown scholar of considerable genius. The text which this scholar composed is the fifth tractate in the well-preserved Codex II.[1] Schenke has provided a title for this tractate, "Die

It should be noted that students are not the only ones to benefit from Professor Stinespring's scholarly attitudes. His colleagues have also learned much from listening to his scholarly papers, reading the dissertations which he has directed, and participating with him in the oral examinations. His concern for serious scholarship is also reflected in the encouragement and support which he provides for the scholarly interests of his colleagues. Those who seek his advice on scholarly matters have learned to expect a sound and independent judgment. Over the years together he has taught me much. I should like to thank him.

1. The first fourteen pages of this tractate appeared at the end of the famous Labib volume: Pahor Labib, *Coptic Gnostic Papyri in the Coptic Museum at Old Cairo* (Cairo, 1956), vol. 1. Three years later, Hans-Martin Schenke published a German translation of that portion of the text together with a brief introduction and notes in *TLZ* (1959). In the same year, W. C. van Unnik's German edition of *Evangelien aus dem Nilsand* came to the attention of Hans Quecke, and he noticed that it contained three photographs (plates 5, 7, and 9) of an additional page of the manuscript, which he correctly identified and published in *Le Museon*, 72 (1959). The remainder of the text was made available in 1962, when Alexander Böhlig published a critical text of the entire tractate together with an introduction and a brief commentary in the form of footnotes to the text and translation. The *editio princeps* which Böhlig produced was made possible

Abhandlung [λόγος] über den Ursprung [ἀρχή] der Welt [κόσμος]." [2]
This has been shortened in English to "On the Origin of the
World," and is abbreviated here as OW.

Despite his anonymity, the author of OW reveals himself to be
a scholar of considerable ability. He impresses the reader with his
ability to move between abstract argument and a more familiar
recitation of the Gnostic myths. [3] He has a great interest in etiological notes, [4] a fondness for linguistic arguments, [5] a rich store of
mythological data, [6] and a considerable talent for correlating certain theoretical views about the nature of man and the cosmos
with inherited mythological traditions. [7] Like scholars of every

---

through the cooperation of Pahor Labib. The full title of the work is *Die Koptisch-
Gnostische Schrifte ohne Titel aus Codex II von Nag Hammadi* (Berlin, 1962).

The method of citing tractates has been confused for some time. Böhlig and Schenke
both followed the pagination established by the page sequence in the Labib volume
of photographic prints, but since the pagination in that volume did not correspond to
that of the original codex its deficiency is obvious. A great deal of work has been done
by Krause and Robinson in an effort to recover the original sequence of pages for all
of the codices in the library. The pagination cited in the present study will follow that
provided by James M. Robinson in his study of "The Coptic Gnostic Library Today,"
NTS, 14 (1967/1968), 356–401. It is hoped that this system will prevail in all future
studies.

2. Hans-Martin Schenke, p. 246.

3. The tractate begins with an argument that Chaos cannot be the origin of all
things (97:27–98:7). The author first argues in an abstract manner that Chaos is
darkness and darkness is shadow. Therefore there must have been something prior to
Chaos since there must have been something to cast the shadow. In line 98:8, the
author begins to repeat the same argument in mythological form, describing how a
veil (παραπέτασμα) arose between the eon of truth and that boundless Chaos which
lies beneath the veil and from which this world was finally created.

4. The author explains in line 109:28–29, for example, that the grape vine grew
up from blood poured upon the earth by the virgin Pronoia in her lust for pneumatic
Adam. It is because of the passionate origin of the grape that "those who drink it
acquire for themselves the desire (ἐπιθυμία) for coitus (συνουσία)." There are a
number of other etiologies of this sort in the text.

5. The author's linguistic arguments play a significant role in his exegetical method,
and a number of examples will be given in the discussion which follows. Compare,
for example, pp. 254–55 below.

6. In addition to the basic store of Gnostic mythology, this writer has preserved
from Jewish sources an account of Sabaoth's exaltation and a description of his throne
chariot (103:32 ff.). His discussion of the Phoenix (124:3 ff.) reflects Egyptian contacts, and from Greek sources he has preserved variations on the theme of Eros-Psyche
(109:1 ff. and 111:8 ff.) and Aphrodite-Hermaphrodites (113:21 ff.).

7. The attempt to discover a basis for certain theoretical views within inherited
mythological data is one of the motivating principles for his work. In line 117:28 ff.,
the author states his view of tripartite man, who is pneumatic, psychic, and choic.
Elsewhere within the tractate, it is obvious that his reinterpretation of Genesis 1–2 is
guided by this theoretical view of man with the result that his own exegetical skills

age, the author wanted the reader to understand that he knew far more than he had time to discuss. Therefore he subtly refers the reader to other authoritative works in which a particular subject was treated more exhaustively.[8] As a result of this tendency to refer the reader to other works in search of detail, his tractate is often more interesting than many of the other Gnostic texts because he has spared the reader long lists of meaningless names and frequent repetitions.

The scholarship of the author has contributed significantly to the historical importance of this document. It accounts for the relative clarity with which he presents his case[9] and the richness of the material which he has preserved for us. It also accounts for the manner in which he has preserved his material. Since he was apparently much more interested in preserving his sources accurately than he was in creating a smooth composition, the seams which join the several sources together are frequently transparent.[10] The document is constructed in such a manner that it will prove to be a fertile text for both source criticism and form criticism. Ultimately, scholars should be able to write a fairly precise history

---

lead him to discover within the Old Testament mythological data which supports that theoretical view.

The use of the term *mythological* to describe the literature found in Genesis 1–3 is not simply the reflection of a contemporary perspective. Although the author does not use the term himself, he treats biblical episodes in the same manner that he deals with motifs drawn from Greek mythology. Placing them side by side, he accords them equal reverence. By so doing, he appears to be attributing the same status to biblical traditions that he would assign to the Greek tales, whatever that status may have been, e. g., myth, sacred stories, divine mysteries.

8. The list of works cited by this author includes the following: *The First Book* (βιβλός) *of Norea* (102:10), which may be the same as *The First Logos* (λόγος) *of Norea* (102:24), *The Archangelikè of Moses* (102:8), *The Book of Solomon* (107:3), *The Seventh Cosmos of Shieralais the Prophet* (112:23), *The Schemas of Heimarmene* (107:16), and *The Holy Book* (110:30 and 122:12).

9. This is a judgment based on a comparison of this work with works such as *Pistis Sophia* or *The Apocryphon of John*. The initial impression which this tractate makes on an uninitiated reader is hardly one of clarity. Nevertheless, careful rereading and study lead one to appreciate the author's logic.

10. In some cases the writer finds it necessary to insert a phrase at the end of a particularly long digression in order to help the reader recall the prior sequence from which he digressed. Thus, for example, after he interrupted his discussion of Light-Adam's appearance in order to insert a long digression dealing with Psyche and Eros, he drew the reader's attention back to the earlier account of Light-Adam by writing, "But before all these (things), when he (i. e. Light-Adam) appeared on the first day, he remained upon the earth thus two days" (111:29–31). The text contains many other seams which are equally obvious.

of many of the traditions which are found in this document, an
achievement that would amount to describing the history of a very
significant sector of Gnosticism since many of the basic motifs
which are found in this text are shared by both "The Hypostasis
of the Archons" (HA)[11] and "The Apocryphon of John" (AJ).[12]

The nature of the relationship between AJ, OW, and HA may
be illustrated in various ways. One perspective is provided by a
brief survey of three themes which appear in these texts. Each of
the texts 1) describes the origin of the demiurge, Yaldabaoth,
who began to create eons and archons, declared himself to be the
only god, and was renounced for his hybris; 2) reinterprets the
traditions found in Genesis 2–3; and 3) discusses the present
plight of the pneumatics together with their ultimate release,
which may be described in the context of an eschatological destruction of the powers of darkness.

In HA the first of these three themes is dealt with twice. It is
treated in an abbreviated form near the beginning of the tractate
(86:28–87:6) and again in a more expanded form (94:2–96:17) at
the end of an extended reinterpretation of Genesis. The second of
these passages (94:2–96:17) contains a digression in which Yaldabaoth's son, Sabaoth, repents and is redeemed after he witnesses
the renunciation of his father. The reinterpretation of Genesis in
HA extends beyond the third chapter of Genesis to include the
story of Cain and Abel as well as the building of the ark in the time

11. "The Hypostasis of the Archons" is found in the same codex (II) as the tractate
"On the Origin of the World." It is the fourth tractate in Codex II. The Coptic text
appeared in the Labib volume. It was translated into German by Hans-Martin Schenke,
"Das Wesen der Archonten: Eine gnostische Originalschrift aus dem Funde von
Nag-Hamadi," *TLZ*, 83 (1958), 661–670. There is also an English translation by
Roger Bullard, "The Hypostasis of the Archons: The Coptic Text with Translation
and Commentary" (Ph.D. diss., Vanderbilt University, 1965).

12. This is one of the better known tractates. There are four copies of the text now
available for study. It is written as the first tractate in Codices II, III, and IV. There
is also a copy of the tractate preserved in the Berlin Gnostic Codes 8502 (BG 8502).
The Berlin text was published by Walter Till in *Die gnostischen Schriften des koptischen
Papyrus Berolinensis 8502*, (Berlin, 1955). The copy of the text from Codex II subsequently (1956) appeared in the Labib volume. More recently M. Krause has coop-
erated with Labib to produce *Die Drei Versionen des Apokryphon des Johannes im koptischen
Museum zu Alt-Kairo*. Abhandlungen des Deutschen Archäologischen Instituts Kairo,
Koptische Reihe, vol. 1 (Wiesbaden, 1962). That work provides a critical text of the
copy which first appeared in the Labib volume plus the copies from Codices III and IV
hitherto unpublished. In the present study, the majority of quotations are taken from
the Berlin Codex.

of Noah. HA concludes with a discussion of pneumatics and the eschatological destruction of the lower powers.

AJ is a much longer tractate than HA and contains many additional episodes. Nevertheless, the same three blocks of material can be discovered. AJ begins with a frame narrative which presents the document as a post-Resurrection revelation by the Savior to his disciple, John. The revelation itself begins with a praise of the unknown god in the familiar language of negative theology, followed by a description of the eons from Barbelo to Sophia. Thereafter the story follows the pattern outlined above: the story of Yaldabaoth, the reinterpretation of Genesis 2–3, and the discussion of the pneumatics. In the last of these three sections AJ has incorporated an allegorized version of the flood story, but the description of an eschatological downfall of powers is lacking.

OW is also much longer than HA, incorporating a large number of digressions. The longest of these digressions contains the tale of Eros and Psyche (109:1–111:24) and a series of comments on the phoenix (122:2–123:2). Nevertheless, the three themes outlined above are still discernable. After a rather formal opening in which the author argues that Chaos cannot be considered original, but rather implies a previous work on which it depends, the author begins to tell of the manner in which Yaldabaoth proceeded from Sophia. Like HA, this tractate contains an expanded version of the Yaldabaoth tale which includes the traditions concerning Sabaoth. The reinterpretation of Genesis follows, and the tractate ends with a discussion of pneumatics and the eschatological downfall of the powers of darkness.

A slightly different perspective on the relationship of these three tractates to one another is gained if one examines more closely the manner in which each of them reinterprets the material found in Genesis 2–3. Since English translations of HA and OW are not yet easily available, the relevant passages have been provided in an appendix to the present study. On the basis of a reading of these parallel sections, it is possible to make certain general observations. With regard to Genesis 2–3 it appears that OW falls somewhere between HA and AJ in terms of its distance from the original biblical narrative. In this respect it is clearly closer to HA than to AJ.

In HA the role of the God of the Old Testament is filled by the chief archon, an episode in which the archons attempt to sexually pollute Eve has been introduced,[13] and there are numerous minor exegetical notes; for instance, Adam's sleep must be understood as ignorance, and the nakedness of Adam and Eve was a spiritual nakedness. The order of events, however, is essentially that of Genesis 2–3.

In OW, the pollution of Eve is included, but that episode together with the rib incident is placed before the command that man should not eat of the tree of knowledge. The naming of the animals has also been shifted in OW to follow the cursing of man. In this new position it is used to provide a new explanation for man's fall from Paradise, namely, the archons were jealous of the knowledge that man revealed in naming the animals. Finally, there is a more persistent attempt to expose the ignorance and powerlessness of the archons by means of exegetical comment. In other respects OW is quite close to HA.

When one turns to AJ, however, the variation in order and detail is so extensive that a detailed discussion would lead far beyond the bounds of the present paper. By way of illustration one may compare the excerpt dealing with Eve, which is found at the end of the appendix. In this excerpt, which is typical of the section in AJ which parallels Genesis 2–3, the Gnostic theological perspective has become so consciously authoritative that it provides a basis for correcting the Mosaic traditions. The statement, "Not as Moses said" illustrates the manner in which the author of this material has come to the outer limits of exegetical tolerance.

As surprising as this statement is, however, it becomes far less shocking when seen in the light of two earlier exegetical trends. One trend is represented by Philo, who assumed that there were two levels of meaning in the scriptural texts: a literal meaning and an allegorical meaning. In Philo, however, there seems to be a note of folly imputed to those who might be tempted to take certain texts in their simplest literal sense. Speaking of the account in which woman is produced from the rib of man, he describes the literal sense ($\tau\grave{o}$ $\dot{\rho}\eta\tau\acute{o}\nu$) as being in the nature of "myth." He con-

---

13. This episode is well known elsewhere in Gnostic writings. Its ancestry is to be sought in Jewish speculation. See R. McL. Wilson, *The Gnostic Problem* (London, 1958), p. 166, for references.

tinues, "For how could any one concede that a woman or any person at all came into being out of a man's side?" (*Leg. Alleg.* II, 19). In a similar manner the author of AJ has rejected any crass literalism in favor of an allegorical interpretation.

A second exegetical trend can be traced back to the statement of Jesus concerning divorce (Matt. 19:4–9), in which Jesus appeals to the text of Gen. 2:24: "For this reason a man shall leave his father and mother and be joined to his wife, and the two shall become one," in order to provide the basic model for marriage. With regard to the Mosaic legislation, he seemed to imply that it was simply an accommodation to the hardness of men's hearts. The drastic implications of Jesus' exegetical method did not escape the notice of Gnostic scholars. In his "Letter to Flora," Ptolemaeus uses these words of Jesus to prove that the Old Testament contains three different levels of law: divine law, Mosaic law, and the traditions of the elders. Even more significantly for the history of exegesis he argues that in the case of the divorce legislation the law of Moses is actually contrary to the law of God. Thus Moses, who is held in respect by Ptolemaeus, is shown to be technically in error concerning the highest law.[14] This leads one to the natural conclusion that Moses may have technically misstated certain other matters. For the author of AJ, the fantastic story about Adam's rib needed to be corrected. It appeared to him to have been poorly stated so as to lead the unwary into a literal interpretation. He corrected any such tendency with the blunt comment, "Not as Moses said."

A direct study of quotations from the Old Testament enables us to see these three tractates from a third perspective. Søren Giversen described the usage which he found in AJ in terms of the following four categories: 1) quotations which are introduced by citing the source; 2) quotations which are set forth without indication of the source; 3) sentences in which biblical expressions are recalled without actually quoting the Old Testament; and 4) one passage in which a single word alludes to an Old Testament passage. OW provides examples of all but the first of these categories.

---

14. Ptolemaeus' "Letter to Flora" is preserved in Epiphanius, *Panaria*, xxxiii 3–7. A translation appears in Robert Grant's anthology, *Gnosticism: A Source Book of Heretical Writings from the Early Christian Period* (New York, 1961), pp. 184–90.

In discussing the last of his four categories Giversen wrote:

In BG 44, 16–45, 1 it is stated, "The mother began to ἐπιφέρεσθαι." . . . Nothing indicates a biblical passage. The solution is provided by the work itself, a little further on, BG 45, 6–19: John there asks Christ the meaning of the words: "But I said: Christ, what does ἐπιφέρεσθαι mean? But he smiled, and said: Do you think that it is as Moses said: upon the face of the waters?" . . . Thanks to AJ's own explanation we thus see that a single word, which is not given in the form of a quotation, and which is not in itself suggestive enough to enable one to say immediately what it refers to, may very well be used with special reference to an expression in the OT.[15]

His point is well taken. Within the history of Gnostic exegesis there is a level of familiarity with certain biblical texts which enables the writers to allude to them with considerable subtlety. In OW, the reference to Gen. 1:2 is more explicit. It is found in 100:33 ff. "His thought was completed by means of the word, and it appeared as a spirit which went to and fro over the waters." This type of allusion to the Old Testament is similar to the third of Giversen's categories. The reference to "the word," however, more nearly approximates the example which Giversen provided for his fourth category. Nevertheless, "the word" is so theologically pregnant that it is rather obvious in this case that the writer is exegeting Gen. 1:2 in terms of the prologue to the Fourth Gospel.

This particular method of exegeting scriptures by means of conflated readings in which a detail from one portion of scripture is added to details found elsewhere provides us with another example of the subtle employment of the Old Testament, in which the briefest sort of expression is clearly intended to be understood by readers steeped in certain critical texts from the Old Testament. Consider the following quote from OW:

Then [τότε] Justice [δικαιοσύνη] created Paradise [παράδεισος]. It was beautiful and outside the circuit [κύκλος] of the moon and the circuit [κύκλος] of the sun in the luxuriant [τρυφή] earth, which is in the East in the midst of the stones. (110:2–6)

15. Giversen, S., "The Apocryphon of John and Genesis," *StTh* 17 (1963), pp. 64–65.

This description of Paradise, somewhere beyond the sun and moon, rests upon a long tradition of speculation which grew in apocalyptic circles such as we meet in II Enoch or III Baruch, but despite its complex history the description has retained or reintroduced the eastward reference of Gen. 2:8 and the "stones" of Ezek. 28:14. A fuller understanding of Paradise is thus made possible by adding Scripture to Scripture, but the method is so subtle that contemporary scholars have tended to miss the allusion to Ezek. 28:14 in this passage.[16]

There are a number of passages in OW in which biblical expressions are used apart from direct quotes. Compare, for example, 103:21 ff., "He will trample upon [καταπατεῖν] you like potter's [-κεραμευς] clay, which one treads, and you will go with those who are yours down to your mother, the abyss." This recalls the language of Isa. 41:29. Such a use of biblical language would seem to suggest an easy familiarity with the text, which enables the writer to clothe his own thoughts in biblical language.

There are a number of clear quotes in OW although the context is generally changed and there is a frequent tendency to expand. Thus it is the archons who say, "Adam, where are you?" (119:27), adding the vocative to the quote. Nevertheless, the dependence on the biblical text is sometimes extremely literal. Thus "the wild beast" says to Eve, "Don't fear. You will surely not die, for he knows that when you eat from it your mind will be sobered, and you will become like the gods" (118:33–119:1). Although the injunction, "Don't fear," is not part of the text of Gen. 3:4–5, the brief phrase "You will surely not die," is a precise quote. It is stated somewhat awkwardly in Coptic. If rendered literally in English, it would read, "You will not die in a death," a literal rendering of the Greek, οὐ θανάτῳ ἀποθανεῖσθε, which in its turn represents an attempt to reproduce the infinitive absolute construction of Hebrew. This wooden literalness is then followed by an interpretive rendering which replaces the opening of the eyes with a sobering of the mind. The full quotation illustrates quite well the most frequent method of using material quoted from the

16. The stones which are mentioned in both Ezekiel and OW are probably "thunderstones," bright, fiery stones which flash through the sky and thunder to the earth in the midst of a summer storm.

Old Testament: partially expanded, partially literal, partially rendered in an interpretive manner.

As noted above, OW does not contain the first type of scriptural quotation mentioned by Giversen, i. e. quotes in which the source is explicitly cited. There are several ways to interpret this fact. It could be simply a matter of personal style on the part of the authors. It could reflect the needs of the intended readers; the more sophisticated readers would not need to be informed of the source. In the case of HA, the reason for including a quotation of this type is transparent. There is a single citation quote at the beginning of that tractate, in which the author cites "the great apostle," who said, "Our contending is not against flesh [σάρξ] and blood, but rather [ἀλλά] against the powers [ἐξουσία] of the world [κόσμος] and what pertains to the spirit [πνευματικόν] of wickedness [πονηρία]. . . ." (86:23–25).[17] In this context, the citation quote serves as a "proof-text," as if to say that Paul also alluded to the matters which are discussed in HA. A citation of this sort would most logically arise in a segment of the Gnostic community which was seeking to win favor among churches where Paul was held in esteem. By way of contrast, OW seems uninterested in that type of proof-text argument.

Except for the single citation quote in HA, neither HA nor OW contains any citation quotes within the material which parallels Genesis, but it is precisely within this parallel material that AJ introduces quotes of this type, both positively and negatively, as the following example dealing with Adam's sleep will show.

> But he said, "Not as Moses said, 'He caused him to sleep,' "
> but [ἀλλά] he covered over his perceptions [αἴσθησις] with
> a covering. He dulled him with imperception [ἀναισθησία].
> For [γάρ] he also [καί] spoke through the prophet [προφήτης]
> saying, "I will make thick the ears of their hearts in order
> that they might not understand [νοεῖν] and in order that they
> might not see." (BG 58:15–59:5)[18]

Two observations appear to be justified on the basis of this passage. On the one hand, the author appears to be acutely conscious

17. Cf. Eph. 6:12.
18. Cf. Isa. 6:10.

that his exegesis of Genesis is in conflict with other, more literal, traditional readings of the text. In rejecting them, he assumes an attitude of superiority vis-à-vis the text with the surprising statement, "Not as Moses said." On the other hand, he feels called upon to support his own exegesis by supplying a proof-text from the prophet (cf. Isa. 6:10). Such a use of scripture would suggest that a debate over the proper exegesis of Genesis took place within circles where a proof-text from the prophet would still represent a reasonably persuasive argument.

The evidence provided by biblical quotations tends to offer a mild support for earlier conclusions that the group for which AJ was written is somewhat further removed from easy familiarity with the Old Testament text than the readers of either OW or HA. Although Giversen was able to illustrate a very subtle use of the word ἐπιφέρεσθαι, that the author immediately explained the allusion suggests that he may have guessed that his readers would not recognize it.

OW and HA both reinterpret the Genesis material, but neither document appears to be as self-conscious about it as AJ. We hope to show that in the case of OW much of the reinterpretation came about by applying traditional methods of exegesis to the biblical text. If that is true, there would have been no particular reason to defend the new interpretation by inserting a proof-text. In OW and HA it was sufficient to set two scriptures side by side in order to exegete one by means of another. It is only in a community where exegetical methods are not self-evident that a new interpretation needs to be defended by citing the authority of someone such as "the prophet."

The parallels between HA, OW, and AJ are helpful inasmuch as they reveal the manner in which the several texts rework a common body of traditional material, providing an external reference which may help to determine what the unique contribution of each author may have been. Despite the help provided by parallel texts, however, the task of separating the author from his sources is enormously difficult. As we turn to consider the text of OW by itself, it is immediately obvious that much of the material which it contains has a considerable history. A hint of the complexity of materials assembled by the author of OW is provided by the linguistic and geographical spread of references within the text. Many

of the oldest materials embedded in this text come from the Semitic
world. For example, a primitive type of exegesis which assigned
Aramaic meanings to words found in the Hebrew text gave rise to
reading ḤYH "wild animal" in Genesis 3 as an Aramaic participle
meaning "instructor" (114:2 ff.). Many other examples of an
Aramaic background are also available. A similar example illustrates the Greek background of materials found in this text, for the
author has passed along an attempt to interpret Adam in terms of
ἀδαμαντίνη, "steel-like" (108:24). An example such as this shows
that the material was not simply translated into Greek, but it was
carefully reworked in Greek. Again, there are many examples of
material derived from Greek sources. There is also clear evidence
that the author is drawing on sources which are peculiar to Egypt.
He concludes his interpretation of the Phoenix and the three baptisms in 122:9 ff. with the following statement. "These great signs
[σημεῖον] appeared only in Egypt, not in other lands [χώρα], signi-
fying [σημαίνειν] that it is like the Paradise [παράδεισος] of God"
(122:33–123:2).

If there were no parallel texts, it would be tempting to assume
that the text of OW grew with the geographical expansion of the
sect which produced it. One might assume that the earliest stratum
was created within the Aramaic-speaking community. As the sect
moved away from its Aramaic-speaking homeland the Greek and
finally the Egyptian strata were added. Such a thesis might actually be valid for some of the material contained in OW, but a
comparison with HA, which appears to be an earlier, briefer text,
reveals that the supplementary material found in OW is derived
from all three sources: Aramaic, Greek, and Egyptian. The additional material in OW is often introduced in the form of an expansion or commentary on material of briefer compass attested in HA.
Thus, for example, HA mentions the chariot of Sabaoth briefly:

He made himself a great chariot [ἅρμα], cherubin [χερουβίν],
with four faces [πρόσωπον], and numerous angels [ἄγγελος],
without number, in order that they might serve [ὑπηρετεῖν].
(95:26–30)

OW, by way of contrast, contains an expanded version of this
material:

Then in front of his dwelling place he created a great throne [θρόνος] on a chariot [ἅρμα]; it was four-faced [-πρόσωπον] and called Cherubin [χερουβίν]. And [δέ] the Cherubin [χερουβίν] has eight forms [μορφή] at each [κατά] of the four corners—lion forms [-μορφη] and bull forms [-μορφη] and human forms [-μορφη] and eagle [ἀετός] forms [μορφη] so that [ὥστε] all of the forms [μορφη] amount to sixty-four forms [μορφη] plus seven archangels [ἀρχάγγελος] who stand before him. He is the eighth, having authority [ἐξουσία]. All of the forms [μορφη] amount to seventy-two, for [γάρ] from this chariot [ἅρμα] the seventy-two gods received a pattern [τύπος]. . . . (104:35–105:14)

The parallel passage in OW actually continues through line 106:5, describing the angelic host which surrounds the chariot, but the nature of the expanded material is clear from the excerpt cited above.

In most instances the material introduced by OW appears to be later than the material found in HA. There are, however, a few examples in which material preserved by OW is clearly presupposed by HA. Thus one is able to understand more fully the role of the "wild beast" (θηρίον) who speaks to Eve in the garden (OW 118:24 ff.) because the interpretation of "wild beast" as instructor was provided beforehand. In HA, however, the spiritual woman who enters the serpent to speak with the fleshly woman is also called "the instructor" (90:11), but the reader would never have guessed that such a casual allusion was based on close biblical exegesis had not OW incidentally preserved the tradition that Eve (ḤWH) also means "instructor" on the basis of an Aramaic reading of the root. The etymology is found in OW 113:13 where it is preserved in relation to the spiritual Eve. It thus appears that the relative age and peculiar history of many of the materials contained in OW will require many years of labor to unravel.

Another way of illustrating the complexity of materials within this tractate is to review the evidence for literary sources which lie behind both HA and OW. Source criticism of the documents has scarcely begun, but A. Böhlig has already shown that the basic account of the demiurge together with the parallel discussion of Genesis 2–3 must have circulated in two parallel accounts, one of which made use of the term *archons* (ἄρχοντες) whereas the other used *authorities* (ἐξουσίαι). Both HA and OW depend on these two sources, sometimes following one version, sometimes the other. One of the surprises which emerges from a comparison of sources within OW and HA is the fact that both documents contain a digression dealing with the redemption of Sabaoth. The material clearly falls outside both the *archon* and the *authorities* sources and is so obviously tendentious in OW that one would have quite naturally assumed its insertion to have been an original contribution of the author of that tractate had not the author of HA inserted the same digression at exactly the same point. Unexpected parallels of this sort make judgments about what is unique within a particular document particularly tentative.

With such reservations in mind, it is possible to consider the exegetical labors of the author of OW. There are two ways of viewing his work; one may consider the exegetical methods employed in the document or one may seek to discover the attitudes and presuppositions which led the author to certain conclusions about the biblical text. With regard to exegetical methods, certain observations have already been made. The author is particularly fond of interpreting a text by means of introducing an etymology for names appearing in the text. This method is based on biblical examples such as "The man called his wife's name Eve, because she was the mother of all living" (Gen. 3:20).[19] This method of exegesis permits the meaning which is concealed in a name to be added to the literal meaning of the text or to serve as the starting point for an allegorical interpretation. Sometimes the etymologies were arrived at by relating two meanings to a common root. Thus ḤYH yields both "wild animals" and "instructor." Sometimes a similar sounding word is suggestive. This is the case with the interpretation of ʾ*Adam*, "man," in light of *dam*, "blood," and ἀδαμαντίνη "steel-like" (108:20 ff.).

Words are capable of yielding new meanings in still other ways. In the case of words which are homographs, it is always possible to substitute one meaning for another. Thus φοῖνιξ, which means "date-palm" in Ps. 91:13 (LXX) is interpreted in terms of "the

19. This, of course, involves the similarity between the root ḤYH, from which "life, living" is derived, and a root ḤWH, on which the name "Eve" appears to be based.

Phoenix bird" in (122:29). Likewise, if a word has a well known figurative meaning, it is subject to the same principle of substituting one meaning of a word for another. Since "to see" in certain contexts clearly means "to intellectually perceive," "to see with the mind's eye," it is possible to apply that meaning to the serpent's words, "your eyes shall be opened," in Gen. 3:5. Thus OW reads the serpent's words as "your mind [νοῦς] will be sobered [νήφειν]" (119:1), an interpretation which was surely suggested to a careful exegete on the basis of Gen. 3:7, "And the eyes of both of them were opened, and they *knew*. . . ."

Another method of exegesis involved the interpretation of one text by means of another. An example has already been given which involves adding a detail from Ezek. 28:14 to the description of Paradise. Another example is provided in 116:20 ff. "Let us teach him [Adam] in his sleep as though [ὡς] she came to be from his rib so that woman will serve [ὑποτάσσειν] and he will be lord over her." The exegesis in this case takes into account two difficulties. On the one hand, the Gnostic found it hard to understand the rib episode in Gen. 2:21 ff. On the other hand, it was equally difficult for the Gnostic to see why the act of eating from the tree of knowledge—a positively good act for the Gnostic—in which both Adam and Eve participated jointly should result in subjecting one to another as stated in Gen. 3:16. Nevertheless, within his world women were apparently subjected to men. All these problems are solved by exegeting Gen. 2:21 ff. in the light of Gen. 3:16.

These are some of the more frequent methods of exegesis found in the text of OW. There are undoubtedly a number of other methods employed in this text, awaiting the research of scholars who are thoroughly familiar with the exegetical techniques of the first two centuries of the Christian era.

The exegetical methods illustrated thus far are not peculiar to this text. Although the author may have understood and approved of most of the exegesis discussed up to this point, it is probable that most of the exegetical work had been done on this material before he inherited it in his sources. At one point, the author appears to have made his own exegetical contribution. A type of allegorical interpretation was well known to the author. He applied it to non-biblical material in the phoenix passage (122:2 ff.), arguing that the three phoenixes stand for three races of men and three baptisms.

The two bulls in Egypt also contain a mystery (μυστήριον), apparently representing the sun and the moon. With regard to biblical
exegesis, the author seems to make the equation light = fire =
πνεῦμα in such a way that he understands the appearance of light
in Gen. 1:3 to stand for the advent of pneumatic Adam.[20] The
author's doctrine of three Adams is discussed below.

There are two groups of presuppositions with which the author
of OW approaches the text. The first group of presuppositions the
author shares with other Gnostic exegetes. There are at least three
of these: 1) a basic assumption that the biblical text contains
knowledge about the true character of God and man; 2) an assumption that baser powers of the universe are also exposed therein
in accord with truth about their nature; and 3) a reluctance to
predicate anything inferior of the true God. The second group of
presuppositions are those which are peculiar to this text. Two of
these are particularly significant: 1) the author brings to the text
a prefabricated, tripartite anthropology; and 2) the author has a
strong aniconic view which resulted in a peculiar exegesis of Gen.
1:26.

The assumption that the biblical text contains knowledge about
the true character of God and man led to a respect for the text and
an assiduous attempt to interpret it skillfully in order to demonstrate the wisdom which it contained. This perspective, which in
many ways parallels that of Philo, stands in contrast to a rabbinic
attempt to find within the Old Testament texts a basis for legislation or the attempt of Qumran sectaries to discover a prophetic
message outlining details of their own eschatological time of crises.

The Gnostic writers, of course, had more than one perspective
on scripture. They knew how to exploit a proof-text in order to
buttress theological assumptions which appear to have arisen elsewhere. Nevertheless, there are two texts—Genesis 2–3 and Isa.
45:18(?)—which the Gnostics quote in a manner which indicates
that the text itself had unique authority within Gnostic circles rep-

20. The author's understanding of Gen. 1:3 is somewhat complex. He apparently
began his work on the basis of the homograph φῶς which means both "light" and
"man." When he read φῶς as "man" in that passage, however, he did not give up
the meaning "light." The result was his "Light-Adam." The question which next
needs to be considered is, "How does Light-Adam come to stand for pneumatic-
Adam?" and the answer is to be sought in the general Gnostic tendency to symbolize
pneuma in terms of fire or light.

resented by AJ, OW, and HA. The fact that AJ, OW, and HA represent different strains within Gnosticism simply proves that these two passages of Scripture exercised authority within a rather broad segment of Gnosticism, an observation that should be confirmed and amplified as more texts from Nag² Hammadi are published.

AJ, OW, and HA each exegete Genesis 2–3 in different ways, but in each case the text of Genesis 2–3 appears to be a given factor, a text which they cannot ignore or in any way pass by. They must stop and exegete it. They are forced to take it seriously because it is a real source of wisdom about the nature of man. In this respect their regard for the authority of the Old Testament appears to be as vigorous as that of their orthodox opponents.

With regard to the quotation from Isa. 45:18(?), the three tractates, AJ, OW, and HA, are equally emphatic. It appears in OW as a quotation placed in the mouth of the Archigenetor, "I am god and no other one exists apart from me" (103:12). This boast takes place "after the heavens established themselves and their powers" and is interpreted in all Gnostic texts as an act of hybris on the part of the Demiurge. Sometimes it is a boast made in partial ignorance, and sometimes it is made in open revolt, but its importance for the Gnostics cannot be denied. It is quoted three times in OW (103:12, 107:30, 112:28), twice in HA (86:30, 94:21) as well as once in AJ, where it is expanded in the light of Exod. 20:3–5 (cf. Deut. 5:7–9) to read, "I am a jealous God, beside me there is no other" (BG 44:14). There are several Old Testament passages which may be regarded as the source of this quotation. Compare Isa. 43:11; 44:6, 8; 45:21–22 or Hos. 13:4. The context of Isa. 45:18 (LXX version) is strikingly similar to that which is found in OW. It reads, "Thus says the Lord who made the heaven, this God who established the earth . . ." (ἐγώ εἰμι, καὶ οὐκ ἔστιν ἔτι). In a number of manuscripts the text is expanded to read ἐγώ εἰμι κύριος. There are even Sahidic fragments which attest a reading ὁ θέος for the expanded κύριος and add πλὴν ἐμοῦ to the text. There is no justification for putting undue stress on the Sahidic manuscript tradition which provides a precise parallel to the Gnostic text, nor is there any need to insist on a precise parallel. The text in its simplest form would have been read by a Gnostic as the boast of the Demiurge, "the lord who made heaven."

The text of Isaiah may well have been understood by the Gnostics in the light of an exegetical tradition which began in Dan. 11:36 ff. where we read of a king who will magnify himself "above every god." The theme is resumed in II Thess. 2:3 ff. The text speaks of "the son of perdition, who opposes and exalts himself against every so-called god or object of worship, so that he takes his seat in the temple of God, proclaiming himself to be God." The theme is carried one step further in the "Ascension of Isaiah" 4:2 ff., where it is reported that Beliar, who has ruled this world since it came into being, will descend and enter an earthly monarch who will boast, "I am God and before me there has been no other" (4:6). In light of this sort of exegetical development, it is not difficult to understand how a Gnostic theologian might come to interpret Isa. 45:18 as the boastful words of a Demiurge, who would certainly deserve to be punished at the end of this age.

The repeated appeal to this text in Gnostic circles[21] suggests that this particular interpretation of the Old Testament text established something of a landmark in the history of Gnostic exegesis. Although the interpretation given to this text is understandable in view of earlier exegetical trends, it is nevertheless a bold interpretation, establishing the fact that the Old Testament contains unworthy statements made by the Demiurge as well as the truth about the nature of God and man. The exegete henceforth needed to discern between the good and evil which appeared in the biblical text. Thus Gnostic exegesis of the passage from Isaiah[22] provided a manifesto encouraging the reader to have a wary eye for traces of the Demiurge lurking behind every text in the Old Testament.

Gnostic exegesis should not be considered in isolation at this point. Pseudepigraphic writings beginning with the *Book of Jubilees* tended to find fallen angels, Satan, Beliar, or Mastema behind

21. From the earlier Gnostics, an episode describing the Demiurge's boasting is preserved in Irenaeus' report on the Barbelo-Gnostics (*Adv. haer* I.29) and the Sethian-Ophites (*Adv. haer* I.30). In the first of these, the quotation is influenced by Exod. 20:3–5 and has strong parallels to AJ.

22. Since the statement of the Demiurge was influenced by Exod. 20:3–5 as early as the time of Irenaeus' contact with the Barbelo-Gnostics, the texts from Nagᵓ Hammadi (AJ, HA, OW) must be used with caution in seeking to determine the precise text which has thus been reworked by the Gnostics. The earliest Gnostic texts dealing with the hybris of the Demiurge show evidence of conflating Old Testament passages.

most of the sins and human misfortunes of the Old Testament. *The Apocalypse of Moses*, for example, describes in some detail the manner in which Satan persuaded the serpent to serve as a vessel through which he might speak to Eve. In view of this it is hardly surprising to discover that the Gnostic writer of HA understood that a spiritual woman entered the serpent to speak with Eve.[23] In general, however, the Gnostic exegetes believed that the Old Testament contained information about inferior powers who came into being on this side of the veil which separates our cosmos from the pleroma. More orthodox(?) exegetes of the Old Testament believed that it bore witness to the works of Satan. Satan was implicated wherever there was wickedness, cruelty, or senseless suffering. The key to Gnostic exegesis is equally straightforward. A reference to some inferior deity is recognizable wherever something inferior is predicated of a deity. One of the clearest presuppositions of the Gnostics is the assumption that nothing inferior could ever be attributed to the highest deity. In so much as the created world falls short of perfection it cannot be either the work or the will of the highest deity. The highest deity cannot be ignorant, jealous, angry, or vengeful. In fact any anthropomorphism is considered degrading. The Gnostic god doesn't love anyone.

In order to set this Gnostic position in perspective it is helpful to begin with Philo. In dealing with the problem of relating a transcendent deity to the created world, Philo appealed to both the Divine Reason (Logos) and the "Powers" of God. According to Philo, two of the "Powers" are represented by the divine names "God" and "Lord," names which designate his goodness and sov-

---

23. For the Gnostics it was a good thing for Eve to eat the fruit of Gnosis. Therefore, a good power, "spiritual woman," entered the serpent. *The Apocalypse of Moses* is more orthodox in viewing the eating of the fruit as harmful to man. Thus the author understood that an evil power, Satan, entered the serpent. In describing the manner whereby the power came to enter the serpent, however, the author of *The Apocalypse of Moses* permits his imagination free rein in order to fill in the dialogue between the serpent and Satan, as Satan tricks the serpent into permitting the use of his body. In OW, the writer simply states that the "spiritual woman" entered the serpent. Behind both interpretations, however, there is probably a similar assumption. If the serpent was able to speak with man in such a way that he could be understood, it was only possible through the agency of a higher power which had entered the serpent.

In OW the basic identity of "the one who is wiser than ($\pi\alpha\rho\dot{\alpha}$) all of them" is "the instructor." It is only of secondary significance that "he was called the wild beast ($\theta\eta\rho\dot{\iota}o\nu$)" (118:25–26). Therefore it is not surprising that the "instructor" should speak in his own right.

ereignty. In two passages, however, Philo charges the "Powers" with the creation of evil (see *De Opificio Mundi* 73–75 and *De Fuga* 65–72). In both cases Philo attempts to exegete Gen. 1:26, "Let us make man in our image." He explains that Moses used the plural to indicate that God was holding parley with his "Powers." God who created the rational, ruling part of the soul considered it proper that his subservient powers create the subservient, mortal portion of the soul. Philo then adds a second reason for the plural. Since the human soul is open to conceptions of both good and evil, it is not fitting that a God who is totally good should create it alone. The text continues, "Therefore he considered it necessary to distribute the creating of evil (things) to other craftsmen [δημιουργοῖς]" (*De Fuga* 70).

Philo, the Platonist, has thus exegeted Gen. 1:26 in terms of the doctrine found in *Timaeus*. His great concern for the transcendent goodness of God has led him to state his own position so sharply that the "craftsmen" in this text receive an independent status which enables them to bear the responsibility for an action which is too degrading to predicate of God. Gnostic exegesis involves carrying a number of the separate notions expressed in Philo to their logical conclusions. Philo would never have named Yahweh and Elohim as the creators of evil. The context in which he identifies them as "Powers" of God is separated from the passages in which he assigns the creation of evil to the "Powers." Nevertheless, the world view which Philo reflects was shared by many others so that it was simply a matter of time until some unknown scholar who was working with similar data and presuppositions would make the sort of judgment which Philo did not care to make, giving rise to a type of exegesis which is characteristically Gnostic.

Once a first step was made, everything within the text confirmed the inferiority of the "Powers" discussed in Genesis 2–3. In the mind of the Gnostic exegete, God did not want man to eat of the tree of knowledge and become "like the gods" because he was "jealous" (OW 119:5). When Adam hid, the archon had to ask, "Adam where are you?" because he didn't know (HA 90:20 ff.). The archons cursed the serpent because they were powerless to do anything else (OW 120:5, 6). Straightforward exegesis of the text clearly reveals the inferiority of the deities described there. It was obvious to the Gnostic exegete that Yahweh and Elohim were inferior powers. A literal reading of the text reveals that they were petty, jealous, and even hostile to man.

In addition to the exegetical presuppositions shared with other Gnostic writers, the author of OW has certain unique views. These may be illustrated by a discussion of two passages in the tractate. The first of these reads as follows:

> Moreover the first Adam of the light is pneumatic [πνευμα-τικός]. He appeared on the first day. The second Adam is Psychic [ψυχικός]. He appeared on the fourth day, which is called "Aphrodite." The third Adam is Choic [χοϊκός], i. e. "man of law" [-νομος]. He appeared on the eighth day, i. e. "the rest [ἀνάπαυσις] of the poverty," which is called "sunday" [ἡμέρα ἡλίου]. (117:28–118:2)

This understanding is obviously based on the presupposition that man is a tripartite creature: pneumatic, psychic, and choic. There is also a reference to a span of eight days. In order to interpret this passage it is worth recalling that as early as the *Book of Jubilees* there was developed a scheme for reading Genesis 1–2 in sequence. The author of that work considers the creative activity described in Gen. 1:1–2:3 to be a description of the events of the first seven days whereas Gen. 2:4 ff. describes events which began on the eighth day. Although it would have been logical to place the creation of man "of the dust from the ground" (Gen. 2:7) on the eighth day, *Jubilees* brushes over the fact that there are two accounts of the creation of man by accepting the view that man was created in the first week and ignoring Gen. 2:7 (*Jubilees* 3). By the time of Philo, however, the two different accounts of creation are explained. The creation of 1:27 is the creation of a heavenly man, man viewed as a "genus" consisting of both male and female, and the account of 2:7 deals with the creation of an earthly man, an individual man who is molded of clay. Thus the number of Adams has grown to two. If one were to apply the chronology of *Jubilees* to the system of Philo he would conclude that the first Adam was created on the sixth day and the second Adam was created on the eighth day. The author of OW adds yet another Adam. Moving backward from the choic Adam, who was created on the eighth day, he reinterpreted the Adam of 1:27 as a psychic, and then he discovered an earlier pneumatic Adam in Gen. 1:3 created on the first day. For reasons of his own—perhaps just a sense of balance—he moved the creation of psychic Adam, who is mentioned in Gen. 1:27, from the sixth day to the fourth day.

The Gnostic author of OW seems to have been motivated by a presupposition that man is a tripartite creature. He sought to confirm this opinion by means of an allegorical interpretation of Gen. 1:3. Within the Gnostic world view the equation Light = Fire = Pneuma is so widely understood that it was possible to see in the first appearance of light a reference to the advent of pneumatic Adam. On the basis of such an equation, the author of OW replaces the terse Hebrew phrase "and God said 'let there be light,' and there was light," with a rather lengthy paraphrase, " 'If someone exists before me, let him appear in order that we might see his light.' And immediately, behold a light came out of the eighth, which is above. It passed through all of the heavens of the earth. When the archigenetor [ἀρχιγενέτωρ] saw the light, that it was beautiful [and] radiant, he was amazed. And he was very much ashamed. When the light appeared, a human likeness, which was very wonderful, was revealed within it" (107:36–108:9). Despite the poetic expansion, it is still possible to see that this text is based on Gen. 1:3.

A second passage which reveals a unique presupposition of this author is the passage in which he deals with Gen. 1:26. This follows the episode which describes the hybris of the Demiurge and the appearance of the heavenly light. When the archons saw Light-Adam, they recognized him as one who destroyed their work. They immediately questioned the Demiurge, who replied:

"Yes, if you desire that he not be able to destroy our work [ἔργον], come, let us create a man from the earth according to [κατά] the image [εἰκών] of our body [σῶμα] and according to the likeness of that [one], and let him serve us in order that whenever that one sees his likeness and loves it he will no longer [οὐκέτι] destroy our work [ἔργον], but [ἀλλά] those who are begotten by the light we will make serve us through all the time [χρόνος] of this eon [αἰών]." (112:32–113:5)

In passing, it may be noted that this text provides an additional example of early attempts to interpret the text by means of conflation. Man is here said to be created in an image and likeness, which is in agreement with Gen. 1:26, but the text also reports that he is "from the earth," a detail taken from Gen. 2:7. The same type of conflation is attested in HA (87:23), a fact which suggests that a conflated form of the text came to the author of OW in his sources. Actually it is here somewhat out of place in the text of OW, since the molding (πλάσσειν) of man, which corresponds to Gen. 2:7, is not discussed in OW until 114:29 ff.

Excluding the reference to Gen. 2:7, the quotation cited above reveals several themes which are significant for the author of the tractate. He understood that man contained within himself both good and evil. The theme appears in the quotation just cited as well as elsewhere in the tractate. It is described in many different ways. In mythological terms, the author understood that man was subjected to afflictions at the hand of his zoomorphic (θηρίον, μορφή) makers (πλάστης), whose form he shared. Nevertheless, the gift of illumination from on high, which came as the result of eating the fruit of Gnosis, enabled him to loathe (σικχαίνειν) his makers (119:11–19). Man is the scene of a cosmic drama, for it is within man that heavenly Gnosis confronts and rebukes the powers of this world. On the basis of his exegesis of Gen. 1:26, the author of this tractate was able to show that man is ontologically structured in conformity with his special role in that drama. On the one hand, he is created in the likeness of the heavenly Light-Adam, while on the other hand, he is created in the image of the powers of this world.

Several factors are involved in the author's strange exegesis, which separates the likeness from the image. The writer is obviously conditioned by his own dualistic presupposition about the nature of man. Within Gen. 1:26, however, the Gnostic imagination was stimulated by the plural possessive pronoun in the Greek text: ποιήσωμεν ἄνθρωπον κατ' εἰκόνα ἡμέτερον καὶ καθ' ὁμοίωσιν. A Gnostic exegete would find it difficult to think of the supreme, unknown god as a plurality. Therefore it was obvious to him that the biblical text referred to the "image" of lesser beings. An intense aniconic feeling in certain circles may have encouraged placing a negative value on the word εἰκών. The reason for treating ὁμοίωσις as a positive term is a bit more elusive. It is difficult to believe that the Gnostics were so ignorant of Greek as to be unaware of the fact that the plural pronoun might also apply to the "likeness." No, they purposely read the text as they did because of their pre-supposition about the nature of man. They were certainly encouraged to give a positive value to the "likeness" by the LXX reading of Gen. 5:3, where we are told that Adam begot Seth: κατὰ τὴν ἰδέαν αὐτοῦ, καὶ κατὰ τὴν εἰκόνα αὐτοῦ. In this text the dualistic structure of man, who was created in Gen. 1:26, is passed on from Adam to Seth, but the word ἰδέα has been substituted for ὁμοίωσις. In the Massoretic text, the same words are used in Gen. 1:26 and 5:3, "image" (ṣĕlĕm) and "likeness" (dᵊmūth). Speculation as to why the LXX translated dᵊmūth as ἰδέα in Gen. 5:3 would lead us too far astray, but it is certainly safe to assume that the Gnostic exegete would be inclined to understand the term ἰδέα in light of hellenistic reinterpretation of Platonic philosophy. That would explain the Gnostic readiness to postulate a transcendent origin for the ἰδέα / ὁμοίωσις, "likeness" in man.

Once the basic structure of man has been confirmed through exegesis of Gen. 1:26, the author expands on the biblical account, explaining that the archons made man in their "image" and according to the "likeness" of Light-Adam so that he (Light-Adam) might be enticed by means of his own likeness to refrain from destroying the work of the archons. Thus "their moulded image [πλάσμα] became a hedge for the light" (113:9–10). The scheme of the archons failed, however, because the heavenly man is destined to "appear in the presence of his likeness and condemn them [the archons] by [means of] their moulded image [πλάσμα]." Why does man have to have a nature inherited from both the archons of this world and the heavenly man? It is because the primary task of man in the world is to repudiate the archons. He must participate in that which is from above because the archons can only be repudiated by a higher power. Man must also participate in that which belongs to the archons because he is the agent of a peculiar justice which demands that the archons be repudiated by means of their own work. At this point, however, the Gnostic theology has gone far beyond simple exegesis.

APPENDIX

In the texts which follow, a | is used to indicate the end of a line of Coptic text. Every fifth line is indicated by ‖.

Excerpt from "The Hypostasis of the Archons"

(88:11) After | these (things) the Spirit (πνεῦμα) saw the psychic (ψυχικός) man | upon the earth. And the Spirit (πνεῦμα) came out of | the steel-like earth (ἀδαμάντινη). He (the Spirit) descended and dwelt ‖¹⁵ within him, and that man became a | living soul (ψυχή). He called his name Adam because (γάρ) | he was found moving upon the earth. A voice | came out of the Incomprehensibility for the help (βοήθεια) of Adam.

And then the Archons assembled ‖²⁰ all of the beasts (θηρίον) of the earth and | all of the birds of the sky, and they brought them to Adam | in order to see what Adam would call them | (and) in order that he might name each of the birds | and all of the cattle. (Then) they took Adam ‖²⁵ and left him in Paradise in order that he might work | it and guard it. And the Archons commanded | him, saying, "From | [every] tree which is in Paradise you may eat. | But (δέ) from the tree of knowledge of ‖³⁰ good and evil, don't eat! and don't (οὐδέ) | [touch] it! because (on) the day which you eat | of it you will surely die." They | [say] this to [Adam] but they do not know what it is | [which they have spoken] to him. But (ἀλλά) by the will of ‖⁸⁹:¹ the Father they said this in this manner so that | it might be eaten, and Adam might see them, esteeming them | as material (beings) (ὑλικός).

The Archons took counsel together | and said, "Come, let us bring a ‖⁵ sleep upon Adam." And (then) he slept |—but (δέ) the sleep is the ignorance which | they brought upon him—and (then) he slept. They laid open | his rib like a living woman. | And they (re)built his side with flesh (σάρξ) ‖¹⁰ in its place.

And (then) Adam came to be | wholly psychic (ψυχικός). And (then) the spiritual (πνευματική) woman | came to him. She spoke with him and said | "Arise, Adam." And when he saw her | he said, "You are the one who gave me life; ‖¹⁵ you will be called 'the mother of the living' | because she is my mother, (and) she is the physician | and the wife and the one who gave birth." |

Then (δέ) the Authorities (ἐξουσία) came to their Adam | But (δέ) when they saw his companion-likeness (fem.) speaking with ‖²⁰ him, they were greatly agitated, | and they loved her. They said to one another, | "Come, let us cast our seed (σπέρμα) | upon her." They pursued (διώκειν) her, and | she laughed at them because of their ‖²⁵ senselessness and their blindness. And (then) she became a tree | beside them. She left her shadow | before them, and they defiled it | in an abominable manner. And they polluted the seal (σφραγίς) | of her voice in order that (ἵνα) they might be themselves condemned ‖³⁰ by means of their moulded image (πλάσμα) of her | likeness.

Then (δέ) the spiritual (πνευματική) woman came [into] | the serpent, the Instructor (masc.). And he instructed [them], | saying, "What did [he say] to you? 'From every tree in ‖³⁵ Paradise you may eat, [but (δέ) from the tree] ‖⁹⁰:¹ of knowledge of evil and good | don't eat!' " The woman of flesh (σαρκική) said, | "He not only (οὐ μόνον) said, 'Don't eat,' but (ἀλλά) | 'Don't touch it because in the day which you ‖⁵ eat of it you will surely die.' " | And the serpent, the Instructor (masc.), said, | "You will surely not die since (γάρ) he said this to you | in jealousy (φθονεῖν), but rather (μᾶλλον) your eyes will be opened | and you will become like the gods, ‖¹⁰ knowing evil and good." | And (then) the Instructor (fem.) was removed from the serpent, | and she left him alone as an earthly (creature). |

And the woman of flesh (σαρκική) took from the tree, | and she ate, and she gave to her husband also. ‖¹⁵ And the psychic (beings) (ψυχικός) ate, and their baseness (κακία) | was exposed within their ignorance. And | they knew that they were naked with respect to that which is of the Spirit (πνευματικόν). They took fig leaves and bound them | on their loins. Then (τότε) the Chief ‖²⁰ Archon came, and said, "Adam, where are you?" | since (γάρ) he was not aware of what happened. | And Adam said, "I heard your voice, and I was | afraid because I was naked, and I hid." | The Archon said, "Why did you hide? unless perchance ‖²⁵ (εἰμήτι) you ate from the tree | (concerning) which I ordered you, 'Don't eat | of it alone!' and (then) you ate." | Adam said, "The woman whom you gave to me, [she gave] to me, and I ate." And the Wilful (one) (αὐθάδης) ‖³⁰ of the Archons cursed the woman. (Then) the woman said, | "The serpent is the one who enticed (ἀπατᾶν) me, and I ate." |

[And (then) they (the Authorities) came] to the serpent and cursed his shadow | [but (δέ) they were] powerless since they did not know | that it was (only) a moulded image (πλάσμα). From that day ‖⁹¹:¹ the serpent came to be under the curse of the Authorities (ἐξουσία) | until the perfect (τέλειος) man comes. | (As For) that curse, it came upon the serpent. (Then) they turned | to their Adam and seized him and cast him and his wife out of ‖⁵ Paradise.

Excerpt from "On the Origin of the World"

(114:24) But (δέ) in ‖²⁵ that time (καιρός), then (τότε) the Archigenetor | gave a decree (γνώμη) to those who were with him concerning | the man. Then (τότε) each one of them cast | his seed (σπέρμα) on the midst of the navel of the | earth. From that day, the seven ‖³⁰ Archons moulded (πλάσσειν) the man. His body (σῶμα) (+μέν) | is like their body (σῶμα), but (δέ) his likeness is | like the man who appeared to them. | His moulded image (πλάσμα) came to be according to (κατά) a part (μέρος) of each one. Their (δέ) chief created ‖³⁵ the brain (ἐγκέφαλον) and the marrow. Afterward | he appeared as (ὡς) (the one) before him. He became ‖¹¹⁵:¹ a psychic (ψυχικός) man, and they called | him "Adam," i. e. "the father," according to (κατά) | the name of the one who was before him. But (δέ) after | Adam was completed, he left him in a vessel (σκεῦος) since he had ‖⁵ received a form (μορφή) like the miscarriage, having no spirit (πνεῦμα) in him. | Because of this deed, when the Chief Archon | remembered the word of Pistis, he was afraid | lest perhaps (μήπως) the true (man) come into | his moulded image (πλάσμα) and rule over it. Because of this he ‖¹⁰ left his moulded image (πλάσμα) forty days without (χωρίς) | psyche (ψυχή) and he withdrew (ἀναχωρεῖν), and left him.

But (δέ) in the | forty days Zoe-Sophia sent | her breath into Adam, who had no psyche (ψυχή). He began to (ἄρχεσθαι) move upon the earth ‖¹⁵ And he was not able to rise . . . (Line 115:15–30 contains a description of the Archons' concern at seeing Adam move. When they questioned him, he responded in such a way as to give them rest.)

(115:31) Sophia | sent Zoe, her daughter, who is called | "Eve," as (ὡς) an instructor in order that she might | raise up Adam, in whom there is no psyche (ψυχή) ‖³⁵ so that those whom he would beget might become | vessels (ἀγγεῖον) of the light. When ‖¹¹⁶:¹ Eve saw her companion-likeness cast down, she | pitied him, and she said, "Adam, live! | rise up upon the earth!" Immediately, her | word became a work (ἔργον), for (γάρ) when Adam ‖⁵ rose up, immediately he opened his eyes | When he saw her, he said, "You will be called | 'the mother of the living' because you are the one who | gave life to me."

Then (τότε) the authorities (ἐξουσία) were informed | that their moulded image (πλάσμα) was alive, and had raised up. ‖¹⁰ They were very agitated, and they sent seven | archangels to see that which had come to be. They came | to Adam. When they saw Eve speaking with | him they said to one another, "What is this (female) | light being? for truly (καὶ γάρ) she is like the likeness which ‖¹⁵ appeared to us in the light. Now, | come! let us seize her and let us cast | our seed (σπέρμα) on her so that if she is polluted | she will not be able to go up to her light, | but (ἀλλά) those whom she will produce will serve (ὑποτάσσειν) ‖²⁰ us. But (δέ) let us not tell Adam because he is not | from us, but (ἀλλά) let us bring a sleep | upon him. And let us teach him in his | sleep as though (ὡς) she came to be from | his rib so that the woman will serve (ὑποτάσσειν) ‖²⁵ and he will be lord over her.

Then (τότε) Eve, being | a power (δύναμις), laughed at their purpose (γνώμη). | She darkened their eyes. She left | her likeness there stealthily beside Adam. She entered | the Tree of Gnosis. She remained there, ‖³⁰ but (δέ) they followed her. It appeared | to them that she had entered the tree and became | tree. But (δέ) when they came to be in a great | fear, the blind ones ran away. Afterward | when they sobered (νήφειν) up from their sleep, they came ‖³⁵ to Adam, and when they saw the likeness of that one ‖¹¹⁷:¹ with him, they were agitated, thinking that this |

was the true (ἀληθινή) Eve. And they acted recklessly (τολμᾶν). They came
to her; they seized her, and they | cast their seed (σπέρμα) upon her. They
did it ||⁵ villainously (πανοῦργος), polluting (her) not only (οὐ μόνον) |
naturally (φυσικῶς), but (ἀλλά) corruptibly, | polluting the seal (σφραγίς)
of her first voice, | which spoke with them, saying, "What is the (one)
who exists | before you?" (They did this) in order that they might pollute
those who say ||¹⁰ that they are begotten through the word | by means of
of the true (ἀληθινός) man in the consummation (συντέλεια). | But they
erred (πλανᾶσθαι), not knowing | that they were polluting their (own)
body (σῶμα). It is the likeness | which the authorities (ἐξουσία) in every
form polluted ||¹⁵ with (the aid of) their angels (ἄγγελος). (Line 117:15–
118:16 reports that Abel was born to the Chief Archon and the other
children of Eve to the seven Authorities. The author then continues to
spell out his own peculiar theological conclusions, stating that Eve contained all seed in accord with Heimarmene. This is followed by his systematic description of the three Adams, who are created in eight days.
At the end of this section, the Archons are again discussed. They stand
before Adam in fear, suspecting that he might be the true man who
blinded them.)

(118:16) Then (τότε) they | took counsel (συμβούλιον) among the seven.
They came to | Adam and Eve fearfully (φόβος). They said to him |
"Every tree which is in Paradise ||²⁰ whose fruit (καρπός) may be eaten,
was created for you. But (δέ) the Tree | of Gnosis, beware! don't eat |
from it. If you do eat, you will | die." After they gave them a great fright
(ψόβος) | they withdrew (ἀναχωρεῖν) up to their authorities (ἐξουσία). ||²⁵

Then (τότε) the one who is wiser than (παρά) all of them, | one who
was called "the wild beast" (θηρίον), came. | And when he saw the likeness
of their mother, | Eve, he said to her "What is it that god said to you?
'Don't eat from the tree ||³⁰ of Gnosis!' " She said, "He not only (οὐ
μόνον) said, | 'Don't eat from it,' but (ἀλλά) 'Don't touch it lest (ἵνα) you
die.' " He said | to her, "Don't be afraid. You will surely | not [die], for
(γάρ) [he knows] that when you eat ||¹¹⁹:¹ from it your mind (νοῦς) will
be sobered (νήφειν) and | you will become like the gods, | knowing the
distinctions (διαφορά) which exist between | the human evil (πονηρός)
and the good (ἀγαθός). For (γάρ) he said ||⁵ this to you, being jealous
(φθονεῖν) lest you eat from it." Then (δέ) Eve was confident (θαρρεῖν) of |
the words of the Instructor, and she peered into | the tree. She saw that
it was beautiful and | tall. She desired it, and took some of ||¹⁰ its fruit
(καρπός) and ate. She gave to her | husband also, and he ate. Then (τότε)
their mind (νοῦς) | was opened. For (γάρ) when they ate, the light | of
Gnosis illuminated them. When they put | on shame, they knew that
they were naked ||¹⁵ with regard to Gnosis. When they sobered up (νήφειν)
they saw themselves, | that they were naked, and they loved one an-
other. | When they saw their makers (πλάστης), since they were | wild
animal (θηρίον) forms (μορφή), they loathed (σικχαίνειν) them.

Then (τότε) when the Archons knew that ‖²⁰ they had transgressed (παραβαίνειν) their commandment (ἐντολή), they came in an earthquake | with a great threat (ἀπειλή) into | Paradise to Adam and Eve in order to see | the result (ἀποτέλεσμα) of the help (βοήθεια). Then (τότε) Adam and Eve were very much disturbed. ‖²⁵ They hid under the trees which are in Paradise. | Then (τότε) the Archons did not know where they were. | They said, "Adam, where are you?" He said, "I am in | this place. But (δέ) because of your fear, I hid | when I was ashamed." But (δέ) they said to him, in ‖³⁰ ignorance, "Who is the one who spoke to you of the shame which you put on unless (εἰμήτι) | you have eaten from the tree?" He said | "The woman whom you gave me, she is the one who | gave to me, and I ate." And (δέ) then (τότε) they said ‖¹²⁰:¹ "What is this which you did?" She answered and said, "The Informer is the one who enticed me, and I | ate." Then (τότε) the Archons came to the Informer, | and their eyes were blinded by him. ‖⁵ They were not able to do anything to him. They cursed | him since (ὡς) they were powerless. Afterward they came to | the woman, and they cursed her and her sons. After the woman they cursed Adam and the earth because of him | and the fruit (καρπός). And everything which they created ‖¹⁰ they cursed. There is no blessing | from them. It is impossible that good (ἀγαθόν) be produced from | evil (πονηρόν).

From that day the authorities (ἐξουσία) | knew that truly (ἀληθῶς) the strong one is | before them. They would not have known except (εἰμήτι) that ‖¹⁵ their command (ἐντολή) was not kept (τηρεῖν). They brought a great | envy into the world (κόσμος) only (μόνον) because of | the deathless man. But (δέ) when the Archons saw | their Adam, he came to be in another Gnosis | (and) they desired to test (πειράζειν) him. They gathered ‖²⁰ all of the beasts and the wild animals (θηρίον) of the | earth and the birds of the heaven, and they brought them to | Adam in order that they might see what he would call them. | When he saw them, he named their | creatures (κτίσμα). They were troubled because Adam had sobered (νήφειν) ‖²⁵ from all anguish (ἀγωνία). They gathered together and | took counsel (συμβούλιον). They said, "Behold, Adam | has become like one of us to | know the distinction (διαφορά) of the light and the | darkness. Now lest perhaps (μήπως) he be deceived in the manner of ‖³⁰ the Tree of Gnosis, and he comes also | to the Tree of Life and eats from it | and becomes immortal and rules and condemns (καταφρονεῖν) | us and regards all our glories as folly | (and) afterward passes judgment (κατακρίνειν) on ‖³⁵ us and the world (κόσμος), come let us cast him ‖¹²³:¹ out of Paradise down upon the earth, | the place from whence he was brought so that he | will not be able henceforth to know anything more | about us." And thus they cast Adam and his wife ‖⁵ out of Paradise. And this | which they did did not suffice them. But (ἀλλά) when they were frightened | they came to the Tree of Life and they set great terrors around it, fiery living (ζῷον) beings | called "Cherubin." And they left ‖¹⁰ a flaming sword in their midst, turning | continually in a great terror in order that (ἵνα) no one among earthmen might ever enter to | that place (τόπος).

Excerpt from "The Apocryphon of John"

(Line 58:1–12 contains a discussion of the role of the serpent. It was his desire to withdraw the power which was found within Adam, and it is at this point that the present excerpt begins. The Christ is speaking.)

(58:12) And (then) | he cast a BSHE (n.b. this Coptic word can mean either "sleep" or "forgetfulness.") over | Adam. I said to him, ‖15 "O Christ, what is the BSHE?" Then (δέ) he | said, "(It is) not as (κατά) | Moses said, 'He | caused him to sleep,' but (ἀλλά) he | covered over his perception (αἴσθησις) ‖20 with a covering and he made him dull through ‖59:1 the lack of perception (ἀναισθησία). For truly (καὶ γάρ) | he spoke through the prophet (προφήτης) | saying, 'I will make dull | the ears of their hearts (= minds) lest ‖5 they perceive (νοεῖν) and see.' " |

Then (τότε) the Thought (fem.) (ἐπίνοια) of the | light hid within him, and by | his will he desired to bring her | out of the rib. But (δέ) (as for) her, the ‖10 Thought (ἐπίνοια) of the light, since | she is unattainable, when the darkness pursued | her it did not catch her. (Then) he (the serpent) desired | to bring the power out of him (Adam) | to make once more a moulded image (πλάσις) ‖15 with a feminine form (μορφή). And he set (her) up before him. | (It was) not as (κατά) Moses said, "He took a rib (and) created the woman beside him." ‖20

Immediately, he was sobered (νήφειν) from | the drunkenness of the darkness, (and) ‖60:1 the Thought (ἐπίνοια) of the light | removed the covering which was over his heart (= mind). | Immediately, as soon as he knew | his substance (οὐσία) he said, "This ‖5 now is bone of my | bone and flesh (σάρξ) of | my flesh (σάρξ)." Therefore man will leave his father | and his mother and cleave to ‖10 his wife and the two of them will become | one flesh (σάρξ). Because they will be sent forth | from the consort (σύζυγος) of the mother, and she will be established, therefore Adam named her, "the mother of all the living."

(The text used in this excerpt is that of the *Coptic Papyrus Berolinensis* 8502.)

בעותא IN EARLIEST CHRISTIANITY

J. H. CHARLESWORTH

Almost thirty years ago Professor W. F. Stinespring's mentor, C. C. Torrey, speculated on the meaning of בעותא among the earliest Aramaic-speaking Christians. His conjecture has been subsequently ignored both by Semitists and historians. Recent discoveries of Aramaic manuscripts and contemporary research on related subjects show that a reassessment of Torrey's speculation is opportune.

In the present essay we shall discuss the following: the definition of בעותא customarily held by Semitists today; Torrey's position; the meaning of this noun in an apocryphal Syriac psalm; the use of בעותא[1] in the Sinaitic Palimpsest; the derivation of the Arabic word *ᵃlbâ ͨûth*; and finally the probable meaning of בעותא in the earliest Christian hymnbook, the so-called Odes of Solomon.

The denotation of בעותא that is usually given is "petition," and this meaning is said to derive etymologically from the familiar verb בעא ("to ask," "to pray"). There is no question that this definition is supported by the expression in Dan. 6:14 [13]: בעא בעותא "petitioning his petition." The meaning "petition" for בעותא, however, does not apply in some later texts, viz. the Sinaitic Palimpsest and the Odes of Solomon, as we shall see.

Professor Torrey's speculation regarding the meaning of this noun was that בעותא also meant "resurrection," but that this meaning was peculiar to the earliest Aramaic-speaking Christians.[2] He obtained this meaning from the use of בעותא in the Sinaitic Palimpsest, a variant reading found also in Aphraates, and from an etymological examination of the Arabic word *ᵃlbâ ͨûth*. In the following pages we shall attempt to revive Torrey's inference. At the outset it is important to observe that he did not challenge the meaning of this noun in Jewish circles.

---

1. Printing costs demand that the Syriac script be put into square characters. It is hoped, however, that this practice will not give the impression that the writer believes the Sinaitic Palimpsest and the Odes of Solomon were originally composed in the square script.

2. *Documents of the Primitive Church* (New York, London: Harper and Brothers, 1941), pp. 257–62.

While בעותא is not found in the Genesis Apocryphon, it is present in the five apocryphal Syriac psalms[3] recently described by M. Delcor as "Cinq Psaumes Syriaques Esséniens."[4] We are in agreement with Delcor's judgment "que ces cinq psaumes trouvent leur explication normale sinon dans le milieu essénien proprement dit, du moins dans un milieu essénisant. . . ."[5]

Our attention is drawn to the third psalm, the fifth line of which is as follows:

בעותי לא תכלא מני.

My בעותא do not withhold from me.

What is the denotation of בעותא in this line? The answer is clarified by the corresponding word in the first line of the synonymous parallelism: שאלתי ("my request").[6] The meaning of this stich, therefore, is as follows:

And give me my request,
My petition withhold not from me.

Consequently, as in Dan. 6:14 [13] so in this Jewish, Syriac psalm בעותא signifies "petition." The denotation is precisely the one Torrey would expect since the psalm is not Christian. For example, see line 11: נמוסך and lines 37–38:

פרוק ליסריל גביך
ולדבית יעקוב בחירך

When we turn to the early Christian, Syriac literature, we discover that another meaning is given to this noun.

In the earliest Syriac recension of the gospels, the Sinaitic

---

3. These psalms have been known to western scholars since Assemani's publication in 1759 (*Bibliothecae Apostolicae Vaticanae Codicum manuscriptorum Catalogus* [1759], vol. 1, 3:385 f.). For a succinct bibliographical statement regarding the extant manuscripts of these psalms, see M. Delcor, *Les Hymns de Qumran* (*Hodayot*) (Paris: Letouzey et Ané, 1962), p. 299.

4. Delcor, p. 299.

5. Delcor, pp. 299–300. The most important parallel with Qumran ideology is the emphasis that praise is more important than cultic sacrifices (Psalm 2, lines 17–21). Also of importance is the meaning of the communal meal (Psalm 2, lines 24–25) and the intermittent use of words that have an Essene connotation (see Delcor, p. 303).

6. Martin Noth brings out this meaning through his translation of the line into Hebrew: תְּחִנָּתִי ("my supplication for favor"). See Noth's important study, "Die fünfsyrisch überlieferten apocryphen Psalmen," *ZAW*, 47 (1930), 1–23.

Palimpsest, we find the following unusual uses of בעותא (juxtaposed with the parallel passages in the Greek and the Peshiṭta):

Luke 2:25

προσδεχόμενος παράκλησιν τοῦ 'Ισραήλ,	GK
ומקבל הוא בעותא דאיסריל	Sy^s
ומסכא הוא לבויאה דאיסריל	Peshiṭta
looking for the consolation of Israel	RSV

Luke 6:24

Πλὴν οὐαὶ ὑμῖν τοῖς πλουσίοις,	GK
ὅτι ἀπέχετε τὴν παράκλησιν ὑμῶν.	
ברם וי לכון עתירא דקבלתון בעותכון	Sy^s
ברם וי לכון עתירא דקבלתון בויאכון	Peshiṭta
But woe to you that are rich, for you have received your consolation.	RSV

It is important to note that the Peshiṭta follows the Greek and that the Sinaitic Palimpsest alone attests to this use of בעותא (the Curetonian version has neither passage).

In attempting to understand the meaning of this noun, it is first necessary to note that in the Sinaitic Palimpsest it translates (or corresponds to) παράκλησις, which means "summons, imploring, invocation, request, exhortation, consolation." (Liddell-Scott-Jones-McKenzie). In the New Testament it is conceptually linked with παράκλητος, "the helper, intercessor." The latter Greek noun is used only by John (four times); the former is peculiar to Luke (two times in the Gospel, four times in Acts) and Paul (twenty).[7] The two passages cited above, consequently, are the only ones in the Gospels in which we find the noun παράκλησις. In both passages it means "consolation." The translator of the Sinaitic Palimpsest would have rendered παράκλησις, if this noun was in his *Vorlage* and all the evidence leads to that presupposition, with a Syriac noun of similar meaning. Hence בעותא in early western, Christian Aramaic[8] probably obtained the meaning "consolation."

---

7. R. Morgenthaler, *Statistik des neutestamentlichen Wortschatzes* (Zürich: Gotthelf-Verlag, 1958).

8. No evidence has been found nor reason given to weaken or disprove C. C. Torrey's contention that the Sinaitic Palimpsest was written "at or near Antioch, early in the second century." *Documents* p. 275. Also see A. S. Lewis's comments in *The Old*

It should be observed that the Greek noun means both
"petition" and "consolation." In Jewish Aramaic and Edessene
Syriac בעותא means only "petition." Of the numerous Aramaic
and Syriac lexicons only those by R. Köbert, S.J., and C. Brockelmann record the meaning *solatium* for בעותא. Brockelmann alone
cites textual evidence; he lists the two passages in the Sinaitic
Palimpsest given above.

What is the relationship between παράκλησις in the Greek
New Testament and בעותא in the Sinaitic Palimpsest? There are
three reasonable possibilities. The first is that the Syriac translator chose בעותא because it corresponded to one meaning of the
Greek word, viz. "petition." This possibility is highly unlikely. It
would demand the unfounded presupposition that the translator
of the Sinaitic Palimpsest was unskillful. The second possibility is
that בעותא obtained a new meaning from παράκλησις, viz. "consolation." This possibility seems unlikely because there were
Aramaic and Syriac words that meant "consolation," for example,
נֶחָמָה (a Hebrew loanword, it is frequently used as a verb in the
Hodayoth, e. g. 5:3, 6:7, 9:13 [bis], 11:32, 16:17) and בוייאא (not
found in the Gen.Ap. but used in the Peshitta at Luke 2:25 and
6:24).[9] The third possibility is that בעותא in the Sinaitic Palimpsest
goes behind the Greek to the selfsame word in Palestinian Aramaic.

Syriac Gospels or Evangelion da-Mepharreshê (London: Williams and Norgate, 1910),
pp. v, xiii. P. E. Kahle "fully" agreed with Torrey's conclusions regarding the date
of the Old Syriac Gospels (OSG) but changed "in the region of Antioch" to "in
Adiabene." *The Cairo Geniza*, 2nd ed. (Oxford: Basil Blackwell, 1959), pp. 287 f. Cf.
Arthur Vööbus, *Studies in the History of the Gospel Text in Syriac* (Louvain: Imprimerie
Orientaliste, 1951), pp. 26 ff. Kahle rightly sees the weaknesses in Torrey's comment
about Antioch but his own conjecture about Adiabene is burdened with more difficulties. That a palimpsest, whose upper script was written near Antioch and contains
numerous Western features itself, was composed east of Edessa is a possibility which
appears extremely improbable to the present writer. Matthew Black's discussion of
the sources and antiquity of the OSG raises the possibility that a Palestinian Aramaic
Gospel or Gospel tradition influenced the OSG; for example, the Sinaitic Syriac alone
retains in John 10:12 a paronomasia characteristic of Jesus (*sakhir shaqqar*). While
Principal Black states that Torrey's conclusion goes beyond the evidence, he nonetheless amasses data to support the suggestion that the OSG were directly influenced
by Palestinian Aramaic. We are in total agreement with his comment that "it is certainly difficult to believe . . . that in bilingual Antioch the Gospels were not translated
in Syriac early in the second century." *An Aramaic Approach to the Gospels and Acts*,
3rd ed. (Oxford: Clarendon Press, 1967), pp. 262–70.

9. It is highly unlikely that בעותא is a corruption of בוייאא. The second and fourth
consonants in each word are too dissimilar. Likewise, it is improbable that the supposed error would be repeated precisely the same way four chapters later.

This suggestion would demand that בעותא in Palestinian Aramaic during the first Christian century meant both "petition" and "consolation." The possibility seems conjectural, but the following discussion tends to confirm it. For the moment, suffice it to state that new ideologies usually coin new words and infuse old words with new meanings. Certainly the earliest Christians used old words in new ways. Unfortunately, we cannot presently prove the third possibility since the earliest Christian Aramaic documents have not been preserved. However, the meaning of the noun בעותא in the extant manuscripts from earliest Aramaic-(Syriac-) speaking Christianity, the Sinaitic Palimpsest and the Odes of Solomon, does reinforce the third possibility, as we shall soon see.

Professor Torrey argued that among the earliest Aramaic-speaking Christians בעותא acquired the meaning "resurrection." The distance from "petition" to "resurrection" is extreme; the separation from "consolation" to "resurrection" is much less, but the two nouns are not exactly synonymous. They are not far from being synonyms, however, when one realizes that the "consolation" Simeon was looking for was certainly the "salvation" of Israel. "Salvation" and "resurrection" were metonyms for the early Christians, as Professor Torrey clearly demonstrated (p. 259; see also John 11:25 in the Sinaitic Palimpsest). Likewise, if one could push aside the veil of history, *et hoc genus omne*, that separates us from the earliest Palestinian Christians, and ask them what was their consolation, or what was their salvation, the answer would probably be the same, viz. the resurrection of the Messiah. The deduction is that for them בעותא denoted "consolation" and connoted "resurrection." The following two observations, one concerning an Arabic word and the other about the use of בעותא in the Odes of Solomon, certainly go a long way to substantiate this inference.

As we turn to Arabic for possible elucidation on this point, we note that two scholars besides Professor Torrey have argued that *ᵃlbāᶜûth* is a Syriac loanword. Both scholars note that the meaning of the Arabic word is connected with Easter. The first, S. Fraenkel, could not etymologically diagnose the origin of this meaning in Arabic, "Wieso aber grade das Osterfest speciell das 'Gebet' genannt wurde, weiss ich nicht zu sagen."[10] The second, Adrien

---

10. *Die Aramäischen Fremdwörter im Arabischen* (Leiden: E. J. Brill, 1886), p. 277.

Barthélemy, reported that the Arabic word meant "prières du lundi de Pâques," and that it derives etymologically from the Syriac בעותא, which comes from the root בעא, "to demand, to pray."[11] The problem with Barthélemy's explanation, however, is that *ɔlbâ ͨ ûth* does have the meaning he suggests, but primarily means "Easter," and it is difficult to see how that meaning came from the verb "to demand."

The attempt to explain the Arabic noun on the basis of the Arabic verb *ba ͨ atha* ("to revive"—a dead person) has been suggested,[12] but to represent the noun *Easter* requires the additional word *yôm*, which means in Arabic "the day of resurrection." There is no need to show that this latter derivation is different from the Syriac loan word which by itself means "Easter." Suffice it to say that *B ͨ Th* in Arabic means "to revive" but the selfsame root in Syriac means "to be formidable."

Perhaps some light will be shed upon a solution if we follow Torrey's lead and turn to a previously unmentioned Aramaic root, namely בוע, which means "to swell, burst forth, rejoice." The derivative בועתא means "rejoicing." It is easy to see how *Easter* could have derived from *rejoicing*, but the waw is in the wrong place. The Targum to Psalm 43:4, however, has the waw after the ͨ ayin: בעותי, as does the Targum to Psalm 42:5: בעותא. It is possible that the first Aramaic-speaking Palestinian Jewish-Christian circles used this noun to signify their Easter, the time of rejoicing, because of the resurrection of their Lord. It is clear why בעותא did not have this meaning for later Syriac-speaking Christians: בוע as a verb with this meaning is found neither in biblical Aramaic nor Edessene Syriac.[13] Moreover, it seems relatively certain that the peculiarly western portions of the Old Syriac Gospels were edited out by Edessene Christians. The evidence, therefore, clearly points in one direction. The Arabic word *ɔlbâ ͨ ûth*, which means Easter, is a Syriac loanword that goes back to the

---

11. *Dictionnaire Arabe-Français* (Paris: Librairie Orientaliste Paul Geuthner, 1935), p. 51.

12. Régis Blachère, Mustafa Chouémi, and Claud Denizeau (eds.), *Dictionnaire Arabe-Français-Anglais*. Vols. in process (Paris: G.-P. Maisonneuve et Larose, 1967–), 1: 697–99.

13. In Syriac another verb has the same radicals (בוע), but is found only in participial forms: מביע. R. Payne Smith reports that the verb signifies *cessavit, tempus trivit* (*Thesaurus Syriacus*, Oxonii: E Typographeo Clarendoniano, 1879, vol. 1, *ad loc.*)

Syriac noun בעותא, that comes from the root בוע, means "rejoicing," and was probably associated with the Resurrection.

In the preceding pages we have intermittently suggested that the meanings "consolation" and "resurrection" were obtained by בעותא only in earliest Christian Aramaic. We now turn to the Odes of Solomon, which was probably composed in an early form of Syriac (Aramaic) around A.D. 100 in or near Antioch,[14] in order to discover if either of these meanings is supported by it.

In Ode 17:13b we find the following difficult line:

ובעותי בחובא דילי

The translations of this line are equivocal and ambiguous. In his final edition of the Odes, J. R. Harris was forced to append the following note: "The sense is very doubtful."[15] The confusion is caused by בעותא. Applying the meaning found in most lexicons, we obtain the following translation of verse 13:

And I offered my knowledge generously,
And my petition through my love.

Obviously something is wrong. Harris's final attempt at solution was to amend the text to read, "And their request to me with my love." This conjecture is unacceptable for three reasons: The manuscripts agree at this point so that an emendation is purely subjective. The conjecture destroys the synonymous parallelism since "my knowledge" is not parallel with "their request." It is not easy to understand the meaning of "I offered . . . their request. . . ."

While the meaning "petition" does not fit into the context of this verse, the meaning "consolation" fulfills the requirements. It restores the parallelistic construction, and makes the verse coherent and lucid. The verse so translated would read as follows:

14. See the author's *The Odes of Solomon* (Oxford: The Clarendon Press, in preparation). The provenance of the Odes will be discussed in a future publication.
15. J. R. Harris and Alphonse Mingana, *The Odes and Psalms of Solomon*, 2 vols. (London, New York: Longmans, Green and Co., 1919-20), 2: 291. In 1911 Harris had translated the verse as follows: "and I imparted my knowledge without grudging: and my prayer was in my love. . . ." *The Odes and Psalms of Solomon* (Cambridge: Cambridge University Press, 1911), p. 114. In 1912 J. H. Bernard presented the same translation. *The Odes of Solomon*, Texts and Studies, vol. 8, no. 3 (Cambridge: Cambridge University Press, 1912), p. 82. Both of these early translations were relegated by the later recognition that the Odes are composed in verse. Verse 12 is constructed according to *parallelismus membrorum*.

And I offered my knowledge generously,
And my consolation through my love.

What is the precise meaning of *consolation* in this passage? Let
us now turn to the Ode with this question in mind.

The evidence points toward the assumption that *consolation* in
this verse means "resurrection." First, we should note that the
particular context favors it. Since the Odist frequently emphasizes
that eternal life is the result or reward of belief in Christ, it is only
natural that he would have written that Christ offered his knowledge and his resurrection (the passage is written *ex ore Christi*).
Note that the first person, singular suffix shows that the "consolation" is not some abstract idea but a personal offering. No emendation is needed, and the synonymous parallelism is palpable.

Second, it is important to observe that the general context adds
great weight to the deduction that בעותא in Ode 17:13 means
"resurrection." Prior to verse 13 the Odist is probably developing
the subtle meanings of the Resurrection of Christ. In verse 11 he
claims that Christ is "the opening of everything" and in verse 12
he states the result of his Resurrection. These verses are as follows:

And nothing appeared closed to me,
Because I was the opening of everything.

And I went towards all my bondsmen in order to loose them;
That I might not leave anyone bound or binding.

The two verses that follow verse 13 speak of "my fruits" and "my
blessing," both of which are parallel to ובעותי. Since the former
two gifts by Christ result in the "bondsmen" being "transformed"
and "saved," it is highly likely that ובעותי meant "and my resurrection." Moreover, if this passage concerns the *descensus ad inferos*
(cf. Ode 42:10 ff.), then the only consolation which would be
effective is the resurrection from the dead.

In conclusion, בעותא probably denoted "consolation" and sometimes connoted "resurrection" among the earliest Aramaic-
speaking Christians in Palestine. These meanings alone explain the
passages in the Sinaitic Palimpsest, clarify the etymology of the
Arabic word *ᵃlbâ ͨûth*, and remove the difficulty in Ode 17.

To sum up, we have found that בעותא in the Odes of Solomon
has precisely the meaning that Torrey speculated it would have in

an early Christian, Aramaic (Syriac) manuscript. Incidentally, we may have found supportive evidence that the provenance of the Odes is not in eastern Syria, as most scholars have argued,[16] but somewhere in western Syria or Palestine.[17]

16. The scholars who have defended this thesis, accompanied with the date of their publication, are the following: Johannes de Zwaan (1937), R. M. Grant (1944), Jean Daniélou (1957), Arthur Vööbus (1958), and Gilles Quispel (1965). Also included in this list are the scholars who contended that Bardaiṣan may be the author of the Odes: W. R. Newbold (1911), Martin Sprengling (1911), and F. M. Braun (1957). Full bibliography for their publications is given in the author's *The Odes of Solomon.*

17. Numerous scholars have told the writer that the word *Syriac* must be used solely for documents written in Edessa. *Aramaic*, on the other hand, should be used to signify western writings. This distinction between early Syriac and Aramaic is no longer tenable. For example, one of the heretofore cherished distinctions between Aramaic and Syriac is that the former uses the preformative *Yôdh* in the imperfect but the latter uses the preformative *Nûn*. This distinction no longer holds. Early Syriac inscriptions have been found containing the preformative *Yôdh*. The two most important publications on this point are the following: Klaus Beyer, "Der reichsaramäische Einschlag in der ältesten syrischen Literatur," *ZDMG*, 116 (1966), 242–43; Ernst Jenni, "Die altsyrischen Inschriften," *TZ*, 21 (1965), 381.

THE OLD TESTAMENT IN MARK'S GOSPEL

HUGH ANDERSON

I count it a privilege to contribute to the honor being paid to my former colleague, Dr. W. F. Stinespring. Having been closely associated with him for almost a decade particularly on many Ph.D. examination committees at Duke University, I came to respect and admire both the range and rigor of his scholarship. I continue to cherish his friendship from across the seas.

The Gospels of Matthew, Mark, and Luke are generally held to subscribe to a "promise-fulfillment" schema: they regard the events they relate about Jesus Christ as fulfillment of corresponding earlier events or of prophetic predictions witnessed to in the Old Testament. This schema is especially evident in Matthew's Gospel, but in Luke's as well.

Matthew has by far the greatest number of "fulfillment" מָלֵא–πληροῦν phrases among the Evangelists. These phrases occur mainly in Matthew's so-called "formula quotations" (1:22 f.; 2:15; 2:17 f.; 2:23; 3:3; 4:14 f.; 8:17; 12:17 ff.; 13:14 f.; 13:35; 21:4 f. [26:56]; 27:9). In his "formula quotations" Matthew reveals a profound concern for the precise fulfillment of certain Scripture passages understood as predictions, and even allows one proof-text at least (Zech. 9:9) to provide circumstantial detail about the presence of two beasts in his account of the Triumphal Entry (Matt. 21:1–7).

Unlike Matthew, Luke rarely cites actual Scripture prophecies, as in the opening sermon of Jesus in Capernaum (Luke 4:17–21). Nevertheless for Luke too the "fulfillment of prophecy" motif is very significant, as may be gathered from his highly articulated "philosophy of the Resurrection" in the Emmaus story. "And beginning with Moses and all the prophets he interpreted to them in all the scriptures the things concerning himself" (Luke 24:27). With Luke the Christ appears not only as the consummation of the entire Scripture but as the mediator of its meaning as a whole. The things concerning Jesus which took place in Jerusalem in those days are the culmination of the plans and promises God initiated long ago with Israel.

What then of Mark? Since Mark's Gospel also is liberally sprinkled with references to the Old Testament, should we without any ado team him with Matthew and Luke as sharing their promise-fulfillment categories and as believing in the divine scheme of salvation which he finds in searching the Scripture? One or two preliminary considerations suggest that we should not judge the matter too hastily. First, in direct contrast with Matthew's Gospel, there is a very low incidence of fulfillment מָלֵא–πληροῦν phrases in Mark: if we exclude 15:28 as *falsa lectio*, he has only two, in 1:15 and 14:49. Second, in Mark it is always Jesus or some other character in the narrative who cites or refers to Scripture. There is only one notable exception. Only at the very beginning of his Gospel does *Mark himself* quote Scripture and come near to the Matthaean type of formula quotation. Third, it is worth noting that in a recent full-scale study of Mark's use of the Old Testament, Alfred Suhl has denied altogether to Mark any promise-fulfillment schema.[1]

Within the limited scope of this paper our purpose is to examine the main features of Mark's use of the Old Testament and to enquire to what extent, if any, this bears upon his aim and intention in his overall portrayal of Jesus Christ.

Most critics would agree that, as with Matthew and Luke, the beginning and ending of Mark's Gospel ought to provide the surest clues to his own intent and design. But the trouble with Mark is that the opening and close of his Gospel, assuming that it ends with 16:8, are typically condensed. Mark's Easter record is short and sharp, relates no appearance of the risen Jesus, and is somewhat cryptic. Lohmeyer's view that Mark means to point to Galilee as the scene of the eschatological fulfillment of the Parousia has found little favor. But what is of interest to us here is that Mark makes no reference to the Old Testament in 16:1–8. Surely very few would be prepared to follow those imaginative typologists who link the stone at the door of the tomb in Mark 16:4 with Jesus' words in Mark 11:23 about the mountain "being

---

1. Alfred Suhl, *Die Funktion der alttestamentlichen Zitate und Anspielungen im Markusevangelium* (Gütersloh: Gerd Mohn, 1965).

taken up and cast into the sea," connect these in turn with the prophecy of the clearing of the Mount of Olives in Zech. 14:4, and see in "the stone rolled back" of Mark 16:5 a symbol of the removal of the whole structure of Pharisaic legal righteousness.[2]

Mark's Easter report in 16:1–8 contains in fact no express allusion to Scripture prophecy, but rather only a retrospective glance in 16:7 at the earlier *prophecy of Jesus* himself: "After I am raised up, I will go before you to Galilee" (Mark 14:28). Very different is it with Luke whose Emmaus story, as we have seen, depicts the risen Christ pointing to himself as the sum of all the Scripture's meaning.

As to the opening of Mark's Gospel, nowhere else is there an explicit *Marcan* quotation of Scripture (Mark 1:2–3). The complex problems of the composite citation in these verses from Mal. 3:1 and Isa. 40:3 have been much debated. Since both together are assigned in Mark to Isaiah, can we regard the words from Malachi in Mark 1:2 as genuine, or are they an early gloss or interpolation? The main argument for the genuineness of the Malachi quotation has been that Mark could have taken over the two texts from an oral or written collection of testimonies, in which they had already been combined under the name of one author, perhaps because of the appearance of the same phrase פִּנָּה דֶרֶךְ in both. Against its genuineness the strongest argument has been that, if Mal. 3:1 had stood in Mark, its omission from the parallel contexts in Matt. 2:3 and Luke 3:4 is most puzzling.[3] The arguments on either side are hardly decisive. Possibly, therefore, some weight may be given to Professor Krister Stendahl's proposal to forsake the testimony hypothesis of such a composite quotation for the simpler view that, since they have to do with John the Baptist, both prophecies may have been taken over into the Gospels from the disciples of John the Baptist *in the form used by them.*[4] The Qumran Sect also used the prophecy of Isa. 40:3, but the sect followed the form of the Hebrew text and so made it apply

2. See, for example, A. G. Hebert, "The Resurrection-Narrative in St. Mark's Gospel," *Scottish Journal of Theology* 15 (Mar., 1962), 66 ff.

3. Mal. 3:1 is of course cited later in a different context in Matt. 11:10 and Luke 7:27, but its inclusion there does not really help to explain its omission in Matt. 3:3 and Luke 3:4, if it stood in Mark 1:2.

4. Krister Stendahl, *The School of St. Matthew* (Lund: C. W. K. Gleerup, 1954), pp. 50 ff., 215 f.

to the life and activity of its own desert community of the Elect
in the Last Days: "Prepare in the desert Yahweh's way" (IQS
8:14). The followers of the Baptist, on the other hand, adopted
the LXX form of the Isa. 40:3 text (on which the New Testament
also in turn relied) and applied it to their own "wilderness-
preacher-leader," "the voice in the wilderness." Could they have
done so in direct opposition to Qumran?

From such an estimate of the situation important results would
follow. First, it would offset the form critics' judgment that the
picture of the Baptist as a wilderness preacher is a purely *Christian*
invention based solely on the Isa. 40:3 prophecy. Second, we
could not so readily assume that the texts had undergone christological adaptation in their fusion in the Marcan context. In this
regard, in any case, it is difficult to say whether, with the *Kyrios*
of Isa. 40:3, Mark has Yahweh or perhaps the Messiah in view, although it is certainly noteworthy that elsewhere in the Gospel
Kyrios is not for Mark a christological title.

The abruptness of Mark's beginning, however, makes it difficult
for us to gauge how the Old Testament prophecies of Mark 1:2 f.
function for him. This question is moreover closely linked with
the rather acute problems of the meaning and scope of the title
of Mark 1:1 (presuming from the anarthrous ἀρχή that it is a title
and that it is Mark's title) and of the place and connections of
Mark 1:14 f.

It is now commonly recognized that there is no great gap between Mark 1:8 and 1:9, as Westcott and Hort's spacing of the
text might have encouraged us to believe, and that Mark's introduction extends from 1:1 to 1:13. Accordingly the consensus is
that with his opening words: "The beginning of the Good News
of Jesus Christ the Son of God," Mark means to describe not
merely the appearance of the Baptist as the punctiliar starting-
point of the Gospel. Rather, he intends his title to refer to the
whole story of Jesus he is going to tell—Jesus and his work (and
of course the Baptist and his work as forerunner) are of the very
stuff of the Gospel for Mark and constitute its ἀρχή or "beginning."

But how does Mark understand this beginning? Does his "prologue" reveal any biographical intent? It is at this point that the
interpretation of the Marcan summary statement in 1:14 f. becomes crucial. The words of Mark 1:14 f. are usually taken as a

preface to the section of the Gospel ending with 3:6 and relating the first stage of the Galilean ministry. In that case the tendency arises to regard chronology as Mark's primary concern in the passage. Vincent Taylor, for example, holds that Mark fastens on to the arrest of John (1:14) as the precise moment of division between the work of John, now over, and the work of Jesus just getting under way. On the other hand he concedes that "Mark's chronology is controlled by the preaching praxis of the church" (as evidenced in Acts 10:37 and 13:14–15).[5] But should we not then give up the term *chronology* altogether as being quite alien to Mark's purpose here? To say simply that Mark wants to stress the instant "when Jesus appeared in Galilee as a new star" (as Johannes Weiss)[6] because he remembers Peter's teaching on the matter is to fail to distinguish between the function of the tradition at its pre-Marcan stage and the aim Mark pursues in using it. And there is really little indication that Mark's aim is to show how Jesus reckoned inwardly that the Baptist's fate must be the signal that his own hour had struck.[7] Matthew's account hereabout, it is true, seems to have a more biographical flavor inasmuch as it gives some prominence to Jesus' personal response to the news of the Baptist's arrest. "When he *heard* that John had been arrested, he withdrew into Galilee" (Matt. 4:12). But we should not interpret Mark by Matthew.

That Mark's treatment of both John and Jesus in his opening verses is dominated by kerygmatic or theological considerations may be borne out in various ways. The absolute use of $\pi\alpha\rho\alpha$-$\delta\omicron\theta\tilde{\eta}\nu\alpha\iota$ in Mark 1:14 ("after John was delivered up") implies for Mark a "delivering up" *that is God's will* (compare 9:31). Accordingly 1:14 does not necessarily denote for Mark the first level of a new historical development. Rather there seems to be already a hint of the Passion of Jesus and "what Mark has done is to set the preaching and the summons of Jesus into the divinely willed deathward work of John."[8] The theme of the conformity

5. Vincent Taylor, *The Gospel According to St. Mark* (London: Macmillan, 1952), p. 165.

6. Johannes Weiss, *Das Markusevangelium*, 3rd ed. rev. W. Bousset (Göttingen, 1917), p. 136. See also Taylor, p. 165.

7. See W. F. Howard, "John the Baptist and Jesus: A Note on Evangelic Chronology," *Amicitiae Corolla* (R. Harris *Festschrift*), (London, 1933), pp. 119 f.

8. L. E. Keck, "The Introduction to Mark's Gospel," *NTS*, 12 (July, 1966), 360. Keck makes a good case for regarding 1:14 f. as tied up with vv. 1–13.

with the divine will of Jesus' work (and John's), constitutive of the Gospel's ἀρχή, appears in fact to be one of the chief preoccupations of Mark's introduction. When, in terms of the Marcan précis of his message, Jesus says that "the time is fulfilled," the time spoken of is the time "willed by God." Similarly, when at the Baptism of Jesus the heavenly voice declares him to be the messianic Son of God in language echoing several Old Testament passages (e.g. Gen. 22:2; Isa. 62:4; Ps. 2:7; Isa. 42:1 and 44:2), Mark is much less interested in divulging the messianic self-consciousness of Jesus than in informing the reader that he is the One singled out directly by the express wish and action of God and his Spirit.[9]

In agreement with all this is also Mark's apparent unconcern, unlike Matthew and Luke, with pointing to John as an independent historical figure, a great champion of social righteousness in his own right, although almost certainly Mark had the requisite information at hand (see Mark 2:18 and 11:32). Mark focuses upon John only on the one hand as the Elijah-like forerunner of the Stronger One (Mark 1:6–7), and on the other hand as the forerunner of the Old Testament prophecies (Mark 1:2 f.). John thus becomes in Mark's presentation the link between the promises of God in Scripture and Jesus the Messiah. It is in such broad terms that we should speak of Mark's intention here, inasmuch as he is not at all inclined to draw out any exact correspondence between *events* surrounding the Baptist and *historical details* lying further back in the Old Testament (although to be sure the prophecies of 1:2 f. enable him to locate the Baptist's activity in the wilderness).

Accordingly there is a grain of truth in Alfred Suhl's contention that in the καθὼς γέγραπται formula of Mark 1:2, "καθὼς does not as yet say much for Mark."[10] Certainly it does not quite measure up to Matthew's rabbinic principle of Scripture interpretation whereby he seeks in general to show how the letter of the Old Testament is fulfilled this way or that.[11] And here in particular Matthew employs a more specific formula of citation

9. See D. E. Nineham, *St. Mark*, Pelican Gospel Commentaries (Baltimore: Penguin Books, 1963), pp. 61 f.
10. Suhl, p. 137.
11. See Oscar Cullmann, *Salvation in History*, trans. S. G. Sowers and the editorial staff of the S.C.M. Press (London: S.C.M. Press, 1967), p. 134.

in introducing the Baptist when he says of him: "This is he who was spoken of by the prophet Isaiah when he said. . . ." (Matt. 3:3). Further, in contrast with Mark, Matthew relates the appearance of Jesus in Galilee directly to the data provided by the Scripture text of Isaiah (Isa. 9:1–2; see Matt. 4:12–16). We might say that in this context at any rate Matthew is "controlled" more by the Old Testament, whereas Mark turns the searchlight more on the essential "newness" of the event of Jesus Christ. In other words, it is not altogether correct to suggest that Mark makes the Old Testament his starting point in the same way as does Matthew.[12]

However, the element of newness in Mark's opening portrayal should not be overemphasized. One cannot easily follow Suhl when he denies to Mark any interest whatever in promise-fulfillment. In rather uncritical dependence on Willi Marxsen's arguments that Mark's view is purely existentialist, that the Gospel is simply addressed to the churches of Mark's time, and that its whole meaning is "I (Christ) am coming soon,"[13] Suhl contends that Mark appeals to the Old Testament only to stamp this contemporaneous address of the Gospel as conforming with the Scripture in the broadest sense.[14] But why then conformity with the Scripture at all? Why bother with relating Jesus to the Old Testament *via* John? We should perhaps rather see Mark trying to persuade his readers that the Gospel's ἀρχή resides not in the post-Easter faith or in the mind of the apostles but in the event of Jesus Christ.[15] The pastness and primacy of this event he secures, in part at least, not by concern with the letter of the Old Testament and its fulfillment, but by connecting it in a profounder way with the will of God expressed in the Old Covenant.

As we observed at the outset, Mark 1:2 f. is the only explicit quotation made by Mark in his own name. Everywhere else in the Gospel, references to the Old Testament by citation or by

---

12. Matthew exhibits a stronger interest in OT events (e. g. 4:12–16) and in the exact correspondence of the NT events with them for the sake of the events themselves. See C. F. D. Moule, "Fulfilment-Words in the New Testament: Use and Abuse," *NTS*, 14 (Apr., 1968), 297.

13. Willi Marxsen, *Der Evangelist Markus*, Forschungen zur Religion und Literatur des Alten und Neuen Testaments, n.f. 49, 2nd ed. (Göttingen, 1959), p. 89.

14. Suhl, *passim.*

15. Keck, p. 366.

allusion are on the lips of a speaker, most frequently Jesus himself. These could be investigated in various ways, either by simply tracing them through the Gospel chapter by chapter or alternatively by dealing with them according to the level of the Gospel tradition in which they occur, for example, the Passion story, the *logia*, the pre-Marcan units or the units built up by the redactor, Mark himself. But the method we shall adopt here is to treat Old Testament usages and references throughout Mark's Gospel under two broad categories: 1) the Old Testament in eschatology; and 2) the Old Testament in parenesis or teaching.

The Old Testament in Eschatology

Some years ago, in examining explicit Old Testament citations in the Qumran literature and in the New Testament, J. A. Fitzmyer described four classes of Old Testament usage, and two of these, namely "eschatological usage" and "modernizing usage," properly fall under the above broad heading.[16] The distinction between them will become evident as we proceed.

Texts labeled "eschatological" normally express in the Old Testament a promise or threat about some thing to be accomplished in the *eschaton*, and the Qumran or New Testament writer then makes the text refer to the new *eschaton* of which he is speaking. We have a good example in Rom. 11:26–27 where Paul quotes Isa. 59:20–21 and 27:9 to support his view that despite Israel's erstwhile rejection of the Christ, all Israel will at last be saved in accordance with Isaiah's prophecy: "The deliverer will come from Zion, he will drive all ungodliness away from Jacob and this will be my agreement with them, when I take away their sins." In the pre-Passion narrative of Mark one text that may belong to this order is the citation on the lips of Jesus of Isa. 56:7 and the allusion to Jer. 7:11 within the context of Jesus' visit to the Temple for its "cleansing" (Mark 11:15–18): "And he taught, and said to them, 'Is it not written, "My house shall be called a house of prayer for all the nations"? But you have made it a den of robbers.' " (Mark 11:17).

16. J. A. Fitzmyer, "The Use of Explicit Old Testament Quotations in Qumran Literature and in the New Testament," *NTS*, 7 (July, 1961).

Within the scope of this paper it is impossible to discuss in any detail the complexities of the cleansing of the Temple. There is no good reason to question the historicity of Jesus' appearance and action in the Temple, although Mark's very condensed account really does not allow us to say whether Jesus' expulsion of the Temple merchants was intended as a social protest, a gesture of Zealot insurrectionism, a blow at the sacrificial system, or whether it was the symbolic act of the eschatological renewer of the cultus. Our primary concern is with the "teaching" of Jesus ascribed to the Temple episode and recorded in Mark 11:17. The indications are that, even if the *logion* of Mark 11:17 were original to Jesus, it could scarcely belong only to the incident of the expulsion of the Temple dealers: the confusion surrounding the expulsion would not easily have provided the setting for such teaching, and additionally, the stylized introductory formula of Mark 11:17 as well as the obscurity of those addressed as "them" and "you" suggests that the saying was a separate unit. In that case, what might have been its *Sitz im Leben?* Mark alone among the Evangelists retains the words "for all the nations" of the Isaianic prophecy, and it has been held that the universalism expressed here must have had its setting in the preaching or apologetic of the Gentile Christian churches. For Mark, as R. H. Lightfoot argues, the Temple would have been the setting for that activity of the messianic king by which the gathering of the Gentiles into the life and worship of the people of God prophesied in Isa. 56:7 was now on the way to being fulfilled. [17]

However, we should possibly think of a quite different *Sitz im Leben* for the saying of Mark 11:17. In the context of Isa. 56:7 "all the nations" refers specifically to those converted pagans who would come on pilgrimage to offer sacrifices in the Jerusalem Temple restored at the End. Now there is nothing Gentile Christian in the idea of a universal pilgrimage to a restored Temple, and it may be that Matthew and Luke have suppressed the words "for all the nations" because for them they could have applied only to the Christian Church and not to the Temple. Nor could Mark, in view of his hostility to the Temple, have wanted

17. R. H. Lightfoot, *The Gospel Message of St. Mark* (Oxford: The Clarendon Press, 1950), pp. 60 ff.

to glorify it in this way. Consequently E. Trocmé has recently proposed that we should seek a *Sitz im Leben* for the saying of Mark 11:17 in the early debates of the primitive Jewish-Christian communities about how the Temple courts and particularly the Court of the Gentiles ought to be used. The debates would have been responsible for appending the saying to the incident of the expulsion of the Temple dealers as an explanatory comment showing how the commercial transactions in the Court of the Gentiles were tantamount to rebellion against the divine will.[18] Probably Mark sees in these verses and especially in 11:17 Christ's judgment upon the Temple which in actual practice was promoting a false sense of security and stood in stark contrast to the plans God had for it. By inserting the Temple pericope between the two parts of the enigmatic fig tree story, Mark seems to reveal that for him the Temple is synonymous with Jewish life and religion, both in their fruitlessness now calling down God's *ultimate* judgment upon Israel.[19] Possibly in Mark's understanding the pronouncement of 11:17 is not unrelated to Jesus' words about the coming destruction of the Temple in 14:58.[20] But, however Mark 11:17 is construed, perhaps enough has been said to show that it may be included in the class of eschatological texts.

Mark's Gospel, like the rest of the New Testament, appears to be lacking in instances of the eschatological use of the Old Testament. The inference drawn by Fitzmyer and others from the dearth of eschatological texts in the New Testament and their relative abundance in the Qumran documents is that "Christian writers were more often looking back at the central event in which salvation had been accomplished rather than forward to a deliverance by Yahweh, which seems to characterize the Qumran literature."[21]

To what extent, we have now to ask, is this generalizing comment about the difference between Qumran and the New Testament true of Mark in particular? How strong is the backward

18. Etienne Trocmé, "L'Expulsion des Marchands du Temple," *NTS*, 15 (Oct., 1968), 12–15.
19. Nineham, pp. 300 f.
20. Eduard Schweizer, *Das Evangelium nach Markus*, Das Neue Testament Deutsch, no. 1 (Göttingen, 1967), p. 131.
21. Fitzmyer, p. 329. See also Moule, pp. 310 f.

look or the sense of eschatological completeness in Mark? We should try to assess this by investigating those Old Testament quotations and references in Mark that might be described as "modernizing usage." Fitzmyer explains that a "modernized text" is one taken over from an analogous situation in the Old Testament and made to speak with a deeper significance to the new situation in Qumran or the early Church. What is important for our purpose is that he includes among such texts the *pesher*-type citations in Matthew and takes especial note of the strong sense of completeness or fulfillment in Matt. 4:15–16 and Luke 4:16–21. In the latter Christ's commentary on Isa. 61:1–2 begins: "This passage of Scripture has been fulfilled here in your hearing today." New meaning is given to the words of Isaiah by the event.[22]

Neither Mark himself nor Mark's Jesus, I think it may be claimed, makes the Old Testament text and the situation it reflects point with the same completeness or directness to the new situation that *has come to prevail* in Jesus. Even in passages where Mark might appear to subscribe to the notion of the literal realization of prophecy in the past situation that had arisen with Jesus, there is in fact a movement toward a near future that is still expected. This is true of the three places in Mark's Passion narrative where there is explicit reference to Scripture. In the story of the betrayal Jesus says: "For the Son of man goes as it is written of him, but woe to that man by whom the Son of man is betrayed!" (Mark 14:21). Here the καθὼς γέγραπται περὶ αὐτοῦ does not imply the completion or verification in the events of Christ's ministry of the details of any particular Scripture prediction. The Johannine verb ὑπάγει ("goes") (e. g., John 8:14, 21 f.; 13:3, 33; 14:4, 28) has the meaning of "going, toward death and through death to the Father," and "as it is written of him" indicates that the Son of man's way to death is in conformity with the purpose of God.[23] The betrayer's irresponsible use of his freedom in a gross act of perfidy brings down the final judgment of God upon him ("woe to that man"), and can neither offset nor arrest God's final plan and purpose for the Son of man.

In Mark 14:27 we find the only express quotation of words of Scripture in Mark's Passion narrative:

22. Fitzmyer, p. 316.
23. M. D. Hooker, *The Son of Man in Mark* (London: S.P.C.K., 1967), p. 159.

And when they had sung a hymn, they went out to the Mount of Olives [v. 26]. And Jesus said to them, "You will all fall away; for it is written, 'I will strike the shepherd, and the sheep will be scattered' [v. 27]. But after I am raised up I will go before you to Galilee" [v. 28]. Peter said to him, "Even though they all fall away, I will not" [v. 29]. And Jesus said to him, "Truly I say to you, this very night, before the cock crows twice, you will deny me three times" [v. 30]. But he said vehemently, "If I must die with you, I will not deny you." And they all said the same. [v. 31]

The seams of this little composition are badly joined. When Peter speaks in verse 29 he takes no notice either of the prediction of Jesus in verse 28 or of the Scripture quotation in verse 27b, but refers back only to Jesus' simple statement in verse 27a: "You will all fall away." Again, the change from the imperative of the Hebrew, Targum, Old Testament Peshitta, and almost all Septuagint texts to the first person indicative of the verb πατάξω in the Marcan text (14:27b) makes the sense more difficult insofar as the subject of the next verb προάξω is Jesus himself. Even so we really think of God as the subject of πατάξω and not of Jesus as "the smiter" and Peter as "the smitten shepherd." Moreover, the cursory mention of the Resurrection (μετὰ τὸ ἐγερθῆναί με) in Jesus' forecast that he would "go before to Galilee" (v. 28) plus the fact that the forecast is matched by Mark 16:17 prompt the conclusion that verse 28 is a Marcan insertion. It is tempting, therefore, to bracket off verses 27b and 28, for without them we have a clear and unified account of Peter's denial. Following this line, Barnabas Lindars maintains that the Zech. 13:7 testimony of Mark 14:27b can be viewed in isolation, but perhaps also in relation to the flight of the disciples. The original application of Zech. 13:7, however, according to Lindars, was not the flight of the disciples, but the Crucifixion: seen within its whole context in Zechariah and in the light of the comparison of Zech. 13:6 with Zech. 12:10, it could readily be applied to the sufferings of Jesus. Only when the verse had been torn from its context could there arise specific identification of the shepherd with Jesus and of the scattered sheep with the fleeing disciples. The verse on its own would then have found its way into the Gospel tradition as showing that what happened with the flight of the disciples had already been predicted in Scripture; it would have furnished an apologetic for the disciples' shameful dereliction as something already foreseen in God's plan.[24]

But does Mark so understand the testimony? Possibly the emphasis lay for him not on detailed proof from prophecy but on Jesus' own prophetic foreknowledge. In verse 28 Jesus himself predicts that he will "go before to Galilee." In verse 27a he foretells his coming lonely ordeal. And the words from Zechariah confirm his own prediction of coming tribulation as being in conformity with Scripture and so in line with God's will. So Mark is trying to convince his readers in these few verses that the *divinely willed* way of Christ (and indeed of the Church which Mark is addressing and keeps close in his sights) is the way ahead through humiliation (v. 27) to vindication in the Resurrection (v. 28).[25]

It may of course be objected that since Matthew has faithfully transcribed these Marcan verses without any deviation (see Matt. 26:30–35) both Mark and he should have had the same understanding of this unit. But that does not inevitably follow. In fact Matthew shows his own hand elsewhere in his Passion narrative, and reveals his own greater inclination to reflect on past events surrounding Jesus as the precise working out of details predicted in Old Testament texts. For instance, in the account of the purchase of the potter's field with the betrayal money, Matthew affirms: "Then was fulfilled what had been spoken by the prophet Jeremiah saying, 'And they took the thirty pieces of silver, the price of him on whom a price had been set by some of the sons of Israel, and they gave them for the potter's field, as the Lord directed me' " (Matt. 27:9–10). Also in regard to the arrest of Jesus Matthew himself reports: "But all this has taken place, that the scriptures of the prophets might be fulfilled" (Matt. 26:56). By contrast, in the parallel passage in Mark it is Jesus who says merely: ἀλλ' ἵνα πληρωθῶσιν αἱ γραφαί (Mark 14:49). The phrase

---

24. Barnabas Lindars, *New Testament Apologetic* (London: S.C.M. Press, 1961), pp. 129 ff.

25. Fitzmyer classifies Mark 14:27 as an "eschatological text" pointing ahead to a coming trial as does the comparable usage of Zech. 13:7 in MS. B of the *Damascus Document* (19:7–9). Lindars, on the contrary, regards it as a *pesher*-type citation of the "modernizing" kind. See Fitzmyer, p. 326; Lindars, p. 131.

is not in Mark's usual manner and so is sometimes held to be a later scribal insertion. If the words are Mark's they should probably be translated as in the RSV.: "But let the scriptures be fulfilled." The difficulty of the phrase is not to be overcome by understanding here something like Matthew's γέγονεν, "all this has taken place that,"[26] for it is not apparently Mark's way, as it is Matthew's, to reflect on past events as the exact fulfillment of Old Testament predictions. For the same reason we should not say either that Mark has thrown the phrase in here for good measure simply because "by the time Mark wrote, it had become a fixed dogma of the Church that all the events of the Saviour's Passion, even down to the details, happened 'according to the scriptures,' and the phrase *that the scriptures might be fulfilled* might be introduced even though there were no very particularly apt passage of scripture to be adduced."[27] On the contrary, just because no particular passage of Scripture appears to be in view here, the phrase on Jesus' lips may have been for Mark the equivalent of "let God's will be done: let there come upon me what God has in store for me."

Our investigation of the three explicit references to Scripture in Mark's Passion story suggests that there are within them elements of futurity, incompleteness, or suspension. They fall, with Mark, into the category of eschatological usage more than of modernizing usage. The same is, I think, true also of earlier indirect scriptural references and citations in Mark's pre-Passion narrative. We have first to consider Mark 9:9–13:

And as they were coming down the mountain, he charged them to tell no one what they had seen, until the Son of man should have risen from the dead [v. 9]. So they kept the matter to themselves, questioning what the rising from the dead meant [v. 10]. And they asked him, "Why do the scribes say that first Elijah must come?" [v. 11]. And he said to them, "Elijah does come first to restore all things; and how is it written of the Son of man, that he should suffer many things and be treated with contempt? [v. 12]. But I tell you that

26. Mark 14:49 is so understood by Taylor; see p. 561.
27. A. E. J. Rawlinson, *The Gospel according to St. Mark*, Westminster Commentaries, 7th ed. (London: Methuen, 1949), p. 214.

Elijah has come, and they did to him whatever they pleased, as it is written of him" [v. 13].

These verses have been a battleground of debate ever since Wrede saw in them the main clue to understanding of the "messianic secret" in Mark's Gospel. We cannot here canvass all the many intricate questions involved. Clearly verses 9–10 connect the section with the Transfiguration story (9:2–8). Beyond that, however, critics have been so worried by the abruptness of the question about Elijah in verse 11 and the interruption of the Elijah theme (resumed in v. 13) with the other question about the Son of man in verse 12b that they have resorted to various rearrangements of the text. But theories of dislocation are perhaps needless if it is at all possible to make sense of Mark's arrangement, no matter how awkward it is. The very awkwardness and tentativeness of the Marcan formulation, seemingly pieced together from several independent strands of tradition, may be the best argument for taking it as it stands. For it may well reflect a church trying, as R. H. Lightfoot described it, "to construct some kind of philosophy of history, in the light of its convictions about the person and office of its Master, and of his work and its results."[28]

In the Transfiguration the disciples are given an anticipatory glimpse of the final vindication and victory of Christ (Mark 9:2–8). On the descent from the mountain silence is enjoined on them about what they had seen until that final vindication should have come to pass in and through the Resurrection of the Son of man (Mark 9:9). Their uncertainty about what "rising from the dead" might mean (Mark 9:10) then leads not unnaturally to their concern about what part Elijah would play in the events preceding the coming of the reign of God referred to in Mark 9:1. The disciples' question to Jesus, "Why do the scribes say that first Elijah must come?" (9:11) has as its background Mal. 4:5: "Behold, I will send you Elijah the prophet before the great and terrible day of the Lord comes." In his reply Jesus in the first instance embraces the traditional expectation of Elijah come back as forerunner of God's reign, based on Malachi: "Elijah does come first to restore all things" (9:12a). But immediately in 9:12b the disciples are also challenged to recognize that alongside the traditional expectation of Elijah as "restorer" (ἀποκαθιστάνει πάντα), founded on Mal. 4:5, stands the much more unexpected word of the prophetic Scriptures about the Son of man's suffering being "set at nothing" (ἐξουδενηθῇ). And finally in verse 13 scriptural evidence is adduced against scriptural evidence to reshape the scribal picture of Elijah as the restorer. For Elijah, now in fact identified in a thinly-veiled way with John the Baptist, has already come and has suffered in conformity with the Scriptures, so that his suffering is the framework for the suffering of the Son of man. Thus in a twofold way, by reference to the will of God for the Son of man himself and for Elijah, it is confirmed that there is no other way toward the Son of man's ultimate vindication and triumph save the way of humiliation.[29]

The foregoing interpretation allows us to make the following comments. First, the statement of Mark 9:12b was most probably an independent statement issuing from the debates of the Christians with the Jews on the fulfillment of scriptural prophecies.[30] However, as Mark has incorporated it in the section 9:9–13, his idea is not to show that Jesus (or in the case of verse 13, Elijah) did certain things and their occurrence proved that the Scripture was exactly fulfilled. The emphasis is rather on what Jesus (and Elijah) suffered, and their *suffering* is held to be in conformity with the Scripture, that is, in accordance with the will of God revealed therein.[31] Mark's aim is to clarify and illustrate the messianic ἐξουσία of Jesus, and this he does by pointing up the contrast between scribal passivity before the Old Testament and the creative grasp that enables Jesus to lift up as crucial the less agreeable or harsher promises of God.

---

29. For recent defences of the logic of Mark's arrangement in 9:9–13, see H. E. Tödt, *The Son of Man in the Synoptic Tradition*, trans. D. M. Barton (London: S.C.M. Press, 1965), pp. 194 ff.; Hooker, pp. 129 ff.

30. See Tödt, p. 196.

31. The difference between actions initiated by Jesus and events experienced or suffered by him and its importance for our notions of "fulfillment" is stated by James Barr, *Old and New in Interpretation* (London: S.C.M. Press, 1966), p. 138. On the view we have taken, we can leave open the much debated questions of what OT texts lie behind the pronouncements about the sufferings of the Son of man and the maltreatment of Elijah. For the former the main proposals have been: (*a*) the Servant Songs of Isaiah especially Isaiah 53; (*b*) the "stone testimony" of Ps. 118:22; (*c*) Daniel 7; and for the latter: (1) a lost apocryphal book; (2) I Kings 19:2–10.

Mention has previously been made of the tentativeness of Mark's formulation and of the fact that in verse 13 the allusion to John the Baptist is partly veiled. In his own rearrangement of the Marcan text, Matthew has articulated his train of thought more clearly and decisively and in particular has made the identification of the suffering of the Baptist with the suffering of Elijah *redivivus* fully explicit. So Matthew appears to have dwelt more on actual fulfillment by highlighting the past fate of the Baptist as the decisive argument against the scribes' objection: "Then the disciples understood that he was speaking to them of John the Baptist" (Matt. 17:13).

Second, though Jesus "speaks with authority" over against scribal understandings of Scripture (Mark 9:9–13), his authority is nevertheless that of one who must suffer many things and be treated with contempt (9:12b). Mark 9:12–13 is complementary to Mark 1:2 ff. in that here once again the coming Passion of Jesus, Son of man, is set down as parallel to the "passion" of the Baptist. Thus there is reaffirmed Mark's desire, from the very beginning of his Gospel and all through, to let the tradition about Jesus fall under the shadow of the Cross that looms ahead.

Third, in Mark 9:1 Jesus promises that God's reign is very near at hand. Forthwith in the Transfiguration the disciples are granted a foretaste of the coming vindication of the Christ. Then in the section 9:9–13 it is made plain that the indispensable precondition of the coming of the kingdom and of Messiah's vindication is the suffering and rejection of Jesus. And the references to Scripture in Mark 9:12–13, so far as Mark is concerned, do not so much denote correspondence between the data of Old Testament texts and past New Testament events as illumine the truth that it is in line with the *express purpose of God* that the kingdom will only come in this way.[32]

The "stone testimony" from Ps. 118:22–23 that comes at the close of the Parable of the Wicked Husbandmen in Mark 12:1–11 exhibits a similar concomitance of "rejection" and "vindication." "The very stone which the builders rejected has become the head of the corner; this was the Lord's doing and it is marvelous in

---

32. See Hans Conzelmann, "Gegenwart und Zukunft in der synoptischen Tradition," *Zeitschrift für Theologie und Kirche*, 54 (1957), 290.

our eyes" (12:10–11). Whereas conceivably Jesus may have cited this passage on a separate occasion, it hardly fits in with the parable itself until a moment when by way of allegorical interpretation the son who is killed at the end of the story (12:8) has become equated with Jesus.[33] As this Scripture stands in Mark, there is an element of futurity in it for him, for as verse 12 ("And they tried to arrest him") and other Marcan phrases in this section of the Gospel indicate, Mark is preparing us for the dénouement and pointing the way forward to the Cross and subsequent vindication of Christ.

Our discussion so far has moved in the direction of showing that in his usage of the Old Testament in eschatology Mark is but little concerned to demonstrate that this and this event in the ministry of Jesus matches this and this event that is told already in the Scripture. Instead, his primary concern is with the will of God witnessed to in Scripture, that will of God under which the Christ goes forward through suffering and death to eventual vindication and victory.

Arguably, such usage is in agreement with the "detainment motif" that is so prominent a feature of Mark's whole Gospel. The detainment motif, by which in Mark's Gospel the Passion of Christ and the final unveiling and consummation of God's reign are permitted to cast their gleam back over all the tradition but are nonetheless held in suspension, figures in the recurrent commands to silence that accompany Jesus' exorcisms and healing miracles (the so-called messianic secret). It figures also in Mark's so-called parable theory in 4:10–12. Mark 4:12 echoes the words of Isa. 6:9–10, which describe those people whose sin and ignorance make it impossible for them to absorb the word of God through the prophet and who are in fact condemned by it. In Mark's view verses 10–12 appear then to regard the teaching of Jesus in parables as a means of carrying over God's will and design toward the *ultimate* division between those who are not destined for salvation and so cannot bear the truth, and the elect to whom the mystery of the kingdom is revealed. By these detaining corrections Mark is able to bring the tradition of Jesus under the control of the coming Passion (and vindication) or to point

33. See Nineham, p. 313.

toward the climax that can only be reached with the Cross and Resurrection.[34] One is inclined to accept Hans Conzelmann's view that some such detainment or secret motif is in any case the indispensable hermeneutical presupposition for the writing of a gospel since this is the "messianic" interpretation of the tradition inherent in the material itself.[35] But there is another side to the picture, and it comes out especially in the thirteenth chapter of Mark, which has been all too frequently overlooked in estimates of Mark's purpose in his Gospel. Mark 13 consists largely of a series of predictions in the style and language of Old Testament prophecies and covered over here with a thin apocalyptic veneer.[36] Beyond the woes and supernatural portents and the gathering of the elect before the Last Days, Mark looks further into the future, to the Parousia itself which will usher in the expected consummation (13:14–32)—but these things shall not be except for the disciples' suffering and endurance for the sake of the Gospel (13:9–13). Mark has his sights firmly on the church of his time that needs to be instructed about its posture as it faces the delay of the Parousia and incipient persecution as well. That the final manifestation of Jesus' messianic authority as the Son of God has to be held back until the Cross is reached has paradigmatic significance for the church of Mark's day, for which discipleship inevitably means the constructive "waiting" that consists of suffering and service and alone leads to the End.

It remains for us to consider at this point the δεῖ that occurs in Mark only in the first of the three Passion predictions at 8:31: "And he began to teach them that the Son of man *must* suffer many things . . ." (italics mine). We can, I think, reject the view of Bultmann, that the δεῖ is an incomprehensible divine "must" applied to the horrible and puzzling event of the Passion which the community at first simply could not understand. Our grounds for doing so are concisely stated by Heinz Eduard Tödt: "The announcements of suffering are not concerned with the enigma of God's will as seen apart from the Scriptures."[37] If, however, we

34. Heinz-Dieter Knigge, "The Meaning of Mark," *Interpretation*, 22 (Jan., 1968), 69 f.

35. Conzelmann, pp. 294 f.

36. See Hooker, pp. 128 ff.

37. Tödt, p. 191.

accept that the δεῖ is related to Scripture, we are at once confronted with the problem of what particular Old Testament text prescribes beforehand the *necessity* of Christ's or rather the Son of man's sufferings. The Servant Songs of Isaiah, the "stone" passage of Ps. 118:22, and Daniel 7 have each in particular had their recent advocates.[38] But more likely than not Mark for his part did not begin with a specific Old Testament text and think of it as having mapped out already the course that Christ *must* follow. He was too much aware that with the Christ-event he had something *new* to say for that, and too sensitive to the immediacy of God's presence for Jesus (as in the Baptism and Transfiguration). Consequently none of the passages mentioned above would have stood alone in describing and determining the necessity of the Messiah's suffering. Rather, the δεῖ of Mark 8:31 would have to do with a whole set of Old Testament ideas concerning the persecution of God's true servants and ambassadors by his impenitent people; it would have to do not with *proving* anything from the Old Testament texts but with the paradoxical will of God expressed in Scripture.[39]

Nevertheless the meaning of the δεῖ is not exhausted out of what is given in the Old Testament. The δεῖ of Mark 8:31 has in fact a rich background in the apocalyptic literature, and when we couple that with Mark's twofold use of it in his thirteenth chapter (13:7, 10), it becomes clear that it contains an element of detainment or futurity and relates also to the "apocalyptic law of suffering."[40] God's will stretches out toward certain future events including the coming suffering of the Son of man, by which alone his redemptive purpose for this his world can be brought to final fruition. That the δεῖ of 8:31 should have this kind of futurity for Mark would be in accord with his usage of the Old Testament in eschatology as we have reviewed it.[41]

38. Joachim Jeremias and Walther Zimmerli, *The Servant of God* (London: S.C.M. Press, 1957), p. 90; Tödt, pp. 161 ff.; Hooker, pp. 108 ff.

39. See Erich Fascher, "Theologische Beobachtungen zu δεῖ," *Neutestamentliche Studien für Rudolf Bultmann*, Beihefte zur Z.N.T.W., 21 (Berlin: A. Töpelmann, 1954), 228–54.

40. Ernst Lohmeyer, *Das Evangelium des Markus*, H. A. W. Meyer's Handkommentar z. N.T. (Göttingen: Vandenhoeck & Ruprecht, 1937), vol. 1, pt. 2, 10 aufl.

41. The contrast between Mark and Luke here is striking. Luke uses the "must" in Luke-Acts forty-one times. If Conzelmann is right in attributing this frequency to Luke's desire to apply the "must" to certain situations within salvation-history (*The*

THE OLD TESTAMENT IN PARENESIS AND TEACHING

The majority of Mark's references to the Old Testament in his pre-Passion narrative fall in the above category, e. g., 2:23 ff., 7:6–8, 7:10, 10:3 ff., 10:19, 12:18–27, 12:29 ff., 12:36 f. All of these references occur in the context of the Marcan *Streitgespräche*, which may in general be said to reflect a church rejoicing in its liberation from the Law. In the "conflict stories" Jesus is portrayed as the one who exhibits an intuitive and unrestricted attitude toward the scriptural commands and exercises a sovereign freedom over against them.

It is true that in at least one instance, the Sadducees' question about resurrection in Mark 12:18–27, Jesus' freedom appears as the freedom to be on occasion orthodox in the sense that he here employs the same rabbinic exegetical method as his opponents in order to turn the matter against them. When the Sadducees argue that what the Law says about levirate marriage is incompatible with resurrection (Mark 12:19–23), Jesus first challenges their knowledge of Scripture and of the power of God. He then outsmarts them with an argument that runs against the original sense of Exod. 3:6—since the Law says: "I *am* the God of Abraham, and the God of Isaac, and the God of Jacob," (italics mine), and the "I *am*" applies to a time when they were no longer alive, then they must be alive in a life beyond death. The argument is of course a plea for life beyond death as a life of unbroken communion with God and not for resurrection strictly speaking. Although some commentators would want to replace the strange Pharisaic argumentation of Mark 12:26–27 with a more typical terse pronouncement of Jesus, it may be that beyond the apparent "orthodoxy" in exegesis of these verses, Mark saw something of profound didactic significance for the Gentile church, namely instruction in a more spiritual and refined as against a crudely materialistic view of resurrection.[42]

Again in the scribe's question about the first commandment of

Theology of St. Luke, trans. G. Buswell [London: 1960], p. 153), and we are right in thinking of the solitary "must" of Mark 8:31 as possessing something of the character of an apocalyptic-eschatological "must" formula, then the difference between Mark and Luke is indeed notable.

42. See Nineham, p. 321.

all and Jesus' reply that the whole Law is summed up in love to God and love to neighbor (Mark 12:29 ff.), Jesus seems on the face of it to accept the absolute supremacy of the Law's commands (Deut. 6:4–5 and Lev. 19:18) without any demur. Assuming that the words of Mark 12:29–31 were spoken by Jesus and not by the scribe as in Luke's version (10:27), we need not here discuss to what extent their summing up of the distilled essence of the Law represented a unique creative insight on Jesus' part or had been anticipated by the rabbis near his time. Presumably from the evangelist's standpoint the way the spirit of the Law is highlighted in Jesus' summary implied a critique of and disregard for the letter of the Law and its manifold injunctions. So for Mark Christ's authority over the Law shines forth.

In Mark 2:23 ff. when the Pharisees protest about the disciples breaking the sabbath by plucking ears of grain, Jesus meets them with an argument in the normal rabbinic style about the precedent set by the good and pious King David: even he had transgressed the Law (I Sam. 21:1–6 and II Sam. 8:17), under the constraint of hunger by eating the shewbread. So far what is substantiated is the familiar enough rabbinic principle that in exceptional circumstances of great human need the Law may have to give way. But Mark, probably taking over an earlier comment of the church, administers the coup de grâce to any such rabbinic principle as the true norm of this section in verse 28. Christ's lordship or authority over the sabbath is the real justification for his disciples' freedom to break it (2:28).[43]

The section of the Gospel 7:1–23 presents enormous difficulties, not least in respect to Mark's evidently erroneous views of prevailing Jewish custom. These difficulties we cannot even touch here. Mark 7:1–23 consists of three segments, on handwashing (1–8), on Corban (9–13), and on food laws or ritual defilement (12–23). It is by no means easy to trace the various stages by which these segments and their parts were built up into a unified discourse, or to decide how much of the composition in its present form we owe to the Evangelist himself.[44]

---

43. This freedom so constituted may be the ground for Mark's silence about any physical need on the disciples' part (Mark 2:23). Matthew says openly, on the contrary: "the disciples were hungry" (12:1).

44. See Taylor, pp. 334 ff.; Nineham, pp. 187 ff.; Ernst Haenchen, *Der Weg Jesu*

In the first segment, the Pharisees notice that Jesus' disciples eat without ritual cleansing of the hands (v. 2) and this leads to the broad question of why the disciples do not in general conform to the tradition of the elders, i. e. the oral law that had grown up through the discussions of rabbis or scribes over many years alongside the written Law (v. 5). Jesus' response comprises first a citation from Isa. 29:13 introduced with a rather elaborate formula, "Well did Isaiah prophesy of you hypocrites, as it is written," and then a charge against the Pharisees that they follow the oral tradition to the neglect of the "commandment of God." The form of the quotation of Isa. 29:13 deviates extensively from the Hebrew and follows the LXX with one or two minor modifications. In this Greek form it could hardly have come from the lips of Jesus and probably has its *Sitz* in the polemic of Gentile Christians against Jews. Precisely at the point where it departs most significantly from the Hebrew does it possess its relevance to the Marcan context: "The doctrines they teach are nothing more than human precepts."[45] And this affords a clue as to how the quotation functions here: it is hardly a "proof from prophecy" marking out the Pharisees as the very hypocrites described far in advance by Isaiah,[46] but rather functions as a description of Jesus' opponents whose activity now brings them under condemnation. The problem Jesus' reply in verses 6–8 leaves us with is that the Pharisees of his day certainly did not think of the oral tradition as opposing or negating the Law but as making possible its more exact performance.

The segment that follows on Corban (9–13) in a sense compounds the problem because, whereas it purports to provide a concrete illustration of how the Pharisees let their oral tradition take precedence over Moses or the Torah, what it really does is to show Jesus opposing the practice of obeying one provision of the written Law on oaths (Deut. 23:21–23; Num. 30:2) by canceling out another provision on filial responsibilities (Exod. 20:12; Deut. 5:16; etc.). What particular Jewish practice of the day is

---

(Berlin: A. Töpelmann, 1966), pp. 260 ff. Possibly v. 14, vv. 17–18a and 20–23 are Marcan since they reflect Mark's parable theory and include the Marcan-style private interpretation of a parable in vv. 20–23.

45. Nineham, pp. 194 f.
46. See Suhl, p. 81.

reflected in the reference to the Corban vow (v. 11) it is not easy to say. At all events the equation of the commandment of the Law on oaths with the tradition of men and of the commandment on filial responsibility possibly implied for Mark at least that the Pharisees were failing to grasp the true essential spirit of the Law and so were guilty of moral insensitivity in the all important sphere of human relationships (now they are "hypocrites" and now "lacking in filial responsibility").

The crux of Mark 7:1–23 lies in the parabolic saying of verse 15: "There is nothing outside a man which by going into him can defile him; but the things which come out of a man are what defile him." The radicality of the saying with its severe blow at the Law's written commands is in rather stark contrast with the positive appeal to Moses against the Jews in verses 9 f. And it is very questionable whether the bold and broad pronouncement of verse 15 could go back to Jesus in that form: if Jesus had so un-ambiguously swept aside large areas of the written Law, it is hard to see why the early church, with such an absolute word of the Lord to guide it, should have continued to engage in disputes about the Law's validity.[47] We ought possibly to regard the say-ing of verse 15, coupled with the explanation of verses 18–19, as representing for Mark the final solution to the church's contro-versies over the keeping of the Law. Such a final solution need not of course have been inconsistent with the original attitude of Jesus himself, since Jesus may well on particular occasions and specific issues have upheld the primacy of *moral* probity over the Law's injunctions to ritual cleanliness.[48]

Comparison of Mark 7:1–23 with the Matthaean parallel (15:1–20) is instructive. Neither there nor elsewhere does Matthew appear to place a higher estimate than Mark upon the observance of all the scriptural food laws. But by the same token neither does he take up and repeat those unequivocal Marcan statements that simply throw out or abandon the biblical commands (e. g., Mark 7:19c). In the section Mark 7:1–23 there is no overt reference to Jesus' messiahship, and D. E. Nineham is quite right to point out that in this passage neither Mark nor his sources gives any hint

---

47. See recently C. E. Carlston, "The Things that Defile," *NTS*, 15 (Oct., 1968), 95.
48. See Nineham, p. 191.

that Jesus felt free to abrogate the Law *"because he was Messiah."*[49]
However, if indeed Jesus' messiahship is not the ground of the
freedom he here assumes over against the Law, we may say that
in the Marcan understanding and presentation this same freedom
points to and is the ground of the messianic ἐξουσία of Jesus. The
same can be said of the Marcan pericope on divorce (10:2–12). In
the corresponding passage in Matthew (19:3–12) the atmosphere
is more casuistic (e. g., the much debated exceptive clause in
verse 9), and Jesus merely brings together the Old Testament
texts of Deut. 24:1 and Gen. 1:27; 2:24. In Mark, on the contrary, Jesus virtually overthrows Moses by appealing from the
concession made by Moses to the hard hearts of the Jewish people
in Deut. 24:1–4 to God's original design in so ordering the creation of the race ("God made them male and female" [10:6]) as
to ensure the indissolubility of marriage. Although in the use he
makes of Gen. 1:27 and 2:24 Jesus may be said to follow the rabbinic mode of interpretation, in his rejection of Deut. 24:1 he has
"taken up a position which virtually abrogated a Pentateuchal
Law"[50] and to that extent has gone far beyond the rabbis. Once
again the supreme freedom that Jesus assumes over against the
Scripture is consonant with the Marcan emphasis on his messianic
ἐξουσία.[51]

On balance the Jesus of Mark's Gospel appears as one who in
his teaching supersedes and transcends Scripture more than as one
who makes the Scripture point to himself as its fulfillment.[52] Indeed
the relative lack of testimonies is a feature of Mark's Gospel. It
is sometimes attributed to the influence of external circumstances
upon Mark at the time when he wrote his Gospel. It is suggested,
for example, that Mark did not employ testimonies like Matthew

49. *Ibid.*, p. 192.
50. Rawlinson, p. 134, n. 2.
51. The messianic ἐξουσία of Jesus is reflected again in Mark 11:10.
52. *Mark's Jesus* hardly lends support to C. H. Dodd's tentative proposal that it
was our Lord himself whose own creative mind singled out those passages of Scripture
which would become the foundation of the Church's testimony-oriented theology.
See *According to the Scriptures* (London: Nisbet and Co., 1952), p. 110. See also Lindars,
p. 30: "On the whole one gains the impression that Jesus used the Bible or referred
to it as occasion arose, but generally preferred to teach in terms of real-life situations
without appealing to the written word. This may well have contributed to the impression of authority which distinguished his preaching from that of the scribes (Mark
1:22)."

because his work was written for Gentiles. On the other hand John Bowman maintains that Mark simply *presupposes* the testimonies either because his Gospel "represents a stage in the tradition when the scaffolding of 'that it might be fulfilled', 'as it is written' is mainly dismantled or because it belongs to an early period when the Jewish Christians being well versed in the Scriptures did not need the Old Testament prophecies fulfilled, to be pointed out."[53]

None of these explanations seems very satisfactory. Just as likely is it that the relative dearth of testimonies in Mark was conditioned by inner theological or christological convictions on his part. Mark gives the impression of being acutely conscious of having something new to say: the Christ he portrays is one whose words and work cannot be fully explained out of the Old Testament. Mark's Gospel is oriented toward that future in which the *as yet undisclosed* secret of who Jesus really is will be finally revealed. In short Mark's comparative neglect of testimonies may well have to do with the detainment motif by which he seeks to hold up the disclosure until the *Cross* reveals what it means to be the Christ promised by God and to follow him as his disciple.

However, when all this is said, we have still to account for the fact that there is also considerable recourse to the Old Testament in Mark. The Gospel opens with a formula-quotation; "that it might be fulfilled" and "as it is written" occurs in the Passion narrative, which in fact as a whole is painted in Old Testament colors[54] (as of course also is chapter 13 with its catena of biblical phrases). Mark obviously valued the Old Testament highly enough to be unable to present Christ as altogether a *novum*: rather for him Christ's historical appearance and destiny are in conformity with the will of God revealed in Scripture, so that the event of Jesus Christ is thus stamped with an objective priority to the inward imagination and faith of the disciples.

We may think of Mark as standing, *vis-à-vis* Matthew and Luke, at a rudimentary stage of the Christian community's apolo-

---

53. John Bowman, *The Gospel of Mark, The New Christian Jewish Passover Haggadah* (Leiden: E. J. Brill, 1965), pp. 19 f.

54. C. H. Dodd finds seventeen certain or probable references to *testimonia* from the OT in Mark's Passion narrative; see *Historical Tradition in the Fourth Gospel* (Cambridge: The University Press, 1963), pp. 31 f.

getic endeavors to demonstrate from the Old Testament the relations between Jesus and that which is the messianic vocation. The development of the notion of fulfillment in Matthew and Luke reflects not so much that they inhabit a different world of thought from Mark but rather, no doubt, that they are moved by the developing interest of apologetic.[55]

The main intent of this essay has been to show that only with qualifications and reservations can we regard Mark and Matthew and Luke as all subscribing to the same degree and in the same way to a promise-fulfillment schema. We should take seriously C. F. D. Moule's recent timely reminder that we should aim at much greater precision in our use of the promise-fulfillment category.[56]

---

55. See Erich Grässer's critical review of Suhl, *Die Funktion* in *Theologische Literaturzeitung*, 91 (1966), 667–69.
56. Moule, p. 320.

NOTE ON MARK 5:43

JAMES M. EFIRD

In an article in the *Journal of Biblical Literature*[1] Dr. W. F. Stine-spring demonstrated that the active infinitive can be and is used with passive meaning in biblical Aramaic. This usage he called the "hidden third-person plural indefinite."[2] The construction, found most frequently in Daniel, is used in places where someone *commands* that something be done, but the *active* infinitive is used.

It has long been noted though not accepted by all textual scholars that the so-called Western text, especially represented by Codex D (Bezae), is characterized by Semitisms.[3] The late A. J. Wensinck, some of whose work in this area has not yet been published, has demonstrated that there are many Semitisms in Codex Bezae. Matthew Black cites a conclusion of Wensinck's which is quite apropos to our discussion:

> In view of the attestation in Classical and later Greek of λέγειν in the meaning 'to enjoin', 'to command', it might seem a work of supererogation on Wensinck's part to trace this usage in the New Testament to Semitic influence. The broad distinction, however, between the two languages appears to be that, whereas in Greek the meaning is (comparatively) rare, in the Semitic group (so in Arabic) it is regular.[4]

1. "The Active Infinitive With Passive Meaning in Biblical Aramaic," *JBL*, 81, pt. 4 (Dec., 1962), 391–94.
2. *Ibid.*, p. 393.
3. Cf. discussions in Matthew Black, *An Aramaic Approach to the Gospels and Acts*, 3rd ed. (Oxford: Clarendon Press, 1967); E. J. Epp, *The Theological Tendency of Codex Bezae Cantabrigiensis in Acts*, Society for New Testament Studies: Monograph Series, no. 3 (Cambridge: Cambridge University Press, 1966). B. M. Metzger, *The Text of the New Testament: Its Transmission, Corruption, and Restoration* (New York: Oxford University Press, 1964). The reader is referred to t'e arguments and bibliographies found in these three works for fuller explication of the problem. For a discussion of the whole question of "Semitism" the reader is referred to E. P. Sanders, *The Tendencies of the Synoptic Tradition*, Society for New Testament Studies: Monograph Series, no. 9 (Cambridge: Cambridge University Press, 1969). See especially pp. 190 ff.
4. P. 301. Subsequent references to Black are in the text.

The conclusion at which Wensinck arrived from his study of
the Semitisms in Bezan Luke holds good for all the synoptics:
D represents the Aramaic background of the synoptic tradition
more faithfully than do non-Western manuscripts. [p. 277]

In what may be termed the "Bezan redaction" more of the
primitive "Aramaized" Greek text has been left unrevised
than in the redaction . . . represented by the Vatican and
Sinaitic Uncials. [p. 279]

It has been further noted by many commentators of the Gospel
of Mark that 5:43 has Semitic characteristics. Vincent Taylor
comments:

In καὶ εἶπεν δοθῆναι αὐτῇ φαγεῖν the verb εἶπεν is used in
the sense of 'told' or 'command'. Allen, . . . sees a Semitism
here, corresponding to the late use of אֲמַר, 'to command' followed by לְ c. infin. . . . The same usage is found in the papyri
. . . and in Cl. Gk. the simple infin. is used in a jussive sense
after λέγω and εἶπον. . . . These considerations do not exclude
the possibility that Semitic idiom is reflected, especially when
several elements in the narrative point in this direction. [5]

The problem seems to be that there appears to be Semitic idiom
here but the exact nature of it is not apparent! Giving added difficulty is the variant reading in Codex D, i. e., δοῦναι (the active
infinitive) for δοθῆναι (passive). In commenting on this phenomenon Blass, Debrunner, and Funk state that Bultmann "*rightly*
rejects the v. l. δοῦναι (D) instead of δοθῆναι Mk 5:43." [6] Taylor
says, "The passive infinitive δοθῆναι is used because the one who
is to execute the order is not named. . . ." [7] It may be, however,
that the curious variant in D, the active infinitive, is the clue to
the Semitism here. For this passage as read in D is an exact copy
of the pattern found in Daniel. A figure in authority speaks (εἶπεν),
ordering that something *be* done (active infinitive).

---

5. *The Gospel According to St. Mark*, 2nd ed. (New York: St. Martin's Press, 1966),
p. 298.

6. Friedrich Wilhelm Blass and Albert Debrunner, *A Greek Grammar of the New
Testament and Other Early Christian Literature*, trans. and rev. R. W. Funk (Chicago:
University of Chicago Press, 1961), p. 201, para. 392, #4. Italics mine.

7. Taylor, p. 298.

It is the contention of this short note that the reading δοῦναι, the active infinitive, is illustrative of the linguistic phenomenon pointed out by Professor Stinespring as the "hidden third-person plural indefinite." If this is true, the active infinitive is, of course, explained as a Semitism illustrated in biblical Aramaic. Further the exact nature of the Semitism is made plain for the commentators who find "Semitic influence" but are not exactly certain what it is. Finally this is simply one more illustration to suggest that Codex D may reflect the Aramaic background of the Gospel tradition to a much greater degree than do the other recensions (as Black and Wensinck have argued) and therefore deserves much more careful consideration than it has been afforded in the past.

THE MORAL TEACHING OF THE
EARLY CHURCH

W. D. DAVIES

My friend and colleague, Professor William F. Stinespring, is best known as a philologist, a teacher of Semitic languages and a translator of significant studies from modern Hebrew. But to those who share his daily life, he is also known for the warmth of his humanity. In particular, his colleagues have been made aware of his concern with the social and moral issues that have confronted this country. It is, therefore, not unfitting that in this volume there should be one essay dealing with the biblical grounds of that concern which has so much governed him. And it is a real pleasure for me to be able to offer in his honor, not a technical study, but one in which I seek to set forth the broad outlines of the moral teaching of the early church. My aim is to present, not so much a detailed analysis, as the way in which that teaching has impressed itself upon me after years of preoccupation with it.

I

The title of this essay—"The Moral Teaching of the Early Church"—is meant to suggest, rightly, that the term *ethics*, which connotes philosophic reflection upon human conduct, is inappropriate for a description of the moral teaching of the early church; but it implies that in the early church there was a clearly defined body of teaching on morality, which can be neatly described. Let me begin by emphasizing that this was not so. In its moral teaching, as in other matters, the early church presents a coat of many colors. The documents of the New Testament reveal varying emphases.

This essay is one of the Haskell Lectures which, along with Dean Krister Stendahl, I delivered at Oberlin College, Oberlin, Ohio, in March 1968. Its companion lecture, "The Relevance of the Moral Teaching of the Early Church,"—which presupposes the contents of the present one—was published in *Neotestamentica et Semitica, Studies in Honour of Matthew Black*, ed. E. Earle Ellis and Max Wilcox (Edinburgh: T & T Clark, 1969), pp. 30–49. Both lectures should be read together. It is felicitous in this indirect way to link together two such distinguished Semitic scholars to whom I owe so much.

Any neat presentation of early Christian teaching must immediately be suspect. But having said this, it is possible to point out certain themes which do convey the moral seriousness of much of the primitive church, and I shall now attempt to point out what these themes are.[1]

I begin with a central fact: through the life, death and Resurrection of Jesus of Nazareth, early Christians believed that they were living "in the end of the days," in the time of fulfillment.[2] This conviction is to be understood, as is made evident in all the New Testament, in the light of the expectations, expressed in the Old Testament and in Judaism, that, at some future date, God would act for the salvation of his people.[3] The life, death and Resurrection of Jesus of Nazareth were the fulfillment of these expectations. And this fulfillment did not ignore the moral content of those expectations. The ethical aspirations of the Old Testament and Judaism, the Prophets and the Law, were not annulled in the Christian dispensation; they were fulfilled.[4] The early church consciously accepted the moral concern of Israel as it was illumined and completed in the light of the life, death and Resurrection of Jesus.

This acceptance emerges clearly in that in much of the New Testament the experience of the church was understood as parallel to that of the Jewish people. The emergence of the church was, if not the emergence of a New Israel, at least the entrance of Israel on a new stage of its history.[5] In the creation of the church the

1. The moral teaching of the New Testament in recent years has not been given the attention it deserves: "theological" or "kerygmatic" interests have led to its neglect. See J. M. Gustafson, "Christian Ethics" in *Religion*, ed. Paul Ramsey (Englewood Cliffs, N. J., 1965), pp. 337 f.; and my *Setting of the Sermon on the Mount* (Cambridge, 1966), pp. 436 ff. V. P. Furnish, *Theology and Ethics in Paul* (Nashville, 1968), by far the most stimulating volume in this field in recent years, on p. 7 quotes Thomas C. Ogden, who suggests that "the simple task of honest and clear exegesis may be the undiscovered beginning point for contemporary Protestant ethics"; see Ogden, *Radical Obedience: The Ethics of Rudolf Bultmann* (Philadelphia, 1964), pp. 18, 21. For the works which have been found most useful, apart, of course, from the standard works on New Testament Theology and Ethics: See *IDB*, vol. E–J, on "Ethics in the New Testament." Furnish supplies a most helpful bibliography, *op. cit.*, pp. 280–94.

2. Gal. 4:4.

3. Isa. 10:22; 35:4; 43:3; 45:17–22; 60:16. See "Eschatology of the Old Testament" by J. Hempel in *IDB*, E–J, 153 ff.; for Apocalyptic and Ethics, see H. H. Rowley, *The Relevance of Apocalyptic* (London, 1944); D. S. Russell, *The Method and Message of Jewish Apocalyptic, 200 B.C.–A.D. 100* (Philadelphia, 1964).

4. Matt. 4:4, 6–7; 5:17–18; Mark 12:28–37; etc.

5. On this see now Peter Richardson, *Israel in the Apostolic Church*, Society for New

Exodus was repeated as it were. And as a corollary to the experience of a new Exodus, the church understood itself as standing under the new Sinai of a new Moses. This complex of ideas—Exodus, Sinai, Moses[6]—largely governs Paul's references to the New Covenant,[7] Matthew's[8] presentation of the Sermon on the

---

Testament Studies, Monograph Series, no. 10 (Cambridge, 1969). According to him the designation of the Church as "the true Israel" does not occur until the mid-second century in the works of Justin Martyr. The phrase "the New Israel" used of the church is not found in the New Testament.

6. On this see the following: *Cahiers Sioniens: Revue Trimestrielle viii année*, no. 2–3–4 (Paris, 1954), on Moïse, *L'Homme de L'Alliance*, especially sec. 3 by Albert Déscamps, *Moïse dans les Évangiles et dans la tradition Apostolique*, pp. 171–80 and Paul Démann, *Moïse dans la Pensée de Saint Paul*, pp. 189–241; Harold Sahlin, "The New Exodus of Salvation According to St. Paul," in *The Root of the Vine*, ed. Anton Fridrichsen (New York, 1953), pp. 81 ff.; *The Setting of the Sermon on the Mount*; H. M. Teeple, *The Mosaic Eschatological Prophet* (Philadelphia, 1957); and for the Fourth Gospel, R. H. Smith, "Exodus Typology in the Fourth Gospel," *JBL*, 81 (1962), 329–42; J. L. Martyn, *History and Theology in the Fourth Gospel* (New York, 1968), pp. 88, 91 ff.; T. F. Glasson, *Moses in the Fourth Gospel* (London, 1963); W. A. Meeks, *The Prophet-King: Moses Traditions and the Johannine Christology*, Supplements to Novum Testamentum, 14 (Leiden, 1967); H. J. Schoeps, *Theologie und Geschichte des Judenchristentums* (Tübingen, 1949); David Daube, *The Exodus Pattern in the Bible* (London, 1963); Joachim Jeremias on Moses in Kittel's *Theologisches Wörterbuch zum N.T.* On the "wilderness" motif, see Ulrich W. Mauser, *Christ in the Wilderness: The Wilderness Theme in the Second Gospel and its Basis in the Biblical Tradition* (London, 1963); contrast Ernest Edwin Best, *The Temptation and the Passion* (Cambridge, 1965), pp. 25 ff. But see also Jacques Dupont, "L'arrière-fond biblique du récit des tentations de Jésus," *NTS*, 3 (1956–1957), 287–304; G. H. P. Thompson, "Called-Proved-Obedient: A Study in the Baptism and Temptation Narratives of Matthew and Luke," *Journal of Theological Studies*, 11 (1960), 1–12. On "Law" in Paul, see also the suggestive essay by W. R. Schoedel, "Pauline Thought: Some Basic Issues," in *Transitions in Biblical Scholarship*, ed. J. C. Rylaarsdam (Chicago, 1968), pp. 263 ff.

7. See W. C. Van Unnik, "La conception paulinienne de la nouvelle alliance," in *Litterature et Theologie Pauliniennes*, Recherches Biblique, V (Bruges, 1960), pp. 109–126, 224 f.; see also his "Ἡ Καινὴ Διαθήκη: A Problem in the early history of the Canon," in *Studia Patristica*, 4; and in F. L. Cross, ed., *Texte und Untersuchungen zur Geschichte der altchristlichen Literatur*, vol. 79 (Berlin, 1961). He notes the neglect of this theme in Pauline studies. Emphasis on the notion of the New Covenant was so strong in early Christianity that both Joseph Bonsirven, *Le Judaïsme Palestinien* (Paris, 1934–1935), 1: 79 f., and H. J. Schoeps, p. 90, claim that it led to a neglect or muting of that theme in rabbinic Judaism. Compare also Gottfried Quell, *Theologisches Wörterbuch zum N. T.*, 2. See also Roy A. Harrisville, *The Concept of Newness in the New Testament* (Minneapolis, 1960), pp. 46 ff. For the Covenant in Judaism see the exhaustive study by Annie Jaubert, *La Notion d'Alliance dans le Judaïsme aux abords de l'ère Chrétienne* (Paris, 1963). On the presence of Law in the early church as in the OT, see Gerhard Von Rad, *Old Testament Theology*, trans. D. M. G. Stalker (Edinburgh, 1962), 2: 391 ff. "The saving event whereby Israel became Yahweh's is indissolubly bound up with the obligation to obey certain norms which clearly mark out the chosen people's sphere, particularly at its circumference. The same thing, however, occurs in the early Christian community. From the very beginning it too was conscious of being bound to certain legal norms and it put them into practice unreservedly. . . ." See I Cor. 5:5; 16:22;

Mount, and Mark's[9] reference to a new teaching which John presents as a new commandment.[10] In its vital contents the moral teaching of primitive Christianity must be understood in relation to the teaching which Judaism traced back to Sinai: this relationship is variously expressed, sometimes in terms of reform, sometimes in terms of antithesis, and sometimes in terms of fulfillment. What is clear is that "Law" is bound up with the Christian Gospel, as it was bound up with the message of the Old Testament and Judaism.[11] To put this in technical terms, the structure of primitive Christianity is, in some aspects at least, modelled upon, or grows out of, the structure of Judaism. This means that Law is integral to the Gospel of the New Testament as it was to that of the Old.[12]

---

cf. Acts 8:20; II Tim. 2:19. Important are Günther Bornkamm, "Das Anathema in der urchristliche Abendmahls Theologie" in *Das Ende des Gesetzes: Paulus Studien* (Munich, 1952), pp. 123 ff.; E. Käsemann, "Satze Heiligen Rechts in Neuen Testament," *NTS*, 1 (1955), 248 ff. On the difficulty which Protestants have in doing justice to the Mosaic element in the NT, see the brilliant work of F. J. Leenhardt, *Two Biblical Faiths: Protestant and Catholic*, trans. Harold Knight (Philadelphia, 1964), pp. 42 f. "Protestants have the greatest difficulty in not underestimating the value of the Mosaic tradition in the corpus of revelation . . . the Pauline polemic against the threat of Judaism and Judaic Christianity often remains, in the mentality of Protestant readers of the apostle, the sole key to the understanding of the Gospel. What is argued by St. Paul against the Judaic and Judaizing interpretation of the Law is applied by them in the most massive way to the whole structure of the Mosaic faith."

8. See Davies, *The Setting of the Sermon on the Mount*.

9. Mark 1:27 ff. The emphasis on "teaching" in Mark emerges from R. Morgenthaler, *Statistik des neutestamentlichen Wortschatzes* (Zürich, 1959); his data are given on p. 97, n. 1 of *The Setting of the Sermon on the Mount*. See Eduard Schweizer, "Anmerkungen zur Theologie des Markus" in *Neotestamentica et Patristica, Freundesgabe Oscar Cullmann* (Leiden, 1962), pp. 37 f.

10. John 13:34; the context of this new commandment within the last supper, which at least has Passover undertones, is important.

11. See my article "Torah and Dogma," *The Harvard Theological Review*, 61 (1968), 700 ff.

12. One of the most illuminating developments in Old Testament studies has been the rehabilitation of the Law. Through the work of Alt, Von Rad, Martin Noth, Buber, Zimmerli, Clements, and others, the influence of the covenant tradition, with its Law, on the prophets has become clear. And just as the prophets have been connected with the Law that preceded them, so Finkelstein in a brilliant study has connected them with the Law that followed them in Judaism. The old antithesis of Law and Prophet has been challenged. The prophets are emerging as "teachers." This has an important bearing on our understanding of Jesus. To place him among the prophets is not to displace him from the role of teacher. On the above, see Albrecht Alt, *Die Ursprünge des Israelitischen Rechts* (Leipzig, 1934); Gerhard Von Rad, *Das Formgeschichtliche Problem des Hexateuch* (Stuttgart, 1938); reprinted in *Gesammelte Studien zum A. T.* (Munich, 1958), pp. 9–86; and his *Old Testament Theology* (2 vols.); Martin Noth, *Die Gesetze im Pentateuch* (Munich, 1958), pp. 9–141. Walther Zimmerli in a

II

But in what sense can this be asserted? What Law is integral to the Gospel? This brings us to the motif which most governs early Christian thought on morality. I have already asserted that the early church reinterpreted the moral tradition of the Old Testament and Judaism in the light of Christ; and it is the Person of Christ that is normative for the understanding of morality, as of all other aspects of life, in the New Testament.[13] Just as early Christians reinterpreted the temple,[14] Jerusalem,[15] the sabbath[16] and

series of lectures *The Law and the Prophets: A Study of the Meaning of the Old Testament* (New York, 1965), gives a fascinating account of the theme in scholarship; see also R. E. Clements, *Prophecy and Covenant* (London, 1965). On the prophets in Judaism, see my article, "Reflexions on Tradition: The Aboth Revisited" in *Christian History and Interpretation: Studies presented to John Knox* (Cambridge, 1967), pp. 127 ff. Martin Buber in his work *The Prophetic Faith* (New York, 1960), pp. 24 ff., puts great emphasis on the influence of the Sinai tradition on the prophets.

13. This essay was completed before V. P. Furnish's work *Theology and Ethics in Paul* (Abingdon, 1968), reached me. On p. 114, he writes: "In the discussion of Paul's preaching which follows, the traditional 'chronological-dogmatic' approach has been abandoned altogether. Instead, it is suggested at least as a working hypothesis, that the heuristic key to Pauline theology as a whole [and therefore to Pauline ethics (my addition)] the point in which his major themes are rooted and to which they are ultimately oriented, is the apostle's eschatological perspective. Eschatology, therefore, is properly the *first*, not the last, section in an exposition of Paul's theology." Furnish refers in support of his position to H. D. Wendland, "Ethik und Eschatologie in der Theologie des Paulus," *Neue kirchliche Zeitschrift*, 10 (1930), 757 ff., 793 ff.; and Henry M. Shires, *The Eschatology of Paul in the Light of Modern Scholarship* (Philadelphia, 1966). It will be noticed that I, too, have begun to discuss the moral teaching of the New Testament with its eschatology, and particularly with an aspect of that eschatology—that of the new Exodus, a motif to which Furnish pays little attention. So far the emphasis of Furnish is to be accepted. But I immediately went on to assert that the central fact in the moral teaching of the New Testament is the Person of Jesus Christ. This means that even the eschatology of the New Testament and, therefore, its ethic, is subordinate to its Christology. Here I find myself in much sympathy with the position urged by Joseph A. Fitzmyer in a review of his work, which Dr. Furnish himself kindly sent me, published in *The Perkins School of Theology Journal* (Spring, 1969), pp. 113 ff. Fitzmyer writes: "To my way of thinking, such labels as 'the heuristic key to Pauline theology' or 'the fundamental perspective (Furnish, *op. cit.*, p. 214)' should be applied to what Paul himself says: 'we proclaim a Christ who has been crucified' (see I Cor. 1:21–25; cf. Rom. 1:16; II Cor. 4:4). In other words, the starting-point is the preaching of the Christ event, a redemptive christology" (p. 114b). Such an emphasis on the centrality of Christ himself is not new; and it is more likely that his Person, rather than any perspective, should govern our understanding of New Testament theology and ethics. Furnish does allow the importance of the christological motif in the Pauline ethic (p. 216), but not, in our view, its primacy. This has results in the understanding of that ethic as it is related to Jesus' own teaching.

14. See Alan Cole, *The New Temple* (London, 1950); R. J. McKelvey, *The New Temple: The Church in the New Testament* (Oxford, 1969), with excellent bibliographies.

all the significant symbols of Jewish self-identity in terms of Christ, so they reinterpreted the Law. They found "in Christ" a new demand under which they stood, so that—although the precise phrase does not occur—Christ became their Law. I have argued elsewhere that for Paul Jesus took the place of Torah. The demand of Christianity is concentrated in the Person of Christ.[17]

But what precisely does this mean? I think that it has three aspects which are exceedingly difficult to hold in proper balance. First, the moral life of Christians bears constant reference to, or is moulded by, the actual life of Jesus of Nazareth, that is, his ministry of forgiveness, judgment, healing, and teaching.[18] Second, the moral teaching has its point of departure not only in the ministry of Jesus but also in his Resurrection. The Resurrection was the ground for the emergence of the primitive community, as a well-knit and self-conscious group. But the Resurrection was also the immediate inspiration of its morality. The Resurrection was not only a triumph of life over death, it was also a triumph of forgiveness over sin. The Resurrection was an expression, perhaps *the* expression of God's grace in Christ, because the Risen Christ came back to those who had forsaken him and fled, who had slept during his agony. He forgave their failure. The Resurrection as forgive-

---

See John 1:14; 2:21 f.; 4:21 ff.; 7:37–38; 10:16; 11:52; etc. See especially John C. Meagher, "John 1:14 and the New Temple," *JBL*, 88 (Mar., 1969), 57. For him the community is the locus of the Word, that is, the New Temple, in John 1:14; contrast McKelvey, pp. 60 ff.; II Cor. 6:14–7:1; I Cor. 3:16–17; Eph. 2:19–22; 1 Pet. 2:4–10; Heb. 12:22–24 *et passim*; and Revelation, *passim*. See also Bertil Gärtner, *The Temple and the Community in Qumran and the New Testament* (Cambridge, 1965).

15. Gal. 4:25, 26; Heb. 12:22; Rev. 3:12; 21:10. Possibly also Matt. 5:14.

16. Heb. 4:9.

17. See *Paul and Rabbinic Judaism*; Oscar Cullmann, "Paradosis et Kyrios: Le problème de la tradition dans le paulisme," *Revue d'histoire et de philosophie religieuses*, no. 1 (1950), 12 ff.; for the "new torah" in later Judaism, see M. Simon, *Verus Israel* (Paris, 1948), pp. 100 ff. The best critique of the position advocated in *Paul and Rabbinic Judaism* is by P. Démann, "Moïse et la Loi dans la pensée de Saint Paul," *Cahiers Sioniens* (1954), pp. 239 ff. It should be recalled that some have found ideas connected with the Torah applied to Christ in the Prologue of the Fourth Gospel also, see e. g., C. H. Dodd, *The Interpretation of the Fourth Gospel* (Cambridge, 1953), pp. 270 ff.

18. Apart from some such assumption the preservation of the tradition about the works and deeds of Jesus in the Gospels is difficult to understand. Even granted that much of that tradition is a creation of the primitive community, its attachment to the figure of Jesus is itself significant. Cf. Günther Bornkamm, *Jesus of Nazareth*, trans. 3rd German ed. Irene and Fraser McLuskey with James M. Robinson (New York, 1960).

ness emerges clearly in Paul and elsewhere.[19] The Resurrection, which reassembled the scattered disciples to form the church, was founded in the grace of Christ and of God in Christ. It was of a piece with the whole ministry of Jesus, and the morality of the community, like that of his ministry, was to be a morality governed by grace—that is, it was the morality of forgiven men who had known the Risen Lord as a forgiving Lord, and who in gratitude (the most ethical of all the emotions) gave themselves to the good life in his name.[20]

But, third, the mode of the presence of this Risen Lord in the community was that of "the Spirit." There have been attempts to maintain that the Spirit, in the earliest days of the church, had no ethical significance, that it was merely a wonder-working power, mysterious and nonmoral. But these attempts are vain. It was the Spirit that had inspired the greatest teachers of morality, the prophets, who had discerned between the precious and the vile; it was the Spirit that would create a new heart in the new Israel of Ezekiel's vision, and inspire the messianic times with counsel, wisdom and righteousness. And, above all else, the Spirit was the inspirer of the Scriptures. This in itself implied the ethicization of the Spirit, because it was through these that Israel knew the demands made upon it. Through the Resurrection, the Spirit was again experienced.

The coming of the Spirit in primitive Christianity should never be separated from the Resurrection as grace. Like the Resurrection itself, the coming of the Spirit is "an energy of forgiveness." Thus it became the source of morality because gratitude for forgiveness is the ground of Christian being. Love, joy, peace, righteousness, and every victory "in the moral sphere" are the fruit of the Spirit.

19. To connect the Resurrection with morality is not usual. But this is implicit in I Cor. 15:7 ff. It is significant that in I Cor. 15:5 the Risen Lord is said to have appeared first to Cephas who had betrayed Jesus three times, and then to the twelve who had all forsaken him and fled. We must assume that Paul knew the tradition about the betrayals. In the Fourth Gospel Jesus first appears to Mary Magdalene whose sins were well known. It is no accident that in the Sermon on the Mount, the Beatitudes, which are the expression of God's grace, precede the statement of the demands of Jesus, which are thus deliberately set in a context of grace. James T. Cleland in his Th.D. diss., "The Religious Ethic of St. Paul" (Union Theological Seminary, Feb., 1954), deals with the connection between the Resurrection and ethics from another angle; see pp. 196–473, pts. 2 and 3.

20. On this see further IDB, E–J, 168; John Knox, The Jesus in the Teaching of the Church (Nashville, 1961), pp. 73 ff.

The enthusiasm of the Spirit, much as it was open to more superficial expressions, found its true fruit in love.[21]

When, therefore, we say that for the early church the Law had been Christified, we recognize that the earthly ministry of Jesus, the Risen Lord, and the Spirit—inextricably bound together as they are, so that often what was uttered in the Spirit could be ascribed to the earthly Jesus himself—that all these together became the source of the demand under which the early church lived. Christian morality, in short, always has as its point of reference the life, Resurrection and living Spirit of Jesus Christ. And it is this that determines its manifold dimensions. These can be conveniently gathered under two main heads: its vertical dimensions and its horizontal dimensions.[22]

III

The vertical dimensions of Christian morality

As we have seen, then, the ground on which the early church stood was the life, death, Resurrection and Spirit of Jesus Christ. To put the matter geometrically, it was their relation vertically with the Risen Lord, the participation of the early Christians in the experience of being forgiven by the Risen Lord and the Spirit, that lent to them a common grace wherein they stood. They had been grasped by him and their response was primarily, through the promptings of this Spirit, to him. All Christian fellowship was rooted in a particular event—immediately in the Resurrection and behind this, in the life and death of Jesus, with which the Resurrection, as we have seen, as an expression of grace, was wholly congruous. The ethic of the community is linked to the understanding of an event—the life, death and Resurrection of Jesus. In this the church saw the act of God himself in history.

21. On all this see W. D. Davies, *Paul and Rabbinic Judaism*, pp. 215 ff. and references to literature there given. In the Fourth Gospel the Spirit, which is "holy," is to teach and to recall what Jesus had taught: see John 14:25 ff. See also Gal. 5:22; I Cor. 13; John 14:15–17; 15:9–10; 16:8–11.

22. This division of the material, although adopted for the sake of convenience, is not accidental. To some degree at least it corresponds to the distinction which Furnish, p. 279, has rightly emphasized—that between the concrete moral teaching of Paul in ethical warnings, prohibitions, exhortations, etc., and his preaching as a whole, especially to his theological presuppositions and convictions, as constituting the essential problem of the Pauline ethic, although this cannot be pressed.

Now in much of the New Testament, though not in all, morality is understood in terms of the appropriation of this event, the recapitulation of it in the life of the believer. To put it in other words, the moral life is a life "in Christ"; it is the living out in daily conduct what it means to have died and risen with Christ. This is true of Paul and, it is arguable, of Matthew also.[23] For Paul, morality is inseparable from the life, death and Resurrection of Jesus. He divided his own life clearly into two parts: first, his life under the Law when he was a Jew, and second, his life in Christ. The two parts were distinctly separated by his experience on the road to Damascus. The act by which a Christian acknowledged his faith and really began to live "in Christ" was baptism. This act symbolized a death to the old life under the Law and a rising to newness of life "in Christ" or "in the Spirit." By baptism[24] the Christian through faith had died, had risen, had been justified: he was a new creation. And what was now necessary for him was to become what he was. His moral life is rooted in what he *is*—a new creation in Christ. Just as we call on each other to "play the man," so Christians are called upon to "play the Christian"—to be what they are. To use theological jargon—the imperative in Paul is rooted in the indicative. There is a vertical dimension to Christian living—an attachment to the fact of Christ, his life, death and Resurrection.[25]

23. See Davies, *The Setting of the Sermon on the Mount*, pp. 341 ff.

24. Rom. 6:3; I Cor. 12:13; Gal. 3:27. But baptism was not universal, Acts 1:14–15; 19:1–7.

25. II Cor. 8:9; 12:1; Phil. 2:5–8; Rom. 8:11; and especially Rom. 6:1–7:6. On the history of the emphasis on what is generally referred to as the "Indicative-Imperative" motif in Paul, see the excellent appendix by Furnish, pp. 242 ff.: "A Survey of Nineteenth- and Twentieth-Century Interpretations of the Pauline Ethic." Like him, I, too, found the work of Maurice Goguel in *The Primitive Church*, trans. H. C. Snape (London, 1964), especially original and provocative. In the discussion at Oberlin, Stendahl objected to connecting the motif of "dying and rising with Christ" with morality, on the grounds that while the tense of the verbs referring to dying with Christ is in the aorist, that of those referring to rising with Christ is in the future. The matter is discussed by Furnish, pp. 171 ff. The future tenses in Rom. 6:5, 8 are important: "We *shall be* united in his resurrection"; "we *shall* also live with him." But, as Furnish also makes clear, the newness of life *is* associated with the Resurrection. Rom. 6:4 reads: "We were buried therefore with him by baptism into death, so that as Christ was raised from the dead by the glory of the Father, we too might walk in the newness of life." The power of the future life is already at work in the present. The Christian is to walk in the power of that life here and now. Rom. 8:4–5; II Cor. 10:2–3; I Cor. 3:3; Rom. 13:13; Phil. 3:18, etc. See Furnish, pp. 214 ff.; and especially W. R. Schoedel, "Pauline Thought: Some Basic Issues," in *Transitions in Biblical Scholarship*,

And so, too, in the Fourth Gospel the life of the Christian man is to reenact the self-giving of God in sending Christ into the world. The "love" which exists between the Father and the Son is to be reproduced in the relationship of the disciples to one another. Here again there is a vertical relationship between the believer and Christ and God which determines his relationship with others.[26]

ed. J. C. Rylaarsdam (Chicago, 1968), p. 279, n. 34. On the understanding of the "indicative-imperative" relation as not only an individual one, I wholeheartedly agree with Ernst Käsemann, who writes in his essay on " 'The Righteousness of God' in Paul," translated by W. S. Montague and W. F. Bunge in *New Testament Questions of Today* (Philadelphia, 1969), as follows:

> In many quarters today we hear the relationship between indicative and imperative in Paul described in terms of the formula 'Become what you are'; while this is certainly not wrong, it is yet, in view of the origin of the formula in idealism, not without its dangers. Paul was not primarily concerned with the Christian in some purely notional individual capacity, much less with the Christian personality. To say that a man only believes as an individual is simply to say that here, as in the case of ministry in the world, he cannot shrug off responsibility. But I find myself totally unable to assent to the view that Paul's theology and his philosophy of history are orientated towards the individual. To understand the righteousness of God exclusively in terms of gift is to ask for trouble: the inevitable result is that the Pauline anthropology is sucked under by the pull of an individualistic outlook. The sense of the parenetic imperative as the logical implication and the verification of the indicative is much better described in terms of the formula 'Abide by the Lord who has been given to you and by his lordship', which constitutes the core of the conception of 'abiding' in the Johannine farewell discourses. This is the way in which the Christian really does become what he is. For Paul sees our existence as determined at any given time by the Lord whom we are serving. If a transformation of our existence is really effected in baptism and if God's Word does posit a new creation, this cannot help but mean a change of lordship. The new Lord cuts us off from what we were before and never allows us to remain what we are at any given time, for otherwise he might be the First Cause but he would not be our Lord in the true sense. In this particular theological context, man is never seen as free in the sense of autonomous. But he does receive—eschatologically—the possibility of choosing between the kingdom of Christ and the kingdom of Satan, and the ordeal of temptation, like the call sounded in preaching, is for ever demanding that the Christian should make this choice anew; thus the Christian life may rightly be seen as a perpetual return to baptism. (pp. 175–76)

Compare my introduction to *Paul and Rabbinic Judaism* (New York, 1965), pp. xii f.

26. This is brought out in C. H. Dodd, *The Interpretation of the Fourth Gospel*, p. 418, in his treatment of the Prayer of Christ in John 17:

> We have now to enquire in what precise way this prayer is related to the discourses which preceded it. If we look back on these discourses, we see that they turn upon one central theme—what it means to be united with Christ (with Christ crucified and risen). This theme is treated in a kaleidoscopic variety of aspects. Let us briefly recapitulate a few of them. Jesus washes His disciples' feet that they may "have part with Him" (μέρος ἔχεις μετ' ἐμοῦ, xiii. 8). They are to be bound together with the ἀγάπη which is a reflection, or reproduction, of His

But this vertical dimension of morality in the early church has another aspect which is simpler to understand. Not only the imitation of God's act through dying and rising with Christ, but also the imitation of the Jesus of history (if we may so put it) played a real part in the moral development of the early church. Early Christians looked up to Jesus of Nazareth—so a modern educationist would put it—as their "identifying figure." Part of the reason for the preservation of stories about the life of Jesus, such as we have in the Gospels, was the desire to imitate Jesus in his acts.[27] During his ministry, Jesus had demanded readiness to enter upon his way of suffering: his followers were literally to take up the Cross (Mark 8:34 ff.). In the life of the early church, while persecution (walking the way of the Cross literally) was always a possibility, more often Christians were called upon to imitate their Lord, in the witness of the common way, less spectacular perhaps, but no less arduous, than readiness to die—in love, forbearance, patience, mercy—in messianic grace. Luke's change of Mark 8:34 in 9:23 is significant.[28] The degree to which the imitation of Jesus informed

---

ἀγάπη (xiii. 34). Such ἀγάπη is capable of transcending the separation made by death between Christ and His own: His "return" to them is a realization of ἀγάπη (xiv. 19–24). After He has passed through death they will be united with Him as branches of the true Vine (xv. 1–9), and the fruit which the branches yield is once again ἀγάπη proceeding from the ἀγάπη of God revealed in Christ (xv. 8–10).

27. It has been pointed out that Paul and Peter and other figures in the early church were regarded as "models" to be imitated; see Julius Wagenmann, *Die Stelling des Apostels Paulus neben den Zwölf* (Giessen, 1926), pp. 52–76. The Paul of the Pastorals— who finished his course—was a "model." John 13 makes clear that specific acts in the life of Jesus were "models"; 13:15 reads: "For I have given you an example, that you should do as I have done to you." Moody Smith referred me also to John 14:12 where "imitation" of some kind seems to be involved.

28. Again in the discussion at Oberlin, Stendahl raised the question whether the Cross, as such, was made the ground of an appeal for the moral life in the New Testament. If we exclude all moral considerations from discipleship, such a question might be answered in the negative. If we do not, as is surely more likely, then as Harald Riesenfeld has pointed out, it is significant that discipleship is closely related to the Cross not only in the synoptics, but in the Fourth Gospel. (Compare Matt. 16:21–27 and parallels; John 12:31 ff.). See his *Gospel Tradition*, trans. E. Margaret Rowley and R. A. Kraft (Philadelphia: Fortress Press, 1970). The obedience of Christ in death (Rom. 5:19; cf. Phil. 2:8) is an "act of righteousness" (Rom. 5:18), and preeminently an expression of God's love (Gal. 2:19 ff.; 5:6 ff.). Christ crucified becomes "wisdom, righteousness, sanctification and redemption for us" (I Cor. 1:30–31). God's love revealed in the Cross forgives, renews and sustains (II Cor. 5:14). See further Furnish, p. 168. It is difficult to divorce the appeal to the Cross from an appeal to the good life.

the lives of early Christians has been variously assessed. But it is difficult to deny its presence. Christ is an object of imitation to Paul as Paul expects to be such an object to his own followers (I Cor. 11:1). The apostle holds up certain qualities of the historic Jesus which were to be imitated: he points to Jesus who pleased not himself (Rom. 15:3), to his meekness and gentleness (II Cor. 10:1), and he commands liberality through a reminder of him who was rich and became poor (II Cor. 8:8–9).[29] The description of love in I Cor. 13 which is probably based upon the life of Jesus, is, in short, a character sketch of him. There can be little question that for Paul every Christian is pledged to an attempted moral conformity to Christ. So also is it with the Fourth Gospel (John 13)

Furnish, rightly in my judgment, thinks that Paul's use of the hymn in Phil. 2:5 ff. is at least partly used in a hortatory sense; some have denied that the Cross has moral implications even in Phil. 2:5 ff.: see, for the literature, R. P. Martin, *Carmen Christi* (Cambridge, 1967), pp. 68 ff., 84 ff.

29. On this question, see Johannes Weiss, *Die Nachfolge Christi und die Predigt der Gegenwart* (1895); Edvin Larsson, *Christus als Vorbild* (1962), pp. 29–47; Anselm Schulz, *Nachfolgen und Nachahmen* (Munich, 1962), pp. 270 ff.; W. P. deBoer, *The Imitation of Paul: An Exegetical Study* (1962); Eduard Lohse, "Nachfolge Christi," in *RGG*, 3rd ed., IV, cols. 1286 ff.; D. M. Stanley, " 'Become imitators of Me': The Pauline Conception of Apostolic Tradition," *Biblica*, 40 (1959), 859 ff.; E. J. Tinsley, *The Imitation of God in Christ* (Philadelphia, 1960). For further details, see Martin Hengel, *Nachfolge und Charisma: Eine exegetisch-religionsgeschichtliche Studie zu Mt 8:21f und Jesu Ruf in die Nachfolge* (Berlin, 1968), p. 1, n. 2, and a forthcoming volume on *Imitation and Tradition in Paul* by Donald Williams (Fortress Press). Furnish discusses the matter acutely and with a wealth of bibliographical detail, pp. 217 ff. He speaks of Christ's obedience as "paradigmatic for the believer's new life in Christ" (p. 218), but rejects any reference in this paradigm to "any particular qualities of the earthly Jesus with the insistence that they be emulated" (p. 223). He endorses Dibelius's view that "when Paul speaks of following Christ, he is not thinking first of all of the historical person Jesus of Nazareth, but of the Son of God who emptied himself and lived and died for others (*RGG*, 2nd ed., IV, cols. 395–96)," p. 224 n. It is this so sharp dichotomy which is difficult to accept: it was precisely in Jesus of Nazareth that early Christians saw the Son of God: it was the actuality of his life that lay behind their Christological and Mythological assertions about him. To separate the historical person, Jesus of Nazareth, so sharply from the Son of God or the Kurios is to make the myth govern the history rather than the history the ground of the myth. On the relation of "Jesus" to the "Lord" in Paul, see Davies, *The Setting of the Sermon on the Mount*, pp. 341 ff. Furnish writes: "W. D. Davies goes so far as to contend that the preservation of Jesus' sayings and stories about him was due largely to the importance his followers attached to imitating his example" (p. 219). But is this so very different from what is now a common assumption of most New Testament scholars that the needs of the church are reflected in the tradition, except that for some form critics the church, to serve those needs, "created" a tradition and a history while I prefer to think of a "history"— fashioned, indeed, by the church—transmitted by the tradition, that is, given in the ministry of Jesus? I agree with what Furnish affirms, but not with what he denies.

and I Peter 2:2.[30] The life of Jesus is a paradigm of the Christian life.

So far we have noted two aspects of the vertical dimensions of Christian morality in the early church: The Christian is raised up with Christ to newness of life and is to live out his resurrection daily; and he looks to Jesus as an object of imitation. There is a third aspect to this vertical dimension. The Christian is taken up into the purpose of God in Christ. To be a believer was to be directed to and by Jesus of Nazareth as the Messiah. That is, there is always an eschatological reference to Christian living: the Christian shares in the purpose of God in the salvation revealed in Jesus. This comes out most clearly in Paul's understanding of his call to be an apostle. This meant for him that he was taken up by God's grace to share in the redemptive activity of God now at work through Christ in the church. True, the apostolic consciousness of Paul was more intense than that of most Christians and his calling as the apostle to the Gentiles, perhaps, unique. But the whole community also was called, that is, caught up into the large counsel of God. Christians were delivered from futility; they shared in the work of salvation (including their own) inaugurated by Jesus and to be completed in the future. In the light of the redemptive purpose revealed in Christ, they made their decisions, they discerned the things that further and that hinder this purpose, and they became fellow-workers with God.[31] The life of early Christians was a life born of the grace of God in the Resurrection and sustained by the hope of the End: Christian morality is rooted in a "lively hope,"[32] even as it is informed by the earthly Jesus. It is governed by a memory and an anticipation.

Perhaps we differ over what we consider to be historically probable. For a discussion of H. D. Betz, *Nachfolge und Nachahmung Christi im Neuen Testament* (1967), see Hengel, pp. 94 ff. The pertinent texts on "imitation" are discussed by Furnish, pp. 220 ff.

30. See E. G. Selwyn, *The First Epistle of St. Peter*, 2nd ed. (London, 1947), pp. 90 ff., on "The Imitation of Christ and the Atonement," especially I Pet. 2:20b f.: "But if when you do right and suffer for it you take it patiently, you have God's approval. For to this you have been called, 'because Christ also suffered for you, leaving you an example, that you should follow in his steps. He committed no sin; no guile was found in his lips. When he was reviled, he did not revile in return, when he suffered he did not threaten. . . .'" See also I Pet. 4:1 ff.

31. See especially on all this Oscar Cullmann, *Christ and Time* (Philadelphia, 1962); Oscar Cullmann, *Salvation in History*, trans. G. S. Sowers *et al.* (London, 1967); Furnish, p. 235, rightly emphasizes that all Christian "discerning" is informed by *agapê*.

32. Explicitly expressed in I Pet. 1:1, but implied throughout the New Testament.

The horizontal dimensions of Christian morality

So far, in describing the moral life of early Christianity, I have emphasized what I have called its vertical dimension—its attachment to the Risen Christ who was one with the Jesus of history; its contemplation of him in imitation and its participation in the Divine purpose in him. But the early Christians were not exclusively oriented to these vertical realities, and early Christian morality contains an horizontal or, if I may put it, a human, societary dimension: it is the morality of a community born of the grace of the Resurrection. The New Testament knows nothing of solitary religion and it knows nothing of an individual morality: it points to a community with a life to live. This community was not to luxuriate in grace, absorbed in irrelevant, vertical privileges. As a community of grace, it took practical steps to give expression to grace in its life. How was this achieved? We may summarize the answer to this question under two main heads.

The emphasis on the Christian community. First, there was a constant concern among early Christians for the quality of their common life. This it was that led to the experiment usually referred to as the "communism" of the early chapters of Acts.[33] This experiment of having all things common was the natural, spontaneous expression of life in the Spirit with which the neglect of the poor was incompatible. This appears from the naiveté of the experiment. Owners sold their property and handed over the proceeds to the apostles, who administered a common fund from which the needs of the poor were met, presumably in the form of common meals. The contributions to the common pool were voluntary (Acts 5:1–11). The experiment failed, not to be repeated in this form; but it witnessed to the societary or communal morality of the primitive community in its realism and its impracticability. That experiment took place in the light of an absolute demand for love informed by the intensity of the church's experience of forgiveness and, therefore, of grace.

And the emphasis on the communal nature of the Christian way persists throughout the New Testament. It is rooted in a communal emphasis found in the ministry of Jesus himself who gathered the

33. See C. H. Dodd, "Communism in the New Testament," *Interpreter*, 18 (1921).

Twelve as the representatives of the new community of Israel to follow him.[34] It is from this probably that there developed Paul's "Christ-Mysticism" which issued not in "a flight of the alone to the Alone"; but in the building up of the church, the new community.[35] Along with rationality[36] and the recognition of personal integrity[37] Paul sets forth as the criterion of Christian action the building up of the church.[38] Similarly, in the Johannine literature one finds the love of the brethren as the mark of the church. "If you love not your brother whom you have seen how can you love God whom you have not seen?"[39]

But the same impulse which led to the experiment in communism, the awareness of the horizontal significance of the life in grace, in part at least, led to other developments:

The emphasis on specific moral teaching. (a) At first, in the awareness of its resources in grace, the church attempted to live in the light of the absolutes, in messianic license, as Stendahl has characterized this. The absolutes constitute the peculiarity, though not the totality, of the teaching of Jesus. For certain elements in the early church, the commandments of Jesus in their absolute form were guides for conduct. But under inevitable pressures, it became necessary for the church to apply these absolutes to life. There began that process which tended to transform the absolutes into practical rules of conduct, Christian casuistry.[40] The classic example is the way in which the prohibition of divorce was made practicable by the addition of the exceptive clause: "except on the ground of un-

34. I find no reason to reject the historicity of the Twelve; see Wagenmann.

35. This is one of the important insights of Albert Schweitzer, *The Mysticism of Paul the Apostle*, English trans. W. Montgomery (London, 1931), pp. 105 ff. But for the caution necessary in accepting Schweitzer, see *Paul and Rabbinic Judaism*, 2nd ed., pp. 98 ff.

36. Thus knowledge is placed by Paul as the second of the gifts of the spirit, after wisdom (I Cor. 12:8). In I Cor. 14:13 ff. the importance of "rationality" is clear as in I Corinthians 14. The necessity of the renewal of the mind is recognized, Rom. 12:2. In the Fourth Gospel emphasis on "the truth" of the witness to Christ is frequent, 10:41; 19:35; 21:24, etc. Rationality is included in this truth although it does not exhaust it. Compare I Pet. 3:15; II Tim. 1:27.

37. Cf. Philemon, 15, 16.

38. For Paul the criterion of love among the brethren is normative; Rom. 14:21; I Corinthians 12–14. See also Eph. 4:1–16. H. A. A. Kennedy, *The Theology of the Epistles* (London, 1923), p. 145.

39. I John 4:20; John 17, *et passim*.

40. I have dealt with this at length in *The Setting of the Sermon on the Mount*, pp. 366–93, where I refer to the crisis character of material from Q and the *gemaric* character of much in Matthew.

chastity" (Matt. 5:32 ff.). Because it is Matthew that reveals this best, it has been claimed that the words of Jesus as such played a significant part in the moral development of the church only in Jewish Christian circles. But this is not so. The Pauline letters also appeal to the words of Jesus as authoritative. These words were at least one source for Paul's moral teaching. The extent to which the Pauline letters are reminiscent of the tradition as represented in the synoptics has been insufficiently recognized. The matter has been the subject of acute debate and continues to be so.

Two factors emerge clearly: first, Paul interweaves words of Jesus almost "unconsciously," as it were, into his exhortations, which suggests that these words were bone of his bone. The following parallels are clear:

Rom. 12:14	Matthew 5:43
Bless those who persecute you; bless and do not curse them.	You have heard that it was said, "You shall love your neighbor and hate your enemy."
Rom. 12:17	Matthew 5:39 ff.
Repay no one evil for evil, but take thought for what is noble in the sight of all.	But I say to you, Do not resist one who is evil. But if any one strikes you on the right cheek, turn to him the other also;
Rom. 13:7	Matthew 22:15–22
Pay all of them their dues, taxes to whom taxes are due, revenue to whom revenue is due, respect to whom respect is due, honor to whom honor is due.	Render therefore to Caesar the things that are Caesar's, and to God the things that are God's. (22:21b)
Rom. 14:13	Matthew 18:7
Then let us no more pass judgment on one another, but rather decide never to put a stumbling block or hindrance in the way of a brother.	Woe to the world for temptations to sin! For it is necessary that temptations come, but woe to the man by whom the temptation comes!

Rom. 14:14

I know and am persuaded
in the Lord Jesus that nothing is unclean in itself; but
it is unclean for any one who
thinks it unclean.

Matthew 15:11

not what goes into the mouth
defiles a man, but what
comes out of the mouth, this
defiles a man.

1 Thess. 5:2

For you yourselves know
well that the day of the Lord
will come like a thief in the
night.

Matthew 24:43–44

But know this, that if the
householder had known in
what part of the night the
thief was coming, he would
have watched and would not
have let his house be broken
into. Therefore you also must
be ready; for the Son of man
is coming at an hour you do
not expect.

1 Thess. 5:13

and to esteem them very
highly in love because of
their work. Be at peace
among yourselves.

Mark 9:50

Salt is good; but if the salt
has lost its saltness, how will
you season it? Have salt in
yourselves, and be at peace
with one another.

1 Thess. 5:15

See that none of you repays
evil for evil, but always seek
to do good to one another
and to all.

Matthew 5:39–47

But I say to you, Love your
enemies and pray for those
who persecute you. . . . (5:44)

In addition to these clear parallels there are many other possible
or probable ones. The evidence for these is given elsewhere.[41]

Second, there is also clear evidence that there was a collection
of sayings of the Lord to which Paul appealed (Acts 20:35; I Cor.
7:10; 9:14; 11:23 ff.; 14:37; I Thess. 4:15–16; see especially I Cor.
7:25). Not only in matters of a legislative character does Paul find
guidance in the words of Jesus, but also in more personal matters

41. See my *Paul and Rabbinic Judaism.*

(Romans 7), where possibly his discovery of the supreme importance of motive goes back to Jesus. In I Cor. 7:25 he refers to a word of Christ as a commandment; in two places, once explicitly and once implicitly, he uses the very words "the law of Christ"[42] where the reference is, in part at least, to the teaching of Jesus. This is no declension on Paul's part to a primitive legalism, but the recognition of the fact that his exalted Lord was never, in his mind, divorced from Jesus, the teacher, that the Spirit is never divorced from the historic teaching of Jesus. And, although in the Fourth Gospel the moral teaching of Jesus as such plays little part, the function of the Spirit is to recall the words of Jesus.[43] The same emphasis appears in I John, where there is constant appeal to the commandments of the Lord and frequent echoes of them.[44]

---

42. Explicitly in Gal. 6:2 and implicitly in Rom. 8:2. I Cor. 9:20–22 reads:

To the Jews I became as a Jew, in order to win Jews; to those under the law I became as one under the law—though not being myself under the law—that I might win those under the law. To those outside the law I became as one outside the law—not being without law toward God but under the law of Christ—that I might win those outside the law. To the weak I became weak, that I might win the weak. I have become all things to all men, that I might by all means save some.

Furnish points out that there is only one certain rabbinic reference to "the Law of the Messiah," that from Midrash Qoheleth 11:8 (52a). But it is surely implied in other passages. See *The Setting of the Sermon on the Mount*, pp. 172 ff. And, in the recently discovered *Targum Yerushalmi to the Pentateuch* of the *Codex Neofiti I* of the Vatican Library, the contents of which have been traced by Diez Macho to the second century A.D. at least, Isa. 11:3 reads:

Behold, the Messiah who is to come
shall be one who teaches the Law
and will judge in the fear of the Lord.

On the *Codex Neofiti*, see A. Diez Macho, "The Recently Discovered Palestinian Targum: its Antiquity . . .", *Supplement Vetus Testamentum*, 7 (1960). In Diez Macho's view Codex Neofiti shows that the Palestinian Targum is of pre-Christian origin. There is no New Torah in the D.S.S.; see my *Sermon on the Mount* (Cambridge, 1966), p. 63. Contrast Norman Perrin, *The Kingdom of God in The Teaching of Jesus* (Philadelphia, 1963), pp. 76 f.
43. John 14:25–26.
44. On this see C. H. Dodd, *The Johannine Epistles*, Moffatt New Testament Commentaries (London, 1946), p. xxxviii. The whole problem is dealt with by Furnish, pp. 51 ff., and by F. W. Beare, "Sayings of the Risen Jesus in the Gospel Tradition: An Inquiry into their Origin and Significance," in *Christian History and Interpretation: Studies Presented to John Knox*, ed. W. R. Farmer, C. F. D. Moule, R. R. Niebuhr (Cambridge, 1967), pp. 161–82; see also his article, "Concerning Jesus of Nazareth," *JBL*, 87 (1968), 125 ff. Furnish finds only eight convincing parallels to the materials in the synoptic Gospels in the whole of Paul (he regards Colossians, Ephesians, II Thessa-

Nevertheless, there is a difference of emphasis (but only of emphasis) in Matthew and Paul, as over against the Johannine literature. The words of Jesus appear in the former two over their wide range. But even there they are summed up in one word, *agapê*.

---

lonians, the Pastorals as deutero-Pauline: he does not consider his omission of these as significant; *op. cit.*, pp. 11–12). The other "allusions" usually cited he does not find persuasive. He dismisses the work of Alfred Resch, *Der Paulinismus und die Logia Jesu in ihrem gegenseitigen Verhaltnis untersucht in Texte und Untersuchungen zur Geschichte der altchristlichen Literatur* (1904), vol. 27, as "imaginary" (p. 59), as he criticizes C. H. Dodd's treatment of the phrase *Ennomos Christou* in *Studia Paulina* (1953). Furnish's treatment is salutary; but it does not convince me that the words of Jesus were not highly significant for Paul if not "his primary" source for moral teaching. Does Furnish deal justly with the richness of the oral tradition which prevailed in the early church and which finally coalesced, in part, in the Gospels? Here the method employed by H. Riesenfeld, in his articles, "Parabolic Language in the Pauline Epistles," and "Paul's 'Grain of Wheat' Analogy and the Argument of 1 Cor. 15," and "The Parables in the Synoptic and in the Johannine Traditions," all to appear in a forthcoming volume, *The Gospel Tradition* (Fortress Press), is more appropriate or sensitive in dealing with tradition. The detection and dismissal of allusions are not as simple as Furnish suggests, particularly in a milieu where the reception and transmission of tradition were so living. The work of A. M. Hunter, *Paul and His Predecessors* (London, 1940), and P. Carrington, *The Primitive Christian Catechism* (Cambridge, 1940), Furnish refers to only in bare footnotes. See pp. 38 n., 261 n. A very useful and balanced discussion by David L. Dungan under the title *Logia Kyriou and Community Regulations* is forthcoming under the imprint of the Fortress Press. As for the imperative participle the evidence of the Scrolls demands more attention than is given to it, see p. 39, n. 33. The role of Jesus as moral teacher is less difficult to understand in the light of the recent brilliant work of L. Finkelstein, *New Light from the Prophets* (London, 1969). Dr. Finkelstein writes that "to the magnificence of the poetry of the Prophets and the inspiration of their rhetoric, must now be added the greatness of their academic teaching which raised disciples who became teachers of succeeding generations of teachers" (p. 1). They are the precursors of the Sages of Israel (*ibid.*). His work should warn us against thinking that the prophetic, charismatic, eschatological aspects of Jesus's ministry precluded his role as patient teacher. See *The Setting of the Sermon on the Mount*, pp. 415 ff. Rudolf Bultmann recognized Jesus as rabbi, in *Jesus and the Word* (New York & London, 1934). This is questioned by M. Hengel in his fascinating study, already cited, n. 30, pp. 41 ff. But he does recognize a continuity between the teaching of Jesus and that of the early church. He writes:

> Die Diagnose 'Gemeinde-bildung' musste so im Munde des Forschers nicht unbedingt immer nur im Sinne eines grossen Abstandes zum historischen Jesu verstanden werden. Die darin sichtbar werdende, vom prophetischen Geist geleitete, Freiheit der Gemeinde könnte auch ein Ausdruck dafür sein, dass diese sich selbst in ihrer missionarischen Verkündigung ihrem Ausgangspunkt, dem Handeln des historischen Jesus, besonders nahe wusste. Diese Linie liesse sich bis zu Paulus ausziehen. Wenn dieser 1 Cor. 3:9 von sich und Apollos sagt: θεοῦ γάρ ἐσμεν συνεργοί oder auch pointierter 2 Cor. 5:20: ὑπὲρ Χριστοῦ οὖν πρεσβεύομεν ὡς τοῦ θεοῦ παρακαλοῦντος δι' ἡμῶν so steht er bewusst oder unbewusst—direkt in der Linie jenes Geschehens, das Jesus durch seinen Ruf in die Nachfolge und seine Jüngeraussendung eingeleitet hatte. [p. 93]

See further C. H. Dodd, "Some Johannine 'Herrenworte' with parallels in the Synoptic Gospels," *NTS* 11, 2 (Nov., 1955), 75 ff., and A. Schlatter, *Die Parallelen in*

Thus the climax of the Sermon on the Mount at Matt. 7:12 is the Golden Rule. And Paul and John, like the synoptics, emphasize the centrality of "love" (Rom. 13:8–10; I Cor. 8:1; 13; Col. 3:14; John 13:34–35; I John 3:1; 2:7–10; 4:7–16). The meaning of *love* has again to be carefully noted. Partaking more of active good will than of emotion, it can be commanded, as emotions cannot. In I John it is used in a "down-to-earth" manner as involving willingness to share one's goods (I John 3:17). For Paul it is the fulfillment of the Law and the principle of cohesion in the Christian community. The expression of love is multiple (I Cor. 13), but its essential nature is revealed in Christ's dying for men. It is this kind of act that is demanded of those who love.[45]

(b) The necessity which led to the application of the absolutes of Jesus to life led the church to take over for its own use codal material whether from Hellenism or from Judaism or both. Most of the letters reveal a twofold structure: a first part, dealing with "doctrine," is followed by a second, dealing with "ethics." Romans is typical. Chapters 1–11 deal with doctrine, 12:1 ff. deals with ethics, and it is casually connected with chapters 1–11. The ethical sections of the various letters reveal a common tradition of catechesis, which may have been used in the instruction of converts, especially at baptism (cf. Rom. 12:1; Eph. 4:20–6:19; Col. 3:8–4:12; Heb. 12:1–2; James 1:1–4:10; I Pet. 1:1–4:11; 4:12–5:14).[46] This common tradition must not be regarded as having a fixed pattern, but the similarity in the order and contents of the material in the above sections is too marked to be accidental. The presence in them of the imperative participle (e. g., Rom. 12:9–19), a form found, but not common, in Hellenistic Greek but familiar in Hebrew legal documents, suggests that Paul, and other Christian writers, drew upon codal material, such as is found in the Dead

---

den *Worten Jesu by Johannes und Matthaus* (Gütersloh, 1898). See *The Setting of the Sermon on the Mount*, appendix xiv, pp. 463 f. The whole matter is bound up with the question of the relation between Jesus and Paul which is surveyed by Furnish in *The Bulletin of the John Rylands Library*, 47, no. 2 (Mar., 1965), 342, in "The Jesus–Paul Debate: From Baur to Bultmann." I remain unconvinced that Paul was not interested in the historical Jesus: it does not seem to me that the interpretation of II Cor. 5:16 and Gal. 1:11 f. and the argument from silence appealed to, demand such a conclusion.

45. On all this see *The Setting of the Sermon on the Mount*, pp. 401 ff., where James, and the Johannine sources are considered. See the monumental study of C. Spicq, *Agape dans le Nouveau Testament: Analyse des Textes*, 3 vols. (Paris, 1958, 1959).

46. See Carrington and Selwyn.

Sea Scrolls (The Manual of Discipline, 1:18 ff. actually has the imperative participle), Mishna Demai and Derek Eretz Rabba and Zuta.[47] There are also parallels to the tradition in Hellenistic sources. The church probably took over much pagan moral convention from the Jewish Diaspora. Whatever the exact source of the material, the church found it necessary to borrow from non-Christian sources. It not only domesticated the absolutes of Jesus; it also took over domestic virtues from the world.[48]

This brings us to the last aspect of New Testament moral teaching with which we shall deal here. That the church was able to draw upon moral teaching from Judaism and Hellenism means that there was a continuity between the moral awareness of Christians and of the non-Christian world. Wherein did this continuity lie? It lay probably in the doctrine of creation which the early church held. It cannot be overemphasized that creation and redemption are congenial in the New Testament, as indeed in Judaism. The messianic age had cosmic dimensions for Judaism. So too in the New Testament the Creator and the Redeemer are one. It is this that explains the ease with which Jesus can discover redemptive, spiritual truth in the natural order as in Matt. 5:43–48 and in his parables; it explains how Paul can find in Christ the wisdom—the creative agent—of God, and how John and Hebrews can find in him the Word by which all things were made. For the New Testament writers the good life is the truly natural life. Morality is rooted in creation.[49]

47. See *Paul and Rabbinic Judaism*; S. Wibbing, *Die Tugend und Lasterkataloge im Neuen Testament* (Berlin, 1959).

48. See B. S. Easton, *The Pastoral Epistles* (New York, 1948), p. 98; Martin Dibelius, *Die Pastoralbriefe* (1931). On conscience in the New Testament, see my article in *IDB*.

49. I have dealt very briefly with this theme in the companion lecture, "The Relevance of the Moral Teaching of the Early Church," in *Neotestamentica et Semitica: Studies in honour of Matthew Black*, pp. 35 ff. Here it can only be touched upon; see the especially rich contribution of N. A. Dahl, "Christ, Creation and the Church," in *The Background of the New Testament and its Eschatology: Studies in honour of C. H. Dodd* (Cambridge, 1956), pp. 422 ff., and the bibliography on p. 423, n. 1. See also W. R. Schoedel, pp. 272–75, especially p. 274, n. 22. That the Christian life can be regarded as the truly natural life may not sound as strange as it once did to judge from much in modern biology. These are the words of a recent writer, Robert Ardrey, in *The Territorial Imperative* (New York, 1966): "The portrait of life being painted by the new biology bears small resemblance to that natural world of anarchistic instinct and relentless self-interest which, depressed a Tennyson, inspired a Freud, perturbed a Darwin, and confused a century. It is a world of order and ordained self sacrifice to

In the above I have sketched in very broad strokes the context, center of gravity and dimensions of the moral teaching of the early church; its context in primitive Christian eschatology; its center of gravity in the life, death and Resurrection of Jesus of Nazareth, the Christ; its dimensions both in its vertical concentration in

---

greater and longer goods. . . ." But Ardrey has another emphasis which seems to contradict this. In *African Genesis* (New York, 1961), p. 316, he claims that "man is a predator whose natural instinct is to kill with a weapon." Man like the animal has an innate compulsion to gain and defend his property—this is the major motif of his work, *The Territorial Imperative*. For this emphasis he has been severely criticized by M. F. Ashley Montagu in "The New Litany of 'Innate Depravity' or Original Sin Revisited" in *Man and Aggression*, ed. M. F. Ashley Montagu (New York, 1968), pp. 3–16. Montagu takes an even more sanguine view of man than is implied in the first quotation given above from Ardrey: "It is not man's nature, but his nurture, in such a world (overcrowded, highly competitive, threatening) that requires our attention" (p. 16). See further H. Loewe, *The Rabbinic Anthology*, selected by C. G. Montefiore and H. Loewe, p. lxix: "What is true in nature is true in religion: what is false in science cannot be true in religion. Truth is one and indivisible. God is bound by His own laws. . . . It is indeed ironical to note that the unity of the 19th Psalm has been impugned by some people for the very reason that it asserts, first, God's supremacy alike in the natural and in the religious spheres and, secondly, the congruence of those spheres. The sun, in going forth on its daily round, is fulfilling Torah as much as is a human being who worships God, as much as is a Jew when he performs the commandments, which are 'pure and enlightening to the eyes.' Ps. 19.8." He refers to *Sifre Deut.* on 32:1 §306; see *The Rabbinic Anthology*, p. 208. I recognize that there is in the New Testament something of an antinomy: there is on the one hand the belief that through the fall, creation itself has been affected, and on the other, the belief that in creation is visible "the eternal power of God." Cf. J. Weiss, *The History of Primitive Christianity*, trans. four friends and ed. F. C. Grant (N. Y., 1937), 2: 597. Both views are native to Judaism. Stendahl reminded me that there is a certain "unnaturalness" in the operations of grace in the parables of Jesus, as when the seed in the parable of the Sower increases a hundredfold. But, in fact, this is not so much "unnatural" as "the natural enhanced, or intensified." I suggest in my companion essay that it is the understanding of creation that provides a bridge between the moral teaching of the church and the world. See *Neotestamentica et Semitica*, pp. 35 ff. The work of Teilhard de Chardin and, before him, of C. E. Raven, who have both emphasized the cosmic continuities in Christian theology may be connected with this. The danger in the position of both is a possible neglect of the sense of the transcendent and of the antinomy to which I have referred above. See Christopher F. Mooney, *Teilhard de Chardin and the Mystery of Christ* (New York, 1966), p. 207, who notes that while the *concept* of the transcendent is never absent in Chardin's work, the *sense* of it gets lost; and my critique of Raven in *Paul and Rabbinic Judaism*, p. 190, and the reply to it in Raven's Gifford Lectures. The rich words of Donald M. Mackinnon, *Borderlands of Theology and Other Essays*, ed. G. W. Roberts and D. E. Smucker (New York, 1968), pp. 44 ff., on the significance of Raven and Chardin, deserve serious consideration. On Law and Nature in Plato and Hellenistic Judaism, see H. A. Wolfson, *Philo*, 2: 170 f.; for Philo the law of nature and the Mosaic law, being derived from the same source—God—are in harmony. Wolfson, 2: 192. This is why God put the creation of world as preface to his laws in Genesis. Note that in Philo πρόνοια ("Providence") and νόμος τῆς φύσεως are interchangeable. Philo's sense of the Law and order of nature is keen (Mos. ii. 48). He commands living according to

Christ, the Risen Lord, and in its horizontal concern with the community and its cosmic affinities. We have not touched upon the relevance of this teaching to the life of the world outside the church, but that theme is dealt with elsewhere in a lecture which, as previously indicated in the first footnote, presupposes this, and to which the reader is referred.

---

nature: πρὸς τὸ βούλημα τῆς φύσεως (Op. Mundi. 3). For the Stoic root of these ideas, see Diogenes Laertius vii. 87 in Stoicorum Veterum Fragmenta, ed. H. F. A. von Arnim (Leipzig, 1903–1924), 1: 262. On eschatology and creation as illuminating the meaning of the Law in Matthew, see Bornkamm, "Enderwartung und Kirche im Matthäusevangelium," pp. 222–60.